# Exploring International Human Rights

# Critical Connections:
## Studies in Peace, Democracy, and Human Rights

T. DAVID MASON, SERIES EDITOR

*Revolution and Political Violence: Theories and Cases*
edited by T. David Mason and John A. Booth

*Exploring International Human Rights: Essential Readings*
edited by Rhonda L. Callaway and Julie Harrelson-Stephens

# Exploring International Human Rights

## Essential Readings

edited by
Rhonda L. Callaway
Julie Harrelson-Stephens

LYNNE
RIENNER
PUBLISHERS

BOULDER
LONDON

Published in the United States of America in 2007 by
Lynne Rienner Publishers, Inc.
1800 30th Street, Boulder, Colorado 80301
www.rienner.com

and in the United Kingdom by
Lynne Rienner Publishers, Inc.
3 Henrietta Street, Covent Garden, London WC2E 8LU

**Library of Congress Cataloging-in-Publication Data**
Exploring international human rights : essential readings / Rhonda L.
Callaway and Julie Harrelson-Stephens, editors.
    p. cm. — (Critical connections: studies in peace, democracy, and
human rights)
  Includes bibliographical references and index.
  ISBN 978-1-58826-412-1 (hardcover : alk. paper) — ISBN 978-1-58826-437-4
(pbk. : alk. paper)
  1. Human rights.  I. Callaway, Rhonda L., 1965–  II. Harrelson-Stephens,
Julie, 1969–
  K3240.E975 2007
  341.4'8—dc22

                                         2006102357

**British Cataloguing in Publication Data**
A Cataloguing in Publication record for this book
is available from the British Library.


Printed and bound in the United States of America

The paper used in this publication meets the requirements
of the American National Standard for Permanence of
Paper for Printed Library Materials Z39.48-1992.

5   4   3   2

# Contents

# Preface

In teaching introductory courses on international human rights, we were constantly searching for compelling, accessible articles that illustrate the main themes and tensions in the field. This collection is the culmination of that search.

While some of the selections in the book cover basic issues in human rights, others were chosen to put a face on the realities of repression, and still others deal with current issues such as the relationship between human rights and terrorism or globalization. To cover many of the most timely topics, we commissioned several original pieces. The result of our efforts, we believe, is a well-rounded anthology that can be used in a variety of contexts and human rights courses.

This volume was a collaborative effort, and we owe a deep thanks to several notable individuals. Steven C. Poe provided constant guidance and reviewed the outline for this anthology. Both Steve and David Mason provided us with valuable advice and assistance throughout the process. We also want to thank Marilyn Grobschmidt, acquisitions editor at Lynne Rienner Pubishers, whose guidance was appreciated and essential throughout. We owe a debt of gratitude to our home institutions, Sam Houston State University and Stephen F. Austin State University, for their continued encouragement. In addition, we particularly thank the Peace Studies Program at the University of North Texas for financial support of this project. Finally, we thank our families, Carl and Barbara Callaway and Mark Stephens, for their unwavering patience and support during this process.

# 1 | What Are Human Rights?

## 1.1 ⎯⎯⎯

## Introduction
*The Editors*

Since the Holocaust, human rights have increasingly emerged as an international norm. Atrocities committed by the Nazi regime led the international community to examine the idea of human rights and prompted world leaders to begin to recognize limits on the sovereignty of states. As a result, states have become more attentive to the values of human rights and, in much of the world, to their actual realization. Citizens are also more apt to claim such rights as theirs, not on the basis of their legal status or the color of their skin, but merely because they are human. Thus, in the last half century, human rights have become increasingly accepted in international discourse and increasingly claimed by citizens and world leaders alike.

The transformation toward an acceptance of human rights has been accompanied by an increase in scholarly research devoted to the study of those rights. Although the study of human rights is still seen as a fringe topic by many international relations scholars, research devoted to its study has increased, particularly since the 1980s. Research in human rights today examines a variety of questions, including what is meant by human rights, what are the causes of gross human rights violations, and how are these rights important in formulating foreign policy?

This section seeks to address a fundamental issue: What are human rights? This question remains highly contested within both political discourse and the field of human rights research. Before we can engage in a meaningful dialogue regarding human rights, we must first agree on what we mean by human rights. In the first selection, Julie Harrelson-Stephens and Rhonda L. Callaway illustrate the difficulty in defining and conceptualizing human rights. We begin with a discussion of the evolution of human rights as an international norm since the end of World War II. Cold War divisions resulted in a theoretical rift in terms of economic and political rights, positive and negative rights, and first generation and second generation rights. In practice, the resulting typologies have been used to further political agendas and undermine certain types of rights in favor of others. That rift continues today, with developed states advocating security rights while developing states promote subsistence rights. This debate leads to the fundamental question in human rights research today: Are human rights universal or culturally relative? We examine the arguments on each side of this debate and discuss the prospects for the future realization of human rights.

David Beetham's piece specifically addresses the Cold War ideological division pitting economic and social rights against civil and political rights. He argues that economic and social rights should be included in the conception of human rights and then turns to the question of the resulting duties correlated to the realization of human rights. Beetham affirms a duty related to economic and social rights as the primary responsibility of a citizen's government. To the extent that the government is unable to fulfill this duty, he argues that the developed world has an obligation to support these individuals through international organizations.

Henry Shue also questions whether there is a hierarchy of rights. He challenges the prevailing typologies of human rights, asserting instead that there are certain basic rights. Basic rights are those rights that are necessary for the enjoyment of other rights and therefore must be provided by society. Ultimately, Shue argues that both security rights and subsistence rights are basic rights in that a denial of these rights precludes the enjoyment of all other rights.

While the previous articles survey the typologies of human rights, Jerome Shestack addresses what is meant by human rights from a philosophical perspective. To fully explore this, he examines possible sources of human rights claims, including the moral basis encompassing both religion and natural law. For instance, Shestack argues that most religions are based on the idea that man is created in God's image and therefore has intrinsic value. From this perspective, human rights flow naturally from religion. By contrast, natural law suggests that individuals have inherent rights based on their humanity rather than a divine gift. He moves beyond these traditional sources to include theories where the state is the source of human rights based on legal positivism or Marxism, as well as sociological and utilitarian approaches to human rights. For a positivist, human rights are based in law, rather than derived from what "ought" to be. Similarly, Marxism also recognizes rights as those granted by the state, emphasizing duty to society rather than individuality. Next, Shestack addresses the current sociological approach, which emphasizes prevailing social and economic conditions and the resulting societal preferences for specific rights. Last, utilitarianism is based on the idea that governments should promote the greatest happiness for the greatest number. Thus, individual rights are sometimes sacrificed for collective welfare.

This section explores the difficult and continuously divisive question of what we mean by human rights, specifically how individuals in different cultures and distinct political systems around the world may come to very different conclusions. Each of the above pieces illustrates the difficulties in conceptualizing and realizing human rights around the world. The remaining articles in this book deal with specific stories and issues in the study of human rights. The typologies, philosophical foundations, and ideological divisions discussed in this section will continue to come up in the remaining articles in this book.

# 1.2 _____

# What Are Human Rights?
# Definitions and Typologies of
# Today's Human Rights Discourse
*Julie Harrelson-Stephens and Rhonda L. Callaway*

The issue of human rights is frequently discussed in international discourse, among world leaders, and in the international media. At any given time, there are world conferences on human rights, speeches from presidents and popes alike about the need for tolerance and respect for human rights, and media outlets airing one program after another on the poverty and poor living conditions around the world. Although what is exactly meant by human rights remains controversial and ambiguous, it is increasingly clear that there is some international concept of human rights. In societies where citizens are by and large free to participate in the political process and express opposition to their government, where they do not simply disappear in the blink of an eye and are generally free from hunger and poverty, human rights may never be a chief consideration or concern. Unfortunately, this only describes the situation of a minority of the world's population.

The acknowledgment of human rights as an issue by the international community has led to the creation of a vast network of laws, treaties, and international organizations. Moreover, most states today recognize some limits to their sovereignty and, at least ostensibly, acquiesce to treaties and covenants designed to protect those rights. Prior to World War II, such a concept would have been deemed untenable, as state sovereignty remained the norm of international relations. This meant that states were the final arbiter in the treatment of their citizens and other states should refrain from intervening in their affairs. The Holocaust and atrocities associated with the Nazi regime served as a catalyst for the human rights movement, propelling the issue into the international arena. After the Nazis attempted to systematically eliminate the Jewish population from Europe, as well as targeting gypsies, the handicapped, elderly, and homosexuals, the world's response was one of horror. It was the extermination of over six million people by the Nazi regime that created the political will to mount the first true challenge to the idea of sovereignty with respect to human rights.

However, while international discourse on the importance of human rights has continually increased since the end of World War II, many states continue to violate a wide range of rights. In fact, some of the worst human rights violations have occurred in modern times: the atrocities committed by the Khmer

4

Rouge in Cambodia, the ethnic cleansing in the former Yugoslavia, the slaughter in Rwanda, and the current genocide in the Darfur region of Sudan. Food insecurity, lack of clean water, and lack of basic healthcare continue to be everyday realities for much of the world. Slavery is on the rise today: in Eastern Europe, women are trafficked as sex slaves; in the Democratic Republic of Congo, children are being forced to fight in wars; and in Nepal, children are being forced to work in sweatshops for subsistence wages instead of attending school. For many people, the lack of human rights is a daily reality. This suggests that while citizens in parts of the world are experiencing greater respect for human rights, the majority have yet to realize and enjoy the full spectrum of human rights. The disjuncture between the discourse on human rights and the realization of human rights is one of the important paradoxes of the study of human rights.

## ■ Beyond a Definition of Human Rights: Developing a Human Rights Regime

The beginning of any formal recognition of the human rights regime came in 1948 when the UN General Assembly unanimously adopted the Universal Declaration of Human Rights (UDHR).[1] This declaration (Preamble, 1948), which still provides one of the most sweeping guarantees of human rights worldwide, begins with the recognition of "the inherent dignity and of the equal and inalienable rights of all members of the human family is the foundation of freedom, justice and peace in the world." At least theoretically, states would no longer be allowed to hide behind the veil of sovereignty regarding the treatment of citizens. A new generation of international cooperation was forming with the UN serving as a forum to push for the advancement of human rights in existing as well as newly emerging states.

The major dilemma facing the international community, however, is the term itself. What are *human rights*? The inability to come to any consensus has led to definitions of convenience as states carve out meanings and conceptions that serve their best interests. From a theoretical and philosophical perspective, we find one prevalent definition of human rights as simply the rights one has because one is human (Donnelly 1989, 1998). Donnelly (1998, 18) further explains that human rights "are held by all human beings, irrespective of any rights or duties individuals may (or may not) have as citizens, members of families, workers, or parts of any public or private organization or association. They are universal rights." This definition suggests that human rights apply to all people in all states; however, it still fails to provide any specificity of what actually constitutes a human right.[2]

In a more pragmatic fashion, states have consequently turned to the international treaties and opted for the types of enumerated rights that reflect their respective ideologies. In fact, the UDHR had little chance of progressing beyond a declaration to become a binding treaty. It didn't take long for a dichotomy of rights to emerge out of the UDHR with the fault lines approximating not only the ideological schisms of the Cold War but also the perceived role of the state. In the West, for example, there is a tendency for states to emphasize civil and political rights while marginalizing economic and cultural rights. This is supported by an ideology that is based on liberalism and democracy and which focuses on the rights of the individual in both the political and economic arenas. The ideology of communist states, by contrast, called for an emphasis on economic and social equality, eschewing the needs of the individual for the greater good. This preference has since been expressed by developing countries, often to the extent that they support a short-term suppression of civil and political rights in order to ensure stability necessary for economic prosperity. Ultimately, these divisions provoke a good deal of debate and disagreement over what are, in fact, human rights.

This divide would lead the UN to create two more statements on human rights: the *International Covenant on Civil and Political Rights* and the *International Covenant on Economic, Social and Cultural Rights*, both of which went into force in 1976. These three documents together are collectively known as the International Bill of Human Rights.[3] The *International Covenant on Civil and Political Rights* encompasses, among other rights, the right to self-determination, the right to a fair trial, freedom of expression, and freedom of religion. This covenant also affirms the right to life and includes protections against torture, slavery, or forced servitude. These rights are sometimes referred to as first generation rights. This designation acknowledges the liberal philosophical heritage experienced in Western societies that first extended political and civil rights to society at large.[4] The idea is that civil and political rights are realized first, resulting in the demand for additional types of rights. Weston (1992, 19) points out that the common denominator in these types of rights is the emphasis on the notion of liberty, "a shield that safeguards the individual, alone and in association with others, against the abuse and misuse of political authority. This is the core value." In general, this statute continues to be emphasized and championed by the West, although many non-Western states have adopted this covenant as well.[5]

The *International Covenant on Economic, Social and Cultural Rights* includes the right to work, equal remuneration for work, and the right to fair compensation, as well as the right to join trade unions. The right to an education, along with the right to food, clothing, and shelter, is also specified in the covenant. These rights are often referred to as second generation rights and were championed by Eastern Bloc states during the Cold War. Today, developing countries tend to underscore the importance of these types of rights. From the Western perspective, the demands associated with economic and social rights came after their political and civil rights were achieved. Conversely, socialist states, and now many non-Western states, focus on the primacy of these types of rights as part of the reaction against the liberal emphasis on individual rights.

Some states, as well as certain groups within states, contend that there is yet a third generation of rights, or solidarity rights. In succinct terms, these types of rights are sought after by groups or collectivities and are closely related to the development of the nation-state (Weston 1992). As such, groups claim the right to self-determination and economic development as well as more abstract objectives such as the right to a healthy environment and peace. Examples of the quest for self-determination sought after by groups include the Kurds in Iraq and Turkey, Palestinians in Israel, as well as the Chechens in Russia. The realization of third generation rights requires, in part, the cooperation of institutions beyond the state, and as a result, they tend to be more difficult to obtain.

Beyond the divisions that seem to flow naturally out of the UDHR and related documents, researchers often distinguish between positive and negative rights. Positive rights are those rights that require the state to be proactive in the provision of something, such as the right to food or healthcare. In terms of the two UN covenants, positive rights are mostly reflected in the *International Covenant on Economic, Social and Cultural Rights* and, as previously discussed, advocated and pursued by developing states. Negative rights, by contrast, are those rights that require the government to refrain from some action, such as torture or genocide. These types of rights are, again, typically championed by the West and are articulated in the *International Covenant on Civil and Political Rights.* However, Donnelly (1998) makes a stinging critique of such divisions, arguing that most rights can be conceived as both positive and negative. Moreover, he argues that "the moral basis of the positive-negative distinction is also questionable. Does it really make a moral difference if one kills someone through neglect or by positive action?" (Donnelly 1998, 25). Attempts to create such a hierarchy of rights are often motivated by political and ideological differences. For instance, Western states often make the distinction between positive and negative rights to reinforce their partiality for civil and political (and presumably negative) rights.

While each of the above typologies implies some hierarchy among rights, critiques, such as Donnelly's, suggest that it is useful to distinguish among basic types of rights, absent any such hierarchy.[6] Here, we can conceive of three broad categories of rights. The first is political rights such as the right of participation, assembly, and expression. These are generally found to be more fully realized in democratic states. A second category of rights is security rights. Security rights, which are sometimes referred to as rights respecting the integrity of the person, consist of the right not to be tortured, imprisoned for one's political views, disappeared, or murdered by your state. A final category of basic rights is basic human needs or subsistence rights, which take into account the right to food, clothing, and shelter. Rather than a hierarchy, some scholars suggest that these rights are actually achieved somewhat simultaneously (Donnelly 1989; Milner, Poe, and Leblang 1999).

## ■ Universalism vs. Cultural Relativism

Perhaps the most important theoretical, if not the most prevailing, controversy in international human rights is the question of cultural relativism. In particular, the question is raised, do universal rights exist or are human rights culturally specific? Universalism suggests that human rights are inherent in the individual, regardless of his or her nationality, ethnicity, or socioeconomic standing. From this perspective, human rights are not granted by the state or law; rather such rights are intrinsic in humanity. Every individual is born with the same rights, regardless of where or when that birth takes place, making human rights inalienable for all human beings.[7] The UDHR, at its core, seems to support the idea that there are certain universal human rights that the international community has accepted.

While the adoption of the UDHR binds the states of the world together and seeks to address human rights under one umbrella, it does so only in a political and moral way. The legal weight it carries is not a heavy one. In addition, the developing countries are quick to dispute the universality of human rights, arguing three main points. First, developing countries had little input in the drafting of the document due to their colonial status at the time. Second, these same countries contend that the rights outlined in the declaration are ethnocentric, reflecting Western conceptions and omitting non-Western views on human rights. Last, critics contend that too much emphasis is placed on the rights of the individual often at the expense of the rights of groups and collectivities. As a result, many states pursue alternatives to the universal model of human rights.

Cultural relativism is the argument that human rights are culturally or historically defined and will likely change over time. According to this point of view, moral values, or what is socially acceptable, are defined by one's culture. As one example, slavery was once an accepted practice among most states in the West; however, today those same states argue that this is a violation of human rights. Moreover, cultural relativists contend that what one society calls a human rights violation, another society might claim as a legitimate cultural practice. Typically, cultural relativists argue that advocates of universalism are, by and large, propagating Western moral standards, and any attempt to establish or impose universal human rights standards amounts to cultural imperialism. As a consequence, we have witnessed the emergence of a variety of human rights perspectives, including Asian values, African values, and Islamic values.

Today, the international community is faced with specific examples of cultural practices leading to a perpetuation of the debate on the twin issues of sovereignty and the universality of human rights. In the twenty-first century, many states still view the human rights regime as an assault on their sovereignty, and many societies see this as a threat to their way of life. In Mauritania, for instance, chattel slavery continues as an accepted institution within its society. The removal of female genitalia (referred to as female circumcision or female genital mutilation) is a long-held tradition in places across Africa, Asia, and the Middle East. Many Islamic cultures prescribe subservient roles for females, often denying them basic civil rights. In the United States, many citizens believe in the right to utilize the death penalty as a punishment. These are just a few cases where strongly held cultural beliefs deny the existence of universal human rights.

The resulting tension between cultural relativity and universalism continues to dominate the human rights debate around the world. While great strides have been made in human rights in the past few decades, there continues to be contention among states and groups as to what constitutes human rights; what types of rights, if any, are the most important; and to what extent the international community can enforce these rights on sovereign states. These issues will inform the rest of the readings in this book.

## ▨ Notes

1. Notably, several countries, including South Africa, Saudi Arabia, and the Eastern Bloc states, abstained from the vote.

2. For a complete discussion of the definition of human rights, see Cranston (1973), Shue (1980), Donnelly (1989, 1998), Howard (1983), and Forsythe (2006).

3. Additional international human rights covenants include the *United Nations Convention on the Prevention of and Punishment for the Crime of Genocide* (1951), *International Convention on the Elimination of All Forms of Racial Discrimination* (1965), *Convention on the Elimination of All Forms of Discrimination Against Women* (1979), *Convention Against Torture and Other Cruel, Inhuman or Degrading Treatment or Punishment* (1984), and *Convention on the Rights of the Child* (1989). For an exhaustive list of all international treaties and covenants pertaining to human rights, see the website of the Office of the United Nations High Commissioner for Human Rights at www.ohchr.org/english/law.

4. This bifurcation of rights into three generations was first articulated by French jurist and human rights scholar Karel Vasek (1977), who associated these three generations of rights with the French slogan *liberté, égalité et fraternité*. First generation rights reflect the notion of liberty, second generation rights encompass the idea of equality, while third generation rights, according to Vasek, signal the rights of the community (Claude and Weston 1992, 6).

5. As of November 2006, there are 160 parties to the covenant and 67 signatories. A complete listing can be found at the Office of the United Nations High Commissioner for Human Rights (www.ohchr.org/english/countries/ratification/4.htm).

6. Shue (1980) offers a complete discussion of basic rights that can be found later in this chapter.

7. As previously mentioned, this very idea is embodied in one of the most popular definitions of human rights, that human rights are rights that one has because one is human (Donnelly 1989).

## ■ References

Claude, Richard Pierre, and Burns H. Weston. 1992. *Human Rights in the World Community: Issues and Action,* 2nd Edition. Philadelphia: University of Pennsylvania Press.

Cranston, Maurice. 1973. *What Are Human Rights.* London: Bodley Head.

Donnelly, Jack. 1998. *International Human Rights,* 2nd Edition. Boulder, CO: Westview Press.

———. 1989. *Universal Human Rights in Theory and Practice.* Ithaca and London: Cornell University Press.

Forsythe, David. 2006. *Human Rights in International Relations,* 2nd Edition. Cambridge: Cambridge University Press.

Howard, Rhoda. 1983. "The Full-Belly Thesis: Should Economic Rights Take Priority over Civil and Political Rights? Evidence from Sub-Saharan Africa." *Human Rights Quarterly* 5:467–490.

Milner, Wesley, Steven C. Poe, and David Leblang. 1999. "Security Rights, Subsistence Rights, and Liberties: A Theoretical Survey of the Empirical Landscape." *Human Rights Quarterly* 21:403–443.

Shue, Henry. 1980. *Basic Rights: Subsistence, Affluence, and U.S. Foreign Policy.* Princeton: Princeton University Press.

Vasek, Karel. 1977. "A 30-Year Struggle: The Sustained Efforts to Give Force of Law to the Universal Declaration of Human Rights." *UNESCO Courier*, pp. 29–32.

Weston, Burns H. 1992. "Human Rights," in Richard Pierre Claude and Burns Weston, eds. *Human Rights in the World Community: Issues and Action.* Philadelphia: University of Pennsylvania Press.

# 1.3 ⸻

# What Future for Economic and Social Rights?

*David Beetham*

## ◼ Corresponding Duties

Among the most substantial objections which the theory of human rights has to face is that it is impossible to specify the duties which correspond to rights claimed, to show who should fulfill them or to demonstrate that they can realistically be fulfilled. In the absence of a satisfactory theory of obligation, it is urged, human rights must remain merely 'manifesto' claims, not properly rights. This objection is held to be particularly damaging to economic and social rights, which require from individuals and governments, not merely that they refrain from harming others or undermining their security, but that they act positively to promote their well-being. This requirement not only presupposes resources which they may not possess. It also contradicts a widely held moral conviction to the effect that, while we may have a general negative duty not to harm others, the only positive duties we have are *special* duties to aid those to whom we stand in a particular personal, professional or contractual relationship. There can be no general duty to aid unspecified others; and, insofar as it presupposes such a duty, the inclusion of economic and social rights in the human rights agenda is basically flawed.

This formidable charge-sheet rests, I hope to show, on a number of fallacies. Easiest to refute is the assumption of a principled difference between the two sets of rights in the character of the obligations each entails, negative and positive respectively. As many commentators have shown, this difference will not hold up.[1] Certainly the so-called 'liberty' rights require the state to refrain from invading the freedom and security of its citizens. However, since governments were established, according to classical liberal theory itself, to protect people from the violation of their liberty and security at the hands of one another, it requires considerable government expenditure to meet this elementary purpose. Establishing "the police forces, judicial systems and prisons that are necessary to maintain the highest achievable degree of security of these (sc.

Excerpted from David Beetham, "What Future for Economic and Social Rights?" *Political Studies* 43, Special Issue. © 1995 Blackwell Publishing. Reprinted with permission. Some of the author's notes have been omitted.

civil and political) rights . . . is enormously expensive and involves the maintenance of complex bureaucratic systems."[2]

Henry Shue has developed this argument furthest in his distinction between three different kinds of duty that are required to make a human right effective. There is, first, the duty to *avoid* depriving a person of some necessity;
the duty to *protect* them from deprivation; and the duty to *aid* them when deprived. All three types of duty, he argues, are required to secure human rights,
whether these be civil and political, or social and economic. Personal security,
for example, requires that states refrain from torturing or otherwise injuring
their citizens; that they protect them from injury at the hands of others; and
that they provide a system of justice for the injured, to which all equally have
access. Similarly, subsistence rights require that states do not deprive citizens
of their means of livelihood; that they protect them against deprivation at the
hands of others; and that they provide a system of basic social security for the
deprived. The examples are entirely parallel. The difference is not between
different categories of *right*, but between different types of *duty* necessary to
their protection, Shue concludes. "The attempted division of rights, rather than
duties, into forbearance and aid . . . can only breed confusion. It is impossible
for any basic right—however 'negative' it has come to seem—to be fully guaranteed unless all three types of duties are fulfilled."[3]

Shue's argument is persuasive. However, two opposite conclusions can be
drawn from it. One (the conclusion which Shue and others who argue similarly, invite us to draw) is that economic and social rights have to be considered as equally solid as civil and political rights, since there is no difference of
principle between the state's provision of security for the vulnerable and social security for the deprived. Those who are prepared to defend the one have
to treat the other with equal seriousness. The opposite response, however, is to
conclude that Shue's argument makes civil and political rights every bit as pre-
carious as economic and social ones. If the most that can realistically be required from governments with limited resources, as from individuals with limited moral capacities, is duties of restraint or avoidance of harm to others; and
if these negative duties are on their own insufficient to guarantee any human
rights, as Shue has ably demonstrated: then no human right can be regarded as
secure, since they all remain unanchored by the full range of corresponding
duties. In other words, to make the case for human rights it is not enough simply to show what range of duties *would be* required to make the rights effective; it has also to be shown that these are duties which appropriate agents can
reasonably be expected to fulfil.

The argument has therefore to be engaged at a deeper level, and a second
assumption—that we have no general duty to aid others—needs examination.
This is particularly important to economic and social rights, because the suspicion remains, despite all Shue's endeavors, that the two sets of rights are not
after all symmetrical. More seems able to be achieved comparatively in the

civil and political field by government abstention; and more seems required comparatively in the economic and social sphere by way of positive aid and provision. Moreover, while the provision of defence and law and order can readily be presented as a public good, from which all benefit, key elements of a basic economic and social agenda more readily assume the aspect of a particular good, which benefits definable sections of the population through transfer from the rest. Examining the logic of duties, therefore, is particularly necessary in respect of economic and social rights.

The argument that the only general duties we owe to unspecified others are negative ones, to refrain from harming them, not positively to give aid, is rooted not merely in liberal categories of politics, which prioritize non-interference, but also in a basic moral intuition about what we can reasonably be held responsible for. The objections to holding people responsible (and therefore morally reprehensible) for all the good that they could do, but do not, as well as for the harm they actually do, are twofold. Whereas the latter, sins of commission, are clearly assignable (to *our* actions), and to avoid them entails a clearly delimited responsibility (we can reasonably be required to take care not to harm others, and it is usually evident what this involves), a general duty to aid others is both potentially *limitless*, and also *non-assignable* (why us rather than millions of others?). By contrast, special duties to give aid—to family, friends, clients, etc.—derive their moral weight precisely from the fact that they are both clearly assignable and delimited, and in this they share with the general negative duty to avoid harming others the necessary characteristics of *circumscription* for a duty which a person can reasonably be required to fulfil.[4]

There is much force in these considerations. Most of us remain unconvinced by philosophical arguments which show that inaction is simply another form of action, and omissions therefore as culpable as commissions. A morality which requires us to go on giving up to the point where our condition is equal to that of the poorest of those we are aiding is morality for saints and heroes, perhaps, but not for ordinary mortals; and not one, therefore, on which the delivery of basic rights can rely. However, it does not follow from these arguments that there can be *no* general duty to aid the needy, or that such a duty cannot be specified in a form sufficiently circumscribed to meet the criteria outlined above.

Consider an elementary example. All would surely agree that children have a variety of needs which they are unable to meet by themselves, and that a duty therefore falls on adults to aid and protect them. In most cases this responsibility is fulfilled by their parents or other close relatives as a 'special' duty by virtue of their relationship. However, where there is no one alive to perform this duty, or those who have the responsibility are incapable of meeting it, then it falls as a general duty on the community as a whole. Here is an example of a general duty to aid the needy, whose ground lies in the manifest needs of the child. Yet it is neither limitless nor unassignable. It is not a duty to all children, but only those for whom no one is able to care as their 'special' duty; they are, so to say, a residual rather than a bottomless category. And the duty falls upon members of the society in which they live as those most appropriately placed to help, just as when someone is in danger of drowning those most appropriately placed to help, and therefore with the duty to do so, are those present at the incident. In the case of children, however, those responsible will typically fufil their duty, not as individuals in an *ad hoc* manner, but collectively, by establishing arrangements whereby the children are placed in the care of professionals or foster parents, and paid for by a levy on all members capable of contributing. A publicly acknowledged duty so to aid those in need, with whom we stand in no special relationships, forms one of the principles of the modern welfare state.[5]

It is mistaken therefore to assume that, if there is a general duty to aid those in need, it can only be unlimited and unassignable, and so must be either unrealistically burdensome or inadequate to guarantee any universal rights. We incur general duties to aid the needy in a social world already structured with special relationships and special duties, and in which most people meet their basic needs for themselves either individually or collectively. . . .

As the ICESCR recognizes, it is governments that have the overarching duty to ensure a division of labour in the matter of positive duties, and one that is both appropriate to their own societies and sufficient to ensure that the rights are effectively secured. This is an obligation on all states, but one with quasi-legal or contractual status for the 130 (as of 1994) that have ratified the Covenant. As the so-called Limburg principles of interpretation of the Covenant insist, states are "accountable both to the international community and to their own people for their compliance with the obligations under the Covenant."[6] In other words, the obligations corresponding to the rights are not merely derivable from a general moral duty, on the part of both individuals and governments, to aid those in need; they are also publicly acknowledged by international agreement.

But what if states are unable to meet their obligation to realize a minimum agenda of basic rights? Whose duty does it then become to assist them, and to aid the deprived to realize their rights? By a logical extension of the general duty to aid those in need, and the principle of a division of labour in fulfilling that duty, it clearly falls to other governments with the resources to do so, coordinated by an international body such as the UN and its agencies. A prior duty to aid those within our own country—whether we argue this on the 'kith and kin' principle, or, more plausibly, from the logic of a world organized into territorial citizenships[7]—does not absolve us of any wider duty. This is indeed publicly acknowledged in internationally agreed aid targets for the developed countries, in their contributions to UN agencies, in the continuous public support for the work of NGOs, in the massive (if spasmodic) public response to emergency appeals, and so on. These may be all insufficient, but the duty is at least generally acknowledged.

A clear answer can thus be given to the objection that economic and social rights remain unanchored by any corresponding duties. The ground of the duty is the same as for the rights themselves: in human needs. The general duty to aid those in need is, however, neither unlimited nor unassignable. It falls in the first instance upon governments, from societal resources, to ensure that basic rights are realized where individuals, families or groups prove insufficient by themselves; and to the international organizations in turn, from the resources of the developed world, to support this effort where national resources prove insufficient. Such duties are widely acknowledged.

## ▨ Notes

1. S. M. Okin, 'Liberty and welfare: some issues in human rights theory,' in J. R. Pennock and J.W. Chapman (eds), *Human Rights: Nomos XXIII* (New York: New York University Press, 1981), pp. 230–56; R. Plant, 'A defence of welfare rights,' in R. Beddard and D. M. Hill (eds), *Economic, Social and Cultural Rights* (Basingstoke: Macmillan, 1992), pp. 22–46; R. Plant, *Modern Political Thought* (Oxford: Blackwell, 1991), pp. 267–86; H. Shue, *Basic Rights: Subsistence, Affluences and U.S. Foreign Policy* (New Jersey: Princeton University Press, 1980), ch. 2.

2. Okin, 'Liberty and welfare,' p. 240.

3. Shue, *Basic Rights*, p. 53.

4. See P. Foot, *Virtues and Vice* (Oxford: Blackwell, 1978); H. L. A. Hart, 'Are there any natural rights?', *Philosophical Review* (1955) 64:2, 175–191.

5. R. E. Goodin, *Protecting the Vulnerable* (Chicago: University of Chicago Press, 1985), pp. 134–144; see also Plant, *Modern Political Thought*, pp. 284–285.

6. UN Doc. E/C/1987/17, Annex, principle 10.

7. R. E. Goodin, 'What is so special about our fellow countrymen?', *Ethics*. 98 (1988). 663–686.

# 1.4 _____

# Basic Rights
*Henry Shue*

## ■ Basic Rights

Basic rights, then, are everyone's minimum reasonable demands upon the rest of humanity. They are the rational basis for justified demands the denial of which no self-respecting person can reasonably be expected to accept. Why should anything be so important? The reason is that rights are basic in the sense used here only if enjoyment of them is essential to the enjoyment of all other rights. This is what is distinctive about a basic right. When a right is genuinely basic, any attempt to enjoy any other right by sacrificing the basic right would be quite literally self-defeating, cutting the ground from beneath itself. Therefore, if a right is basic, other, non-basic rights may be sacrificed, if necessary, in order to secure the basic right. But the protection of a basic right may not be sacrificed in order to secure the enjoyment of a non-basic right. It may not be sacrificed because it cannot be sacrificed successfully. If the right sacrificed is indeed basic, then no right for which it might be sacrificed can actually be enjoyed in the absence of the basic right. The sacrifice would have proven self-defeating.

In practice, what this priority for basic rights usually means is that basic rights need to be established securely before other rights can be secured. The point is that people should be able to *enjoy*, or *exercise*, their other rights. The point is simple but vital. It is not merely that people should "have" their other rights in some merely legalistic or otherwise abstract sense compatible with being unable to make any use of the substance of the right. For example, if people have rights to free association, they ought not merely to "have" the rights to free association but also to enjoy their free association itself. Their freedom of association ought to be provided for by the relevant social institutions. This distinction between merely having a right and actually enjoying a right may seem a fine point, but it turns out later to be critical.

What is not meant by saying that a right is basic is that the right is more valuable or intrinsically more satisfying to enjoy than some other rights. For example, I shall soon suggest that rights to physical security, such as the right not to be assaulted, are basic, and I shall not include the right to publicly supported education as basic. But I do not mean by this to deny that enjoyment of the right to education is much greater and richer—more distinctively human, perhaps—than merely going through life without ever being assaulted. I mean only that, if a choice must be made, the prevention of assault ought to supersede the provision of education. Whether a right is basic is independent of whether its enjoyment is also valuable in itself. Intrinsically valuable rights may or may not also be basic rights, but intrinsically valuable rights can be enjoyed only when basic rights are enjoyed. Clearly few rights could be basic in this precise sense. . . .

## ■ Security Rights

If we had to justify our belief that people have a basic right to physical security to someone who challenged this fundamental conviction, we could in fact give a strong argument that shows that if there are any rights (basic or not basic) at all, there are basic rights to physical security:

> No one can fully enjoy any right that is supposedly protected by society if someone can credibly threaten him or her with murder, rape, beating, etc., when he or she tries to enjoy the alleged right. Such threats to physical security are among the most serious and—in much of the world—the most wide-spread hindrances to the enjoyment of any right. If any right is to be exercised except at great risk, physical security must be protected. In the absence of physical security people are unable to use any other rights that society may be said to be protecting without being liable to encounter many of the worst dangers they would encounter if society were not protecting the rights.
>
> A right to full physical security belongs, then, among the basic rights—not because the enjoyment of it would be more satisfying to someone who was also enjoying a full range of other rights, but because its absence would leave available extremely effective means for others, including the government, to interfere with or prevent the actual exercise of any other rights that were supposedly protected. Regardless of whether the enjoyment of physical security is also desirable for its own sake, it is desirable as part of the enjoyment of every other right. No rights other than a right to physical security can in fact be enjoyed if a right to physical security is not protected. Being physically secure is a necessary condition for the exercise of any other right, and guaranteeing physical security must be part of guaranteeing anything else as a right. . . .

## ▪ Subsistence Rights

By a "right to subsistence" I shall always mean a right to at least subsistence. People may or may not have economic rights that go beyond subsistence rights, and I do not want to prejudge that question here. But people may have rights to subsistence even if they do not have any strict rights to economic well-being extending beyond subsistence. Subsistence rights and broader economic rights are separate questions, and I want to focus here on subsistence.

I also do not want to prejudge the issue of whether healthy adults are entitled to be provided with subsistence *only* if they cannot provide subsistence for themselves. Most of the world's malnourished, for example, are probably also diseased, since malnutrition lowers resistance to disease, and hunger and infestation normally form a tight vicious circle. Hundreds of millions of the malnourished are very young children. A large percentage of the adults, besides being ill and hungry, are also chronically unemployed, so the issue of policy toward healthy adults who refuse to work is largely irrelevant. By a "right to subsistence," then, I shall mean a right to subsistence that includes the provision of subsistence at least to those who cannot provide for themselves. I do not assume that no one else is also entitled to receive subsistence—I simply do not discuss cases of healthy adults who could support themselves but refuse to do so. If there is a right to subsistence in the sense discussed here, at least the people who cannot provide for themselves, including the children, are entitled to receive at least subsistence. Nothing follows one way or the other about anyone else. . . .

The same considerations that support the conclusion that physical security is a basic right support the conclusion that subsistence is a basic right. Since the argument is now familiar, it can be given fairly briefly.

It is quite obvious why, if we still assume that there are some rights that society ought to protect and still mean by this the removal of the most serious and general hindrances to the actual enjoyment of the rights, subsistence ought to be protected as a basic right:

> No one can fully, if at all, enjoy any right that is supposedly protected by society if he or she lacks the essential for a reasonably healthy and active life. Deficiencies in the means of subsistence can be just as fatal, incapacitating, or painful as violations of physical security. The resulting damage or death can at least as decisively prevent the enjoyment of any right as the effects of security violations. Any form of malnutrition, or fever due to exposure, that causes severe and irreversible brain damage, for example, can effectively prevent the exercise of any right requiring clear thought and may, like brain injuries caused by assault, profoundly disturb personality. And,

obviously, any fatal deficiencies end all possibility of the enjoyment of rights as firmly as an arbitrary execution.

Indeed, prevention of deficiencies in the essentials for survival is, if anything, more basic than prevention of violations of physical security. People who lack protection against violations of their physical security can, if they are free, fight back against their attackers or flee, but people who lack essentials, such as food, because of forces beyond their control, often can do nothing and are on their own utterly helpless.

The scope of subsistence rights must not be taken to be broader than it is. In particular, this step of the argument does not make the following absurd claim: since death and serious illness prevent or interfere with the enjoyment of rights, everyone has a basic right not to be allowed to die or to be seriously ill. Many causes of death and illness are outside the control of society, and many deaths and illnesses are the result of very particular conjunctions of circumstances that general social policies cannot control. But it is not impractical to expect some level of social organization to protect the minimal cleanliness of air and water and to oversee the adequate production, or import, and the proper distribution of minimal food, clothing, shelter, and elementary health care. It is not impractical, in short, to expect effective management, when necessary, of the supplies of the essentials of life. So the argument is: when death and serious illness could be prevented by different social policies regarding the essentials of life, the protection of any human right involves avoidance of fatal or debilitating deficiencies in these essential commodities. And this means fulfilling subsistence rights as basic rights. This is society's business because the problems are serious and general. This is a basic right because failure to deal with it would hinder the enjoyment of all other rights.

Thus, the same considerations that establish that security rights are basic for everyone also support the conclusion that subsistence rights are basic for everyone. It is not being claimed or assumed that security and subsistence are parallel in all, or even very many, respects. The only parallel being relied upon is that guarantees of security and guarantees of subsistence are equally essential to providing for the actual exercise of any other rights. As long as security and subsistence are parallel in this respect, the argument applies equally to both cases, and other respects in which security and subsistence are not parallel are irrelevant.

It is not enough that people merely happen to be secure or happen to be subsisting. They must have a right to security and a right to subsistence—the continued enjoyment of the security and the subsistence must be socially guaranteed. Otherwise a person is readily open to coercion and intimidation through threats of the deprivation of one or the other, and credible threats can paralyze a person and prevent the exercise of any other right as surely as actual beatings and actual protein/calorie deficiencies can. Credible threats can be reduced only by the actual establishment of social arrangements that will bring assistance to those confronted by forces that they themselves cannot handle.

Consequently the guaranteed security and guaranteed subsistence are what we might initially be tempted to call "simultaneous necessities" for the exercise of any other right. They must be present at any time that any other right is to be exercised, or people can be prevented from enjoying the other right by deprivations or threatened deprivations of security or of subsistence. But to think in terms of simultaneity would be largely to miss the point. A better label, if any is needed, would be "inherent necessities." For it is not that security from beatings, for instance, is separate from freedom of peaceful assembly but that it always needs to accompany it. Being secure from beatings if one chooses to hold a meeting is part of being free to assemble. If one cannot safely assemble, one is not free to assemble. One is, on the contrary, being coerced not to assemble by the threat of the beatings.

The same is true if taking part in the meeting would lead to dismissal by the only available employer when employment is the only source of income for the purchase of food. Guarantees of security and subsistence are not added advantages over and above enjoyment of the right to assemble. They are essential parts of it. For this reason it would be misleading to construe security or subsistence—or the substance of any other basic right—merely as "means" to the enjoyment of all other rights. The enjoyment of security and subsistence is an essential part of the enjoyment of all other rights. Part of what it means to enjoy any other right is to be able to exercise that right without, as a consequence, suffering the actual or threatened loss of one's physical security or one's subsistence. And part of what it means to be able to enjoy any other right is not to be prevented from exercising it by lack of security or of subsistence. To claim to guarantee people a right that they are in fact unable to exercise is fraudulent, like furnishing people with meal tickets but providing no food.

# 1.5 _____

# The Philosophical Foundations of Human Rights
*Jerome J. Shestack*

## ■ Sources of Human Rights

### Religion
To be sure, the term "human rights" as such is not found in traditional religions. Nonetheless, theology presents the basis for a human rights theory stemming from a law higher than that of the state and whose source is the Supreme Being.

If one accepts the premise of the Old Testament that Adam was created in the "image of God," this implies that the divine stamp gives human beings a high value of worth. In a similar vein the Quran says, "surely we have accorded dignity to the sons of man." So too, in the Bhagavad-Gita, "Who sees his Lord/Within every creature/ Deathlessly dwelling/Amidst the mortal: That man sees truly. . . ."

In a religious context every human being is considered sacred. Accepting a universal common father gives rise to a common humanity, and from this flows a universality of certain rights. Because rights stem from a divine source, they are inalienable by mortal authority. This concept is found not only in the Judeo-Christian tradition, but also in Islam and other religions with a deistic base.[1]

Even if one accepts the revealed truth of the fatherhood of God and the brotherhood of all humans, the problem of which human rights flow therefrom remains. Equality of all human beings in the eyes of God would seem a necessary development from the common creation by God, but freedom to live as one prefers is not. Indeed, religions generally impose severe limitations on individual freedom. For most religions, the emphasis falls on duties rather than rights. Moreover, revelation is capable of differing interpretations, and some religions have been quite restrictive toward slaves, women, and nonbelievers, even though all are God's creations. Thus, at least as practiced, serious incompatibilities exist

Excerpted from Jerome J. Shestack, "The Philosophical Foundations of Human Rights," *Human Rights Quarterly* 20 (2): 201–234. © 1998 The Johns Hopkins University Press. Reprinted with permission of The Johns Hopkins University Press. Some of the author's notes have been omitted.

between various religious practices and the scope of human rights structured by the United Nations.

However, religious philosophers of all faiths are engaged in the process of interpreting religious doctrines toward the end of effecting a reconciliation with basic human rights prescriptions. This process is largely via hermeneutic exercise, namely reinterpretation of a religion's sacred texts through both historical explication and a type of prophetic application to modern conditions.

Thus, religious doctrine offers a promising possibility of constructing a broad intercultural rationale that supports the various fundamental principles of equality and justice that underlie international human rights. Indeed, once the leap to belief has been made, religion may be the most attractive of the theoretical approaches. When human beings are not visualized in God's image then their basic rights may well lose their metaphysical *raison d'être*. On the other hand, the concept of human beings created in the image of God certainly endows men and women with a worth and dignity from which the components of a comprehensive human rights system can flow logically. . . .

### Natural Law: The Autonomous Individual

Natural law theory led to natural rights theory—the theory most closely associated with modern human rights. The chief exponent of this theory was John Locke, who developed his philosophy within the framework of seventeenth century humanism and political activity, known as the Age of Enlightenment. Locke imagined the existence of human beings in a state of nature. In that state men and women were in a state of freedom, able to determine their actions, and also in a state of equality in the sense that no one was subjected to the will or authority of another. However, to end the hazards and inconveniences of the state of nature, men and women entered into a "social contract" by which they mutually agreed to form a community and set up a body politic. Still, in setting up that political authority, individuals retained the natural rights of life, liberty, and property. Government was obliged to protect the natural rights of its subjects, and if government neglected this obligation, it forfeited its validity and office.

Natural rights theory was the philosophic impetus for the wave of revolt against absolutism during the late eighteenth century. It is visible in the French Declaration of the Rights of Man, in the US Declaration of Independence, in the constitutions of numerous states created upon liberation from colonialism, and in the principal UN human rights documents.

Natural rights theory makes an important contribution to human rights. It affords an appeal from the realities of naked power to a higher authority that is asserted for the protection of human rights. It identifies with and provides security for human freedom and equality, from which other human rights easily flow. It also provides properties of security and support for a human rights system, both domestically and internationally.

From a philosophical viewpoint, the critical problem that natural rights doctrine faced is how to determine the norms that are to be considered as part of the law of nature and therefore inalienable, or at least prima facie inalienable.

Under Locke's view of human beings in the state of nature, all that was needed was the opportunity to be self-dependent; life, liberty, and property were the inherent rights that met this demand. But what about a world unlike the times of Locke, in which ample resources are not available to satisfy human needs? Does natural law theory have the flexibility to satisfy new claims based on contemporary conditions and modern human understanding? Perhaps it does, but that very potential for flexibility has formed the basis for the chief criticism of natural rights theory. Critics pointed out that most of the norm setting of natural rights theories contain *a priori* elements deduced by the norm setter. In short, the principal problem with natural law is that the rights considered to be natural can differ from theorist to theorist, depending upon their conceptions of nature. . . .

### Positivism: The Authority of the State

Classical positivist philosophers deny an *a priori* source of rights and assume that all authority stems from what the state and officials have prescribed. This approach rejects any attempt to discern and articulate an idea of law transcending the empirical realities of existing legal systems. Under positivist theory, the source of human rights is found only in the enactments of a system of law with sanctions attached to it. Views on what the law "ought" to be have no place in law and are cognitively worthless. The theme that haunts positivist exponents is the need to distinguish with maximum clarity law as it is from law as it ought to be, and they condemned natural law thinkers because they had blurred this vital distinction. In its essence, positivism negates the moral philosophic basis of human rights.[2]

By divorcing a legal system from the ethical and moral foundations of society, positive law encourages the belief that the law must be obeyed, no matter how immoral it may be, or however it disregards the world of the individual. The anti-Semitic edicts of the Nazis, although abhorrent to moral law, were obeyed as positive law. The same is true of the immoral apartheid practices that prevailed in South Africa for many years. The fact that positivist philosophy has been used to justify obedience to iniquitous laws has been a central focus for much of the modern criticism of that doctrine. Critics of positivism maintain that unjust laws not only lack a capacity to demand fidelity, but also do not deserve the name of law because they lack internal morality.

Even granting the validity of the criticism, the positivist contribution can still be significant. If the state's processes can be brought to bear in the protection of human rights, it becomes easier to focus upon the specific implementation that is necessary for the protection of particular rights. Indeed, positivist thinkers such as Jeremy Bentham and John Austin were often in the vanguard of those who sought to bring about reform in the law. Always under human control, a positivist system also offers flexibility to meet changing needs. . . .

### Marxism: Man as a Specie Being

Marx regarded the law of nature approach to human rights as idealistic and ahistorical. He saw nothing natural or inalienable about human rights. In a society in which capitalists monopolize the means of production, Marx regarded the notion of individual rights as a bourgeois illusion. Concepts such as law, justice, morality, democracy, freedom, etc., were considered historical categories, whose content was determined by the material conditions and the social circumstances of a people. As the conditions of life change, so the content of notions and ideas may change.

Marxism sees a person's essence as the potential to use one's abilities to the fullest and to satisfy one's needs.[3] In capitalist society, production is controlled by a few. Consequently, such a society cannot satisfy those individual needs. An actualization of potential is contingent on the return of men and women to themselves as social beings, which occurs in a communist society devoid of class conflict. However, until that stage is reached, the state is a social collectivity and is the vehicle for the transformation of society. Such a conceptualization of the nature of society precludes the existence of individual rights rooted in the state of nature that are prior to the state. The only rights are those granted by the state, and their exercise is contingent on the fulfillment of obligations to society and to the state.

The Marxist system of rights has often been referred to as "parental," with the authoritarian political body providing the sole guidance in value choice. The creation of such a "specie being" is a type of paternalism that not only ignores transcendental reason, but negates individuality. In practice, pursuit of the prior claims of society as reflected in the interests of the Communist state has resulted in systematic suppression of individual civil and political rights. . . .

### The Sociological Approach: Process and Interest

To many scholars, each of the theories of rights discussed thus far is deficient. Moreover, the twentieth century is quite a different place from the nineteenth. Natural and social sciences have developed and begun to increase understanding about people and their cultures, their conflicts, and their interests. Anthropology, psychology, and other disciplines lent their insights. These developments inspired what has been called the sociological school of jurisprudence. "School" is perhaps a misnomer, because what has evolved is a number of disparate theories that have the common denominator of trying to line up the law with the facts of human life in society. Sociological jurisprudence tends to move away from both *a priori* theories and analytical types of jurisprudence. This approach, insofar as it relates to human rights, sometimes directs attention to the questions of institutional development, sometimes focuses on specific problems of public policy that have a bearing on human rights, and sometimes aims at classifying behavioral dimensions of law and society. In a human rights context, the approach is useful because it identifies the empirical components of a human rights system in the context of the social process.[4]

A primary contribution of the sociological school is its emphasis on obtaining a just equilibrium of interests among prevailing moral sentiments and the social and economic conditions of time and place. In many ways this approach can be said to build on William James' pragmatic principle that "the essence of good is simply to satisfy demand."[5] This approach also was related to the development in twentieth century society of increased demands for a variety of wants beyond classical civil and political liberties—such matters as help for the unemployed, the handicapped, the underprivileged, minorities, and other elements of society. . . .

### Rights Based on the Value of Utility

Utilitarianism is a *maximizing* and *collectivizing* principle that requires governments to maximize the total net sum of the happiness of all their subjects. This principle is in contrast to natural rights theory, which is a *distributive* and *individualizing* principle that assigns priority to specific basic interests of each individual subject.

Classic utilitarianism, the most explored branch of this school, is a moral theory that judges the rightness of actions affecting outcomes in terms of securing the greatest happiness to all concerned. Utilitarian theory played a commanding role in the philosophy and political theory of the nineteenth century and continues with some vigor in the twentieth.

Jeremy Bentham, who expounded classical utilitarianism, believed that every human decision was motivated by some calculation of pleasure and pain. He thought that every political decision should be made on the same calculation, that is, to maximize the net produce of pleasure over pain. Hence, both governments and the limits of governments were to be judged not by reference to abstract individual rights, but in terms of what tends to promote the greatest happiness of the greatest number. Because all count equally at the primary level, anyone may have to accept sacrifices if the benefits they yield to others are large enough to outweigh such sacrifices.

Bentham's happiness principle enjoyed enormous popularity and influence during the first half of the nineteenth century when most reformers spoke the language of utilitarianism. Nonetheless, Bentham's principle met with no shortage of criticism. His "felicific calculus," that is, adding and subtracting the pleasure and pain units of different persons to determine what would produce the greatest net balance of happiness, has come to be viewed as a practical, if not a theoretic, impossibility.

Later utilitarian thinkers have restated the doctrine in terms of "revealed preferences."[6] Here, the utilitarian guide for governmental conduct would not be pleasure or happiness, but an economically focused value of general welfare, reflecting the maximum satisfaction and minimum frustration of wants and preferences. Such restatements of utilitarian theory have an obvious appeal in the sphere of economic decision making. Even then, conceptual and practical problems plague utilitarian value theory: the ambiguities of the welfare concept, the nature of the person who is the subject of welfare, the uncertain basis of individual preference of one whose satisfaction is at issue, and other problems inherent in the process of identifying the consequences of an act and in estimating the value of the consequences. . . .

The essential criticism of utilitarianism is that it fails to recognize individual autonomy; it fails to take rights seriously. Utilitarianism, however refined, retains the central principle of maximizing the aggregate desires or general welfare as the ultimate criterion of value. While utilitarianism treats persons as equals, it does so only in the sense of including them in the mathematical equation, but not in the sense of attributing worth to each individual. Under the utilitarian equation, one individual's desires or welfare may be sacrificed as long as aggregate satisfaction or welfare is increased. Utilitarianism thus fails to treat persons as equals, in that it literally dissolves moral personality into utilitarian aggregates. Moreover, the mere increase in aggregate happiness or welfare, if abstracted from questions of distribution and worth of the individual, is not a real value or true moral goal.

Hence, despite the egalitarian pretensions of utilitarian doctrine, it has a sinister side in which the well-being of the individual may be sacrificed for what are claimed to be aggregate interests, and justice and right have no secure place. Utilitarian philosophy thus leaves liberty and rights vulnerable to contingencies, and therefore at risk.

## ▀ Notes

1. *See generally* Simon Greenberg, *Foundations of a Faith* (1967); Leonard Swidler, *Religious Liberty and Human Rights: In Nations and in Religions* (1986); Ann Elizabeth Mayer, *Islam and Human Rights* (1991).

2. *See, e.g.,* Herbert Lionel Hart, *Positivism and the Separation of Law and Morals*, 71 Harv. L. Rev. 593 (1955); John Austin, *The Province of Jurisprudence Determined* (Wilfrid E. Rumble ed., 1985).

3. Karl Marx, *The Economic and Philosophic Manuscripts of 1844* (Martin Milligan trans., Dirk J. Struik ed., 1969).

4. *See* Karl Llewellyn, *Jurisprudence: Realism in Theory and Practice* (1962).

5. William James, *Pragmatism* (1975).

6. *See* Joseph Raz, *The Morality of Freedom* 267–87 (1986).

# 2 Measuring Human Rights

## 2.1 _____

# Introduction
*The Editors*

In this section, we explore the empirical study of human rights. With the behavioral revolution, the study of politics was transformed as scholars began to apply the principles of the scientific method. This revolution eventually reached the study of human rights, but not without controversy. Should we study human rights empirically, or does this move us away from the emotional stories and normative policy emphases that motivate the study of human rights in the first place? Can we define human rights, or are human rights culturally bound and therefore impossible to capture in a single definition? Perhaps more problematic, is it possible to measure human rights abuse? These questions continue to pervade the study of human rights. At the same time, there has been a general move in the study of human rights toward more empirical research. Definitions of human rights, though contentious, have been put forth. Measurements, though not perfect, have been created. As a result, the study of human rights continues to be increasingly empirical in nature.

The first group of articles examines measurement issues in the study of human rights. The excerpt from Robert Goldstein examines the general difficulty in defining and measuring human rights, particularly security rights. According to Goldstein, even if we could agree on a definition of human rights, there are real barriers to actually collecting such data. Goldstein points out that data are the least reliable in the most repressive regimes, as these states often have an incentive to cover up atrocities. Goldstein does an excellent job of elucidating the possible pitfalls of empirical human rights research. Even with all of its problems, though, he does not suggest that empirical research should never be pursued. Instead, Goldstein prescribes that empirical studies should be supplemented with normative ones.

David Richards addresses the concepts of scope, validity, reliability, and level of aggregation as they apply to measuring human rights. He discusses several existing human rights measures in terms of these concepts. Richards provides a thorough explanation of how basic statistical properties must be addressed in social science measurement.

The next piece is an excerpt from an article by Mark Gibney and Matthew Dalton discussing the measurement of security rights using the Political Terror Scale (PTS). The PTS is one of the prevalent measures of security rights used in empirical study. This piece illustrates how researchers might address the difficulties discussed in the Goldstein piece. Gibney and Dalton specify the method and criteria for translating Amnesty International reports and US State Department reports into a single human rights score for a country. They discuss the coding criteria for each level of the PTS, as well as instructions given to the coders. They also indicate how this particular scale deals with problems in measuring security rights.

Steven C. Poe, Sabine C. Carey, and Tanya C. Vazquez systematically compare reports generated by the US State Department with those from Amnesty International. Utilizing the same PTS scale as Gibney and Dalton, these researchers look for differences in country scores across time. They find that State Department reports may be colored by security concerns, whereas early Amnesty reports covered only the worst offenders. Although they find substantive differences between the two reports, they also see a convergence of the two scores over time.

These same types of measurement issues are dealt with in the selection by Wesley T. Milner and Rhonda L. Callaway, which outlines the criteria used to create the Physical Quality of Life Index. This measure attempts to capture the level of subsistence rights or basic human needs within a state. One of the primary dilemmas in measuring subsistence is determining if a single measure adequately reflects the concept. Milner and Callaway discuss the disadvantages of single indicators, particularly per capita gross domestic product (GDP), and argue in favor of utilizing an index. After presenting the criteria used to evaluate such indices, they illustrate how the Physical Quality of Life Index qualifies as a reliable and valid measure of basic human needs.

# 2.2 ───────

# The Limitations of Using Quantitative Data in Studying Human Rights Abuses
*Robert Justin Goldstein*

## ▣ Problems in Obtaining Reliable Data

### Historical Studies

An insistence upon relying heavily on quantitative data rules out or strongly limits significant scholarly pre-twentieth-century analysis of human rights problems. Cross-nationally comparable and longitudinal quantitative data for entire countries, as opposed to small geographic regions, are scarce for any area before 1800. When available, the data are often of dubious reliability until well after 1900. Much of what reasonably reliable data exist before the late nineteenth century are available only for Europe; even then, the vast bulk of them are aggregate economic data such as agricultural and industrial output. Data useful for social and economic human rights studies such as information on infant mortality, life expectancy, standards of living, literacy, and unemployment become available for Europe around 1850 but are far more fragmentary and unreliable.[1]

Measures of political human rights violations such as numbers of political prisoners and killings of protesters by the police and military (there were many such violations) simply do not exist in any systematic form for pre-twentieth-century Europe. Although large-scale massacres and executions presumably would be easiest to measure, invariably one must rely solely upon gross estimates of those killed or upon government figures which scholars agree are serious underestimations. For example, although the "Bloody Sunday" massacre of 9 January 1905, which touched off the Russian Revolution of that year, has been extensively studied, all that scholars can agree upon is that the official government count of 130 killed is a ludicrous underestimate.

---

The most thorough attempt to calculate casualties resulting from American labor disputes in the 1873–1937 period produced a tally of over 700 deaths and thousands of serious injuries but also a warning that the data are gross underestimates. The authors state that the United States has had the "bloodiest and most violent labor history of any industrial nation in the world"; however, as there are no comparable studies, this conclusion may be quite misleading. Depending upon the definition of labor dispute, casualties may well have been higher in France, Russia, Spain, and Italy.[2]

Obtaining human rights–related data, aside from deaths for the pre-1900 period, is usually even more difficult. For the United States and Europe, data on such subjects as politically motivated arrests, police brutality, incidents involving censorship, numbers of political exiles, and so forth, are generally either not available or are accessible only in highly decentralized police archives or in hundreds of newspapers (which, at least in Europe, were often censored). Outside of Europe and the Anglo-American lands, even basic population data are unavailable, and data concerning political, civil, social, or economic rights before 1900 are for all practical purposes nonexistent.

### Contemporary Studies

The availability and reliability of various forms of quantitative data for the twentieth century far exceed those for the pre-1900 period. This is markedly less so, however, for the underdeveloped world where statistical reporting procedures are often embryonic; embarrassing information is also often deliberately suppressed. Thus, there has never been a complete national census conducted in either Chad or Afghanistan. Although it is widely believed that the highest concentration of AIDS disease occurs in central Africa, African governments have refused to cooperate in releasing statistics for fear of bad publicity. Also, surveillance systems for communicable diseases in the region are inadequate. Much data on world hunger and malnutrition (including those for the United States) are inadequate; estimates of the number of persons who starved to death in the Ethiopian famine of 1984–1985 range from several hundred thousand to over one million.[3] . . .

*Social and economic human rights data.* Contemporary quantitative data are clearly far more available and reliable in the areas of social and economic rights than in political, civil, and personal security rights. Thus, data on such clearly definable and relatively easily countable subjects as mortality rates, infant mortality rates, and life expectancy are available for almost all countries, although the quality of these data deteriorates for some of the poorest nations (notably those in sub-Saharan Africa). Other data, such as measures of poverty, literacy, unemployment, and homelessness, present major problems of conceptualization, interpretation, and measurement. In some cases, data may be unavailable for cross-national comparative purposes, due to definitional differences or lack of compilation, but may be adequate for the purpose of tracking trends within individual countries. . . .

*Political, civil, and personal security human rights data.* The availability and reliability of data for contemporary human rights studies deteriorate markedly when the focus shifts to the political, civil, and personal security areas. This is especially true for some of the worst human rights violations such as torture and arbitrary executions, and for candidates for worst violators, such as, in the 1965–1985 period, Guatemala, Indonesia, Uganda, Argentina, and Cambodia. Occasionally modern governments, especially those in the developed world, which claim to value adherence to legal norms, do publish data related to political human rights violations. South Africa, for example, reports enough data that AI [Amnesty International] could estimate 238,000 arrests of blacks for pass-law violations occurring in 1984 and could report that South Africa led the world in 1985 with 137 "confirmed" executions.[4] In general, however, the problem is quite simply that governments do not generally publish statistics on how repressive they are (much less in forms comparable across countries or time!), and it is virtually an axiom that the more repressive the regime, the more difficult it makes access to information about its human rights atrocities to researchers (or anyone else).

Thus, it is astonishing, but true, that it was years after the mass executions in Stalin's Russia, Hitler's Germany, Idi Amin's Uganda and Pol Pot's Cambodia before authenticated information about the extent of the crimes there became available—and then only after the death or ouster of the dictator. Even today, however, what presumably would be the easiest quantitative indicator to gather and verify—the number of deaths—remains a mystery, with estimates varying not only by hundreds of thousands but in some cases by millions. Reliable information about torture is only rarely available when it is occurring, especially since it cannot generally be proved, even through medical examination. Confirmed information about torture emerged in the 1970s only after changes in the regimes of Portugal, Greece, Iran, Nicaragua, Equatorial Guinea, Cambodia, and Rhodesia.[5] A 1979 study that attempted to use the number of political prisoners per capita as a measure of repression was greatly hindered (aside from the problem of comparable definition across countries) by the total lack of such data for many countries; for example, data were available for only half the Latin American countries.[6] Often what data are available for political prisoners vary widely from source to source. Thus the Rumanian government reported 7,674 political prisoners in 1960 but AI reported 12,000; for 1971, the Indonesian government claimed 45,000 while AI reported 116,000; for the same country the U.S. State Department reported 31,000 political prisoners in 1976 while AI found 55,000.[7] After the fall of the Marcos regime in the Philippines, the new government was for days unable even to find many political prisoners because it could find no single master list.

In general, obstruction is the normal contemporary governmental response to attempts to gather data on human rights violations and has often made it impossible to investigate charges of grave abuses. Thus, Iranian opposition groups have charged the Khomeini regime with over 40,000 executions and thousands of tortures since 1979, but a November 1984 United Nations report could only say such allegations "cannot be dismissed as groundless" since U.N. officials were not allowed to visit Iran and requests for information about 299 persons alleged to have been killed were ignored.[8] Amnesty International, in its October 1985 annual report, stated it could reach no conclusions as to whether more or fewer human rights violations had occurred than in the previous year because, "secrecy concealed many deaths and governments denied responsibility for killings carried out on their orders or with their complicity."[9]

## ■ Difficulties in Interpreting Data

Even if human rights terms can be adequately defined and reliable quantitative information can be obtained, making intelligent assessments of such data will often be extraordinarily difficult, especially if the data are interpreted out of the context of other, nonquantitative sources, such as interviews, on-the-spot observation, and background reading. Measuring and comparing or assessing the impact of different kinds of human rights violations will be extraordinarily difficult because they come in so many forms. Clearly just a raw count of human rights violations (as in the *Handbook*) or any analyses or correlations based on such raw counts will not be terribly revealing without differentiating among different types of violations, since, as Freedom House notes, it is "the pattern of rights, and not a simple checklist of pluses or minuses, that is critical for evaluation."[10] But any form of weighting different types of violations will be even more problematic than a raw count, suggesting that any single summary measure of political human rights violations will be either impossible or meaningless. . . .

Barnett Rubin and Paula Newberg seriously state that a fundamental "dilemma" in human rights research is to determine "how many reports of torture are equivalent to a murder"; Gloria Valencia-Weber and Robert Weber suggest a formula which answers such a question by equating 70 murders with 100 "disappearances"; and Kenneth Bollen suggests creating a system whereby a hypothetical country might be assigned a baseline score of 100 with regard to, for example, freedom of party organization, and then "a real country judged to have party liberties a fifth of the standard would receive a score of 20 while one 18 times greater would have 1800 as a value." John McCamant reports having actually carried out such an endeavor, and that, for example, with regard to the overall human rights climate, he concluded that East Germany was "probably 200 times more severe in 1976 than was the Federal Republic of Germany, but Uganda was still 100 times worse." Chile under Pinochet was assessed as 10 times more repressive than the Philippines and "100 times worse than India."[11]

How can such determinations even be rationally attempted, much less calculated? What does it *mean* to say that there is 18 times more freedom to organize a political party in one country than in another? Or that one country is 200 times more repressive than another? How can one possibly arrive at a theoretically sound formula for equating a certain number of people injured by police at a political demonstration with one killed? How can one reasonably conclude that one newspaper suppressed counts as more than or less than one person killed or one labor union banned? When Lech Walesa or Benjamin Spock is arrested for antigovernment activity, can this possibly be counted as the same as when John Doe (or Jan Doesky) is? Is there any real point in trying to measure degrees of political repression with such exactness, especially given that the underlying data are almost certainly incomplete and noncomparable across countries?

Even if one avoids trying to create overall "indexes" of repression of the sort just discussed, instead sticking to raw counts of human rights abuses, numerous problems of comparability, context, and interpretation remain that statistical data alone cannot resolve. Thus, examples of the difficulties arising from relying on raw counts of political arrests or detentions can easily be found in American history, even though these detentions are some of the more easily measured and cross-nationally common types of violations. During the Alien and Sedition Acts crises of 1798, only about twenty-five arrests were made, a figure which suggests mild repression indeed. One cannot understand the threat these arrests posed to the fledgling American democracy and the uproar they caused without knowing that many were directed against editors of leading opposition newspapers at a time when newspapers were the central element in organized party behavior.

Does the fact that the federal government arrested about 2,100 people for written and oral opposition to World War I compared to only about 200 arrested for similar opposition to World War II indicate that repression was less (as most scholars suggest) during World War II? Probably it simply reflects the fact that hardly anyone opposed the latter war, although those who did often suffered multiple prosecutions. This suggests the need to somehow quantify and measure protest activity and then construct a ratio of repression to protest, tasks which verge on the theoretically gargantuan and the practically impossible.[12] How would the incarceration (but not formal arrest) of 110,000 Japanese-Americans during World War II affect the equation? One scholar has termed this event "the most widespread disregard of personal rights in the nation's history since the abolition of slavery,"[13] yet it conveyed a repressive message only to those with yellow skins. . . .

There are enormous conceptual and practical difficulties in trying to measure the impact that human rights violations have of frightening people into not doing what they might have done otherwise. In some cases, data suggesting few human rights abuses such as few political arrests may actually reflect the success of previous repression or a general but unmeasurable atmosphere of intimidation. This idea is captured in the Chinese proverb, "Kill one, frighten 10,000." Professors Scoble and Wiseberg have noted, however, that in a society with a poorly developed communications network many such actions are needed to attain a "given level of deterrence," while in a more sophisticated setting "the marginal utility of each repressive act is considerably higher."[14] The point is that past repression, as Professor Stohl writes, "seems to radiate a kind of 'afterlife' which lingers and has effects for some time after the observable use of coercion by state agents."[15] Thus, little dissent may reflect either a terrorized or a satisfied society. Statistics alone are unable to tell us which.[16]

To take some concrete examples, low figures for political prisoners being held "may well denote the very opposite of the contented, peaceful conditions they appear to indicate," since "in Amin's Uganda and Pol Pot's Kampuchea, for example, there were less protracted ways of dealing with opponents than confining them to jail."[17] Scholars unanimously agree that the Hapsburg Empire was the leading police state of Europe in the 1815–1830 period, yet there were no political trials or executions during this period because the atmosphere of oppression stifled dissent in the bud. Thus a visitor to Vienna noted, "You can visit public places for months without hearing a single word about politics, so strict is the watch maintained over orthodoxy in both state and church. In all the coffee-houses, there reigns such a reverent silence that you might think High Mass was being celebrated."[18] . . .

## ▨ A Concluding Word

Despite all the problems discussed above, it is not my argument that quantitative data should never be used in human rights studies or that they are never helpful. What must be avoided is a dependence on statistics alone in an area such as human rights, where needed data either are not available or are not meaningful unless interpreted within a historical and political context, which alone can tell us the significance of even negative data such as the lack of dissent in Metternich's Austria and McCarthyite America. What must also be avoided is the orientation that suggests "if you can't measure it, you can't study it" and the disease labeled statistical "moreitis" by former American Statistical Association (ASA) President William Shaw, that more statistics are necessarily better.[19] (That can be true of course—if they are relevant and reliable.)

# ▓ Notes

1. See generally B. R. Mitchell, *European Historical Studies, 1750–1970* (New York: Columbia University Press, 1978).

2. Philip Taft and Philip Ros, "American Labor Violence," in *Violence in America*, ed. Hugh Graham and Ted Gurr (New York: Bantam, 1969), p. 281.

3. Nicholas Eberstadt and Clifford M. Lewis, "How Many Are Hungry?" *Atlantic*, May 1986, 34; "Hunger in US Is Widening, Study of 'New Poor' Reports," *New York Times*, 20 April 1986.

4. "1,125 World Executions Are Documented in 1985," *New York Times,* 16 April 1986, 11; "Pretoria Rescinds Pass-Law Control on Black's Moves," *New York Times,* 19 April 1986, 1.

5. Amnesty International, *Torture in the Eighties* (London: Amnesty International, 1984), p. 9, 84.

6. James Seymour, "Indices of Political Imprisonment," *Universal Human Rights* 1, No. 1 (January–March 1979), p. 99.

7. Jorge I. Dominguez, "Assessing Human Rights Conditions," in *Enhancing Global Human Rights*, ed. Jorge Dominguez et al. (New York: McGraw-Hill, 1979), p. 97–98.

8. "UN Rights Report on Iran Assailed," *New York Times,* 24 November 1984, p. 8.

9. Quoted in "Rights Unit Reviews 123 Nations," *New York Times*, 9 October 1985, p. 4.

10. Raymond D. Gastil, ed., *Freedom in the World: Political Rights and Civil Liberties, 1983–1984* (Westport, CT: Greenwood Press, Freedom House Books, 1984), p. 19–22.

11. Barnett R. Rubin and Paula R. Newberg, "Statistical Analysis for Implementing Human Rights Policy," in *The Politics of Human Rights*, ed. Paula R. Newberg (New York: New York University Press, 1980), p. 280; Gloria Valencia-Weber and Robert Weber, "El Salvador: Methods Used to Document Human Rights Violations," *Human Rights Quarterly* 8, no. 4 (November 1986): 767; Kenneth Bollen, "Political Rights and Political Liberties in Nations: An Evaluation of Human Rights Measures, 1950 to 1984," *Human Rights Quarterly* 8, no. 4 (November 1986): p. 590; John F. McCamant, "A Critique of Present Measures of 'Human Rights Development' and an Alternative," in *Global Human Rights: Public Policies, Comparative Measures, and NGO Strategies*, ed. Ved P. Nanda, James R. Scarritt, and George W. Shepherd, Jr. (Boulder, CO: Westview Press, 1981), p. 136, 144.

12. See J. M. Smith, *Freedom's Fetters* (Ithaca, NY: Cornell University Press, 1956); Robert Justin Goldstein, *Political Repression in Modern America: From 1870 to Present* (Cambridge, MA: Schenkman Publishing, 1978).

13. Russell A. Buchanan, *The United States and World War II* (New York, NY: Harper & Row, 1964), vol. 2, p. 236.

14. Harry M. Scoble and Laurie S. Wiseberg, "Problems of Comparative Research on Human Rights," in *Global Human Rights: Public Policies, Comparative Measures, and NGO Strategies*, ed. Ved P. Nanda, James R. Scarritt, and George W. Shepherd, Jr. (Boulder, CO: Westview Press, 1981), p. 152.

15. Michael Stohl et al., "State Violations of Human Rights: Issues and Problems of Measurement," *Human Rights Quarterly* 8, no. 4 (November 1986), p. 594–595.

16. Richard Rose, *Governing Without Consensus: An Irish Perspective* (Boston, MA: Beacon Press, 1971), p. 32–41.

17. Michael Kidron and Ronald Segal, *The State of the World Atlas* (New York: Simon and Schuster, 1981), text accompanying table 31 (no pagination).

18. E. Wangerman, *The Austrian Achievement, 1700–1800* (New York: Harcourt Brace, 1973), p. 184.

19. William Shaw, "Paradoxes, Problems and Progress," *Journal of the American Statistical Association* 68 (March 1973), p. 9.

# 2.3 _____

# Measuring Human Rights:
# Some Issues and Options
*David L. Richards*

## ▦ Why Measure Human Rights?

Why measure human rights? Measuring human rights is part of the effort to attain human dignity for all persons worldwide. This is so as human rights measures allow policymakers, researchers, teachers, and students to systematically explore a variety of important questions, including:

- What type of regime is most/least likely to respect human rights?
- Do international human rights treaties affect government respect for human rights?
- How has globalization affected respect for human rights?
- What particular human rights are the most and least respected, and have patterns of respect for these rights changed over time?
- Can we predict human rights disasters?

## ▦ Social Science Measurement vs. Other Types

Understanding how human rights measures allow for the exploration of questions such as those above, and understanding what the important issues are in creating and selecting such measures, begin with a simple understanding of two important differences between social science measurement and other types of measurement. In one sense, social science measures (including measures of human rights) are like other measures with which you are already familiar. For example, just as a tape measure allows a carpenter to label and classify, social science measurements allow researchers to label and classify. There is an important difference, however. Unlike the carpenter, who is measuring things that can be seen and observed directly, such as a cedar chest, social scientists often must label and classify rather abstract concepts such as democracy, women's status, human development, and many others. This difference is actually the first challenge of human rights measurement: to find a way to reliably label/classify both the level or quantity of an abstract concept (e.g., women's status) and the behavior of some real entity with regard to an abstract concept (e.g., level of government respect for women's status in Country A).

A second important difference is that neither a cook using measuring spoons nor a carpenter using a tape measure must invent a particular measurement system in order to proceed with his or her work. Nor do they typically have to invest a great deal of thought in what measurement system to use. The carpenter or cook may have to decide between using the metric system of measurement and the English system, but once they have made this choice, an entire standardized system of measurement (feet, inches, ounces, and pounds, or centimeters, millimeters, grams, and kilograms) is readily available to them. Furthermore, either measurement system, used properly, should yield identical results. The choice is not always so simple in social science measurement. A social scientist oftentimes must create his/her own measurement system. Even should that not be the case, a single concept, say democracy, will often have many different available measures—all differing based on how the concept is defined, how quantities are measured, and other factors. Using different measures of the same concept can produce different results from otherwise identical statistical analyses and result in different inferences about the world. Thus, one's choice of a particular social science measure for use in one's work might lead to incorrect or biased inferences or might even be hotly debated and/or criticized. This fact certainly makes understanding the issues involved with, and options available for, human rights measurement all the more important.

## Scope

There are many different human rights recognized by international law. In order to study and understand all these human rights, measures must exist for the full range of human rights. Having measures for all human rights is important for a couple of reasons. First, in particular times and places, a particular right or type of right might assume great importance or attention. This means that information about a wide variety of rights is necessary to properly study and understand human rights worldwide. This also assumes an element of equity, in that we must not ignore the study of issues of a particular place/time due to a lack of adequate measurements. Second, human rights do not exist in isolation of one another—they are interdependent—and fully understanding any one type of right requires an understanding of other types of rights.

Indeed, it is a challenge to create such a wide variety of measures. There exists the creative challenge of inventing a measurement scheme; the resource challenge that one needs a great deal of reliable, systematic information to implement a measurement scheme; and the challenge of actually applying a measurement scheme to every country in the world on an annual basis to produce the data. Luckily, there exists a broad range of human rights measures and they cover a variety of human rights.

One major source of human rights data is the Cingranelli-Richards (CIRI) Human Rights Data Project (www.humanrightsdata.org), which offers information about the level of government respect for fourteen human rights in 195 countries from 1981 to the present (Cingranelli and Richards 2005). CIRI measures respect for a variety of types of human rights, including physical integrity rights (freedoms from extrajudicial killing, torture, disappearance, and political imprisonment), empowerment rights (political participation, workers' rights, religious freedom, freedom of movement, freedom of association), women's rights (economic, political, and social), and economic rights (Cingranelli and Richards 2007; Richards, Gelleny, and Sacko 2001; Cingranelli and Richards 1999).

Another measure, the Political Terror Scale, is an index that measures physical integrity rights violations from 1980 to 2005 for almost every country in the world (Poe, Carey, and Vazquez 2001; Gibney and Dalton 1996). Since 1978, Freedom House has offered ratings of government respect for political rights and civil liberties for almost every country and territory in the world in its annual *Freedom in the World* reports (Freedom House 2005). The Polity IV Project offers a variety of indicators about country characteristics, such as competitiveness of political participation, level of democracy, and others for every country in the world, from 1800 to 2003 (Marshall and Jaggers 2005).

Because of the suppression of their importance by the Cold War's emphasis on political and civil rights, measurement of economic and social human rights, women's rights, and children's rights is less developed. Since the early 1990s, the UN has produced a variety of widely used measures as part of its annual *Human Development Report*, which offers development statistics and analysis for every country in the world (United Nations Development Programme 2005). The most well-known measure from these reports is the Human Development Index (HDI), which is a measure of "a country's average achievements in three basic aspects of human development: longevity, knowledge, and a decent standard of living" (United Nations Development Programme 2003, www.undp.org/hdr2003/faq.html#21). The Gender Development Index measures the gap between men and women in the same three areas as the HDI. The Gender Empowerment Measure measures gender inequality "in three basic dimensions of empowerment—economic participation and decision-making, political participation and decision-making and power over economic resources" (United Nations Development Programme 2003, www.undp.org/hdr2003/indicator/indic_207_1_1.html).

## ▓ Validity

To be valid, a measure should measure what it claims to measure. One reason a measure might not live up to this standard is incompleteness. That is, the measure does represent all (or enough) of the parts of the concept it claims to measure. Imagine a measure of overall basic mathematical skills that included information about one's ability to do addition, but not subtraction, multiplication, or division (Carlson and Hyde 2003, 159). Is that measure really giving us information about overall basic math ability? Not really. In human rights measurement, both the CIRI Physical Integrity Rights Index (Cingranelli and Richards 1999) and the Political Terror Scale (Gibney and Dalton 1996) use the same four particular human rights—against extrajudicial killing, disappearance, torture, and political imprisonment—to measure a type of human rights known as physical integrity rights. However, Mitchell and McCormick (1988) and McCormick and Mitchell (1997) do not include disappearance in their measurement of this concept. Whose measure of physical integrity rights is more conceptually valid? The answer may well depend upon the use to which the measure is put.

Another reason a measure might lack validity is conceptual incompatibility of components. That is, a measure may include components that do not directly contribute to measuring the concept of interest.[1] Imagine a measure of government respect for civil rights that includes economic inflation level and currency exchange rate. This measure is not only measuring civil rights, as claimed, but also macroeconomic factors, making it invalid as a measure purely of civil rights. Both of these first two paths to lack of validity—incompleteness and incompatibility—demonstrate that when choosing or creating a measure, it is extremely important to have a very clear definition in mind of the concept one is interested in measuring.

Whether a measure is valid for a particular use can also vary with the question being asked. Often, criticisms of published research are based on the premise that the authors used an inappropriate measure of a concept, and, as a result, the findings are biased or wrong. There are many measures of "democracy," for example. Tatu Vanhanen's measure of democracy includes an element of power sharing by political parties (Vanhanen 1990; 2000). Freedom House's overall indicator of freedom created from its political rights and civil liberties measures is often used as a measure of democracy. The Polity IV Project's measure of democracy does not include power sharing or civil liberties but, rather, relies on institutional features of government for its measure of democracy. Which of these three would be a more valid indicator of democracy to use in one's research relies heavily upon what question is being examined.

In the realm of human rights measurement, one's research question might very well affect the validity of a measure. For example, some human rights measures represent the human rights practices of a government only, and some represent overall human rights conditions in a country. Cingranelli (1996, 5) defines human rights practices as "*the actions of government officials* directly affecting the degree to which citizens can exercise various types of human rights . . . [they are] what governments actually do, not what they claim to do."

Human rights conditions, on the other hand, "refer to the degree to which *citizens can exercise* various types of human rights . . . many things will affect human rights conditions besides what governments intend and . . . do" (Cingranelli 1996, 5, emphasis in original).

Consequently, one must be careful. If one is interested in addressing a question regarding the human rights *practices of governments*, an indicator of overall human rights *conditions in a country* is likely invalid for that purpose. That is, it is not purely measuring human rights practices. Luckily, there are a variety of human rights measures from which to choose. The CIRI data set measures the human rights *practices* of governments. The Political Terror Scale combines information about both human rights practices and conditions, making it essentially a measure of *conditions*. The UN's *Human Development Reports* include measures of both *practices* and *conditions*. The Freedom House and Polity IV reports are dominantly about human rights *practices*.

## ▓ Reliability

A reliable measure is a consistent measure. In this selection, *consistent* means that several persons independently applying the same measurement scheme to the same set of observations will all produce the same measurement value (score) in the end. In human rights measurement, this is probably most important when creating what are known as standards-based measures. Some examples of standards-based human rights measures include the CIRI variables, the Political Terror Scale, Freedom House, and Polity IV. The "standards-based" label comes from the way this type of data is produced: trained coders compare a set of predetermined standards with empirical observations about a particular political unit (e.g., country), and the score that best fits the observations is assigned. The predetermined standards are also known as the measurement scheme. While it is possible that two persons may give the same set of observations a different score, it is important that this is kept as rare as possible. Minimizing the number and severity of these disagreements is maximizing reliability.

There are various strategies that social scientists can use to ensure and improve the reliability of the data they create. I will discuss the CIRI Human Rights Data Project's methods as a best practices example for ensuring reliability in creating standards-based data.

The basic unit measured by CIRI is the country-year, which is simply a particular country in a particular year (e.g., Germany 1996, Brazil 1983). Each country-year receives a score on each CIRI variable. The primary sources of information used by CIRI are the annual US Department of State's *Country Reports on Human Rights Practices* (US Department of State, Annual) and Amnesty International's world reports (Amnesty International, Annual).

Coders (persons trained to assign measurement scores to country-years) use a measurement scheme (a set of standards) to assign scores to country-years, based on the coders' reading of source materials. For example, each country-year is assigned a score of either 0 (frequent violations), 1 (some violations), or 2 (no violations) on the CIRI measure of government respect for the right not to be tortured. Coders are given detailed guidelines on what human rights practices constitute a 0, 1, or 2 and are trained how to accurately assign country-years one of these three possible scores.[2] These trained coders read reports on individual countries in the source materials and assign country-years a score on each of the various CIRI human rights measures.

CIRI uses at least two trained coders to code each data point. A data point is a country-year's score on a particular measure. For example, for a set of 195 countries for a single year and thirteen human rights measures, there would be 2,535 individual data points (scores). So each one of these data points is evaluated by at least two different trained coders. When these paired coders have both finished their work, they meet with senior CIRI personnel and their scores on each data point are compared. When coders differ, the reason for the difference is noted and the senior CIRI personnel resolve the disagreement between the coders. The most common source of disagreement is when one of the coders misses a piece of information in the source material. However, sometimes coders have a substantive disagreement about how to apply the measurement scheme to a country-year. In such a case, senior CIRI personnel decide which coder, if either, has most accurately applied the coding rules. A final score is then issued.

The fewer differences between trained coders, the greater the reliability of a standards-based measure. Because CIRI keeps systematic records of coder differences, a statistic can be calculated to ascertain intercoder reliability. For the coding of the year 2004, the Krippendorf's r-bar intercoder reliability statistic was 0.944.[3] The closer r-bar is to 1.0, the greater the reliability. There are many rules of thumb on how much reliability is "enough," but generally, a "reliable" measure's reliability statistic should not dip below .80, and it is preferable to have a reliability statistic of .90 or above in order to call a measure "highly reliable."

Many things can cause the differences between coders that result in reduced reliability. These include coders' personal biases, poor coder training, coder laziness or indifference, coder fatigue, poor written instructions/guidelines for coders, and problems in the measurement scheme itself. By keeping track of reliability-reducing factors, social scientists can pinpoint problems and make important improvements in coder training, documentation, and even measurement schemes themselves. In addition to an overall reliability statistic, CIRI estimates reliability statistics for each of its human rights measures, so that necessary improvements can be identified and made.[4]

## ■ Level of Aggregation

If you were looking for a measure of respect for physical integrity rights, would you rather have a measure that incorporates many particular physical integrity rights into a single measure (that is, use an *aggregated measure*), or would you rather use individual measures of each particular physical integrity right (that is, use *disaggregated measures*)? This question is an example of the level of aggregation issue that confronts both data creators and users. The debate over the proper level of aggregation to be used in human rights research is ongoing, and its full scope goes far beyond what can be addressed here, but I will touch on a few basic issues.

The human rights measures already discussed represent a variety of levels of aggregation. The Political Terror Scale is what could be considered completely aggregated. That is, it takes information about four different physical integrity rights and condenses that information into a single score. The Political Terror Scale cannot be disaggregated. This means one could not deconstruct the measure and see just the information for a single physical integrity right, say torture or disappearance. Freedom House's political rights and civil liberties scores can also be considered completely aggregated. The political rights and civil liberties measures consist of ten and fifteen individual components, respectively. However, Freedom House only publicly offers one final, single score for each. For example, we do not know how a particular country rated on the corruption component of the political rights measure alone. It may be that Freedom House has the disaggregated data, but because they are not released publicly, we must consider their political rights and civil liberties measures as completely aggregated.

The CIRI and Polity IV projects are in a different category of levels of aggregation. Both projects produce a wide variety of disaggregated measures. For example, CIRI produces individual measures of government respect for workers' rights, freedom of association, freedom from torture, and more than ten others. Polity produces individual measures of political competition, openness of executive recruitment, and more than ten others. However, both also offer aggregated measures created from these indicators. CIRI offers the aforementioned CIRI Physical Integrity Rights Index (CPIRI) (created from four individual measures) and also the CIRI Empowerment Rights Index (created from five individual measures). Polity IV offers aggregated indices of autocracy, democracy, and regime type created from their individual measures of state authority characteristics. The same goes for UN measures such as the Human Development Index, Gender Empowerment Index, and Gender Development Index, all of which are composite, but are created from disaggregated public data.

Unlike the Political Terror Scale and Freedom House measures, the CIRI and Polity IV measures are disaggregable, that is, they can be deconstructed to find information about a particular type of right. For example, while the CPIRI might tell us Country A gets a "5" (out of a possible 8 points) on level of government respect for physical integrity, because the CIRI data used to create the CPIRI are disaggregated, we also could look up that Country A got a "0" (out of a possible 2 points) on level of government respect for torture. This extra information can be rather useful.

There are several arguments on behalf of creating disaggregated, or disaggregable, data rather than composite indices that cannot be deconstructed.[5] One compelling reason is that a composite index can hide variation in government respect for human rights. Figure 2.3.1 shows the CPIRI world average from 1981 to 2004. Note that this aggregate index of government respect for physical integrity rights appears rather stable over time, with a slight downward (but not steadily downward) trend during the last half-decade of the Cold War and, beginning in 2000, a jump to what seems to be a slightly higher baseline level of respect.

Due to the level of aggregation of the Physical Integrity Rights Index, however, Figure 2.3.1 leaves several interesting questions unanswered. Did

**Figure 2.3.1    CIRI Physical Integrity Rights Index, 1981–2004**

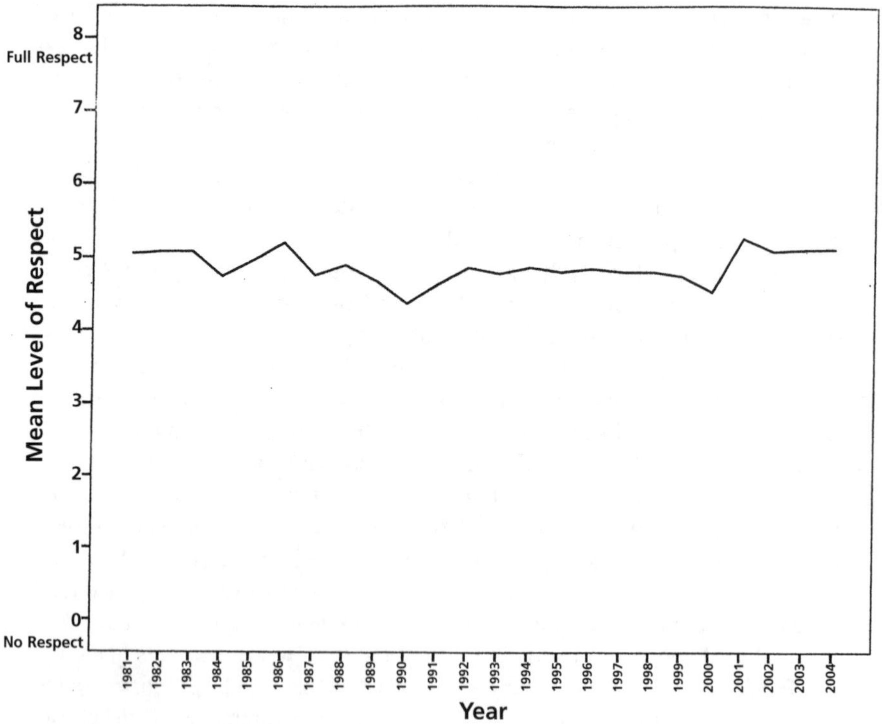

*Source:* CIRI Human Rights Data Project (www.humanrightsdata.org).

nothing interesting happen to respect for physical integrity rights in the 1990s? Did all physical integrity rights improve after 2000? Did respect for all physical integrity rights decline toward the end of the Cold War? Changing the level of aggregation at which we choose to measure government respect for physical integrity rights can help us address these questions.

Figure 2.3.2 shows the four human rights measures that comprise the CIRI Physical Integrity Rights Index graphed individually over the same time period. Right away, we see there is much more variation. While Figure 2.3.1 shows little to no change in the 1990s, Figure 2.3.2 shows that respect for the right against political imprisonment increased dramatically, closely matching the average level of respect for the right against extrajudicial killing by 2000. We see also that respect for the right against torture declines rather steadily throughout the time period shown. We see that among these four rights, respect is steadily the greatest for the right against disappearance.

We have seen that the aggregate index shown in Figure 2.3.1, like all aggregate indices, hides most of the interesting and important variation shown in Figure 2.3.2. This also further illustrates an important distinction between disaggregable data such as those from CIRI and Polity IV and completely aggregated data such as the Political Terror Scale and Freedom House's indicators.

**Figure 2.3.2    Four CIRI Measures Related to Physical Integrity Rights, 1981–2004**

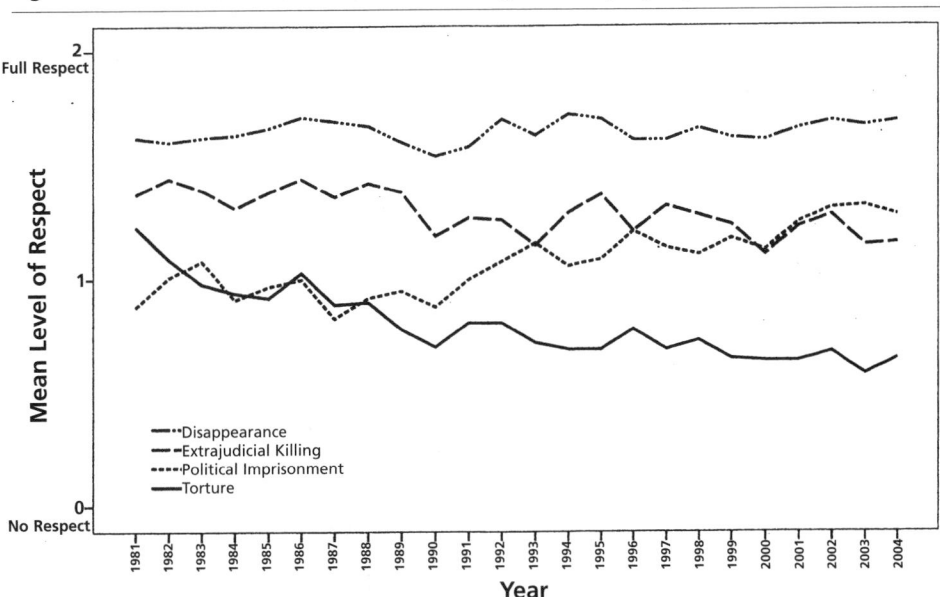

*Source:* CIRI Human Rights Data Project (www.humanrightsdata.org).

This is not to say, however, that aggregate indices are not useful. Aggregate indices allow researchers to measure original abstract concepts from existing data and offer economy in empirically representing a rich concept such as democracy or physical integrity rights. However, when an aggregate index is not made from disaggregated data, and thus is not subject to being deconstructed, it can hide important information (in the form of variation) about what it is purporting to measure. Thus, a researcher, when choosing among competing measures of a concept, must consider level of aggregation.

## Notes

1. We might also say that to the extent a measure includes components not directly related to the concept that is purportedly being measured, the measure is biased.
2. The CIRI Project enhances reliability by basing the coding of its four physical integrity indicators on event counts. For details, see the *CIRI Coding Guide*, found on the CIRI documentation page at www.humanrightsdata.org/ciri_documentation.asp.
3. The Krippendorf's r-bar measure is a statistic designed to measure intercoder reliability for ordinal measures such as CIRI.
4. These detailed reliability statistics can be found on the CIRI documentation page at www.humanrightsdata.org/ciri_documentation.asp.
5. For example, McCormick and Mitchell (1997, 513) make the argument that "human rights violations differ in type not just amount, such that they cannot be clearly represented on a single scale. That is, there is a substantive difference between the use of imprisonment on the one hand and the use of torture and killing on the other."

## References

Amnesty International. Annual. *Annual Report*. Available at www.amnesty.org/ailib/aireport/index.html.
Carlson, James M., and Mark S. Hyde. 2003. *Doing Empirical Political Research*. New York: Houghton Mifflin.
Cingranelli, David L. 1996. "Human Rights Policies, Practices, and Conditions," in David L. Cingranelli, ed. *Human Rights and Developing Countries*. Greenwich, CT: JAI Press.
Cingranelli, David L., and David L. Richards. 2007. "Measuring Government Effort to Respect Economic and Social Rights," in Alanson Minkler and Shareen Hertel, eds. *Measuring Economic Rights*. Cambridge: Cambridge University Press.
————. 2005. *The Cingranelli-Richards (CIRI) Human Rights Dataset*. Version 2005.10.12. Available at www.humanrightsdata.org.
————. 1999. "Measuring the Pattern, Level, and Sequence of Government Respect for Human Rights." *International Studies Quarterly* 43:407–417.
Freedom House. 2005. *Freedom in the World: The Annual Survey of Political Rights and Civil Liberties*. Available at www.freedomhouse.org.
Gibney, Mark, and Matthew Dalton. 1996. "The Political Terror Scale," in David L. Cingranelli, ed. *Human Rights and Developing Countries*. Greenwich, CT: JAI Press.

Marshall, Monty G., and Keith Jaggers. 2005. *Polity IV Project: Political Regime Characteristics and Transitions, 1800–2003.* Available at www.cidcm.umd.edu/inscr/polity.

McCormick, James, and Neil J. Mitchell. 1997. "Human Rights Violations, Umbrella Concepts, and Empirical Analysis." *World Politics* 49:510–525.

Mitchell, Neil J., and James M. McCormick. 1988. "Economic and Political Explanations of Human Rights Violations." *World Politics* 40:476–498.

Poe, Steven C., Sabine C. Carey, and Tanya C. Vazquez. 2001. "How Are These Pictures Different? A Quantitative Comparison of the US State Department and Amnesty International Human Rights Reports, 1976–1995." *Human Rights Quarterly* 23:650–677.

Richards, David L., Ronald D. Gelleny, and David H. Sacko. 2001. "Money with a Mean Streak? Foreign Economic Penetration and Government Respect for Human Rights in Developing Countries." *International Studies Quarterly* 45:219–239.

United Nations Development Programme. 2005. *Human Development Report 2005.* Available at hdr.undp.org/reports/global/2005.

———. 2003. *Human Development Report 2003.* Available at hdr.undp.org/reports/global/2003.

United States Department of State. Annual. *Country Reports on Human Rights Practices.* Available at www.state.gov/g/drl/hr/c1470.htm.

Vanhanen, Tatu. 2000. "A New Dataset for Measuring Democracy, 1810–1998." *Journal of Peace Research* 37:251–265.

———. 1990. *The Process of Democratization: A Comparative Study of 147 States, 1980–1988.* New York: Crane Russak.

# 2.4 _____

# The Political Terror Scale

*Mark Gibney and Matthew Dalton*

Since the early 1980s, a group of human rights scholars and students at Purdue University have produced the Political Terror Scale (PTS). . . . Countries are coded on a scale of 1–5 according to their level of terror the previous year according to the descriptions of these countries provided in the *Amnesty International* and *U.S. State Department Country Reports*. The various levels are set forth below:

> Level 1: Countries . . . under a secure rule of law, people are not imprisoned for their views, and torture is rare or exceptional. . . . Political murders are extraordinarily rare.
>
> Level 2: There is a limited amount of imprisonment for nonviolent political activity. However, few are affected, torture and beatings are exceptional. . . . Political murder is rare.
>
> Level 3: There is extensive political imprisonment, or a recent history of such imprisonment. Execution or other political murders and brutality may be common. Unlimited detention, with or without trial, for political views is accepted. . . .
>
> Level 4: The practices of Level 3 are expanded to larger numbers. Murders, disappearances, and torture are a common part of life. . . . In spite of its generality, on this level violence affects primarily those who interest themselves in politics or ideas.
>
> Level 5: The violence of Level 4 has been extended to the whole population. . . . The leaders of these societies place no limits on the means or thoroughness with which they pursue personal or ideological goals.

In addition, coders are provided with the following additional instructions.

> 1. *Ignore Own Biases.* Coders should make every attempt to keep their own biases out of their work. Thus, coders are instructed to ignore

---

Reprinted from Mark Gibney and Matthew Dalton, "The Political Terror Scale," in *Policy Studies and Developing Nations,* Volume 4, pp. 73–80. © 1996 Elsevier. Reprinted with permission from Elsevier. Some of the author's notes have been omitted.

their preconceptions of a country, and to limit their coding to the information provided in the country report.

2. *Give Countries the Benefit of the Doubt.* Coders also are instructed to give the benefit of the doubt in favor of the countries they are coding. Thus, if a coder thinks that a country could be scored as either a level 2 or a level 3, the country is to receive the lower score. Sometimes coders will not feel comfortable making a choice between two levels. In those instances, coders will oftentimes score a country using both numbers such as a 2/3. If the other coder has either of these numbers, we use the level where there is agreement.

One of the more difficult problems is how to deal with the situation where a country's human rights situation changes dramatically during the course of the year. It is not out of the ordinary for a newly installed regime to pursue policies that are diametrically opposed to that which preceded it. In these instances we instruct the coders to consider when the regime change occurred. For example, if a repressive regime was ousted late in the calendar year, the score probably should reflect the human rights situation that existed for most of the year. On the other hand, if the change occurred anywhere near the middle of the year or before then, the score should reflect this change.

3. *Consider the Size of the Country Being Coded.* Coders are instructed to be sensitive to the size of the countries they are coding. For example, six hundred political prisoners in a small country represents a much different phenomenon than the same number in a much larger country, and thus, should be coded differently.

4. *View the Various Levels as Part of a Continuum.* The PTS provides us with ordinal rankings of levels of human rights abuses. Countries with higher scores should experience higher numbers of deaths, torture, and political imprisonment than those ranked below them. In addition, countries with the same score should experience approximately the same level of political terror (but also reflecting the size of the countries), although it might not occur in the same manner. For example, one country might have a large number of political prisoners, but very few summary executions or disappearances. Another country might have the exact opposite scenario. Still, it is quite possible for both countries to have the same score. Coders are instructed to be sensitive to those kinds of trade-offs, and to attempt to reflect the relative level of human rights abuses in the countries they are coding.

Related to this, it is important that the various levels not be interpreted so literally that one misses the essence of what the PTS is attempting to measure. For example, the essence of what differentiates Level 4 from Level 5 countries is that in the former certain sectors of the population are singled out for widespread terror, while in the latter terror afflicts nearly the entire population. Despite this theoretical distinction, however, sometimes the level of political terror in a country will be so great—although it is only aimed at certain segments of the population—that it still warrants a level 5. To use an illustration, even if Hitler had only singled out one group, Jews, for persecution, the level of terror in Nazi Germany still would have been a level 5.

One of the areas where the PTS seems weakest is in differentiating between countries at the highest level. For example, a medium size country where torture is systematic and upwards of 1300 people have been killed that year, either by summary execution, disappearance, or as casualties in a civil war, will very likely be coded a level 5. A country where ten times that number were killed will also receive a 5. Is political terror in the second country worse than the first? The answer is clearly yes, yet the PTS treats these two countries as essentially experiencing the same levels of political terror. On the other hand, it could be rationalized that life is hell in both countries.

1. *Try to Measure Government Terror, but Ultimately be Sensitive to all Forms of Terror.* The PTS attempts to measure government terror. However, the coders also are instructed not to ignore other forms of terror from non-governmental actors. The aim is to reflect the human rights violations that exist in a country more generally. Usually this does not pose a problem. High levels of human rights abuses by insurgents are all too often matched by similar practices of governments. One country that posed a particular problem for a number of years was Lebanon. For the most part it has been extraordinarily difficult to discern between the terrorist activities of the government (if there was one in anything but name only) and various other factions. As a consequence, for many years Lebanon was not given a score.

2. *Try to Read What the Reports are Trying to Say.* One reason why certain Central American countries such as El Salvador and Guatemala were coded as a 4 rather than as a Level 5 (using the State Department) during the early 1980s is that the Reports on those countries would be replete with praise of the "improvements" occurring in the area of human rights, or else the language with regard to atrocities would be couched in terms of "unconfirmed reports." The point is that it is important to discern what the reports are trying to say. One key is the adjectives employed. For example, "systematic" torture represents a more serious human rights violation than the mention that torture commonly occurs.

In this same vein, there have been some instances where a country's human rights record is described in narrative form as being quite bad, but where there is very little evidence in the report itself of either summary executions, disappearances, torture or substantial numbers of political prisoners (the State Department Reports on Cuba are probably the best example of this). It is important to note that the PTS only measures *actual* terror. Thus, repressive regimes such as the former Eastern-bloc countries that previously had effectively cowered their populations would not have exhibited the highest abuses of terror according to the PTS, although it is very unlikely that they will be coded as a Level 1 or 2 country either.

## ■ The Coding Process

The way we have proceeded is to have at least two people code the pertinent countries, and then a third party (usually Gibney) attempt to resolve any conflicts between the coders by employing a rule of majority vote (invariably two out of three). Coders are asked to provide a score and a few comments rationalizing their decision. Inter-coder reliability between the two original coders is in the range of 70–90 percent. Usually, however, a more informal means of dispute resolution is employed. Oftentimes where there is disagreement the original coders will be asked to re-read certain country reports. After this, it is not unusual for a fair amount of discussion to ensue concerning why certain countries were given the scores they had been given. In nearly every instance, then, there eventually is unanimity. Where the various parties simply cannot agree, the lower score is used.

# 2.5 ⎯⎯⎯⎯

## How Are These Pictures Different? A Quantitative Comparison of the US State Department and Amnesty International Human Rights Reports, 1976–1995

*Steven C. Poe, Sabine C. Carey, and Tanya C. Vazquez*

### ■ About the Human Rights Reports

#### The US Department of State

The *Country Reports* of the US State Department arise out of the historical conflict between the executive and legislative branches of government.[1] During the Nixon administration some members of Congress yearned for a foreign policy that paid more heed to human rights, and took actions to guide presidential actions in that direction. One such act was the Harkin amendment to the Foreign Assistance Act, which prohibited US development assistance to governments that engaged in "a consistent pattern of gross violations of internationally recognized human rights."[2] Publication of the reports began in 1976, as a means for Congress to keep tabs on recipients of US aid in an attempt to verify the wishes of Congress were being followed, but by 1980 the reports were covering a much more comprehensive set of UN member countries. Further, the range of internationally recognized rights discussed in the reports has expanded over the years. The most recent reports cover political and civil rights, the rights of workers, women, minorities, and labor as well as the right to integrity of the person. . . .

These reports are the result of a sizable effort by one of the most far-reaching bureaucracies in the world: the US State Department. They are by far the most complete cataloging of human rights practices around the world, in terms of the number of countries covered, and the range of rights. However,

Excerpted from Steven C. Poe, Sabine C. Carey, and Tanya C. Vazquez, "How Are These Pictures Different? A Quantitative Comparison of the US State Department and Amnesty International Human Rights Reports, 1976–1995," *Human Rights Quarterly* 23 (3): 654–663. © 2001 The Johns Hopkins University Press. Reprinted with permission of The Johns Hopkins University Press. Some of the author's notes have been omitted.

they are not comprehensive. The reports do reflect the traditional US emphasis on so-called first generation rights, for the most part overlooking economic
and social rights in the Universal Declaration, and the Covenant on Economic,
Social and Cultural Rights, as well as third generation rights.

### Amnesty International

Amnesty International is an International Nongovernmental Organization
(NGO), founded in 1961, with the purpose of furthering respect for human
rights. Today, according to its own figures, Amnesty International has "more
than 1,000,000 members, subscribers and regular donors in more than 100
countries and territories,"[3] worldwide. . . .

As for its research methods, according to its own description, it would appear that Amnesty International gathers information on human rights violations much like the US State Department, but focusing on a more limited set
of political and personal integrity rights. The preface and introduction to each
issue of the country reports includes the organization's statement of purpose as
well as a summary of the level of repression around the globe that year. Some
governments are weary of human rights monitors investigating their country
for human rights violations, and thus, Amnesty must tread carefully in order to
paint:

> a picture of human rights abuses by drawing upon a wide range of sources:
> victims or eyewitnesses of abuses, experts like lawyers or doctors and other
> human rights groups. The organization then puts that information in the con-
> text of a country's past pattern of abuses to help determine whether an alle-
> gation is plausible. . . . Researchers or other experts like doctors and lawyers
> will talk to victims or eyewitnesses of abuses to hear their testimonies. They
> will visit prisons, detention centers and places where torture is said to have
> occurred. They attend trials to see if these conform to international fair trial
> standards. Or they may meet government officials and talk to a host of peo-
> ple and groups involved in human rights.[4]

If access into a country is not granted,

> the organization also relies on other sources of information—testimonies
> from refugees or victims who have fled a country; information, such as let-
> ters, smuggled out of a country; a government itself; the more than 1,100
> newspapers, journals, government bulletins and transcripts of radio broad-
> casts which Amnesty International receives; reports from lawyers and other
> humanitarian organizations and letters from prisoners and their families.[5]

Before the initial report is submitted the information is amended "with
knowledge of a country's laws, constitution, and judicial process, and political
and historical background."[6] Upon submission, "all major reports are passed
through several levels of approvals, often up to the Secretary General. It is

standard Amnesty International practice to give its material to governments before publication for their views and additional information, and the organization will publish these in its reports."[7]

The two reports we are investigating empirically in this paper appear, for the most part, to be gathered in a similar fashion. One difference in the discussions is that the State Department makes no mention of giving its material to governments in advance, for feedback, but in fact this is done in many cases. The drafted reports may then be rewritten with the comments and clarifications of the government in mind. Another difference is that rarely, if ever, do US State Department officials follow Amnesty's practice of attending trials, for that would likely be viewed as infringement in another country's affairs.

Why would we expect to find patterns in the differences between the two reports? Reasons for the expected divergences may lie in the differences between the organizations themselves. According to realist doctrine, the United States, as a nation-state, pursues power, and thus weighs security concerns more heavily than the human rights of non-Americans abroad. By contrast, Amnesty International is an international nongovernmental organization whose very motivation and goals are to forward the cause of human rights, worldwide. Further, as an arm of the US government we might expect that the State Department would have to be more concerned with issues of national sovereignty. As such it might have a tendency to tread more lightly than Amnesty International, so as not to interfere unduly in the affairs of other governments. We expect, then, that the State Department reports will be colored by issues of sovereignty, and interests related to national security and power which Amnesty International has little reason to recognize or heed. . . .

## ■ Measuring Human Rights as Depicted by These Two Reports

The main focus of the Political Terror Scales is on personal integrity rights. They do not provide a comprehensive measurement of all of the different categories of rights discussed in either of these reports. What they do provide, however, is coverage of what is probably the subset of human rights featured most prominently in both the Reports of the State Department and Amnesty International.

In order to examine the differences between the reports we first subtracted the values of the State Department scale from those of the Amnesty scale. This created a variable that theoretically could range from –4 to +4, with positive scores indicating the US State Department provided a more positive picture of the human rights situation than did Amnesty International. Negative scores represent cases where the US State Department provided a more negative assessment of human rights conditions than its counterpart.

## ■ Simple Descriptive Analysis

First, in order to gain a better understanding for the data, we performed some descriptive analysis. In Figure 2.5.1, we present the distribution of the difference variable described above. The actual range of this variable in our sample is from −3 to +3. There are 2331 cases in our sample that had values for both the Amnesty and State Department variables. In most cases (54.7 percent) there is no difference between the scores. In the cases where there is a difference, the vast majority differs by an absolute value of one. The State Department had a PTS of one less than that generated for Amnesty in 29 percent of the cases; Amnesty had a PTS score of one less than the State Department in only 12.2 percent of cases. Thus, only in about 4 percent of the cases are the scores different by more than one point. In the relatively rare event in which there was a two-point difference in scales, the majority of those instances involved cases where the US State Department reports were more favorable toward countries (3.1 percent of the sample, as opposed to the .7 percent where Amnesty presented the more favorable report).

**Figure 2.5.1   An Examination of the Differences Between the State Department and Amnesty International Reports**

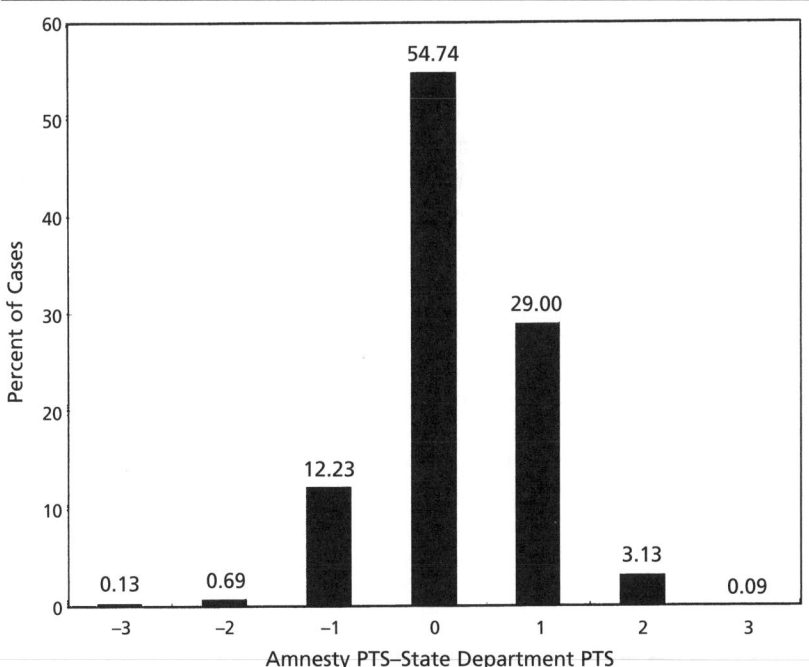

Though it was extremely rare, there were a few cases in which the State and Amnesty scores differed by 3. Among the cases treated relatively more harshly by the State Department, with scores of −3 were Argentina in 1985, Azerbaijan in 1993, and Croatia in 1994. During the years cited above, each of these countries was in, or had recently undergone a period of severe unrest. In the case of Argentina, commissions were established to investigate the "Dirty War." In 1993 Azerbaijan was contending with economic shortages and political disruption, because of the collapse of the former Soviet economic and political systems. In 1994 Croatia suffered from similar political and economic collapses, which apparently resulted in greater increases in repression.

Among the cases treated most favorably by the US State Department, relative to Amnesty, were Israel in 1976, and Guinea in 1983, each of which had a difference score of +3. Israel, of course, is a long time friend of the United States. Among the countries whose human rights practices were consistently treated more negatively by the State Department were: Nicaragua and Mozambique (with negative scores for eleven of the nineteen years in the sample), Laos (nine of sixteen years), Burkina Faso (six of eleven years), Croatia and Tajikistan (three of four years), Ukraine and Azerbaijan (four of four years). After the collapse of the Soviet Union, the difference scores of the newly created countries are mostly −1 or −2. Perhaps the US tended to give these new governments the benefit of the doubt while they were consolidating their power. Alternatively, the degree of unrest in the former Yugoslavia and former USSR might have been such that information about specific human rights violations was more difficult for Amnesty International to obtain consistently with its smaller budget. For whatever reason these differences occur, it seems that the State Department is consistently harsher than Amnesty International in Eastern Europe in the period from 1992–1995.

Countries that were treated more favorably by the State Department's reports 50 percent or more of the time were: Rwanda (ten of sixteen years), Turkey (fifteen of twenty years), Cape Verde (three of four years), Italy and Greece (thirteen of nineteen years), Switzerland (sixteen of nineteen years), France (fourteen of twenty years), Macedonia and Slovenia (one of two years), Egypt (ten of twenty years), Jordan (thirteen of eighteen years), Saudi Arabia (thirteen of fifteen years), Bahrain (eleven of twenty years), Israel (eleven of nineteen years), Sri Lanka (sixteen of twenty years), Philippines (ten of twenty years), Colombia (thirteen of twenty years), Uruguay (eleven of eighteen years), El Salvador (twelve of twenty years), and Brazil, Paraguay, and Venezuela (twelve of nineteen years). Many of these findings are consistent with allegations that the State Department treats with kid gloves, countries in which it has strategic interests (e.g., Israel, Egypt, the Philippines, El Salvador).

The overall distribution of the difference variable indicates that the US has tended to be somewhat less harsh than Amnesty in evaluating the human rights practices of other governments. This is perhaps a result of the greater weight it places on sovereignty issues—seeking to give other governments the benefit of the doubt. Or it may be that the State Department simply has been easier on its allies for security or power political reasons. Additionally, it may be that Amnesty, as an NGO focusing on human rights tends to be harsher in evaluating countries' performance in this regard, because its very subsistence is gained from publicizing human rights difficulties.

In Figure 2.5.2, we present the mean PTS score for both the Amnesty International and State Department reports, and for our difference variable. The results show several interesting trends. First, one notices a slight downward trend in the Amnesty scores across time. This may be attributed to Amnesty's tendency to cover the worst cases. In the early years of their reports, fewer countries were covered and attention tended to be centered mainly on countries that were the worst human rights violators.[8] The countries that were added tended to be nations with less repressive governments. Those changes resulted in a downward trend in the mean repression level in the cases that were covered by Amnesty.[9] In contrast, the US State Department reports have been nearly global in coverage since the early 1980s. There is an obvious trend with those reports as well, as the mean scores climb and are virtually identical to those reported by Amnesty International by 1993. However, the reports diverge again in 1994 and 1995. Consistent with these trends, the mean scores

**Figure 2.5.2    Mean Values of Human Rights Variables, 1976–1995**

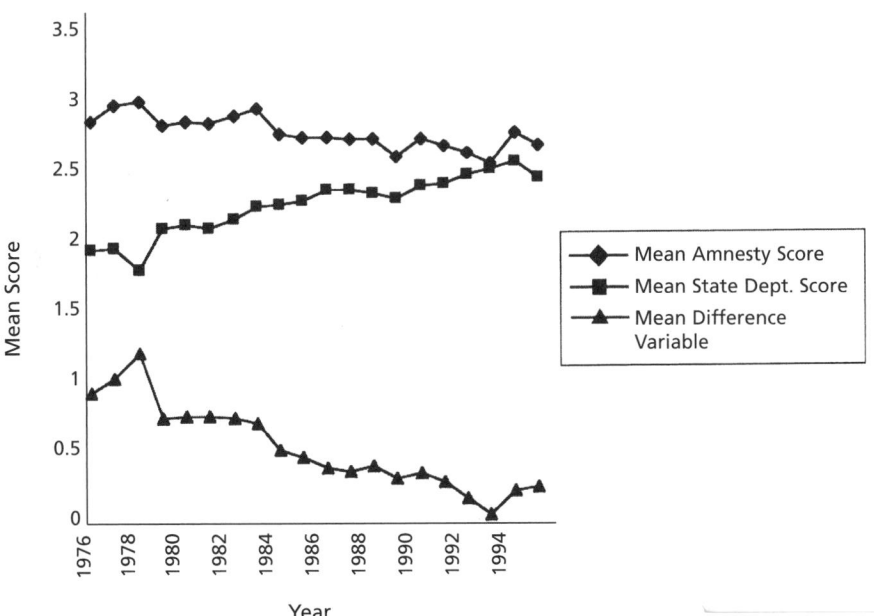

for the difference variable are largest in the earlier years, approaching zero in 1993 and increasing somewhat again, until the end of the series.

Why the increase in the values of the State Department reports? It would be more difficult to argue that the upward trend is due to case coverage. Some relatively repressive countries have been added to the sample in the 1990s, but this does not explain the trend evident throughout the 1980s. Perhaps the upward trend is due to real increases in repression. Alternatively, the convergence of these two lines might be representative of a change in the content of the State Department across time. The latter explanation is most consonant with the arguments of Innes, the Lawyers Committee, and the anecdotal information provided by Forsythe.[10]

## ■ Notes

1. Judith Eleanor Innes, *Human Rights Reporting as a Policy Tool: An Examination of the State Department Country Reports, in* Human Rights and Statistics: Getting the Record Straight 235–57 (Thomas B. Jabine & Richard P. Claude 1992).

2. *Id.* at 237.

3. Amnesty International, *available at* <http://www.amnesty.org/aboutai/factfigr .htm#1> (visited 11 Mar. 1999).

4. Amnesty International, *Searching for the Truth: How Amnesty International Does Its Research* (Mar. 1998), *available at* <http://www.amnesty.org/aboutai/sftt .htm>.

5. Amnesty International, *available at* <http://www.amnesty.org/aboutai/factfigr .htm>.

6. Amnesty International, *available at* <http://www.amnesty.org/aboutai/sftt .htm>.

7. *Id.*

8. Steven C. Poe & C. Neal Tate, *Repression of Personal Integrity in the 1980s: A Global Analysis*, 88 Am. Pol. Sci. Rev. 853–72.

9. Steven C. Poe, C. Neal Tate & Linda Keith, *Repression of the Human Right to Personal Integrity Revisited: A Global Crossnational Study Covering the Years 1976–1993*, 43 Int'l Stud. Q. 291–315 (1999).

10. Innes, *supra* note 1; Lawyers' Committee for Human Rights, Critique: Review of the U.S. Department of States' Country Reports on Human Rights Practices 1992 (1993); and the anecdotal information provided by David P. Forsythe, *Human Rights and World Politics* (1989).

# 2.6 ⸺

# Using the Physical Quality of Life Index to Explore the Level of Subsistence Rights

*Wesley T. Milner and Rhonda L. Callaway*

The 1980s saw researchers focusing on the conditions within states that explained the variation in human rights conditions. Such research requires adequate measures of human rights. While many scholars focused on security rights, or those rights that guarantee the right to be free from government torture, imprisonment due to political or religious views, and murder, a second set of researchers began examining the factors that contribute to a citizen's standard of living, or basic human needs (Dixon 1984; Moon and Dixon 1985, 1992; Dixon and Moon 1987; Moon 1991). Drawing upon the previous selections in this chapter on measurement and human rights, this work discusses the challenges involved in measuring what has been called basic human needs or levels of subsistence.[1]

Before proceeding to the task of measurement, we first must be clear on the concept that we are attempting to measure. Clean air and water; adequate food, clothing, and shelter; and the provision of minimal healthcare are all included in the definition of subsistence rights and collectively constitute basic human needs. While the provision of these rights is somewhat more controversial than security (i.e., integrity of the person) rights, they are nonetheless essential if one is to realize a relatively healthy and substantive life.[2] If a person is lacking in these basic human needs, the result can be just as painful and deleterious as when a person's physical security is violated. Theoretical arguments made by human rights scholars support this notion. For example, Jack Donnelly (1989, 24) asserts that "at minimum, people must be alive. This requires survival rights, such as the rights to life (Universal Declaration, Article 3) and to food (Article 22). And if this survival is to be more than brutish, it requires economic and social rights, such as the right to health care and social insurance." Likewise, Henry Shue (1980, 19) posits that subsistence is one part of a set of basic rights that "are everyone's minimum reasonable demands upon the rest of humanity."

From an international institutions perspective, the UN has long addressed the issue of subsistence and economic development in their various organizations and agencies. More recently, the UN Millennium Development Goals as revealed in the General Assembly resolution in September 2000 (Res. 55/2) called for achieving significant gains in these basic human needs by 2015. In addition, the provision of subsistence rights or basic human needs has long been advocated and championed by developing countries and is specifically addressed in the *International Covenant on Economic, Social, and Cultural Rights.*

## ■ Measuring Subsistence Rights

Assuming that basic needs should be provided (or at least not withheld) by sovereign states, the question of measurement still needs to be solved. Studies focusing on the realization of basic human needs rely primarily on demographic data. For decades, social scientists studying the problems of the developing world have used gross national product (GNP)—and its more contemporary cousin, gross domestic product (GDP)—as a yardstick of progress. Benefits of this measure include its widespread availability for both comparisons across states and time.[3] Researchers hypothesized that the poorest in a society would eventually realize the benefits from increases in societal wealth, or at the least governments would take action to alleviate the inequality. However, history has taught us that growth indeed did not spread to those most in need, and governments did not always step in to assist. This common result therefore questions the validity of GNP as an acceptable measure of basic human needs.

Bruce Moon (1991) presents several arguments regarding the inadequacies of wealth as a measure of basic human needs. First, he argues that wealth, in the form of GNP, is an index of aggregate production and fails to indicate individual income or consumption. The latter would be required in order to evaluate a citizen's basic human needs. Second, the issues involving the evaluation of output from different countries in a common measure are very troublesome. In particular, GNP fails to account for price fluctuations within and between countries such that "the same income buys very different levels of basic needs fulfillment, even within a single country" (Moon 1991, 21).[4] Third, a measure of GNP does not account for how the income is distributed within a society, particularly among women and children. In other words, the economic cost of a good is not a measure of its ability to enhance welfare, particularly to those most in need. Last, Moon argues that measures of wealth fail to account for the fact that crucial items necessary for basic human needs may simply not be available, irrespective of income or GNP (Moon 1991, 22).[5]

As a result of the above shortcomings, there have been numerous attempts by agencies such as the UN, the US Agency for International Development (USAID), the Organisation for Economic Co-operation and Development (OECD), and the UN Educational, Scientific, and Cultural Organization (UNESCO) to find superior measures. The primary focus in this effort has centered on social indicators of certain basic needs. These basic needs and their common indicators are:

*Health:* life expectancy, health expenditures, doctors per thousand population, hospital beds per thousand population
*Education:* literacy, primary school enrollment, education expenditures
*Nutrition:* caloric supply per head, caloric supply as percentage of requirements
*Water supply:* percentage of population with potable water, infant mortality per thousand population
*Sanitation:* percentage of population with access to sanitation facilities, infant mortality per thousand population
*Housing:* no acceptable indicator available

The search for adequate measures can be further broken down into consideration of indicators that reflect either inputs or results. Indicators reflecting results or outcomes are on the whole preferable since we are striving to evaluate the actual performance of governments in providing basic human needs to its citizens. For instance, health expenditures and primary school enrollment tell us nothing about the distribution of these services or the quality and therefore success of the effort[6] (Hicks and Streeten 1979, 571–578; Moon 1991, 24). The question then becomes, which one of these indicators is the most appropriate measure?

The inadequacies of any single measure to capture the concept of basic human needs led to efforts to combine individual indicators into composite indices. Morris David Morris (1979) lays out six criteria that any composite measures should meet. The first two criteria address a fundamental and contentious debate within the human rights literature over universalism. He argues that an index must not assume either that there is only one path to development or that there is a universal understanding of basic human needs. Thus, the measure should be as "unethnocentric" as possible and "allow for differences in cultural experiences and social institutions" (Morris 1979, 22). Third, the indicators or measures employed should reflect results not inputs; that is, the component of an index should reflect the outcome or effectiveness of any governmental policy, not the actual resources contributed. For example, measuring the level of governmental expenditures on education doesn't necessarily accurately reflect literacy levels. A fourth related criterion is that the measure adequately captures how the policy results are distributed within and between states. In other words, any measure must take into account how benefits, particularly welfare benefits, are distributed within society. In addition, an effective index is one that is considered simple, both in construction and interpretation. Last, an index is effective and useful when it can be used for cross-national comparisons. This is particularly important to scholars as they gather data that can be employed in addressing such questions as those presented above.

One promising measure is the Human Development Index offered by the UN (United Nations Development Programme 2006, 393–395). This index combines indicators of national income (adjusted GDP per capita purchasing power parity in US dollars), life expectancy at birth, and educational attainment. The educational component is interesting in that it combines adult literacy and primary, secondary, and tertiary gross enrollment (counter to previous measures that only looked at either literary or student enrollment).[7] Although the overall HDI is an improvement over some previous attempts, it presents several shortcomings. These include only measuring human development since its inception in 1990 and mixing ends and means (i.e., income is means of achieving human development while standards of health and educational achievement are ends). Further, the use of a measure for national income (per capita GDP) as an element of basic human needs will be problematic, as this same concept is often used as an independent variable to explain the provision of basic human needs in a number of cross-national empirical models.[8]

## ▧ The Physical Quality of Life Index

A widely utilized composite, the Physical Quality of Life Index (PQLI), was developed by Morris (1979) under the auspices of the Overseas Development Council. This measure is designed to capture the ability of a country to meet the basic needs of its people. The index consists of three indicators: infant mortality per thousand live births, life expectancy at age one, and basic literacy as the proportion of population fifteen years and over that is literate.[9] Conceptually, the PQLI reflects several principles contained within the various articles in the UN Declaration of Human Rights. For example, Article 25 of the declaration states that "everyone has the right to a standard of living adequate for the health and well-being of himself and his family, including food, clothing, housing, and medical care and necessary social services." Article 26 indicates that the signatories agree that everyone also has a right to education. This right to an adequate standard of living and education is best captured by the Physical Quality of Life Index. Many of these concepts are further clarified and expanded in the *International Covenant of Economic, Social, and Cultural Rights* (1976).

The first two components, infant mortality and life expectancy, together measure the overall health of a society. While these two variables, at first glance, might appear to measure a similar concept, they are actually indicators of different societal phenomena. Infant mortality itself is tied more to water purity, maternal morbidity, and the overall well-being and health of the home environment. Life expectancy at age one, however, addresses the available nutrition and health conditions outside the home. The literacy variable gives an indication of the general level of development within a society and specifically reveals whether social benefits actually extend to women and children (Morris 1979, Dixon 1984). Compared with school enrollment or numbers of classrooms or instructors, literacy reflects overall gains made by the underclass rather than the inputs provided by government.

Empirically, the PQLI composite is the unweighted arithmetic mean of our three indicators. The first indicator, the infant mortality rate (IMR) index, utilizes 250 per 1,000 live births as the "worst" performance and 0 per 1,000 live births as the "best" possible performance. Specific country measures are determined by the formula:[10]

$$\frac{250 - \text{IMR}}{2.50}$$

The second indicator, the measure for life expectancy at age one ($LE^1$), considers 38 years as the "worst" case scenario (since 1950) and 85 years as the "best" performance. The index for each country is thus designated by the formula:

$$\frac{\text{LE}^1 - 38}{0.47}$$

Since most sources usually report data only for life expectancy at birth, $LE^1$ can be calculated by the standard formula:

$$\text{LE}^1 = \frac{\text{LE}^0 - 1 + \text{IMR}(1 - \text{SURV})}{1 - \text{IMR}}$$

where $LE^0$ is life expectancy at birth, IMR is infant mortality rate per 1,000 births, and SURV is the average survival period for the first year and is assumed to be three and one half months (0.3 year).

Morris's (1979) original computation of the index included the early 1970s, as well as indices for males and females for the years 1950, 1964, and 1970 (Morris 1979). This index was updated by Morris in 1996 and included the years 1960, 1981, 1985, and 1990. Wesley Milner (1998) collected additional data and filled in many of the missing years to have a comprehensive cross-sectional time series data set. Thus, Milner (1998) was able to include the years 1980–1993 in his study of globalization and the realization of basic human needs. The data was again updated (Callaway 2001) with the addition of the years 1976–1979 and 1994–1996. In this update, the *World Development Indicators* database was used to gather the initial data for the three separate measures. This source provided a rather comprehensive amount of the data, particularly the rates of illiteracy. This data was compared with the Milner (1998) data set. In instances where data was missing, data from the Milner (1998) data set was added to the initial data from the *World Development Indicators*. Missing data were gathered from the *World Development Report*,

UNESCO, and the *Children of the World Report* from the United Nations Children's Fund (UNICEF).

## ■ Critiquing the PQLI

Some scholars have questioned the index approach in general and the PQLI in particular (Bayless and Bayless 1982; Goldstein 1992; Hicks and Streeten 1979; Larson and Wilford 1979). One argument is that a loss of information may result from an index of indicators that measure similar aspects of basic human needs. Provided the components are indeed highly correlated, then nothing is gained from the index. Conversely, if the components move in different directions, combining them could mask the changes that might be detected by using the individual indicators. Perhaps the most troubling criticism of the PQLI is brought on by the apparent arbitrary nature in equally weighting infant mortality, life expectancy, and literacy (Bayless and Bayless 1982; Goldstein 1992; Hicks and Streeten 1979; Larson and Wilford 1979). While Morris (1979) originally laid out an extensive justification for his index, Moon (1991) succinctly addresses many of these criticisms of the PQLI.

The primary objection is that there is no theoretical basis for assigning equal weights to the components. Morris (1979, 47–49), however, forcefully argues that since there is no overriding theoretical justification for treating any one indicator as more important than another, we must employ equal weights. Moon (1991, 27) echoes this position and stresses that reweighting the components in various plausible alternatives produces measures with a Spearman rank order correlation consistently over .98. The extent of intercorrelation is higher than that usually considered sufficient to warrant a composite index.

First, employing an index instead of a combination of collinear indicators streamlines the analysis and makes reporting more succinct. Second, if it can be assumed that the separate components of the index capture different aspects of a single theoretical construct, Moon (drawing upon previous research) argues that this is indeed justification for a composite index. Comparison studies (Moon and Dixon 1985; Moon 1991) indicate that the intercorrelations among the three ingredients and the overall PQLI are extremely high, indicating that this is indeed the same construct. Third, Moon (1991, 26) suggests that by using a combination of the three indicators, the research can lessen any impact of the anomalies of any single item.

After evaluating the advantages and disadvantages of the numerous approaches to measuring subsistence rights, we are persuaded that the PQLI is the best measure currently available for addressing the concept of basic human needs. Further, we feel that in addition to the important conceptualization and implementation of security rights, the theoretical bases and legal underpinnings for subsistence rights provision are well established both at the domestic and international level. As this important subfield looks to the future, it is imperative that scholars and practitioners alike continue the search for empirical measurements and improved methodologies to assist in the evaluation and promotion of human rights practices.

## ▓ Notes

1. The terms *basic human needs* and *subsistence rights* are often used interchangeably. We use the term *subsistence rights* generally to refer to those rights that are codified in the various international treaties and documents, particularly the *International Covenant on Economic, Cultural, and Social Rights*. The term *basic human needs* provides a better articulation when addressing governmental policies or efforts to address quality of life issues. Moon (1991, 5) indicates that basic human needs are "defined in terms of adequate food, water, health care, shelter, and minimum education," all of which are codified in international treaties and covenants.

2. The controversy rests primarily with the role of the state. For most Western states, less state intervention is the norm, including in the area of human rights. Here, the emphasis is on restraining the state from engaging in certain behavior, such as torture. Conversely, non-Western states place more of an emphasis on state engagement in the provision of certain rights, such as the right to an education.

3. For example, the World Bank and International Monetary Fund provide data for some 200 economies for the past forty-five years.

4. Utilizing an income figure based on purchasing power parity would make this a moot point; however, per capita GDP (purchasing power parity) would still have the additional inherent problems associated with using income as a measure for basic human needs.

5. For a discussion of additional problems with GNP as a measure of overall well-being, see Hicks and Streeten 1979; Morris 1979; Morawetz 1979; Moon and Dixon 1992.

6. At least one attribute in favor of inputs would be in attempting to measure the intention and commitment of a particular government to provide services. Fraser (1994) utilizes both of these approaches in comparing human rights practice versus promise.

7. This measure is calculated with two-thirds weight given to literacy and one-third weight given to combined gross enrollment.

8. In an empirical analysis, independent and dependent variables cannot measure the same concept. In order words, you cannot use per capita GDP to explain why there is a change in per capita GDP. This is considered a tautological argument.

9. Numerous scholars have employed the PQLI, including Morris (1979, 1996), Larson and Wilford (1979), Maizels and Nissanke (1984), Dixon (1984), Moon and Dixon (1985), Spalding (1985, 1996), Rosh (1986), Moon (1991), Tsoutsoplides (1991), Meyer (1996, 1998), Milner (1998, 2000, 2002), Milner, Poe and Leblang (1999), Callaway (2001), Neumayer (2003), Milner, Poe, Leblang, and Smith (2004).

10. For those already familiar with the PQLI, it must be noted here that the original formulas of Morris (1979) have been slightly modified (updated) for methodological reasons. The original index defined life expectancy at age one as $(LE^1 - 38) / .39$ and infant mortality as $(229 - IMR) / 2.22$ (Morris 1979, 45). Because of rapid increases of IMR and $LE^1$ in a number of higher-ranking nations, it was soon possible to obtain a score in excess of 100. If IMR or $LE^1$ rises above 100, its weight in the com-

posite measure will be disproportionate in relation to literacy, which by definition cannot be over 100. Therefore, the high end of the IMR scale has been altered from 7 per 1,000 to 0 per 1,000 live births. The low end of the scale was increased from 229 to 250 per 1,000 live births. The high end of the LE[1] has been increased from 77 to 85 years. The bottom end of the scale remains at 38 years. Finally, the formula used to convert life expectancy at birth data to life expectancy at age one has been slightly altered to where SURV (the average survival period during the first year) is 0.3 rather than 0.2 (Morris 1996, 7).

## ■ References

Bayless, Mark, and Susan Bayless. 1982. "Current Quality of Life Indicators: Some Theoretical and Methodological Concerns." *American Journal of Economics and Sociology* 41:421–437.

Callaway, Rhonda L. 2001. "Is the Road to Hell Paved with Good Intentions? The Effect of U.S. Foreign Assistance and Economic Policy on Human Rights." PhD Dissertation. Denton: University of North Texas.

Dixon, William. 1984. "Trade Concentration, Economic Growth, and the Provision of Basic Human Needs." *Social Science Quarterly* 65:761–764.

Dixon, William J., and Bruce E. Moon. 1987. "The Military Burden and Basic Human Needs." *Journal of Conflict Resolution* 30:660–684.

Donnelly, Jack. 1989. *Universal Human Rights in Theory and Practice*. Ithaca, NY: Cornell University Press.

Fraser, Elvis. 1994. "Reconciling Conceptual and Measurement Problems in the Comparative Study of Human Rights." *International Journal of Comparative Sociology* 35:1–18.

Goldstein, Robert J. 1992. "Limitations of Quantitative Data," in Thomas B. Jabine and Richard P. Claude, eds. *Human Rights and Statistics: Getting the Record Straight*. Philadelphia: University of Pennsylvania Press.

Hicks, Norman, and Paul Streeten. 1979. "Indicators of Development: The Search for a Basic Needs Yardstick." *World Development* 7:567–580.

Larson, David, and Walton Wilford. 1979. "The Physical Quality of Life Index: A Useful Social Indicator?" *World Development* 7:581–584.

Maizels, A., and M. K. Nissanke. 1984. "Motivations for Aid to Developing Countries." *World Development* 7:581–584.

Meyer, William H. 1998. *Human Rights and International Political Economy in Third World Nations: Multinational Corporations, Foreign Aid, and Repression*. Westport, CT: Praeger Publishers.

———. 1996. "Human Rights and MNCs: Theory Versus Quantitative Analysis." *Human Rights Quarterly* 18:368–397.

Milner, Wesley. 2002. "Emerging Human Rights Challenges: The Effects of Globalization and Economic Liberalization," in Alison Brysk, ed. *Globalization and Human Rights: Transnational Problems, Transnational Solutions?* Berkeley: University of California Press.

———. 2000. "Economic Freedom, Globalization and Human Rights: Can We Have It All?" *Journal of Private Enterprise* 15:35–61.

———. 1998. "Progress or Decline? International Political Economy and Basic Human Rights." PhD Dissertation. Denton: University of North Texas.

Milner, Wesley, Steven Poe, and David Leblang. 1999. "Security Rights, Subsistence Rights and Liberties: A Theoretical Survey of the Empirical Landscape." *Human Rights Quarterly* 21:404–443.

Milner, Wesley, Steven Poe, David Leblang, and Kara Smith. 2004. "Providing Subsistence Rights: Do States Make a Difference?" in Sabine Carey and Steven Poe, eds. *Understanding Human Rights Violations: New Systematic Studies*. London: Ashgate.

Moon, Bruce. 1991. *The Political Economy of Basic Human Needs*. Ithaca: Cornell University Press.

Moon, Bruce E., and William J. Dixon. 1992. "Basic Needs and Growth-Welfare Trade-Offs." *International Studies Quarterly* 36:191–212.

———. 1985. "Politics, the State, and Basic Human Needs: A Cross-National Study." *American Journal of Political Science* 29:661–694.

Morawetz, D. 1979. *Twenty-five Years of Economic Development, 1950 to 1975*. Baltimore: Johns Hopkins University Press.

Morris, Morris David. 1996. "Measuring the Condition of the World's Poor: The Physical Quality of Life Index, 1960–1990." Providence, RI: Thomas J. Watson, Jr. Institute for International Studies Working Paper (#23/24).

———. 1979. *Measuring the Condition of the World's Poor: The Physical Quality of Life Index*. New York: Pergamon.

Neumayer, Eric. 2003. "The Determinants of Aid Allocation by Regional Multilateral Development Banks and United Nations Agencies." *International Studies Quarterly* 47:101–122.

Rosh, Robert. 1986. "The Impact of Third World Defense Burdens on Basic Human Needs." *Policy Studies Journal* 15:135–146.

Shue, Henry. 1980. *Basic Rights: Subsistence, Affluence, and U.S. Foreign Policy*. Princeton: Princeton University Press.

Spalding, Nancy L. 1996. "Structural Adjustment Policies and Economic Human Rights in Africa," in David L. Cingranelli, ed. *Human Rights and Developing Countries*. Greenwich, CT: JAI Press.

———. 1985. "Providing for Economic Human Rights: The Case of the Third World." *Policy Studies Journal* 15:123–134.

Tsoutsoplides, C. 1991. "The Determinants of the Geographical Allocation of EC Aid to the Developing Countries." *Applied Economics* 23:647–658.

United Nations Development Programme. 2006. *Human Development Report: Beyond Scarcity*. New York: Palgrave Macmillan.

# 3 International Law and Organizations in the Fight for Human Rights

## 3.1

## Introduction
*The Editors*

The emergence of a human rights regime began after World War II, albeit in small and oftentimes painful steps. As an international response to the horrors of the Holocaust, the UN General Assembly adopted the Universal Declaration of Human Rights in 1948. This was followed by a litany of covenants and treaties aimed at the protection of a whole host of human rights ranging from political rights to the rights of migrant workers. Gaining a consensus on the wording of many of the treaties alone was viewed as progress in the early days of the human rights movement. What followed over the decades was a movement away from the normative basis for the establishment of universally accepted human rights to attempts at gaining international compliance with human rights law. The articles that follow address the evolution of international human rights laws and the role of international organizations and nongovernmental organizations alike in the development of an international human rights regime.

Thomas Buergenthal traces the evolution of both the normative nature and the institutionalization of international human rights laws and organizations. He suggests that there have been a number of steps over the past fifty years that have led to the realization of human rights obligations and limits on state sovereignty. Buergenthal first examines the evolution of a human rights norm, beginning with the adoption of the UN Charter and subsequent covenants on human rights. The second stage in this evolution involved building institutions to enforce international human rights law. The third stage occurred with the end of the Cold War, when the Vienna Declaration moved the international

69

community into further accepting the idea of universal human rights and rejecting arguments based on cultural relativism. The fourth stage shifts the focus from governments to the idea of individual responsibility and the rights of minorities. Although Buergenthal acknowledges limits in the realization of human rights, he reminds us that the concept of human rights has significantly changed and increasingly been accepted in the international community.

Many human rights institutions have emerged in order to facilitate the realization of human rights across the globe. The first attempt at international justice was conducted at the end of World War II in the form of the Nuremburg and Tokyo trials. These international tribunals became templates, both normatively and institutionally, for the future adjudication of human rights abuses. More recently, the war crimes tribunals in Rwanda and the former Yugoslavia have renewed a call for a more permanent court to address heinous acts such as crimes against humanity and genocide. In addition, the inability to initiate a war crimes tribunal for Cambodia suggests that ad hoc tribunals are an inefficient and ineffective means of addressing human rights violations. Thus, the international human rights community renewed the movement toward an International Criminal Court (ICC). Robert W. Tucker outlines the efforts to establish an ICC, including, in particular, initial US opposition to such a court. Based on experiences in the former Yugoslavia and Rwanda, the United States reversed its opposition and began to support the idea of a permanent court. Tucker outlines the controversy over the court's jurisdiction, including the objections made by the United States. In the end, Bill Clinton signed the Rome Treaty establishing the ICC but did not submit the treaty for ratification. Since then, George W. Bush has nullified the signature, and the US Senate has refused to ratify the treaty. Nonetheless, the requisite approval of sixty states necessary to put the treaty into force was acquired in 2002, and the court has been open since 2003.

The next selection, written by Alan Dowty and Gil Loescher, examines the growing international norm of human rights with regard to refugee flows. They argue that it is too costly for governments to ignore refugee crises and that the international community is already bearing the costs of large-scale refugee flows. Moreover, they contend that significant refugee flows across state borders internationalize an otherwise domestic issue and that such flows are an increasingly sufficient justification for international intervention. The excerpt included here argues that intervention can be supported by customary law, by the UN Charter's call for action to preserve peace and security, and by the evolution of norms regarding intervention on behalf of humanitarianism. In each instance, the authors make the case that there is sufficient argument to justify state responsibility and international action to stem refugee flows.

Nongovernmental organizations, or what Margaret Keck and Katherine Sikkink refer to as "transnational advocacy networks," can also play a critical role in transforming the human rights practices of a state. Unlike intergovernmental organizations (IGOs), these types of groups operate outside the purview of state authority and, as such, are able to avoid the obstacle of state sovereignty. Keck and Sikkink compare the campaigns of footbinding and female circumcision to elucidate the power and effectiveness of nonstate actors.

# 3.2 _____

# The Normative and Institutional Evolution of International Human Rights
*Thomas Buergenthal*

## ▓ Stage One: The Normative Foundation

The first stage in this process begins with the entry into force of the UN Charter and continues at least through the adoption in 1966 of the International Covenants on Human Rights. By this time, the Universal Declaration of Human Rights had been adopted by the United Nations, as had the Genocide Convention and the Convention on the Elimination of All Forms of Racial Discrimination, to mention only the principal human rights instruments. During this same period, the European Convention on Human Rights entered into force; the Organization of American States proclaimed the American Declaration on the Rights and Duties of Man; and UNESCO and the ILO [International Labour Organization], respectively, promulgated the Convention against Discrimination in Education and the Convention Concerning Discrimination in Respect of Employment and Occupation.

This period, in short, witnessed the normative consolidation of international human rights law. It is true, of course, that this process continues to this day. It is equally true, however, that in these first 20 years following the establishment of the UN the process had become irreversible. Two very important factors explain this development. First, the human rights provisions of the Charter, supplemented by the Universal Declaration of Human Rights and other human rights instruments, came to be accepted as defining the basic human rights obligations that the Member States of the United Nations had accepted by ratifying the Charter. That is to say, while some states still argued in the early days of the United Nations that the Charter imposed no human rights obligations whatsoever on them, that view was no longer tenable by the end of the 1960s. Second, once it was acknowledged that the Charter, a multilateral

Excerpted from Thomas Buergenthal, "The Normative and Institutional Evolution of International Human Rights," *Human Rights Quarterly* 19 (4): 703–723. © 1997 The Johns Hopkins University Press. Reprinted with permission of The Johns Hopkins University Press. Some of the author's notes have been omitted.

treaty, had created some human rights obligations for the Member States, it followed as a matter of international law that human rights had, to that extent, been internationalized and removed from the protective domain of a subject that previously was essentially within their domestic jurisdiction.

The idea that the United Nations should become the international protector of the rights of the individual grew out of the tragic experience of the Second World War and the horrendous violations of human rights committed in the Holocaust. Many wartime leaders believed that the rise of Hitler could have been averted had there existed in the 1930s a strong international organization with authority to address human rights issues. To them it was critical that the experience with the League of Nations, which was weak and lacked the power to deal with human rights issues, not be repeated. One would therefore have expected the UN Charter to contain provisions establishing an effective international system for the protection of human rights. That did not come to pass because of opposition from the major powers—the United States, the Soviet Union, France, and the United Kingdom. These states all had serious human rights problems of their own at the time[1] and were therefore not prepared to agree to strong commitments in the area of human rights. Although various smaller countries favored the inclusion of a bill of rights in the Charter, they lacked the political influence to prevail. That explains why the human rights provisions of the Charter, as adopted in San Francisco, were purposefully drafted to be weak and vague.[2]

The three major human rights provisions of the Charter are Articles 1(3), 55(c), and 56. The first of these provisions recognizes that one of the "purposes" of the United Nations is international cooperation in solving various international problems, including "humanitarian" problems, and "in promoting and encouraging respect for human rights and fundamental freedoms for all without distinctions as to race, sex, language, or religion." This provision is amplified by Article 55(c), which reads as follows:

> With a view to the creation of conditions of stability and well-being which are necessary for the peaceful and friendly relations among nations based on respect for the principles of equal rights and self-determination of peoples, the United Nations shall promote: . . .
>
> (c) universal respect for, and observance of, human rights and fundamental freedoms for all without distinction as to race, sex, language, or religion.

Article 56 imposes the same obligations on the Member States by providing that "all Members pledge themselves to take joint and separate action in co-operation with the Organisation for the achievement of the purposes set forth in Article 55."[3]

These provisions did not establish an immediate obligation to guarantee or observe human rights, nor did they define what was meant by "human rights and fundamental freedoms." They imposed the much vaguer obligation to "promote . . . universal respect for, and the observance of, human rights" and to take "joint and separate action in co-operation with the Organization" to achieve this purpose. The only unambiguous provision in these articles is the prohibition of discrimination. Despite their vagueness, the human rights provisions of the Charter had a number of important consequences. First, as we have already noted, the Charter internationalized the concept of human rights. This did not mean that as soon as the Charter entered into force, all human rights issues were *ipso facto* no longer matters essentially within the domestic jurisdiction of states. It meant instead that states had assumed some international obligation relating to human rights, although their full scope remained to be defined and that, as far as these obligations were concerned, the states could no longer claim that human rights as such were essentially domestic in character. Second, the obligation of the Member States of the UN to cooperate with the Organization in the promotion of human rights provided the UN with the requisite legal authority to undertake a massive effort to define and codify these rights. The foundation of this codification effort was laid by the proclamation in 1948 of the Universal Declaration of Human Rights. Adopted as a non-binding UN General Assembly resolution, the Declaration was designed, as its preamble indicates, to provide "a common understanding" of the human rights and fundamental freedoms referred to in the Charter and to serve "as a common standard of achievement for all peoples and all nations. . . ."[4] But the Declaration not only gave meaning to the phrase "human rights and fundamental freedoms" used in the Charter, over time it came to be accepted as a normative instrument in its own right which, together with the Charter, spelled out the human rights obligations incumbent upon all UN Member States.[5]

The success of the UN effort is reflected in the adoption of the International Bill of Rights and in the vast number of international human rights instruments in existence today. The entry into force of each new treaty in this field has further internationalized the subject of human rights as between the parties to them. It has also endowed the individuals for whose benefit these treaties were concluded with international legal rights. The state practice spawned by the vast network of human rights treaties continues to create a growing body of customary international law on the subject. Hence, a definition of international law that did not today recognize the individual as the direct beneficiary of international human rights law and, to that extent, a subject of international law, would be blind to contemporary legal and political realities.

## ■ Stage Two: Institution Building

The second stage in the evolution of international human rights law begins in the late 1960s and continues for the next fifteen to twenty years. This is the era of institution building. During these years we find two distinct developments taking place within the UN framework. The first focused on the nature or scope of the human rights obligations that Articles 55 and 56 imposed on the Member States. Only after this issue had been resolved could the UN begin to create institutions and mechanisms to enforce their obligations. From a strictly legal point of view, the answer to the question concerning the obligations of UN Member States turned on the meaning of the phrase "to promote . . . universal respect for, and observance of, human rights and fundamental freedoms. . . ."[6]

It could certainly be argued that this provision did not require states at the time of their ratification of the Charter to stop any and all violations of human rights. It was much too vague for that. Even so, how long could a state go on violating human rights before running afoul of the Charter? Were there at least some human rights violations that had to stop? It took the UN a long time to provide some clear answers to these questions. They were eventually provided and grew out of the UN's struggle to put an end to apartheid. Apartheid came gradually to be characterized as a pervasive violation of all basic human rights, a governmental policy implemented on a massive scale against a large segment of the population. In this context, the meaning of the obligation "to promote," however vague in the abstract, became concrete in the sense that a UN Member State which embarked on or maintained such a policy could certainly not be deemed to be "promoting human rights and fundamental freedoms" and was, therefore, in violation of its Charter obligations. This principle was formally established with the adoption of ECOSOC [Economic and Social Council] Resolution 1235 (XLII) of 6 June 1967. It authorized the UN Human Rights Commission "to make a thorough study of situations which reveal a consistent pattern of violations of human rights, as exemplified by the policy of *apartheid* as practised in the Republic of South Africa . . . and racial discrimination as practised notably in Southern Rhodesia. . . ." This resolution was followed by ECOSOC Resolution 1503 (XLVIII) of 27 May 1970, which empowered the UN Sub-Commission on the Prevention of Discrimination and Protection of Minorities to develop a mechanism for dealing with communications from individuals and groups revealing "a consistent pattern of gross and reliably attested violations of human rights." The Sub-Commission and the UN Human Rights Commission implemented this resolution by establishing the necessary procedures for dealing with such communications.

These two ECOSOC resolutions continue in force to this day and serve as the foundation of the UN Charter–based system for the protection of human rights. They have given birth to an ever expanding institutional mechanism within the UN framework for dealing with large-scale human rights violations that embrace the mushrooming rapporteur and special missions system as well as the UN High Commissioner for Human Rights. These institutions have their juridical basis in the Charter, complemented by the Universal Declaration of Human Rights. Although most of them were created in the late 1960s to respond to the scourge of apartheid, they have been invoked since the early 1980s to address massive violations of human rights in general.[7]

The period here under consideration also saw the emergence and consolidation of universal and regional treaty-based institutions for the protection of human rights. In the mid to late 1970s the UN Human Rights Committee[8] and the Committee on the Elimination of Racial Discrimination (CERD)[9] came into being with the entry into force of the International Covenant on Civil and Political Rights and the International Convention on the Elimination of All Forms of Racial Discrimination. The entry into force in 1978 of the American Convention on Human Rights brought with it the establishment of the Inter-American Commission and Court of Human Rights. Although the European Convention of Human Rights came into effect as early as 1953, it was not until the late 1960s and early 1970s that the institutions it created, particularly the Court, began to play an important role in the implementation of the Convention. In 1978, moreover, UNESCO adopted a special mechanism for dealing with human rights violations falling within its sphere of competence. ILO institutions for dealing with human rights issues predate those referred to above, whereas those established under the African Charter on Human and Peoples' Rights did not come into being until after the entry into force of that instrument in 1986.[10]

The establishment of these and related institutions also contributed to the emergence of nongovernmental human rights organizations and laid the basis for their growing significance. Although some of these groups existed much earlier, their number and strength, and their activism begin in this period.[11] The creation of the intergovernmental human rights institutions referred to above provided the nongovernmental organizations with their *raison d'être* for filing human rights complaints and mounting human rights enforcement campaigns on the national and international plane. In earlier times their principal role consisted of the promotion of normative instruments.

There are a number of interrelated political reasons to explain some of these developments. The end of the colonial era and the vast expansion the UN underwent in the late 1950s and early 1960s resulted in the admission to the UN of many newly independent states, particularly from Africa. These states were unanimous in their commitment to ending apartheid. That could only be achieved by developing and strengthening UN mechanisms for dealing with this egregious human rights problem. By supporting these UN measures with regard to apartheid, the Soviet Union and its allies gave the Western democracies a strong political opening in favor of expanding the jurisdiction of UN human rights mechanisms to embrace not only apartheid but any other massive violations of human rights.

These diverse efforts by the West, the East, and the nonaligned nations focused a great deal of public attention on UN human rights activities. They gave rise to worldwide expectations about the important role the UN and other international organizations should play in addressing human rights violations. Many states now found it increasingly difficult for political and propaganda reasons not to give at least some lip service to international human rights efforts, making it harder for them to oppose the establishment of various international and regional human rights institutions. . . .

## ▓ Stage Three: Implementation in the Post Cold War Era

The institutions referred to in the preceding section did not come fully into their own until the mid to late 1980s when they could begin to focus on adopting effective measures to ensure state compliance with their international obligations. This process continues to this day. It is one thing to establish institutions on the international plane to promote and protect human rights, it is quite another to give them the authority and tools they need to achieve their objective. States are more likely to agree to the creation of human rights institutions than to cooperate with these institutions when they or their allies are charged with human rights violations. It must be recognized, however, that the political factors which contributed in large measure to the creation of human rights institutions in the first place—the ideas that inspired the international human rights movement and captured the imagination of mankind—make it increasingly more difficult for states not to comply with their human rights obligations.

During the period here under consideration, the world underwent dramatic changes to which the human rights revolution contributed significantly and from which the revolution also benefited significantly. The end of the Cold War freed many nations in Europe from Communist rule, permitting them to embark on a process of democratic transformation. What is more, it liberated international efforts to promote human rights from the debilitating ideological conflicts and political sloganeering of the past. These developments have enabled the UN to focus increasingly on obstacles to the implementation of human rights.

The end of the Cold War and its effect on human rights is reflected in part in the text of the 1993 Vienna Declaration on Human Rights. The pervasive scope of the Declaration, evidenced by the fact that it addresses most, if not all, modern human rights concerns, is one of its striking features, as is the fact that it does so, on the whole, in a politically balanced and serious manner. While it does not come up with solutions to the many intractable problems facing the international community in this field, the Declaration identifies them and in the process demonstrates that there are few, if any, human rights issues today that are not of international concern. The catalogue embraces civil and political rights, economic, social and cultural rights, the right to development, the rights of refugees and internally displaced persons, humanitarian law issues, the rights of minorities and of indigenous peoples, the rights of women, the rights of the disabled and of children, etc. It is in this context that the statement in paragraph 4 of the Declaration that "the promotion and protection of *all* human rights is a legitimate concern of the international community" (emphasis added), gains its true significance. Hence, it would appear that the dividing line between domestic and international human rights issues is no more because its factual and legal basis has disappeared. More importantly, the international community is today free to say so.

This same idea also finds expression in another, equally important principle proclaimed in the Vienna Declaration. Paragraph 5 of that instrument declares that

> All human rights are universal, indivisible and interdependent and interrelated. The international community must treat human rights globally in a fair and equal manner, on the same footing, and with the same emphasis. While the significance of national and regional particularities and various historical, cultural and religious backgrounds must be borne in mind, it is the duty of States, regardless of their political, economic and cultural systems, to promote and protect all human rights and fundamental freedoms.[12]

The recognition of the universal character of human rights and the concomitant rejection of cultural relativism, which has traditionally sought to justify violations of human rights by reference to some special religious or cultural imperatives, lays the foundation for global efforts to improve the human rights situation of all human beings.

Read together, paragraphs 4 and 5 of the Vienna Declaration do away with two major impediments to the implementation of human rights which prevented effective international action in the past: the artificial distinctions between domestic and international human rights concerns, on the one hand, and cultural relativism, on the other. The Vienna Declaration also addressed a third obstacle: the myth that all governments, whether democratic or not, can protect human rights and that a state's form of government could not be deemed to affect its compliance with international human rights standards. This legal and political fiction—another product of the Cold War—forced the international community for decades to close its eyes to massive human rights violations having their source in political systems antithetical to the protection of human rights and the rule of law. In paragraph 8, the Vienna Declaration put this myth to rest by proclaiming that "democracy, development and respect for human rights and fundamental freedoms are interdependent and mutually reinforcing." This provision declares further that "democracy is based on the freely expressed will of the people to determine their own political, economic, social and cultural systems and their full participation in all aspects of their lives." Paragraph 8 concludes by urging the international community to "support the strengthening and promoting of democracy, development and respect for human rights and fundamental freedoms in the entire world."

The notion that genuine democracy and the protection of human rights go together, a concept that could not have been proclaimed during the Cold War, found expression some time earlier with the adoption in 1990 of the Copenhagen Concluding Document of the Conference on Security and Cooperation in Europe. Whereas this document laid the foundation for the establishment of a democratic European public order,[13] the Vienna Declaration can be read to have done the same for the world as a whole. This is not to say that all nations of the world have now become democracies or even that they are close to this goal. Unfortunately for the enjoyment of human rights, neither is the case as yet. It does mean, however, that the absence of democracy in a state is today in itself a violation of the human rights of its population and that the international community has the right for that very reason to concern itself with efforts designed to remove obstacles to its democratization.

While the removal of these political myths and legal fictions has enabled the international community to focus more realistically on the task of getting governments to comply with their international human rights obligations, genuine progress in this area will continue to be slow. There is increasing recognition today that the task is a very difficult one even with the best intentions of governments. Underlying many human rights violations are deeply rooted social causes. They cannot be overcome by governmental decrees alone. Poverty, corruption, disease, lack of educational resources, and economic and political underdevelopment are but a few factors that contribute to violations of human rights. These are not problems that can be solved overnight. Solutions often require financial and human resources that are scarce and require international cooperation and development efforts. The fact that various international lending institutions, such as the World Bank, and regional development banks, have begun to channel resources into efforts to create and strengthen national institutions capable of promoting the rule of law and democratic pluralism, in addition to economic development, is an important step in the process of implementing human rights. . . .

## ▓ Stage Four: Individual Criminal Responsibility, Minority Rights and Collective Humanitarian Intervention

In confronting violations of internationally guaranteed human rights, the international community has traditionally focused on holding governments rather than individuals internationally responsible. The assumption here was that governments have a duty not only not to violate human rights, but also to control all activities taking place within their territory, including the obligation to punish human rights violations. Although the post World War II war crimes trials, the Geneva Conventions on humanitarian law, and some international human rights treaties, notably the Genocide Convention, established individual international criminal responsibility for some of the most egregious violations of human rights, such as genocide, crimes against humanity, and war crimes, international human rights law and efforts to enforce it have for the most part dealt with the behavior and obligations of governments.

This focus has shifted to some extent in recent years with the gradual recognition that some governments are simply not able to protect those within their jurisdiction from violations of human rights committed by powerful groups within the state. These groups include terrorist and criminal organizations and, in certain countries, the military establishment. The watchword here is impunity, that is, individuals belonging to these groups are able to engage in large-scale violations of human rights while enjoying *de facto* immunity from prosecution for what in theory at least are criminal acts under the law of the state where these acts take place.[14] Potential violators will obviously not be deterred from engaging in massive human rights abuses in these countries if they know that they will enjoy domestic impunity and that, at most, only the state will be held internationally responsible for their acts.

These realities are increasingly forcing the international community to explore ways not only to hold the state responsible, but also to act directly against individuals whom the state is too weak or unwilling to punish. While various principles of international criminal law have in theory at least always permitted the imposition of individual responsibility for international crimes, including some grave violations of international human rights or humanitarian law, no international tribunals with jurisdiction to apply that law existed for decades after the Nürnberg and Tokyo War Crimes Tribunals were dissolved. This situation has changed in the past few years with the establishment by the United Nations of the International Tribunals for the Former Yugoslavia and for Rwanda with jurisdiction over crimes against humanity, genocide, and war crimes committed in those territories. The United Nations is now also in the process of establishing a permanent international criminal court. In addition, some international investigatory bodies, such as the United Nations Truth Commission for El Salvador, while not international tribunals with criminal jurisdiction, are being created in large measure to pierce national veils of impunity and to fix individual responsibility. The international community is also beginning to develop legal doctrines that would bar governments from granting amnesties to gross violators of human rights, a practice that has tended to be imposed on weak governments by military regimes or other powerful groups before turning over power to civilian authorities. . . .

On the whole . . . the international community showed relatively little interest during the formative years of the United Nations and other post World War II international and regional organizations in the establishment of international systems for the protection of minority rights. The absence of an appropriate clause on this subject in the UN Charter can be attributed, in part at least, to the opposition of some Eastern and Central European nations. These countries believed that various irredentist movements in the 1930s, which had been encouraged by Nazi Germany and its allies, had their source in the League of Nations minorities system. Whether true or not, the omission of any reference to minorities in the UN Charter and the Universal Declaration is attributable to these sentiments.[15]

The break up of the Soviet empire, the inhuman policies of "ethnic cleansing" accompanying the dissolution of the former Yugoslavia, and the threats of similar practices in other parts of the world have again focused international attention on the need for the international protection of minorities. Efforts to lay the normative foundation for a system that would accomplish this objective were initiated in the United Nations with the adoption by the General Assembly of the 1992 Declaration on the Rights of Persons Belonging to National or Ethnic, Religious and Linguistic Minorities. The Council of Europe followed with the adoption in 1994 of the Framework Convention for the Protection of National Minorities. The Organization on Security and Cooperation in Europe pioneered these measures with the 1990 Copenhagen Concluding Document and a number of later OSCE instruments on the subject, culminating in 1992 with the establishment of the office of the OSCE High Commissioner for National Minorities.

Considering that we live in a world in which extreme nationalism and various forms of racial, ethnic, and religious intolerance are on the rise, it is safe to predict that efforts to protect minorities will increasingly occupy the attention of the international community and result in greater legislative and institutional activities in this area. We may thus be coming full circle from the minorities system established by the League of Nations, its abandonment by the founders of the United Nations, back to the realization that contemporary international realities require additional international norms and institutions on the subject.

The UN Security Council is today also increasingly taking action to deal with large-scale human rights violations by authorizing enforcement measures under the powers that Chapter VII of the UN Charter confers on it. This chapter applies to situations determined by the Security Council to constitute a "threat to the peace, breach of the peace, or act of aggression." It has been applied by the Security Council in some of its decisions relating to the Kurds in Iraq, Somalia, the former Yugoslavia, and Haiti, among others. While it is still too early to assert that these and related cases have now firmly established the principle that massive violations of human rights without more will be deemed by the Security Council to constitute a sufficient legal basis for action under Chapter VII, it is clear that the Security Council is moving in that direction. What we are seeing here is the emergence of a modern version of collective humanitarian intervention that has its basis in the convergence of two important developments: the growing power of the Security Council in the post Cold War era and the increasing willingness of the international community to confront massive violations of human rights with force, if necessary. Only time will tell whether this ultimate weapon of the international community for dealing with truly egregious violations of human rights will in fact be used to advance the cause of human rights rather than some extraneous political objectives, a practice which brought the old doctrine of humanitarian intervention into disrepute.

# ■ Notes

1. The United States still had *de jure* racial discrimination, the Soviet Union its Gulag, and France and the United Kingdom their colonies.
2. See Paul Gordon Lauren, "First Principles of Racial Equality: History and the Politics and Diplomacy of Human Rights Provisions in the United Nations Charter," 5 *Hum. Rts. Q.* 1 (1983).
3. U.N. Charter.
4. Universal Declaration of Human Rights.
5. For the different theories that explain the normative status of the Universal Declaration, see Louis B. Sohn, "The New International Law: Protection of the Rights of Individuals Rather Than States," 32 *Am. U.L. Rev.* 1 (1982) at 16–17; Bruno Simma & Philip Alston, "The Sources of Human Rights Law: Custom, Jus Cogens, and General Principles," 12 *Austl. Y.B. Int'l L.* 82 (1992); Thomas Buergenthal, *International Human Rights in a Nutshell* (2d ed. 1995) at 33.
6. U.N. Charter.
7. See Howard B. Tolley, Jr., *The U.N. Commission on Human Rights* (1987); Philip Alston, "The Commission on Human Rights," in *The United Nations and Human Rights: A Critical Appraisal* (1992) at 126, 138; Asborjn Eide, "The Sub-Commission on Prevention of Discrimination and Protection of Minorities," in *A Critical Appraisal*, at 211.
8. See Dominic McGoldrick, *The Human Rights Committee* (1991); Manfred Nowak, *U.N. Covenant on Civil and Political Rights: CCPR Commentary* (1993).
9. See generally Karl Josef Partsch, "The Committee on the Elimination of Racial Discrimination," in *A Critical Appraisal*, supra note 7, at 339.
10. See Cees Flinterman & Evelyn Ankumah, "The African Charter on Human and Peoples' Rights," in *Guide to International Human Rights Practice* 152 (Hurst Hannum ed., 2d ed. 1992); U.O. Umozurike, "Six Years of the African Commission on Human and Peoples' Rights," in *Recht zwischen Umbruch und Bewahrung, Festschrift für Rudolf Bernhardt* 635 (Ulrich Beyerlin et al. eds., 1995); Claude E. Welch, Jr., "Human Rights and African Women: A Comparison of Protection Under Two Major Treaties," 15 *Hum. Rts. Q.* 549 (1993); Burns H. Weston et al., "Regional Human Rights Regimes: A Comparison and Appraisal," 20 *Vand. J. Transnat'l L.* 585 (1987).
11. See Buergenthal, supra note 5, at 318–26; Howard B. Tolley, Jr., *The International Commission of Jurists: Global Advocates for Human Rights* (1994).
12. "Vienna Declaration and Programme of Action, U.N. GAOR, World Conf. on Hum. Rts.," 48th Sess., 22nd plen. mtg., U.N. Doc. A/CONF.157/24 (Part I) (1993) 18 [hereinafter Vienna Declaration].
13. See Thomas Buergenthal, "The CSCE Rights System," 25 *Geo. Wash. J. Int'l L. & Econ.* 333, 355–56 (1991); Thomas Buergenthal, "The Copenhagen CSCE Meeting: A New Public Order for Europe," 11 *Hum. Rts. L.J.* 217 (1990).

14. See *Impunity and Human Rights in International Law and Practice* (Naomi Roht-Arriaza ed., 1995); Juan E. Méndez, "Accountability for Past Abuses," 19 *Hum. Rts. Q.* 255 (1997).

15. See Hersch Lauterpacht, *International Law and Human Rights* 27–47 (1950), at 424; Hurst Hannum, *Autonomy, Sovereignty, and Self-Determination: The Accommodation of Conflicting Rights* 56–57 (1990).

# 3.3

# The International Criminal Court Controversy

*Robert W. Tucker*

In December 1989, the General Assembly, responding to a request from a member state (Trinidad and Tobago, but in connection with illicit trafficking in narcotics across national frontiers), asked the International Law Commission, an organ of the General Assembly, to resume its long abandoned work on an international criminal court. The commission submitted a draft statute to the General Assembly in 1994. Between 1994 and 1998, the draft statute was subject to review and revision.

Prior to 1995, the United States had been at best lukewarm toward establishing a permanent international criminal court. It had supported the creation by the Security Council of ad hoc international criminal tribunals—in 1993 for the former Yugoslavia and in 1994 for Rwanda. (Critics saw the tribunals as substitutes for the interventionary action the American government would not take at the time.) In 1995, however, the United States changed its position and joined other states in supporting the proposal for a permanent court. In his July 23, 1998, statement on the Rome statute to a subcommittee of the Senate Foreign Relations Committee, the chief American negotiator, David Scheffer, U.S. ambassador at large for war crimes issues, gave this explanation: "Our experience with the establishment and operation of the International Criminal Tribunals for the former Yugoslavia and Rwanda had convinced us of the merit of creating a permanent court that would more quickly be available for investigations and prosecutions and more cost effective in its operations."[1] The system of ad hoc justice was too slow, inefficient, and limited in scope, Scheffer argued. A permanent court would also presumably serve as a stronger deterrent.

The crimes over which the court may exercise jurisdiction shall be limited, the Rome statute reads, "to the most serious crimes of concern to the international community as a whole." They are the crimes of genocide, crimes against humanity, war crimes, and the crime of aggression. The definition of genocide, the least contentious crime, duplicates that given in the earlier 1948 Convention. Crimes against humanity are not limited to periods of armed con-

Excerpted from Robert W. Tucker, "The International Criminal Court Controversy," *World Policy Journal* 18, no. 2 (2001): 71–81. Reprinted with permission of The World Policy Institute. Some of the author's notes have been omitted.

flict; but to qualify they must be committed "as part of a widespread or systematic attack directed against any civilian population, with knowledge of the attack." They include "rape, sexual slavery, enforced prostitution, forced pregnancy, enforced sterilization, or any other form of sexual violence of comparable gravity."

The court is, in principle, not to concern itself with every war crime. The Rome statute confers jurisdiction "in respect of war crimes in particular when committed as part of a plan or policy or as part of a large-scale commission of such crimes." War crimes are defined as: "grave breaches" of the 1949 Geneva Conventions; "other serious violations of the laws and customs applicable in international armed conflict, within the established framework of international law"; in the case of an armed conflict not of an international character, serious violations of article 3 of the four 1949 Geneva Conventions (which concerns the humane treatment of noncombatants); and "other serious violations of the laws and customs applicable in armed conflicts not of an international character." . . .

War crimes are given special treatment in the statute in that they are subject to an "opt out" provision. A state, on becoming a party to the statute, may declare that for a period of seven years it does not accept the jurisdiction of the court with respect to war crimes. During that period the state can reassure itself about the court's treatment of war crimes. The United States had initially proposed that the "opt out" provision run without limit, then, when this failed, for a period of ten years.

The last of the core crimes—aggression—remains undefined. Although the statute provides that the court "shall exercise jurisdiction over the crime of aggression," it can do so only after aggression is defined and the conditions set out under which the court shall exercise jurisdiction with respect to this crime. Such provision "shall be consistent with the relevant provisions of the Charter of the United Nations." According to the traditional interpretation of the U.N. charter, aggression is determined by the Security Council, case by case. Whether this will continue to be so for the purposes of the court, whether there will be a link between a Security Council determination of aggression and the court's power to act on this crime, is left in abeyance. In any event, the court will have the competence to consider this crime only if seven-eighths of the states parties to the statute agree on a definition. The difficulty of securing such support comes close to ensuring that the Security Council's role in the determination of aggression will be preserved.

It was not the determination of the crimes falling within the jurisdiction of the court that provoked the greatest controversies but jurisdictional issues. These issues prompted the United States to vote against the treaty. The Rome statute was not what the American government had wanted—a court controlled by the Security Council. The Clinton administration position was simply that the world's greatest military power bore a special responsibility for peacekeeping and the prevention of humanitarian catastrophes. As such, its military personnel would be subject to the potential jurisdiction of an international criminal court. Thus our emphasis on the Security Council, with its reliance on the veto, and our desire to limit other avenues to the court. This might well have meant that action would seldom be taken, since the other four permanent Security Council members—Great Britain, France, Russia and China—have the same veto power. The administration's view, better no action than action over which we might lose control, did not prevail. Instead, the statute provides that the Security Council, by a resolution adopted under Chapter VII of the U.N. charter (which deals with threats of aggression), may halt an investigation or prosecution for a period of 12 months (subject to renewal).

In considerable measure, however, the United States realized its objectives. Provided the Security Council can act under Chapter VII of the U.N. charter, it is the arbiter of the cases that go to the International Criminal Court. The provision authorizing the Security Council to refer to the prosecutor situations in which crimes appear to have been committed is subject to no limitation other than that the Security Council must act under Chapter VII. Moreover, all of the powers at the Security Council's disposal may be applied to enforce the decisions of the court. But this was not the only avenue to the court. The states parties to the statute as well as the court's prosecutor also have access, though it is limited and without the enforcement powers at the Security Council's disposal. It was this access that the United States sought, at Rome and after, to limit still further.

The principle of complementarity provided the means of doing so. That principle, basic to the Rome statute, establishes that the court might assume jurisdiction, absent a Security Council referral, only when national courts are unable or unwilling to prosecute. But when this is the case, the court may exercise jurisdiction with respect to the crimes enumerated in the statute, if it has the consent of the state on the territory of which the conduct in question occurred or the state of which the person accused is a national. . . .

The statute also contains a section dealing with the general principles of criminal law. Among these principles is that first enunciated at Nuremberg, here titled the "irrelevance of official capacity." The statute is to apply equally to all persons without any distinction based on official capacity. A person's position or status shall in no case provide an exemption from criminal responsibility nor mitigate punishment. Military commanders, yet another provision reads, are criminally responsible for crimes committed under their command and control where the commander either knew or should have known that his forces were committing such crimes and failed to take all necessary and reasonable measures to ward off their commission. Nor are superior orders grounds for excluding criminal responsibility unless the person was under a legal obligation to obey orders, the person did not know the order was unlawful, and the order was not manifestly unlawful. Orders to commit genocide or crimes against humanity are manifestly unlawful. . . .

There is a strict order laid out for the law to be applied by the court. The statute was not intended to stand alone, but to be followed by negotiations—subsequently completed—on defining the elements of criminal offenses, the rules of procedure, and the rules of evidence. Second, the court is to apply relevant treaties and the principles and rules of international law. This is followed by the general principles of law derived by the court from national laws of legal systems of the world. The court may also apply principles and rules of law as interpreted in its previous decisions. Finally, the interpretation and application of these sources of law must be consistent with internationally recognized human rights, and be without any adverse distinction founded on grounds such as gender, age, race, color, language, religion or belief, political or other opinion, national, ethnic or social origin, wealth, birth or other status.

Although President Clinton and Secretary of State Madeleine Albright supported the idea of a permanent international criminal court, they apparently did not view with disfavor the Pentagon's opposition to the way in which this court was developing. The Pentagon, as well, had not opposed the idea of a permanent court. It was intent on preventing the creation of the "wrong" kind of court, one that did not give a preferred status to the United States. In practical terms, this could only mean a court controlled by the Security Council. Rome had fallen short of that goal.

Even the International Criminal Tribunal for the Former Yugoslavia had fallen short. An incident had occurred during 1999 that had demonstrated the Pentagon's fears. In December 1999, officials of the international tribunal completed a legal analysis of the possibility that the NATO allies had committed war crimes during their air war with Yugoslavia over Kosovo. The case had been brought to the prosecutor of the tribunal by a delegation of Russian legislators and legal experts who had urged an investigation of NATO's role. A review of the charges and legal issues was undertaken with the result that a formal investigation was not endorsed. But the American government did not dispute the tribunal's legal authority to conduct a review and, had it so decided, to proceed with a formal investigation. The episode served to confirm fears of how a permanent international criminal court would function that was not effectively controlled by the Security Council.

What the Pentagon wanted was the assurance that no American soldier would ever be brought before the court without the American government's consent. In pursuit of this goal, the United States forged a proposal that would alter the basis on which the court may exercise jurisdiction over the personnel of states that are not parties to the treaty. The American proposal would prevent the court from requesting the surrender of a non-party national where that national was acting under the direction of its state and the state acknowledged such action. An issue of individual criminal responsibility would be transformed into one of state responsibility, to be dealt with according to general international law. The proposal would be incorporated into the agreement, required by the Rome Treaty, between the United Nations and the court (the Relationship Agreement).

The American proposal has been the object of a good deal of criticism, not the least being that it is tantamount to an amendment to the statute. As such, it would violate the procedures for amending the treaty. It is clearly inconsistent with certain key provisions of the statute, above all those that deal with the preconditions to the exercise of jurisdiction. And in providing an exemption for acts of state, it contradicts the statute's provision on the irrelevance of official capacity—the principle proclaimed at Nuremberg.

The criticism notwithstanding, the United States maintained its position. In a statement before the Sixth Committee of the U.N. General Assembly on October 18, 2000, David Scheffer reaffirmed that unless there is a referral to the court by the Security Council, acting under Chapter VII of the U.N. charter, "we believe there should be a means to preclude the automatic surrender to the Court of official personnel of a non-party State that acts responsibly in the international community and is willing to exercise and capable of exercising complementarity with respect to its own personnel." Declaring the United States "open to discussion about how to resolve this fundamental issue," Scheffer warned: "If a workable arrangement cannot be negotiated at the next Preparatory Commission session . . . then we envisage a much more difficult relationship with the Court." Despite the fact that the November session of the Preparatory Commission yielded very little in the way of a "workable arrangement," the United States signed the treaty the following month.

In signing the Rome Treaty did the outgoing president tie the hands of his successor? Only in the sense that a disavowal of the treaty must now be explicit, whereas before it need only have been implicit. Apart from this, the situation remains essentially unchanged even granting that signing imposes an obligation to do nothing to undercut a treaty pending decision on ratification. In signing the Rome Treaty, President Clinton did not call for an abandonment of efforts to change it prior to eventually seeking the advice and consent of the Senate. Instead, he declared, "with signature . . . we will be in a position to influence the evolution of the court. Without signature, we will not." Our efforts to alter the treaty are not seen as undercutting but as improving it. Ratification should be considered, Clinton noted, only when we have had the chance "to observe and assess the functioning of the Court, over time," and when our "fundamental concerns are satisfied."

## ■ Note

1. Senate Committee on Foreign Relations, *Is a U.N. International Criminal Court in the U.S. National Interest? Hearing before the Subcommittee on International Operations,* 105th Cong., 2nd sess. July 1998, p. 12.

# 3.4 ─────────

# Refugee Flows as Grounds for International Action
*Alan Dowty and Gil Loescher*

## ■ The Applicability of Customary Law

Customary international law has nothing specific to say about refugees because the issue did not exist in the past. This is not because there were no refugees; numerous acts of persecution and expulsion accompanied the rise of the modern state in Europe and elsewhere. But the simultaneous development of the Westphalian concept of sovereignty created a presumption against interference by other states and—more importantly—there were almost always countries or colonial areas to which refugees could flee. Only in the twentieth century, when refugee flows exploded and came to be regarded as a threat, were legal and institutional responses developed, and these responses understandably focused at first on helping already-existing refugees who were in need of protection and relief. Our first argument is that traditional doctrines do, however, provide a legal basis for action against a state that generates refugees. This was first pointed out in a little-noted article by R. Yewdall Jennings in 1939, a year marking the peak of an earlier "refugee crisis" of our century. Jennings pointed out that "there is one aspect of the refugee problem to which the general customary international law is relevant, and that is the consideration of the legality or illegality of the conduct of the state which creates a refugee population."[1]

Jennings took an approach, like that of this article, "which has regard not so much to the ethics of domestic policy as to the repercussions of that policy on the material interests of third states." Even in cases where a state may not be guilty of illegal act, therefore, by flooding another state with refugees it creates grounds for the affected state to resort to measures of *retorsion*, defined in Oppenheim's classic treatise on international law as "retaliation for discourteous, or unkind, or unfair and inequitable acts by acts of the same or of a similar kind."[2] Such acts of retaliation or reciprocation are commonly used to force states to alter their treatment of aliens or their trade practices. For example, if a nation discriminates against aliens from another state, that state may retaliate against citizens of the first state within its borders. In the context of imposed refugee burdens, retorsion would clearly seem to justify at least economic sanctions designed to impose on the country of origin a cost equivalent to that forced upon the host nation.

Jennings goes further, however, arguing that "the willful flooding of other states with refugees constitutes not merely an inequitable act, but an actual illegality, and a fortiori where the refugees are compelled to enter the country of refuge in a destitute condition."[3] He cites President Benjamin Harrison, who in 1891 based U.S. protests to Russia over its treatment of Jews on the argument that "a decree to leave one country is, in the nature of things, an order to enter another."[4]

The illegality of this action, according to Jennings and subsequent commentators, derives from the generally accepted doctrine of the abuse of rights. In common law this is known as *sic utere tuo ut alienum non laedas* ("use your own property in such a manner as not to injure that of another"), a maxim that according to Oppenheim "is applicable to relations of States no less than to those of individuals" and is "one of those general principles of law recognized by civilized States which [the International Court of Justice] is bound to apply by virtue of Article 38 of its Statute."[5]

The doctrine of abuse of rights, then, establishes the legal responsibility of the state of origin even if this is not stated explicitly in refugee law: "there is ample authority for the proposition that a state is obligated to avoid the generation across its borders of damage to other states."[6] Numerous international treaties, declarations, and adjudications reflect this principle in various contexts. For example, in the Trail Smelter Arbitration (1941), the tribunal ruled that "no state has the right to use or permit the use of its territory in such a manner as to cause injury . . . in or to the territory of another or the properties of persons therein." Similarly, in the Corfu Channel case (1949), the International Court of Justice held that a state from whose territory transboundary damages were generated is responsible if it had knowledge of the harm and the opportunity to act. The 1972 Stockholm Declaration, from the first major UN conference on environmental cooperation, affirmed that "States have . . . the responsibility to ensure that activities within their area of jurisdiction or control do not cause damage to the environment of other States or of areas beyond the limits of territorial jurisdiction."

Expulsion of a state's nationals to the territory of other states is in itself illegal in most cases. The legal right to remain in one's country, or to return to it, has acquired a strong standing. States no longer claim the right to expel citizens who have committed no crime; even exile, as a legal punishment of citizens convicted of a crime, has fallen into disuse. The illegality of expelling nationals is so commonly assumed that international documents, rather surprisingly, do not explicitly forbid it. It is, nevertheless, implicit in the body of conventions and agreements developed during and after World War II. The 1948 Universal Declaration of Human Rights, for example, provides in Article 13(2) that "everyone has the right to leave any country, including his own, and to return to his country." As Jennings had written several years earlier, it is "the undoubted duty of a state to receive back its own nationals."[7] If one has the right to return, then one certainly has the right not to leave in the first place.

Even exile as a legal punishment is conditional, moreover, on the willingness of another state to admit the expellee. This is a point often overlooked in discussions of *de facto* individual or mass expulsions: even where a state may have some justification for expelling one or more of its own citizens, no other state has an automatic obligation to admit them. If no state agrees to take them in, expulsion is not a legal option. There are no acceptable grounds for dumping expellees on the territory of a non-consenting state, including, for example, Israel's 1993 expulsion of Hamas activists from the West Bank and Gaza to an area of Lebanon over which the Lebanese government had no physical control.

The right of states to take away the citizenship of their own citizens—to denationalize them—is severely restricted, and even then a state cannot automatically expel those denationalized if no other state is prepared to receive them. Nor can a state denationalize citizens already out of the country simply in order to prevent their return, which amounts to the same thing. Furthermore, the failure to correct the conditions that led to a refugee outflow can be seen as evasion of a legal duty, since continuation of these conditions renders the right of return meaningless.[8]

To summarize, "established rules of international law . . . permit the conclusion that states are bound by a general principle not to create refugee outflows and to co-operate with other states in the resolution of such problems as may emerge."[9] This suggests an obligation to remedy the cause of the outflow as well as to provide for reparation to the affected parties. About the obligation of reparation there is little debate: violations of human rights that cause specific losses to the victims and to other states are grounds for claims of compensation or indemnity.[10] But can outside parties intervene to prevent tragedy in the first place?

Recent international documents favor a broader definition of "state responsibility" that includes prevention of harm to others as well as reparation. The final report of the "New Flows" group of governmental experts, for example, declared that "averting massive flows of refugees is a matter of serious concern to the international community as a whole" and that such flows "carry adverse consequences for the economies of the countries of origin and entire regions, thus endangering international peace and security."[11] The link to "peace and security" is grounds for invoking Chapter VII of the UN Charter, which overrides claims of domestic jurisdiction. Similarly, the International Law Commission, in its "Draft Articles on State Responsibility," defined an international crime as "an internationally wrongful act which results from the breach by a State of an international obligation so essential for the protection of fundamental interests of the international community that its breach is recognized as a crime by that community as a whole." Included as examples of such crimes, justifying corrective action, are not only threats to peace and security but also "a serious breach on a widespread scale of an international obligation of essential importance for safeguarding the human being, such as those prohibiting slavery, genocide, apartheid."[12]

But how does this expansion of "state responsibility" relate to the traditional principles of non-intervention and domestic jurisdiction? The Permanent Court of International Justice recognized in a 1923 case that the definition of "domestic jurisdiction" is not fixed in perpetuity but changes as other conditions change.[13] In other words, "the sphere of 'domestic jurisdiction' is a relative one that contracts as the sphere of activity governed by international law and other sources of obligation grows."[14] Furthermore, it is a basic principle of international law that a state cannot rely on the provisions of its own laws in defense against a claimed breach of international obligations; international law takes precedence where the two conflict. It would follow, therefore, that as refugee flows impose massively increased burdens on other states, domestic jurisdiction related to such issues would shrink and domestic provisions—even if "legal" by local standards—would come under increased challenge. . . .

### ■ Refugee Flows as Threats to Peace Under the UN Charter

Our second argument is that there is increasing recognition by the international community that massive refugee flows do in fact constitute a threat to international peace and security, and that they therefore justify use of the enforcement powers of the United Nations. . . . A country that forces its people to flee or takes actions that compel them to leave in a manner that threatens regional peace and security has in effect internationalized its internal affairs, and provides a cogent justification for policymakers elsewhere to act directly upon the source of threat. . . .

National and international bodies, and in particular neighboring states, also increasingly regard actions or policies that trigger mass expulsions or refugee movements as an international issue. From this perspective, grievous human rights abuses are not an internal matter when neighboring states must bear the cost of repression by having refugees forced on them. In recent years the Security Council itself has taken an increasingly inclusive view of "threats to peace" where actual hostilities remained limited largely to the territory of a single state (discussed in more detail below).[15] The UN Security Council's Summit Declaration of 1992 identified "nonmilitary sources of instability in the economic, social, humanitarian and ecological fields" as threats to international peace and security, while specifying "election monitoring, human rights verification, and the repatriation of refugees" as "integral parts of the Security Council's efforts to maintain international peace and security."[16] As Rogers and Copeland note, "these expanded notions of what constitute threats to international or national security have important implications for the issue of forced migration: they make it easier to classify forced migration flows or the presence of forced migrants in a host country as security threats."[17]

This new thinking ties in with changing ideas of national sovereignty. While sovereignty is still regarded as a cornerstone of the international political and legal system, domestic matters previously shielded from outside interference are now targets of international action. Since an elementary justification for the state is its ability to provide reasonable security for its citizens, states that force these same citizens to flee call into question the very basis of their sovereignty. . . .

## ▓ Intervention in Practice

Our third argument is that international intervention related to refugee flows has in fact become more frequent in state declaration and practice in the last two decades. Such intervention, in other words, is not only increasingly justifiable, but is actually happening. . . .

Even during the Cold War, unilateral military interventions were carried out without the collective legitimization of the UN Security Council or other international bodies. In . . . such cases, "hideous repression within the target state, and consequent huge refugee flows" provided grounds for action.[18]

The first case was India's intervention in East Pakistan (Bangladesh) in 1971, after an estimated ten million refugees poured into India as a result of fighting sparked when Pakistan's government, dominated by West Pakistan, annulled an election won by a party based in East Pakistan. The burden on India's economy was enormous, and India suspected that the Pakistani government was trying to change the demographic balance between the two parts of Pakistan by forcing massive numbers of East Pakistanis into India. The second case was Vietnam's intervention into Cambodia in late 1978, to overthrow the notorious Pol Pot regime under which large numbers of Cambodians had fled to Vietnam. Also in 1979, Tanzania sent its forces into Uganda in support of Ugandan refugees based in Tanzania; the Tanzanian forces sought to overthrow the Idi Amin regime and to repel Ugandan incursions into Tanzania.

Humanitarian intervention was not the major thrust of any of these actions. While the burden of refugees in the Indian states of West Bengal, Tripura, and

Assam was clearly an important factor, India's objectives also included the strengthening of its regional position *vis-à-vis* its traditional rival Pakistan. Similarly, Vietnam intervened in Cambodia for hegemonic reasons and not to put an end to Pol Pot's genocide. Tanzania intervened in self-defense, but its intervention was also influenced by the presence of active Ugandan exiles in Dar es Salaam.

In all three cases the targeted regime was toppled; Bangladesh became independent, Cambodia acquired a Vietnamese-sponsored government, and in Uganda a previous regime was restored. In all three cases, refugees (at least the original refugee group) were able to return home, relieving the burden on the intervening state. Though all three interventions were widely condemned as violations of national sovereignty, the official international condemnations were on the whole ritualistic and muted in light of the undeniable fact that the interveners had halted widespread massacres and flight. However, the interventions in Bangladesh and Cambodia did provoke strong counter-measures from global powers, who feared potential damage to their interests in these regions. For example, in order to deter India from attempting to extend its gains in the former East Pakistan by an attack on West Pakistan, the Nixon administration moved the U.S. 6th Fleet into the Bay of Bengal. In Cambodia, the Chinese government, furious over the loss of its close ally, the Khmer Rouge, to its historical archenemy, Vietnam, sought to give Hanoi a "bloody nose" by an attack on northern Vietnam in February 1979. Despite these events, it is significant that in all three cases, the international community made no moves to restore the previous regime or even to continue recognizing it (except that many states recognized the successors of the Khmer Rouge because they opposed Vietnam's puppet regime in Phnom Penh).

In dealing with Bangladesh, the General Assembly did not flatly condemn India, but discussed the situation in all its aspects including the return of refugees, and gave priority to condemnation of genocide over reaffirmation of the principle of sovereignty.[19] Subsequently, the International Commission of Jurists, writing on the India-Pakistan case, set out four requirements for unilateral humanitarian intervention: 1) manifest guilt of the target government; 2) lack of practical peaceful means to correct the situation; 3) opportunity for the international community to act first; and 4) use of only necessary force, with accounting to the international community, and withdrawal as soon as practical. . . .

An easier case can be made for unilateral interventions authorized by the Security Council under Chapter VII. After invoking Chapter VII enforcement powers in only two cases (South Africa and Rhodesia) during its first forty-five years of existence, the Security Council has invoked them frequently since 1990. One such case was the authorization of U.S. intervention in Somalia in December 1992. Although the U.S. intervention was basically motivated by humanitarian concerns, the presence of a refugee problem did play some part in UN consideration of the issue. For example, Security Council Resolution 814 (March 1993), took note of the large numbers of refugees displaced by the conflict and of "the difficulties caused to [neighboring countries] due to the presence of refugees in their territories," calling for their reparation as part of the UN operation.

The importance of Somalia as a precedent lies, however, primarily in two other aspects of the UN intervention. This was "the first time the organization has intervened in the domestic affairs of a member state when that state has not presented a military threat to its neighbors."[20] Unlike Iraq in 1991 and Haiti in 1994, the Security Council did not invoke trans-border refugee flows to justify international action. Rather, Security Council Resolution 751 (April 24, 1993) stated that it was "the magnitude of the human suffering" in Somalia which constituted a threat to international peace and security. Second, intervention took place without the "consent" of the target state, on grounds that there was no effective government in Somalia to give or withhold such consent. Both of these conditions are likely to be applicable to refugee-generating crises in the future. . . .

A third category, armed interventions that are multilateral, should be less problematic than unilateral interventions. . . .

The most explicit and far-reaching precedent linking UN enforcement action under Chapter VII with prevention of a refugee crisis was Resolution 688 (April 5, 1991), on Iraqi Kurdistan. Following the end of the Gulf War, Iraqi suppression of widespread revolt in northern Kurdish areas created fears that the entire Kurdish population would be uprooted, a particularly grave prospect for neighboring Turkey, with its own Kurdish minority unrest. Accordingly, the Security Council noted that it was "gravely concerned by the repression of the Iraqi civilian population in many parts of Iraq, including most recently in Kurdish populated areas, which led to a massive flow of refugees towards and across international frontiers and to cross-border incursions, which threaten international peace and security."[21] International forces were deployed to Kurdish areas to protect the population; Iraqi forces were (under pressure) withdrawn from the same areas; and a *de facto* autonomous Kurdish area was established that allowed Kurdish refugees to return, at least, to safe havens in Iraqi Kurdish (not Turkish) territory.

It has been pointed out that this precedent was only possible in the aftermath of Iraq's military defeat; that the resolution attracted significant opposition (ten votes in favor, three opposed, and two abstentions including that of one permanent member, China); that there has been no international commitment to finding a political solution to the Kurds' plight; and that there has been unilateral Turkish intervention in Iraqi Kurdistan during the period of UN operations there.[22] Nevertheless, the fact remained that:

> A precedent has been set . . . for military intervention in the domestic affairs of a state for the purposes of protecting a minority population from the repression

of its own government. . . . A new option to the traditional three solutions for refugees . . . had been created, that is, preventing the refugees from crossing an international border in the first place by "humanitarian intervention," creating safe havens protected by foreign military forces within the national homeland of the refugees.[23]

## ■ Notes

1. R. Yewdall Jennings, "Some International Law Aspects of the Refugee Question," *British Year Book of International Law,* Vol. 20 (1939), p. 110.
2. Ibid., p. 111; L. Oppenheim, *International Law: A Treatise,* Vol. 2: *Disputes, War and Neutrality, 7th ed,* H. Lauterpacht, ed. (New York: David McKay, 1952), pp. 134–135.
3. Jennings, "Some International Law Aspects," p. 111.
4. President's Message to Congress, December 9, 1891, *British and Foreign State Papers,* Vol. 83, pp. 436–437, quoted by Jennings, "Some International Law Aspects," p. 112.
5. Jennings, "Some International Law Aspects," p. 112.
6. Jack I. Garvey, "The New Asylum Seekers: Addressing Their Origin," in David Martin, ed., *The New Asylum Seekers: Refugee Law in the 1980s* (Dordrecht, Netherlands: Martinus Nijhoff, 1988), p. 187.
7. Jennings, "Some International Law Aspects," p. 112.
8. Ibid., pp. 112–113.
9. Guy S. Goodwin-Gill, *The Refugee in International Law* (Oxford: Oxford University Press, 1983), p. 228.
10. Ian Brownlie, *Principles of Public International Law*, 3rd edition (Oxford: Oxford University Press, 1979), p. 520; Daniel H. Derby, "Deterring Refugee-Generating Conduct," in Ved P. Nanda, ed., *Refugee Law and Policy: International and U.S. Responses* (Westport, Conn: Greenwood Press, 1989), pp. 44–45, 53; Luke Lee, "The Right to Compensation: Refugees and Countries of Asylum," *American Journal of International Law,* Vol. 80 (1986), pp. 532–556.
11. UN Document A/41/324 (May 13, 1986), para. 63.
12. International Law Commission, *Report on the Work of the Thirty-third Session, 1981,* Ch. IV, in Ian Brownlie, *State Responsibility, Part I* (Oxford: Oxford University Press, 1983), pp. 289–290.
13. Nationalities Decrees in Tunis and Morocco, Permanent Court of International Justice, Series B, No. 4, 24 (1923), quoted in Kelly Kate Pease and David Forsythe, "Human Rights, Humanitarian Intervention and World Politics," *Human Rights Quarterly,* Vol. 15, No. 2 (May 1993), p. 293.
14. Lori Fisler Damrosch, "Changing Conceptions of Intervention in International Law," in Laura W. Reed and Carl Kaysen, eds., *Emerging Norms of Justified Intervention* (Cambridge: American Academy of Arts and Sciences, 1993), p. 95.
15. Damrosch, "Changing Conceptions," pp. 100ff.
16. *Security Council Summit Declaration* (New York: United Nations, 1992).
17. Rosemarie Rogers and Emily Copeland, *Forced Migration: Policy Issues in the Post–Cold War Period* (Medford: Fletcher School of Law and Diplomacy, 1993), p. 12.
18. Adam Roberts, "Humanitarian War: Military Intervention and Human Rights," *International Affairs,* Vol. 69, No. 3 (July 1993), p. 434.

19. Fernando Teson, *Humanitarian Intervention: An Inquiry into Law and Morality* (Dobbs Ferry: Transnational Publishers, 1988), pp. 187–188; Myron Weiner, "Introduction: Security, Stability, and International Migration," in Weiner, ed., *International Migration and Security* (Boulder, Colo.: Westview Press, 1993), p. 24.

20. Samuel M. Makinda, *Seeking Peace from Chaos: Humanitarian Intervention in Somalia* (Boulder, Colo.: Lynne Rienner, 1993), p. 67.

21. UN Doc. S/RES/688, April 5, 1991.

22. Damrosch, "Changing Conceptions," p. 103; Roberts, "Humanitarian War," pp. 438–439; N.D. White, *Keeping the Peace: The United Nations and the Maintenance of International Peace and Security* (Manchester, UK: Manchester University Press, 1992), pp. 46–47.

23. Howard Adelman, "The Ethics of Humanitarian Intervention: The Case of the Kurdish Refugees," *Public Affairs Quarterly,* Vol. 6, No. 1 (January 1992), p. 62.

# 3.5 _____

## Activists Beyond Borders: Advocacy Networks in International Politics
*Margaret E. Keck and Katherine Sikkink*

### ▪ Early Campaigns Against Footbinding and Female Circumcision

Female circumcision and footbinding were both practices with long-lasting impact on women's health and activity level, practices we would now call violence against women. Both practices were deeply embedded culturally. Both involved highly ritualized rites of passage from girlhood to womanhood, and both were often seen as prerequisites for marriage. . . .

Both of these practices were deeply embedded in domestic life. Both were socially mandated but never legally enforced or required, and mothers and other females performed the rituals on girl children. Both affected girls of diverse classes and backgrounds, and both have been linked to the control of female sexuality and reproductive power. Bound feet had erotic appeal to men, and helped keep women confined to the home. As a result of the connection to sexuality, reformers recognized that feet were "the most risqué subject of conversation in China" during the late 1800s.[1] Female circumcision was even more inherently linked to sexuality because it involved removal of the clitoris, the main female organ of sexual pleasure. After concerted campaigns against both practices, footbinding was eradicated in China in the early twentieth century, while female circumcision continues to be practiced extensively throughout parts of Africa . . .

### ▪ The Campaign Against Footbinding in China, 1874–1911

Footbinding was in some ways analogous to the Western practice of corseting, but it was much more painful. Surrounded by ritual preparations, including making elegant pairs of tiny embroidered shoes, girls had their feet tightly wrapped to prevent growth at between four and eight years old. After years of intense pain, the toes were broken and flesh fell off to produce a narrow foot three to five inches long. Today we would call this a human rights abuse; few forms of modern torture leave such permanent deformation. Yet narratives of women who experienced footbinding testify not only to the pain but to the pride women felt in their small feet. The ritual of footbinding played a central role in female life. Historians stress the functions that footbinding served in socialization, appropriation of female labor, defining nationhood and gender roles, and as a central event in women's domestic culture.[2] "Footbinding prepared a girl physically and psychologically for her future role as wife and a dependent family member. . . . Through footbinding the doctrine of separate spheres was engraved onto the bodies of female children."[3] . . .

A vigorous movement to abolish footbinding originated in the late nineteenth century among foreigners in China's treaty ports, later spreading among those Chinese most exposed to Western ideas.[4] Chinese intellectuals and politicians took over the campaign, which culminated in a decree banning footbinding after the 1911 revolution. The campaign was strongest at the turn of the century, well before the 1919–1920 May Fourth Movement which is often seen as a peak period of political, cultural, and social innovation, and before the formation of the Chinese Communist party in 1921. After the turn of the century progressive literature by and about women moved on to other issues. In other words, changes in footbinding preceded rather than followed the main wave of cultural and political reform.[5]

In 1842 China's defeat in the Opium War led to the opening of treaty ports to foreign nationals and to an influx of missionaries and Western ideas. Chinese intellectuals began to argue that China needed reforms in order to avoid further humiliating defeat. At first, they stressed technological innovations and modern weapons, which were introduced between 1860 and 1894. Following China's defeat by the Japanese in 1895, however, intellectuals began to call for social, cultural and political reforms as well. Goals of a national reform movement emerging in the late 1890s included an end to footbinding and improvement of the status of women. The reform movement spread its message mainly through periodicals and study societies.[6] Male reformers argued that improvements in women's status were a necessary part of their program for national self-strengthening.[7]

In 1898, the imperial authorities repressed the reform movement, leaving key reformers dead or in prison. But despite increased antiforeign sentiment during the Boxer Rebellion, the antifootbinding movement continued to grow. After the Boxer Rebellion the Imperial Court saw the need to implement gradual reforms. One of the first was an antifootbinding edict in 1902.[8] Earlier imperial decrees had no effect, but the 1902 decree was the beginning of the end. When the new republican and nationalist government came into power in 1911, it banned footbinding altogether.

Three groups were involved in the initial campaigns against footbinding: (1) Western missionaries who focused on Chinese Christians; (2) Westerners who led a campaign focused on non-Christian Chinese elites; and (3) Chinese reformers who focused their campaign on non-Christian Chinese elites. A missionary of the London Missionary Society founded the first antifootbinding society in 1874. In 1895 ten women of different nationalities, led by Mrs. Archibald Little, the wife of a British merchant, founded the T'ien tsu hui (Natural Foot Society), a nondenominational umbrella organization. The first Chinese-initiated antifootbinding societies were set up in 1883 and 1895, but local opposition led to their collapse. In 1897 Chinese reformers founded the Pu'ch'an-tsu hui (Antifootbinding Society), China's largest non-Christian antifootbinding organization, which later established many branches and had a membership of 300,000.[9]

Each of the three actors took a characteristic approach to the issue. The missionary approach was the most aggressive and moralistic.[10] Missionary schools promoted "natural feet" first by offering scholarships only to girls with unbound feet; later they refused entry to girls with bound feet and would not employ teachers with bound feet. The missionary schools focused their attention on Christian converts, usually not from the Chinese elite.

Perhaps the most innovative technique of the antifootbinding societies was to take on directly one social issue at the core of footbinding. Chinese families feared that daughters with unbound feet were unmarriageable. So the members of antifootbinding societies pledged not to bind the feet of their daughters and to marry their sons only to women with unbound feet. When registering in the societies, families listed the ages of their children for more convenient matchmaking.[11]

In contrast to the missionaries, Mrs. Little's Natural Foot Society focused on influencing powerful officials and non-Christian Chinese women "of wealth and fashion," thus partially divorcing the issue from the Christian context. Perhaps because Little was not a missionary, she could recognize the campaign's social and cultural implications and take a less rigid, more strategic position on the issue. Her strategy was to work with the upper classes and on footbinding alone, rather than to mix views on the practice with religion.[12] In a country where Christians were less than one percent of the population, this strategy was probably essential to the success of the message. . . .

The members of the Natural Foot Society did engage in some international networking although this was not the central part of their work. At one meeting in China the members decided to contact a U.S. envoy in China and discussed whether there was sufficient interest in footbinding in the United States to pressure the U.S. government to send instructions to him on the issue.[13] This would have been a classic "boomerang" maneuver predating current network tactics by ninety years, but there is no evidence that there was sufficient interest in the United States, or that U.S. or other foreign governments ever got involved in the issue of footbinding. Although most of the initial financial support and labor came from foreigners, by 1908 the Natural Foot Society was operating entirely under the leadership of Chinese women, who continued to campaign with vigor.[14] The foreign leaders of the society argued in 1907 that it was "high time to trust the movement more to Chinese direction."[15] This transfer from foreign to domestic leadership was a mark of the campaign's success.

The Natural Foot Society attempted to turn the tide against footbinding among influential Chinese through lobbying, publications, and speaking engagements, collecting signatures on petitions, essay competitions, and articles in local newspapers. A letter in 1907 summarizing the society's work records 162 meetings in thirty-three different cities, some with as many as 2,000 people present. More than a million tracts, leaflets, and placards were printed and circulated from the Shanghai office alone, in addition to letters to the editor and prize competitions for the best essays against binding.[16]

Only sixteen years passed between the formation of the first umbrella organization and the 1911 ban against footbinding; this is very rapid progress in the history of such campaigns. A corresponding behavioral change evolved slowly but surely. A source in 1905 indicated that 70 percent of female children still had their feet bound.[17] But by 1912 a missionary described footbinding as "on the wane and destined in course of time to disappear."[18] A 1929 study of a region to the south of Peking shows very dramatic change over a short period: "99.2% of those born prior to 1890 had bound feet, only 59.7% of those born between 1905 and 1909, and 19.5% of those born from 1910 to 1914, had bound feet; no new cases at all were found among those born after 1919."[19]

The swift eradication of such a culturally embedded practice is surprising— a practice that had lasted for almost a thousand years gone in little more than a generation. No key economic change occurred around the turn of the century that suddenly rendered the practice additionally dysfunctional from a material standpoint. Nor had industrial change in China yet reached the point where large numbers of women were needed to work outside the home at the time that footbinding began to end. Instead, footbinding ended, just as slavery had ended, because of a concerted moral and political campaign against it. Historians of China differ about the relative weight of international and domestic actors in the campaign; some have stressed the role of foreign missionary groups, while others place more importance on Chinese intellectuals. One Chinese scholar wrote in the 1930s:

In my opinion, for all the wrongs that Western culture might have done in China, one thing alone would have redeemed them, and that is, the conviction that their early missionaries aroused in the Chinese mind that the practice of footbinding was absurd and wrong. Prior to this, scholars did sometimes criticize this absurd custom, but the criticism was always casual, and no serious thought was ever given nor effort made, for the abolishment of this custom until the end of the last century . . . the first rolling of the stone, so to speak, was started by our sisters from the west.[20]

The most thorough treatment of the antifootbinding movement interprets it as part of a reform movement carried on "as a result of contact with the west."[21] The campaign appeared to form a pattern characteristic of modern networks, where both foreign and domestic actors were crucial to the success of the campaign, with foreign actors instrumental in "first rolling the stone" and domestic actors framing the issues to resonate with domestic audiences and generating the broad-based support necessary for success.

Foreign women initiated the antifootbinding movement and nationalist intellectuals and reformers embraced it. In China opposition to footbinding became associated with reform sentiment that was both antifeudal and antiforeign. After military defeat by foreigners, improving the status of women and ending footbinding were seen as tools to modernize and strengthen China so it could resist future intervention. "Not until such efforts were perceived as Chinese phenomena in a nationalistic context did a majority of Chinese . . . espouse them. . . . [T]he foreign and Christian roots of the anti-footbinding campaign had to be renounced in order for victory to be achieved. Yet Western women laid many of the foundations for the eradication of footbinding."[22]

Every campaign to change practices of this sort is a struggle to redefine the meaning of the practice. Foreign or international actors alone rarely succeed in changing embedded practices because they do not understand how to frame debates in convincing and accessible ways for the domestic audience. The Chinese reformers at the forefront of the antifootbinding campaign used arguments that resonated better with discourse of the time in China than did those used by the missionaries. The Chinese message blended appeals to modernity and to tradition. For example, Chinese intellectuals stressed that footbinding was contrary to the ancient way of doing things, and that the Chinese classics did not even mention it.[23] Thus, to eradicate a traditional practice, intellectuals appealed to even more ancient tradition. They referred to issues of filial piety, stressing that footbinding damaged the body—a gift from one's parents—and that a "natural footed woman could buy medicine for a sick parent in less time than it took a bound foot woman."[24] Yet at the same time, they invoked modernity, either by claiming that the custom was "the laughing stock of foreigners" or by citing a pseudo-scientific argument that sons born of deformed women would be weaker.[25] Chinese nationalists argued that one needed to adopt some Western practices in order to better resist Western domination. In an antifootbinding tract a Chinese literati argued: "To learn what the foreigners excel at in order to fight against them doesn't mean to respect or admire them. . . . In fact women with bound feet, who are completely useless, include one half of the population. . . . Useless women are an obstacle to progress."[26] In military defeat, the connection that Chinese reformers made between footbinding and weakness, and between individual weakness and the collective weakness of the country appears to have been a powerful rhetorical weapon against binding.

The successful articulation between antifootbinding and Chinese nationalism at the turn of the century allowed the antifootbinding campaign to succeed rapidly. Once the campaign was launched and embraced by Chinese intellectuals, no strong organized opposition emerged. The Imperial Court had never advocated or practiced footbinding, and thus would not spearhead opposition. The absence of opposition surely helps explain the speed with which the antifootbinding movement achieved its goals.

## ■ The Campaign Against Female Circumcision in Kenya, 1923–1931

The term "female circumcision" has been used to refer to a variety of operations "involving damage to the female sexual and/or reproductive organs," almost always including the removal of part or all of the clitoris (clitoridectomy/excision), and sometimes also involving the removal of the labia minora, the inner walls of the labia majora, and the sewing together of the vulva (infibulation).[27] Calling these operations female circumcision likens them to male circumcision, to which they bear only superficial similarities. Male circumcision leaves neither lasting pain nor health problems, nor does it lessen male sexual pleasure. Female circumcision, on the other hand, carries short-term risks and can lead to chronic infection, painful urination and menstrual difficulty, malformations and scarring, and vaginal abscesses; it also reduces a woman's sexual response and pleasure. . . .

Female circumcision was widely practiced in Kenya, among the Kikuyu and many other related cultural groups. In Kikuyu culture "only a circumcised girl could be considered a woman. It was widely believed that uncircumcised girls would not physically be able to bear children. . . . In Kikuyu eyes an uncircumcised girl of marriageable age was an object of derision, indeed almost of disgust."[28]

Concerted efforts against female circumcision in Kenya began in the 1920s when Protestant missionaries led by the Church of Scotland Missionary Society (CSM) prohibited the operation among their converts and campaigned against it. Unlike the footbinding history, there is no evidence of any internal opposition to female circumcision within the Kikuyu communities before the arrival of the missionaries. . . .

In Kenya, British colonial administrators and missionaries used tactics similar to those used during the antifootbinding campaign in China to try to discourage female circumcision. Missionary schools refused to admit circumcised girls, and church members could be suspended for requiring their girls to be circumcised. The missionaries argued that the operation was medically unnecessary and dangerous, and also that it was unchristian because the associated rituals were pagan and overtly sexual.[29] Many African members of the

CSM chose to leave the church to protest its position on this issue. Some accused church leaders of adding "an eleventh commandment" that was not in the Bible. One leader said, "I was a Christian, but if the choice lay between God and circumcision, we choose circumcision. But it is a false European choice."[30] As the issue became more heated, the CSM and other missionary societies lost substantial numbers of their members. . . .

The campaign took place in the context of increasing African opposition to British colonial practices, such as land alienation for European settlers, heavy hut and poll taxes, and an oppressive labor recruiting system.[31] The Kikuyu Central Association (KCA), set up by young, mainly mission-educated Kikuyu men, represented nascent Kikuyu nationalism. The female circumcision controversy exacerbated an internal Kikuyu political split between the younger, militant KCA and the older Kikuyu leadership represented by chiefs associated with the Christian missions.[32] The KCA embraced some Western values but also attempted to preserve some traditional cultural practices, especially female circumcision; a major conflict developed between the KCA and the missionaries over this issue.[33]

The campaign against female circumcision became a symbol for colonial attempts to impose outside values and rules upon the population. The Kikuyu nationalist elite defended the practice as necessary to the preservation of traditional culture, and attacked foreign efforts to eradicate it. Because the KCA was the leading voice of Kikuyu nationalism, and because it had taken up the crusade in favor of circumcision, female circumcision became associated with Kikuyu nationalism. Since many Protestant leaders opposed the KCA, their opposition to circumcision was viewed as a tool to oppose the association. John Arthur drew up a petition opposing circumcision that asked teachers and other mission employees not only to renounce circumcision, but also to disown the KCA.[34]

Jomo Kenyatta, the general secretary of the KCA and later the main leader of the anticolonial struggle, wrote a stirring defense of female circumcision in his study of Kikuyu culture, *Facing Mount Kenya*, when he was a student of anthropology at the London School of Economics in 1935. "For the present it is impossible for a member of the tribe to imagine an initiation without clitoridectomy. Therefore the abolition of the surgical element in this custom means to the Gikuyu the abolition of the whole institution. . . . [C]litoridectomy, like Jewish circumcision, is a mere bodily mutilation which, however, is regarded as the condition sine qua non of the whole teaching of tribal law, religion, and morality."[35] . . .

In late 1929 the controversy in Kenya became more heated. The pro-circumcision forces circulated a satirical song that ridiculed missionaries, chiefs, and officials, and praised Kenyatta. The government and missionaries, fearing a threat to public order, repressed the singers, flogging them, sentencing them to detention camps, and prohibiting public meetings.[36] In this context, colonial authorities backed off from the missionaries' campaign on female circumcision. Kenyatta and his organization had helped reframe the debate from one about health and Christianity to one over nationalism, land, and the integrity of traditional culture. Convinced that the issue was exacerbating relations between Kikuyu and Europeans, colonial authorities asked Arthur to resign his seat on the Governor's executive council. Some officials advocated more gradual policies stressing education rather than prohibition; one official recommended "masterly inactivity"; another counseled, "the less talked about the operation of circumcision the better."[37] One of the political results of the controversy was to delegitimize Kikuyu leaders associated with the missions and increase the influence and membership of the KCA. It was one of a series of controversies among Kikuyu and between the Kikuyu and the British that contributed to tensions that twenty years later found expression in the mass movement that Europeans called Mau Mau.

In contrast with the nationalism of Chinese reformers, by the mid-twentieth century African intellectuals like Kenyatta were holding up an idealized version of the traditional past as an alternative to Western lifestyles and "progress" that they feared were inappropriate for their countries. The anticircumcision campaign became associated with colonialism and interference, and the practice of female circumcision with independence, nationalism, and tradition. Kenyan nationalists articulated a material vs. spiritual distinction similar to the one made by Indian nationalists in the nineteenth century, where the material corresponded to the outside world, and the spiritual realm to the home. In this paradigm the home and women were to be the main foci for preserving national culture. . . .

[H]ow the activists' message carried and resonated with domestic concerns, culture, and ideology at the particular historical moment in which they campaigned was crucial. Here the footbinding and female circumcision cases offer an especially powerful contrast. One of the most important differences between the two campaigns has to do with how the advocacy campaign articulated with nationalist discourse. Nationalism in China at the turn of the century was quite different from nationalism in colonial Kenya in the 1920s. Chinese nationalism involved a critique of tradition as a source of weakness, and an embrace of modernity—if only to use the tools of modernity to fight off the external enemy. Antifootbinding, once stripped of its missionary origins, thus articulated well with the desire to discard remnants of a feudal past in order to take control of the future. Kenyan nationalism of the 1920s and 1930s had a quite different flavor; it appealed to tradition as a means of strengthening unity and defeating the colonial other. During the Chinese campaign the meanings of footbinding changed; what had been a source of pride for women and a "central motif in her interaction with other women"[38] became a symbol of the past. In Kenya, the opposite occurred; the missionary campaign was associated with a waning colonialism, and the circumcised girl was part of emergent

Kenyan nationalism. Chinese (mainly male) elites assumed leadership of the campaign against footbinding because they saw it as part of the modernization project they advocated. The ideas in the campaign were thus effectively nationalized; their missionary origins mattered less than their contribution to the national project. In Kenya, on the contrary, the anticircumcision campaign never acquired domestic sponsors. Because the missionary origins of the ideas were so deeply associated with the colonial regime, the two could not be dissociated; in fact, the missionaries' desire to intervene in the most intimate practices of the home strengthened the identity between home and nation.

Chinese nationalists did not exempt the home from the nationalist reforms. Especially through the activities of Mrs. Little's Natural Foot Society, the practice of footbinding was singled out and separated from the religious message, and from a range of other cultural issues. Although part of a broader reform movement, natural foot advocates did not demand a comprehensive package of cultural change. In Kenya, on the other hand, where missionaries campaigned against female circumcision in the context of the colonial state, the missionary church demanded "total cultural transformation," excluding the possibility of "selective change, by which the Kikuyu might absorb some elements of Western culture while rejecting others as unacceptable to their values or social institutions."[39]

Strong and dense linkages between domestic and foreign actors do not alone guarantee success. Advocacy campaigns take place in organizational contexts; not only must their ideas resonate and create allies, their organizations must also overcome opposition. In the language of social movement theory, we must consider these campaigns as parts of "multi-organizational fields."[40] . . . In Kenya a group of missionaries with tepid support from colonial authorities confronted a politically weak but ideologically strong opposition in the KCA. In China a well-organized set of antifootbinding societies faced strongly entrenched cultural beliefs, but no effectively organized political opposition. When the societies gained the support of both the Imperial Court and the nationalist reformer politicians, the eventual success of their campaign was assured.

## ■ Notes

1. Mrs. Archibald Little, *Intimate China: The Chinese As I Have Seen Them* (London: Hutchinson, 1899), pp. 147, 150.

2. Dorothy Ko, *Teachers of the Inner Chambers: Women and Culture in Seventeenth-Century China* (Stanford: Stanford University Press, 1994), pp. 148, 150; and C. Fred Blake, "Foot-binding in Neo-Confucian China and the Appropriation of Female Labor," *Signs: Journal of Women and Society* 19 (Spring 1994): 78.

3. Ko, *Teachers of the Inner Chambers*, p. 149.

4. Jane Hunter, *The Gospel of Gentility: American Women Missionaries in Turn of the Century China* (New Haven: Yale University Press, 1984), pp. 23–24.

5. Roxane Witke, "Transformation of Attitudes Towards Women During the May Fourth Era of Modern China." Ph.D. diss., University of California, Berkeley, 1970, pp. 6, 27, 42.

6. Virginia Chui-tin Chau, "The Anti-footbinding Movement in China (1850–1912)," Master's thesis, Columbia University, 1966, p. 28.

7. Hunter, *The Gospel of Gentility*, pp. 23–24.

8. Ibid., p. 24.

9. Alison R. Drucker, "The Influence of Western Women on the Anti-Footbinding Movement 1840–1911," *Historical Reflections* 8:3 (Fall 1981): 194.

10. Witke, "Transformation of Attitudes," p. 20.

11. Chau, "Anti-footbinding Movement," pp. 107, 108.

12. "Anti-Footbinding Society Conference," *North China Herald*, 23 January 1901, pp. 159–160.

13. Ibid., p. 160.

14. Drucker, "Influence of Western Women," pp. 187–189.

15. "Summary of Work Done by the Tien Tsu Hui," *Chinese Recorder* 38 (January 1907): 34.

16. Ibid., pp. 32–33.

17. Ibid., p. 135.

18. Ibid., p. 149.

19. Sidney Gamble, "The Disappearance of Footbinding in Tinghsien," *American Journal of Sociology* 49 (September 1943): 181–183.

20. Ch'en Heng-che, "Influences of Foreign Cultures on the Chinese Woman," 1934, reprinted in *Chinese Women Through Chinese Eyes*, ed. Li Yu-ning (Armonk, N.Y.: M.E. Sharpe, 1992), p. 64.

21. Chau, "Anti-footbinding Movement," p. 26.

22. Drucker, "Influence of Western Women," p. 199.

23. Chau, "Anti-footbinding Movement," pp. 21, 26.

24. Drucker, "Influence of Western Women," p. 182; Witke, "Transformation of Attitudes," p. 27.

25. Chau, "Anti-footbinding Movement," pp. 98, 101, 104.

26. Ibid., pp. 60–61.

27. Leonard J. Kouba and Judith Muasher, "Female Circumcision in Africa: An Overview," *African Studies Review* 28:1 (March 1985): 96.

28. Carl G. Fosberg, Jr. and John Nottingham, *The Myth of "Mau Mau": Nationalism in Kenya* (Stanford: Hoover Institution Press, 1966), p. 112.

29. Marshall S. Clough, *Fighting Two Sides: Kenyan Chiefs and Politicians, 1918–1940* (Niwot, Colo.: University Press of Colorado, 1990), pp. 138–139.

30. Fosberg and Nottingham, *Myth of "Mau Mau,"* p. 119.

31. Bethwell A. Ogot, "Kenya Under the British: 1895–1963," in *Zamani: A Survey of East African History,* ed. Ogot (Nairobi: East African Publishing House, 1974), pp. 266–268, 278; Clough, *Fighting Two Sides*, pp. 66–72.

32. Clough, *Fighting Two Sides*, pp. 142–146.

33. Fosberg and Nottingham, *Myth of "Mau Mau,"* pp. 86–87.

34. Clough, *Fighting Two Sides*, p. 143.

35. Cited in Fosberg and Nottingham, *Myth of "Mau Mau,"* p. 133.

36. Clough, *Fighting Two Sides*, p. 145.

37. Ann Beck, *A History of the British Medical Administration of East Africa, 1900–1950* (Cambridge: Harvard University Press, 1970), pp. 101–102.

38. Ko, *Teachers of the Inner Chambers*, pp. 148, 150.

39. Fosberg and Nottingham, *Myth of "Mau Mau,"* p. 105.

40. Bert Klandermans, "The Social Construction of Protest and Multi-Organizational Fields," in *Frontiers in Social Movement Theory*, ed. Aldon D. Morris and Carol McClurg Mueller (New Haven: Yale University Press, 1992), pp. 77–103.

# 4 Are Human Rights Universal?

## 4.1 _____

## Introduction
### *The Editors*

As international human rights norms emerged, a debate regarding whether cultural attitudes and beliefs would or should supersede the universality of rights surfaced as well. Universalism, in the realm of human rights, suggests that humanity comes before culture and traditions. People are humans first and belong to cultures second. Thus, the rights to life and freedom from torture are universal rights. Advocates of cultural relativism argue in many instances that the culture and traditions of the society take precedence over the rights of the individual, thereby altering or even reducing the specific right in question. This position is most readily evident in the debate over Asian values, and to a lesser extent, Islamic values and African values.

In the first selection, Rhonda L. Callaway focuses on the rhetoric behind the Asian values arguments. Utilizing various speeches and interviews by leading proponents, such as Lee Kuan Yew and Tommy Koh of Singapore, she places the discourse into three major categories. First, Asian values present a leading challenge to the Western paradigm focusing on the role of the individual. Calling on the primacy of state sovereignty, the concept of Asian values is offered as a critique of the West as well as an argument for a unique human rights perspective. Second, the rhetoric suggests that Asian values are a combination of Confucian-based ideals of family, community, frugality, hard work, as well as respect for authority. Third, leaders in many of these Asian countries suggest that due to these Asian values, there is a priority given to social and economic rights over political rights. Asian leaders point to these values in the rationale for the economic growth and development experienced in many of these countries in the 1990s.

Fred Halliday examines the cultural relativism debate in regard to the Islamic Middle East, specifically the issue of whether Islamic values constitute a culturally relative defense of noted human rights violations in the region. He posits that the claim to Islamic values is a modern construct created in response to other international human rights documents, to certain international political questions facing Islamic states, to treatment of certain citizens within Islamic states, to the call for democratization and respect for human rights from the international community, and to a growing grassroots sentiment for the Islamization of society. Halliday argues that the Islamic values position is not grounded in either culture or religion; rather it is a position expressed by other developing countries, particularly in response to pressure from the West to improve human rights. Beyond the political arguments, Islamic states also react to what they view as the moral decline of the West. Upholding Islamic values, thus, will prevent such a decline in the Middle East. Additionally, Halliday contends, in what could be considered a controversial position, that even religious arguments made by Islamic states are universal rather than culturally relativist. Last, Halliday suggests that any violations that do occur in the Middle East are not based on any established traditional, legal, or religious sources but are the result of modern interpretation, and the international society must look at the historical forces that led to these modern interpretations.

Imam Zaid Shakir examines one of these historical forces, the terrorist attacks of September 11, 2001, and the impact on human rights discourse in the United States on the issue of Islamic values. Shakir admits that there are no Islamic legal or philosophical traditions that are consistent with the modern human rights regime, however, Shakir contends that within the religious text and traditions there is a framework for the protection of basic human rights. The problem lies in the inability of modern Muslim discourse to convey this argument. Shakir suggests that there are several reasons for this deficiency: the human rights discourse from the Muslim community is made from a God-centric perspective; it tends to be too general and rhetorical in nature, thereby preventing the creation of any meaningful policy; and perhaps most important, the discourse has presented the protection and preservation of rights for Muslims exclusively. All of these combined, Shakir argues, make it difficult for Muslims in the United States to begin an effective dialogue regarding human rights. In this excerpt, Shakir discusses how the terrorist attacks of September 11 have exacerbated the problems associated with this discourse. The realities of Islamic terrorism seem to belie the cry that Islam respects human rights. In the end, Shakir contends that Muslims must radically alter their approach to human rights discourse in America. Specifically, Shakir proscribes a move from discussing human rights in general terms to a clearly expressed Islamic discourse on human rights.

Bonny Ibhawoh addresses the case of African values, specifically the debate of the concept of human rights in African history and society as well as the contribution of the Africanist position to the globalization of human rights. He suggests that the Africanist discourse on cultural relativism can be divided into three levels or debates. First, similar to arguments made by proponents of Asian and Islamic values, the concept of human rights is a contemporary development with no connection to traditional societies found in Africa. The concept that human rights are individual rights is foreign to traditional societies, which place an emphasis on the community and the notion of human dignity. The second debate questions whether Western conceptions of human rights are applicable to Africa. Ibhawoh contends that many Africanists assert that what is necessary is an "African cultural fingerprint" that applies the African emphasis of the group, community, and duties to the universal model. The author cautions, however, that this position should not be used to justify traditional cultural practices no longer acceptable to modern society. The last level of discourse focuses on the hierarchy of primacy of rights, specifically the argument from the Africanist position that social and economic rights take precedence over political and civil rights. Here Ibhawoh outlines the "full belly thesis" and suggests that from the African perspective a full belly is not the accurate analogy for individuals to care about political and civil rights; rather the belly cannot be empty. It is these three levels of discourse that dominate the African perspective on human rights. From Ibhawoh's perspective, there is room in the international human rights regime for contributions from the Africanist position. Rather than take a narrow view of strong universalism, absent of any cultural flavor, he suggests that the globalization of human rights will be better served with contributions from various cultures.

# 4.2 ─────

# The Rhetoric of Asian Values

*Rhonda L. Callaway*

After the end of the Cold War, many believed that most, if not all, states would finally embrace the liberal political and economic policies modeled by the United States and other Western states. Therefore, when the concept of Asian values emerged, challenging the Western emphasis and even insistence that human rights are universal, many took notice. The economic success of the Asian Tigers caused many to pause as they began to evaluate and dissect the explanation for the so-called Asian economic miracle. The answer from the East was their unique culture encapsulated in the term *Asian values*. Although the East Asian economic crisis has dampened the call for Asian values, it has left an indelible mark on the cultural relativism debate.[1]

The exact date of the emergence of Asian values may be debated; however, one of the international community's first real exposures to the idea of Asian values came with the 1993 Bangkok Declaration.[2] The occasion was the regional meeting for Asia concerning the World Conference on Human Rights. This document, signed by many East and Southeast Asian nations, "stakes out a distinctive Asian point of view" when it comes to human rights. Leading the charge was a trio of Asian leaders: Lee Kuan Yew of Singapore, Mahathir Mohamed of Malaysia, and most recently President Jiang Zemin of China.

While there are many facets to this perspective, I outline three major observations regarding the nature of the Asian values paradigm. First, it provides not only a critique, but an alternative to the Western perspective. Here, the Asian values discourse reflects the predominant debate in human rights: universalism versus cultural relativism. The concept of state sovereignty plays a prominent role as part of this debate. Second, the crux of the Asian values argument lies with certain unique features of Asian culture, specifically the emphasis on family, hard work, frugality, respect for law and authority, and finally deference (and reverence) to authority. Third, stemming from this cultural difference, it is argued that Asian societies place a higher value on social and economic rights than on political rights. In other words, the needs of the collective or community take precedence over the rights of the individual. It is this argument that Asian leaders put forth as an explanation for the level of economic success in many of the booming Asian economies in the 1990s. The following sections address each of these, utilizing speeches and interviews of the leading proponents of Asian values.

## ▨ Three Observations

### *Critique of the West and Cultural Relativism*

First and foremost, Asian values discourse offers a stinging critique of the West, particularly the excesses found in America brought about by capitalism. In the West, human rights have evolved within the liberal paradigm regarding the role of the individual within society. Individual freedoms, in both the political and economic realm, are paramount to the extent that Western states have instituted protection of the individual in state constitutions as well as international treaties. From the Asian values perspective, this individualism has actually served as a detriment to society. In fact, advocates of Asian values suggest that the improvements in their economies are due to their unique values, just as the lack of certain values in the West helps to explain its relative decline. This particular point was made in an interview in *Foreign Affairs* with Fareed Zakaria (1994, 112), where Lee asserted that

> the liberal, intellectual tradition that developed after World War II claimed that human beings had arrived at this perfect state where everybody would be better off if they were allowed to do their own thing and flourish. It has not worked out, and I doubt if it will. Certain basics about human nature do not change. Man needs a certain moral sense of right and wrong. There is such a thing called evil, and it is not the result of being a victim of society. You are just an evil man, prone to do evil things, and you have to be stopped from doing them. Westerners have abandoned an ethical basis for society, believing that all problems are solvable by a good government, which we in the East never believed possible.

Moreover, this emphasis on the individual in the West has led to deleterious conditions, both for the individual and the state. In discussing the United States as a model for other countries, Lee indicated that while he admires some of the qualities of the United States, particularly in comparison with communist states, he was concerned over what he viewed as a crumbling civil society in America. In particular he stated that

> as a total system, I find parts of it totally unacceptable: guns, drugs, violent crime, vagrancy, unbecoming behavior in public—in sum, the breakdown of civil society. The expansion of the right of the individual to behave and misbehave as he pleases has come at the expense of orderly society. In the East the main object is to have a well-ordered society so that everybody can have maximum enjoyment of his freedoms. This freedom can only exist in an ordered state and not in a natural state of contention and anarchy. (Zakaria 1994, 111)

This emphasis on order requires a strong central government. Consequently, the concept of Asian values is predicated on the idea that states, as sovereign entities, have the right to determine priorities within the state, which can range from a whole host of issues, including human rights. In other words, "rights are a matter of national sovereignty" (Li 1996).

The issue of national sovereignty comes to the fore in further criticism of Western views on human rights. Proponents of Asian values argue that Western states are attempting to impose their values on Asia, without respect for its distinct culture, such that the West's insistence on a universal paradigm is tantamount to "cultural imperialism and a remnant of colonial ideology" (Gawlikowski 2000, 183). Beyond that, there is the contention that the attempt to impose universal human rights masks the true intention of the West, which is to cause "instability, economic decline, and poverty" in Asia (Christie 1995, 206).

Consequently, at the heart of the Asian values debate is the tension between universalism and cultural relativism. Any universal idea of human rights, according to this argument, is an attack on their culture (Li 1996). Myanmar's foreign minister U Ohn Gyaw stated in a speech to the United Nations opposing a Western-dominated view of human rights that "there is no unique model of human rights implementation that can be superimposed on a given country" (Christie 1995, 205). General Than Shwe of Myanmar echoed these ideas, adding that the true purpose of the Western insistence on a universal approach was to use democracy and human rights to incite the public. He asserted that Western concepts of "human rights and standards of democracy cannot be the same as our Asian standards. We must choose the human rights standard and the democratic path compatible with the tradition of our country and people" (Christie 1995, 205).

Furthermore, any attempts to try to develop without reference to the unique heritage of Asia will likely fail. As one example, Lee sums up the essence of Asian values:

> We . . . have a different culture, a different way of doing things. The individual is not the building block. It's the family, the extended family, the clan and the state. The five crucial relationships are: you and the prince or ruler, you and your wife, you and your children, you and your parents, you and your friends. If those relationships are right, everything will work out well in society. (quoted in Elliott, Abdoolcarim, and Elegant 2005, 7)

Much earlier, Lee Kuan Yew worried about the impact modernization would have on Singaporean society and culture, particularly the family, suggesting that his nation must not give up one for the sake of the other. He asserted that

> the question leaders of the less developed countries have to answer, is not whether or not to modernize. The question these leaders have to answer is how rapidly they can modernize their societies and equally important, how much of their traditional past can they retain, so that they are not just poor imitators of the West, with all the fads and fetishes, the disorders and aberrations of contemporary Western societies. (Chen 1977, 21–22)

Moreover, attempts by the West to force a set of universal rights on Asian countries implies that there is a consensus on what constitutes rights in the West. The fact is, this consensus does not exist. According to Bilahari Kausikan (1993, 34), the director of the East Asian and Pacific bureau of the Ministry of Foreign Affairs in Singapore,

> the hard core of rights that are truly universal is smaller than many in the West are wont to pretend. Forty-five years after the Universal Declaration was adopted, many of its 30 articles are still subject to debate over interpretation and application—not just between Asia and the West, but within the West itself. Not every one of the 50 states of the United States would apply the provisions of the Universal Declaration in the same way. It is not only pretentious but wrong to insist that everything has been settled once and forever. The Universal Declaration is not a tablet Moses brought down from the mountain. It was drafted by mortals. All international norms must evolve through continuing debate among different points of view if consensus is to be maintained.

Last, proponents of Asian values argue that individual human rights proposed by the West simply are not consistent with their Confucius-based, family-oriented value system. In the end, leaders in Asia reject any attempts to impose a Western philosophy of human rights in the East. Ultimately, Lee argued that other states should not "foist their system indiscriminately on societies in which it will not work" (Zakaria 1994, 110).

### Asian Culture: Family, Hard Work, Frugality, Respect for Law, Order, and Authority

A second aspect of Asian values is the idea that there are certain values and particular characteristics that make Asian societies distinctly different from other societies. For example, in an article in the *International Herald Tribune*, Tommy Koh (1993, 1–2) presents the following ten elements as crucial components of Asian values:[3]

1. East Asians do not believe in the extreme form of individualism practiced in the West . . .
2. East Asians believe in strong families . . .
3. East Asians revere education . . .
4. East Asians believe in the virtues of saving and frugality . . .
5. East Asians consider hard work a virtue—the chief reason this region is outcompeting Europe.
6. East Asians practice national teamwork . . .
7. There is an Asian version of a social contract between the people and the state. The government will maintain law and order and provide citizens with their basic needs for jobs, housing, education, and health care . . .
8. In some Asian countries, governments have sought to make every citizen a stakeholder in the country. More than 90 percent of Singaporeans own their own homes . . .

9. East Asians want their governments to maintain a morally wholesome
   environment in which to bring up their children . . .
10. Good governments in East Asia want a free press but, unlike the West,
    they do not believe that such freedom is an absolute right.

These distinct characteristics are often associated with a common influence
based on Confucianism. Confucianism promotes not only the centrality of the
family, but also an emphasis on individuals' duties to their family and to society (Fukuyama 1998). In other words, individuals should be willing to sacrifice for the benefit of the greater good. This emphasis on communal values is
in sharp contrast to the Western emphasis on individual rights (Li 1996). Lee,
in discussing the primacy of the family, states that the

> fundamental difference between Western concepts of society and govern-
> ment and East Asian concepts . . . is that Eastern societies believe that the in-
> dividual exists in the context of his family. He is not pristine and separate.
> The family is part of the extended family, and then friends and the wider so-
> ciety. The ruler or the government does not try to provide for a person what
> the family best provides. (Zakaria 1994, 113)

Later in the same interview, Lee addressed the connection between the family
and economic success. Here, he highlights many of the attributes commonly
spoken within the Asian values discourse.

> We used the family to push economic growth, factoring the ambitions of a
> person and his family into our planning. We have tried, for example, to im-
> prove the lot of children through education. The government can create a set-
> ting in which people can live happily and succeed and express themselves,
> but finally it is what people do with their lives that determines economic suc-
> cess or failure. Again, we were fortunate we had this cultural backdrop, the
> belief in thrift, hard work, filial piety and loyalty in the extended family, and,
> most of all, the respect for scholarship and learning. (Zakaria 1994, 114)

For Lee, the importance of family in Asian societies, like China, for example,
is paramount, given the nature of many of Asia's dynasties. He contends that
America's civilization has had the benefit of

> the growth of orderly government. History in China is one of dynasties which
> have risen and fallen, of the waxing and waning of societies. And through all
> that turbulence, the family, the extended family, the clan, has provided a kind
> of survival raft for the individual. Civilizations have collapsed, dynasties
> have been swept away by conquering hordes, but this life raft enables the civ-
> ilization to carry on and get to the next phase. (Zakaria 1994, 115)

Moreover, this allegiance to the family and the community results in deference
to the state. The prevailing attitude is one of individual duty to others that

seems to supplant any notion of individual rights. The ultimate result of this cultural predisposition is to sacrifice the individual for the collective good. Thus President Jiang Zemin of China argued that "in today's China, top priority should still be given to ensuring the greatest possible majority of its citizens the rights to subsistence and development . . . there would be no other rights to speak of" (Zemin 1999, 1). The emphasis on family and community leads to a third aspect of Asian values, an emphasis on economic and social rights.

### Emphasis on Economic and Social Rights

The desire for law and order leads naturally to an argument that the rights of the group or collective far outweigh the civil and political rights of the individual (Li 1996). As one Association of Southeast Asian Nations (ASEAN) statesman remarked, "Whether in periods of golden prosperity or in the depths of disorder, Asia has never valued the individual over society. The society has always been more important than the individual. I think that is what has saved Asia from greater misery" (Christie 1995, 208).

This emphasis on economic development and society over individual rights is, at times, in direct conflict with Western values of individual freedom and democracy. Lee illustrates this tension when he remarked in 1992 that "I do not believe that democracy necessarily leads to development. I believe that what a country needs to develop is discipline more than democracy. The exuberance of democracy leads to indiscipline and disorderly conduct which are inimical to development" ("Why Voting Is Good for You" 1994, 15).

The prominence of social and economic rights fits nicely into the emphasis on economic development, which often necessitates and justifies the suppression of individual rights. This rationale for Asian values, as articulated by Amartya Sen (1997, 33), is that it "argues for authoritarian governance in the interest of economic development. Lee Kuan Yew . . . has defended authoritarian arrangements on the ground of their alleged effectiveness in promoting economic success." The general argument is that investment will occur where there is order, making order the prevailing value in society. Thus, governments are more concerned with order than with providing individual freedom. Mark Thompson further articulates the idea that Asian values "were invoked as a form of developmentalism, with the claim that, until prosperity is achieved, democracy remains an unaffordable luxury. This Protestant-ethic-like form of 'Asian values' attributed high growth rates to hard work, frugality, discipline and teamwork which only a 'disciplined' (i.e. authoritarian) regime could provide during the early stages of development" (Thompson 2004, 1085). Thus, the Asian values argument comes full circle. The unique features of Asian values, the emphasis on family, hard work, and authority, unsurprisingly are drawn upon in support of the preference for social and economic rights, which in turn justify the emphasis on law and order for the purpose of economic advancement.

## ■ The Critique of Asian Values

Political dissidents, activists, and scholars alike reject the notion of Asian values. At the height of the rhetoric positing Asian values in the early 1990s, one of the strongest critics was the Dalai Lama. At the UN World Conference on Human Rights, held in Vienna in 1993, he stated that

> no matter what country or continent we come from we are all basically the same human beings. We have the common human needs and concerns. . . . The question of human rights is so fundamentally important that there should be no difference of views on this. We must therefore insist on a global consensus not only on the need to respect human rights world wide but more importantly on the definition of these rights. (Dalai Lama 1993, 1–2)

In response to the argument that Western standards of human rights, as laid out in the UDHR, cannot be applied to countries in East Asia because of cultural, economic, and social differences, the Dalai Lama (1993, 2) remarked,

> I do not share this view and I am convinced that the majority of Asian people do not support this view either, for it is the inherent nature of all human beings to yearn for freedom, equality and dignity . . . I do not see any contradiction between the need for economic development and the need for respect for human rights. The rich diversity of cultures and religions should help to strengthen the fundamental human rights in all communities. Because underlying this diversity are fundamental principles that bind us all as members of the same human family. Diversity and traditions can never justify the violations of human rights. . . .

Ultimately, the Dalai Lama rejects the notion of Asian values and argues that most Asians do as well.

Scholars also critique the concept of Asian values, pointing to several factors. First, the size and diversity of Asia (Sen 1997; Fukuyama 1998, 23), particularly different cultures and traditions (Gawlikowski 2000), make it difficult to gain a consensus on most matters, including the idea of Asian values. Asian values, as a concept, ignore the diversity of the countries within Asia. In addition, emphasis on family is found in many other cultures, including Western countries (Chan 1997). Asian values are built on the assumption that these qualities are unique to that area of the world, which may in fact be a faulty assumption. Moreover, emphasis on the family, collective, or community does not equate to blind devotion to the state. Most importantly, the assumption is that citizens in Asia are choosing between rights and, in fact, are trading off their civil and political rights for subsistence rights. This is inconsistent with current research, which suggests that rights are, in fact, achieved simultaneously (Milner, Poe, and Leblang 1999).

The most damning critique of Asian values is that it is a state's attempt to justify repression.[4] In a 2002 essay, Zakaria (2002, 38–39) explained that the "discussion about Asian values was not simply a scholarly debate. Many Asian dictators used arguments about their region's unique culture to stop Western politicians from pushing them to democratize. The standard rebuttal was that Asians prefer order to the messy chaos of democracy." These criticisms have undermined the legitimacy of Asian values as counter to the idea of human rights.

## ■ Conclusion

Following the financial crisis in the late 1990s, many have questioned the endurance of Asian values. A journalist living in Hong Kong in 2004 noted that the general mood in East Asia was one of "indifference" rather than one of "responsibility to society at large." When he queried a friend from the region on the seemingly contradictory behavior given the rhetoric of Asian values, the friend responded, "Of course we sacrifice for the greater good . . . but that greater good extends no farther than our own clan. The closer the connection, the more we'll sacrifice, so we'll do the most for our families, then perhaps our friends. But without some personal connection, we couldn't care less" (LaMoshi 2004, 3). This statement explains both the appeal of Asian values and the decline of Asian values as a rationale for economic success. On the one hand, the connection to family helps build a stronger society, yet this same connection allowed for the cronyism that many believe led to the economic downturns in the region. Critics of this element of Asian values suggest that "the origins of Asia's financial crisis can be traced to such values as excessive loyalty to family, clan, or otherwise 'in-groups' leading to nepotism, cronyism, and corruption" (Wolf 2000). Others find no evidence of any connection between Asian values and the economic downturn, pointing rather to macroeconomic monetary and fiscal policies in many of the Asian states (Wolf 2000). Whether some form of Asian values will reemerge or there will be a movement toward accepting some degree of universal human rights in Asia remains to be seen.

## ■ Notes

1. In fact, Lee Kuan Yew has since "repudiated" his stance and previous remarks and now prefers the term *Confucian values* (Hirsch 2001).
2. For a complete discussion of the origins of the Asian values debate see Subramaniam (2000). Here, the author suggests that Singapore's Lee Kuan Yew was advocating a unique Asian view as early as 1970.
3. Koh is a professor and formerly Singapore's ambassador-at-large.

4. For example, Francis Fukuyama (1998, 23) argued that "to the 'soft' authoritarian governments ruling Singapore, Malaysia, Indonesia, and increasingly the People's Republic of China, 'Asian values' offered an apparently principled defense of their reluctance to broaden political participation."

## ■ References

Blackburn, Kevin. 1994. "Does the West Need to Learn 'Asian Values'?" *IPA Review* 47 (2): 35–37.

Chan, Joseph. 1997. "An Alternative View." *Journal of Democracy* 8 (2): 25–48.

Chen, Peter S. J. 1977. "Asian Values and Modernization: A Sociological Perspective," in Seah Chee-Meow, ed. *Asian Values and Modernization* (Singapore: Singapore University Press), pp. 21–22.

Christie, Kenneth. 1995. "Regime Security and Human Rights in Southeast Asia." *Political Studies* 43:204–218.

Dalai Lama. 1993. "Human Rights and Universal Responsibility." *The Government of Tibet in Exile*. Available online at www.tibet.com/DL/vienna.html.

Elliott, Michael, Zoher Abdoolcarim, and Simon Elegant. 2005. "Lee Kuan Yew Reflects." *Time Asia,* December 5, 2005. Available at www.time.com/time/asia/covers/501051212/index.html.

Fukuyama, Francis. 1998. "Asian Values and the Asian Crisis." *Commentary* (February): 23–27.

Gawlikowski, Krzysztof. 2000. " 'Asian Values' and Western Universalism." *Dialogue and Universalism* 10 (1/2): 183–187.

Hirsh, Michael. 2001. "Rethinking Confucius: Lee Kuan Yew Recants." *Newsweek,* January 28, 2001.

Kausikan, Bilahari. 1993. "Asia's Different Standard." *Foreign Policy* 92:24–41.

Koh, Tommy. 1993. "The 10 Values That Undergird East Asian Strength and Success." *International Herald Tribune,* December 11, 1993. Available at www.iht.com/bin/print_ipub.php?file=/articles/1993/12/11/edkoh.php.

LaMoshi, Gary. 2004. "Asian Values Behind Singapore Son's Rise." *Asia Times,* August 10, 2004. Available at www.singapore-window.org/sw04/040810at.htm.

Li, Xiaorong. 1996. "Asian Values and the Universality of Human Rights." *Report from the Institute for Philosophy and Public Policy* 16, no. 2 (Spring). Available at www.puaf.umd.edu/IPPP/li.htm.

Milner, Wesley, Steven C. Poe, and David Leblang. 1999. "Security Rights, Subsistence Rights, and Liberties: A Theoretical Survey of the Empirical Landscape." *Human Rights Quarterly* 21:403–443.

Sen, Amartya. 1997. *Human Rights and Asian Values.* New York: Carnegie Council on Ethics and Public Policy.

Subramaniam, Surain. 2000. "The Asian Values Debate: Implications for the Spread of Democracy." *Asian Affairs* 27:19–35.

Thompson, Mark R. 2004. "Pacific Asia After 'Asian Values': Authoritarianism, Democracy, and 'Good Governance,'" *Third World Quarterly* 25 (6): 1079–1095.

"Why Voting Is Good for You." 1994. *The Economist* 332 (7878): 15–17.

Wolf, Charles, Jr., 2000. "Are 'Asian Values' Really Unique?" *Hoover Digest,* no. 2. Available at www.hoover.org/publications/digest/3484341.html.

Zakaria, Fareed. 2002. "Asian Values." *Foreign Policy,* 133:38–40.

————. 1994. "Culture Is Destiny: A Conversation with Lee Kuan Yew." *Foreign Affairs* 73 (March–April): 109–127.

Zemin, Jiang. 1999. "President Jiang Spells out Chinese Values." Reported by the *Renmin Ribao* (People's Daily) on October 22, 1999. East Asian Studies Document, UCLA Center for East Asian Studies. Available at www.isop.ucla.edu/eas/documents/jiangzemin-chinesevalues.htm.

# 4.3 _____

# Relativism and Universalism in Human Rights: The Case of the Islamic Middle East

*Fred Halliday*

Many commentators, Islamic and other, have fallen into the habit of presenting this question as part of a broader, historical and enduring, conflict between two determinate 'civilizations', the Western, or Judaeo-Christian and the Muslim. Convenient, and attractively polemical, as such an argument from transhistorical conflict may be, it has little relevance to the matter in hand. Whatever the philosophical foundations for a theory of human rights, or the historical roots of our modern conception thereof, the discourse of human rights as we express and formulate it today is a recent, post-1945, phenomenon. Hence in explaining how and why particular attitudes to human rights are articulated we are looking above all at influences that have operated since that time, whatever anterior religious or ethical principles they may invoke. While there are some elements in the Islamic tradition and literature that can be drawn on to discuss the issue of human rights, what we are dealing with here is, as in other states, a relatively recent set of arguments, the result of contemporary trends in the international system and within Islamic states.

As such, the debate on human rights in the Islamic context reflects the convergence of at least five distinct processes. First, it is part of, and a response to, the development of the international debate, arising with the Universal Declaration of Human Rights of 1948 and leading on to subsequent, more specific codes, particularly in the 1970s and 1980s. Secondly, the Islamic debate reflects the way in which, partly influenced by the UN-centred debates, a broader set of *political* questions affecting the Muslim world has come to be phrased in human rights terms—the Palestinian, Kashmir and Bosnian issues and the treatment of Muslims in Western European society being cases in point. Thirdly, these discourses are a response to the particular use made of human rights as an issue for criticizing abuses by governments, be this on the part of non-governmental organizations, such as Amnesty, or as with the Carter and subsequent US administrations, and with the UN Human Rights Commission, by governments. Fourthly, the debate reflects the pressure from within Islamic states for greater democratization and respect for human rights, in the direction of an increased compliance with international codes. Finally, and quite separately, it is affected by the current of what one can broadly term 'Islamization', both from above, by governments, and from below, by mass Islamist movements, that has been growing from the 1970s onwards: this tendency seeks to alter legal codes, and state practice, so that they conform more to what is deemed to be 'traditional' or correct Islamic practice.[1]

As this, rather bald, list of trends should suggest, the debate on human rights in the Islamic world has been one that reflects a range of political concerns and ones that are often in rather marked conflict with each other. The result has been a variety of responses, as to the possible relationship of Islam as a religion to the issue of human rights. Indeed at least four distinct responses or themes from within an Islamic discourse may be identified, classifiable as, respectively, *(i) assimilation*: the argument that there is no problem about reconciling Islam with theories of human rights;[2] *(ii) appropriation*: the claim that, far from Islam and human rights being incompatible, it is only under Islam that they can be fully realized;[3] *(iii) confrontation*, i.e. the argument that international human rights doctrines are to be rejected as part of some imperialist or ethnocentric project, and replaced by *shari'a; (iv) incompatibility,* the claim that somehow 'Islam' itself is irreconcilable with human rights, or democratic, principles—a theme present within Islamic societies in the plea for particularism, but also found as well in the non-Muslim world, but outside an Islamic discourse. Given the nature of the discussion, on both sides, these themes are often combined in a particular discourse rather than mutually exclusive positions. However, it is important to note here that whether we are looking at the statements of governments or those of other Muslim entities, it is the first and second arguments that are by far the most frequent.

## ▦ An Alternative Universalism

The argument that follows is one attempt to disentangle this debate, and to cast some light both on the claims of Islamists with regard to human rights, and on the broader issue of relativism in the field of human rights. It will, in the first place, look at the argument that, in some way or another, the Islamic response to the human rights debate is a form of cultural relativism, and show that, in many ways, this is a simplification. It will then proceed to look at some substantive issues underlying this apparent polarization between 'traditions' and at what it is that leads to the conflict between Islamic and universal codes. It will conclude with some reflections on the critique of universalism, based on the Middle Eastern experience.

In writing on the question of Middle Eastern and Islamic responses to the human rights issue it is certainly tempting to contrast a Western, universalistic, approach to the Middle Eastern, particularist, one. Much writing on the subject, be it by Muslims or non-Muslims, operates with such a set of generalities, implying that, in some way, the Islamic approach is comparable to the historicist or communitarian one found in Western thinking.[4] Yet, on closer examination, this is itself a simplification and can serve to confuse rather than illumine the issues at stake. In the first place, if current statements and policies are anything to go by, there is no *one* 'Middle Eastern' or 'Islamic' body of thought on this question. Attempts, declamatory or benign, to identify an 'Islamic' position are as misguided as those seeking to produce an 'African' or an 'Asian' stance. There are over fifty Muslim states in the world, with a variety of legal and political systems, and there is no single body, political or religious, that speaks for the Muslim world as a whole. The Muslim religion itself is not only highly fragmented, but is, in contrast to Christianity, one that operates without even a purported theological and legal central authority: what we have is a range of bodies, some political, some juridical, some academic, such as the al-Azhar University in Cairo, which interpret law and tradition as they see fit and which appeal to all Muslims to follow them.

While many aspire, or claim, to speak in the name of all Muslims, none do, and there are many cases of the factional, the self-appointed, and the political, who speak 'for' the Muslim world. There is, for example, a world of difference between the positions of the government of Saudi Arabia, on the one hand, with its promotion of a conservative 'Islamic' code of rights, and that of Tunisia, which has been in the forefront of the battle *for* universal rights, and which even proposed to the pre-Vienna 'African' conference a denunciation of the threat to human rights posed by religious fundamentalism. In confronting what is said by governments, individual writers or organizations, one has to take them in their specific context and not assume that they speak for an Islamic world, or tradition, or that theirs is the only possible, or legitimate, interpretation of the religion. We are dealing with a diversity of views and interpretations not a single body of thought. . . .

On the issue of human rights itself, those who are the victims of regimes speaking in the name of a legitimating 'Islam', be this in Iran, Saudi Arabia or the Sudan, have often invoked universalistic principles precisely because they contest the very legitimacy of the regimes that are repressing them. In other cases, opposition to Islamization has come from those who want a more moderate, liberal, interpretation of Islam.[5] The debate on the Islamic character of law and the constitution in revolutionary Iran pitted clerical and other Islamic forces against those, many of them involved in years of opposition to the Shah's regime, who wanted a secular approach to these issues: the latter were, in time, silenced by repression, justified in the name of Islam. Indeed, as those concerned with human rights in these states so often point out, what the victims of Islamic states and societies repeatedly ask for is not a different, better or more authentic interpretation of Islamic law, but the consistent application of international, universalistic, principles.

Moreover, if one examines what self-proclaimed Islamic states actually argue then much of it can be said to avoid a culturally relativist position at all. Indeed what is striking about so much of the rhetoric emerging from such regimes, and from writers in the Islamic tradition, is that, with varying shades of explicitness, they are articulating arguments in universal terms. In regard to the overall foreign policy confrontations of the Islamic and non-Islamic worlds, the arguments most frequently heard have little to do with religion or culture. Some pertain to the arguments, heard throughout the third world, on redistribution of wealth, equity in international trade and so forth: on this the Iranians joined hands with the Singaporeans and Chinese at Vienna. Some arguments pertain to the Islamic world, and the Middle East in particular, but for reasons of substance, not formulation: thus the most frequent argument used against Western, particularly US, policy in the region has been that of 'double standards'—expounding the principle of self-determination of peoples, but denying it to Palestinians and Kashmiris, condemning Muslims for violations of international law, while permitting continued Israeli occupation of the Palestinian lands taken in 1967, calling for democracy in communist states, but denying it in such countries as Algeria or Saudi Arabia, condemning one group of nationalist militants as 'terrorists' while encouraging others as 'freedom fighters', and, most recently, upholding the sovereignty of states while denying a Muslim state, Bosnia, the right to self-defence. The underlying principles have not been relativistic at all, and are not comparable to the historicist or communitarian principles articulated elsewhere: here, on the issue of double standards and historical responsibility, the critique emanating from the Muslim world has considerable validity—but this validity is a function of the force of arguments based on universalistic principles.

This is also the case for the very terms in which the critiques of the Western position are articulated. In the first place, many of the rebuttals of Western human rights criticisms start by arguing that states with an imperialistic record, past and continuing, have themselves no right to criticize third world states: in other words, the argument is one that invokes a principle, implicit or explicit, that those who voice human rights criticisms should be themselves countries with a morally defensible record in the field of relations between states. This argument may or may not be valid, or properly applied, but like many of the other views expressed by Muslim states it has nothing particularly to do with Islam. Secondly, in rebutting external criticism, Islamic states, like other objects of such criticism, frequently resort to counter-attack, on the violations by Western states of human rights and indeed on the general moral decline of Western society, be it in regard to crime, relations between sexes, treatment of the aged or whatever. Beneath what appears to be a plea for difference lies a moral critique of the West expressed, with lesser or greater degrees of explicitness, in universalistic terms. Thus the Iranian foreign minister Ali Akbar Velayati, speaking at the UN in 1993, attacked the West for seeking to impose its values on the Islamic and third worlds, but then linked this to the moral crisis in the West, arising from unlimited freedom: ". . . some Western countries intended to impose on other societies their own social ethical decline, to which they themselves confess, within the attractive package of human rights."[6] . . .

Most importantly, however, even where the critique is phrased in terms of Islamic tradition or *shari'a*, and where it is claimed that a different set of moral and legal principles should be applied, this does not take a relativist form: indeed the claim that a particular principle is derived from Islam contains within it, explicitly or implicitly, its own universalism. Islam is a religion without overt ethnic or regional particularism, one that aspires to encompass all of humanity within its compass, and which regards other religions and traditions as, comparatively, inferior. The *da'wa* or call to submit to God, the basis of Islamic faith, is made to all of mankind. Hence, given that the truths of Islam must be applicable to all humans, be they believers or not, any position articulated in Islamic terms is itself universalistic. To imply otherwise, i.e. that in a culturally relativist vein what Muslims believe is no better or worse than what non-Muslims believe, would be a violation of the faith, and of its core doctrine. A consistent Islamic position is *the opposite* of that contained within communitarian Western thinking, since the latter implies that, as between different communities, values can be held to be equal. By contrast, if there is a conflict between 'Western' and internationally established codes of conduct and those of Islamic states it is not one between universalism and particularism, but between two, apparently divergent and contradictory, forms of universalism.

## ■ Notes

1. 'Islamization' refers to policies of governments designed to alter law and social life in accordance with Islamic doctrine. 'Islamism' refers to political movements of a mass populist kind, that challenge established, more secular, states.

2. Kevin Dwyer, *Arab Voices. The Human Rights Debate in the Middle East* (London: Routledge, 1991) and his 'Universal visions, communal visions: human rights and traditions," *Peuples Mediterraneens*, 58–59 (January–July 1992), 205–20, provide rich studies of the varying interpretations of Islamic traditions within the Arab debate.

3. Ann Mayer, *Islam and Human Rights* (London: Westview, 1981).

4. John Vincent, *Human Rights and International Relations* (Cambridge: Cambridge University Press, 1986), pp. 28–30.

5. Saeed Barzin, "Constitutionalism and democracy in the religious ideology of Mehdi Bazargan," *British Journal of Middle Eastern Studies,* 21:1 (1994).

6. BBC Summary of World Broadcasts Part 4 The Middle East, 16 (October 1993), ME/1821 MED/5-6.

# 4.4 _____

## American Muslims and a Meaningful Human Rights Discourse in the Aftermath of September 11, 2001
*Imam Zaid Shakir*

### ■ The Relevance of Human Rights for Islam in America

Islam in America has historically been characterized by a strong advocacy of human rights and social justice issues. This is so because it has been associated with people who would be identified as ethnic minorities. The first significant Muslim population in this country, the enslaved believers of African origin, would certainly fit that description. The various Islamic movements, which arose amongst their descendants, appeared in a social and political context characterized by severe oppression. That socio-political context shaped the way Islam was understood by the people embracing it. It was a religion, in all its variant understandings, which was seen as a source of liberation, justice, and redemption.[1] When the ethnic composition of the Muslim community began to change due to immigration in the 1970s, 1980s, and into the 1990s, the minority composition of the Muslim community remained. These newly arriving non-European immigrant Muslims were generally upwardly mobile; however, their brown and olive complexions, along with their accents, and the vestiges of their original cultures, served to reinforce the reality of their minority status. This fact, combined with the fact that the most religiously active among them were affiliated with Islamic movements in the Muslim world, movements whose agendas were dominated by strong human rights and social justice concerns, affected the nature of the Islamic call in this country, keeping human rights concerns to the fore.

Illustrative of this human rights imperative is the stated mission of the Ahmadiyya Movement when it began active propagation in America. Mufti Muhammad Sadiq, the first Ahmadi missionary to America, consciously called to a multicultural view of Islam, which challenged the entrenched racism

Excerpted from Imam Zaid Shakir, "American Muslims and a Meaningful Human Rights Discourse in the Aftermath of September 11, 2001," *Crosscurrents* 52 (Winter 2003). Reprinted with permission of *Crosscurrents*. Some of the author's notes have been omitted.

prevalent in early twentieth-century American society.[2] This message presented Islam as a just social force, capable of extending to the racial minorities of this country their full human rights. However, there were strong anti-white overtones of the Ahmadi message, shaped by Mufti Muhammad Sadiq's personal experience, and the widespread persecution of people of Indian descent (so-called Hindoos) in America, which dampened the broader appeal of the Ahmadi message. Those overtones were subsequently replaced by the overtly racist proclamations of the Nation of Islam, which declared whites to be devils. In the formulation of the Nation of Islam, Islam came to be viewed as a means for the restoration of the lost preeminence of the "Asiatic" Blackman. This restoration would be effected by a just religion, Islam, which addressed the social, economic and psychological vestiges of American race-based slavery. In other words, Islam was the agent that would grant the Muslims their usurped human rights.

The pivotal figure who was able to synthesize these various pronouncements into a tangible, well-defined human rights agenda was Malcolm X. By continuing to emphasize the failure of American society to effectively work to eliminate the vestiges of slavery, he was an implicit advocate of the justice-driven agenda of the Nation of Islam, even after departing from that movement. His brutal criticism of the racist nature of American society, which he often contrasted with the perceived racial harmony of Islam, highlighted by his famous letter from Mecca,[3] in which he envisioned Islam as a possible cure for this country's inherent racism, was the continuation of the original multi-cultural message of the Ahmadiyya Movement. Finally, his evolving thinking on the true nature of the struggle of the African American people, and his situating that struggle in the context of the Third World human rights struggle, reflected the human rights imperative which figured so prominently in the call of Middle Eastern groups such as Egypt's Muslim Brotherhood, and the Indian Subcontinent's Jamaati Islami, groups which had a strong influence on the founders of this country's Muslim Students Asssociation (MSA) in 1963.

These various groupings, along with the Dar al-Islam Movement, the Islamic Party, and Sheikh Tawfiq's Mosque of Islamic Brotherhood, which would develop in many urban centers during the 1960s and 1970s as the purveyors of an emerging African American "Sunni" tradition, a tradition consolidated by the conversion of Malcolm X to the orthodox faith, represented in their various agendas the crystallization of the sort of human rights agenda which Malcolm was hammering out during the last phase of his life. These groups all saw Islam as the key to liberation from the stultifying weight of racial, social, and economic inequality in America.

The Iranian Revolution of 1979 further strengthened this human rights imperative. The revolution was presented by its advocates in America, who were quite influential at the time, as an uprising of the oppressed Muslim masses to secure their usurped rights from the Shah, an oppressive "Taghut."

This message, conveyed strongly and forcefully through the call of the Muslim Students Association—Persian Speaking Group (MSA–PSG) was extremely influential in shaping the human rights imperative in American Islam, not only because of its direct influence, but also because of the vernacular of struggle it introduced into the conceptual universe of many American Muslims, and the way it shaped the message of contending "Sunni" groups. The combined influence of these forces worked to insure that human rights issues were prominent in the call of Islamic organizations and individuals prior to the tragic events of September 11, 2001.

## ▨ Muslim Human Rights Discourse and the Challenge of September 11, 2001

The tragic events of September 11 present a clear challenge to the human rights/social justice imperative of Muslims in North America. The reasons for this are many and complex. The apocalyptic nature of the attacks of September 11, particularly the assault on and subsequent collapse of the World Trade Center towers, led many observers to question the humaneness of a religion that could encourage such senseless, barbaric slaughter. Islam, the religion identified as providing the motivation for those horrific attacks, was brought into the public spotlight as being, in the view of many of its harshest critics, an anti-intellectual, nihilistic, violent, chauvinistic atavism.

The atavistic nature of Islam, in their view, leads to its inability to realistically accommodate the basic elements of modern human rights philosophy. This inability was highlighted by the September 11 attacks in a number of ways. First of all, the massive and indiscriminant slaughter of civilians belied any Muslim claims that Islam respects the right to life. If so, how could so many innocent, unsuspecting souls be so wantonly sacrificed? Secondly, "Islam's" refusal to allow for the peaceful existence of even remote populations of "infidels," the faceless dehumanized "other," calls into question its respect for the rights of non-Muslims within its socio-political framework. It also highlights its inability to define that "other" in human terms.

As a link between the accused perpetrators of the attacks, Osama bin Laden and the Taliban rulers of Afghanistan, was developed by both the United States government and news media, the human rights position of Islam was called into further question. The Taliban, by any standards of assessment, presided over a regime that showed little consideration for the norms governing international human rights. Much evidence exists which implicates the Taliban in violating the basic rights of women, ethnic minorities (non-Pashtun), the Shi'ite religious minority, detainees, artists, and others, using in some instances, extremely draconian measures. Many of these violations occurred under the rubric of applying what the regime identified as Islamic law. The news of Taliban excesses, coupled with the shock of the events of September 11, combined to create tremendous apprehension towards the ability and willingness of Islam to accommodate a meaningful human rights regime.

The political climate existing in America in the aftermath of September 11 has been exploited by certain elements in American society to call into question any humanitarian tendencies being associated with Islam. For example, in the aftermath of the brutal murder of Daniel Pearl, an act whose implications are as chilling as the attacks of September 11, Mr. Pearl's bosses at the *Wall Street Journal*, Peter Kahn and Paul Steiger remarked, "His murder is an act of barbarism that makes a mockery of everything that Danny's kidnappers claimed to believe in." Responding to those comments, Leon Wieseltier, of *The New Republic*, stated, "The murder of Daniel Pearl did not make a mockery of what his slaughterers believe. It was the perfect expression, the inevitable consequence, of what his slaughterers believe."[4] This, and similar indictments of Islam, challenge the ability of American Muslims to effectively speak on human rights issues in obvious ways.

If we examine the actual nature of American Muslim human rights discourse prior to September 11, we find that it was based in large part on Muslims contrasting the generalities of the *Shari'ah*, with the specific shortcomings of American society and history in relevant areas of domestic and international policy and practice. This discourse ignored the positive human rights strictures contained in sections of the American Constitution, the Bill of Rights, and the UDHR, to which the United States is a signatory. As in other areas, this inadequate approach produced a false sense of moral superiority among Muslims in America. This sense was shattered by the attacks of September 11, in that many Americans were suddenly pointing to what they viewed as the inadequacy of Islamic human rights regimes, their inadequate philosophical basis, and their failure to guarantee basic human rights protection, especially for women, religious, racial, and ethnic minorities living in Muslim lands.

### ■ Moving Ahead

Responding adequately to these charges will require a radical restructuring of current Islamic human rights discourse, and the regimes that discourse informs. The God-centric approach, which can serve as the basis for a strictly Islamic human rights discourse, cannot serve as the basis for such a discourse here in the West, at least in its initial phases. It lacks the necessary universality. Our efforts at such a discourse must be rooted in the UDHR. Although there are elements of the UDHR that we Muslims would object to, they are few, and as demonstrated above, most of the elements of the UDHR have legitimate Islamic parallels. Such an acceptance would not be illegitimate from an Islamic perspective, as virtually every Islamic nation is a signatory to the UDHR. Acceptance of the UDHR as the basis of our discourse, no matter how critical, would immediately give any Islamic discourse a universal base from which to proceed. It would also provide a framework to begin moving beyond generalities and into the realm of effective policy formulations and executive regimes.

Generalities, which formerly sufficed in Islamic human rights discourse will have to be replaced by concrete, developed policy prescriptions, which stipulate in well-defined, legal terms, how viable human rights protections will be extended to groups identified as systematically suffering from human rights abuses in Muslim realms.

An example of the dangerous and inadequate generalities alluded to above, can be glimpsed from a brief examination of the *Cairo Declaration on Human Rights in Islam* (CDHRI). Article 24 of that document states, "All the rights and freedoms stipulated in this Declaration are subject to the Islamic *Shari'ah*." Such a statement is meaningless, considering the vast corpus of subjectively understood literature that could be identified as informing the *Shari'ah*, unless the relevant rulings and principles of the *Shari'ah* are spelled out in exacting detail, and then effective executive regimes are created to guarantee those rights, once they are effectively enunciated. Existing executive regimes, such as that provided by the Helsinki Accords, can serve as viable models for Muslims, once the framework that led to those regimes has been accepted. This provides another incentive to root our discourse in the UDHR.

While this paper has consciously avoided mention of those features of Islam which would be antithetical to the Western concept of personal liberty, such as the lack of freedom to choose one's "sexual orientation," there are major civil liberties issues which must be addressed, in clear and unequivocal terms, if Islam's human rights discourse is to have any credence. Hiding behind Islam's cultural, or civilizational specificity to avoid providing answers to difficult questions will not advance a deeper understanding of our faith amongst enlightened circles in the West. Islam indeed has much to say in the area of human rights. However, much foundational work has to be done before we can speak clearly and authoritatively, especially in the changed post–September 11 political climate.

## ■ Notes

1. See, Robert Dannin, *Black Pilgrimage to Islam* (Oxford, New York: Oxford University Press, 2002). Dannin presents a good summary of the evolution of Islam among African-Americans. His book is especially valuable for its detailed treatment of the evolution of the African-American Sunni Muslim community. See, also Richard Brent Turner, *Islam in the African American Experience* (Bloomington: Indiana University Press, 1997).

2. Turner, 121–131.

3. Alex Haley with Malcolm X, *The Autobiography of Malcolm X* (New York: Ballantine Books, 1964) 338–342.

4. Leon Wieseltier, "The Murder of Daniel Pearl," *The New Republic*, February 25, 2002.

# 4.5 _____

# Restraining Universalism: Africanist Perspectives on Cultural Relativism in the Human Rights Discourse

*Bonny Ibhawoh*

## ■ "African Values" and the Cultural Relativism of Human Rights

The developing world has set its imprint on human rights thought in the 1990s, both by making human rights more socially oriented and also by questioning the focus on the individual that has characterized the human rights discourse in the West. The arguments for the cultural relativity of "Asian values" and lately "African values," in the conception and interpretation of human rights have been central to this trend. The discourse on the cultural relativity of human rights from the Africanist perspective has attracted considerable attention although there remain differences in opinion on the articulation of the Africanist position in relation to the contemporary human rights corpus. . . .

To understand the Africanist discourse on the cultural relativity of human rights in Africa, however, it is necessary to draw attention once again, to the argument by some writers that the contemporary concept of human rights is a modern development which has its roots in the Universal Declaration of Human Rights and was thus alien to traditional societies in Africa or elsewhere. Some of these writers have suggested that the concept of human rights as legal entitlement, which individuals hold in relation to the state, simply did not exist in traditional African societies. As indicated earlier, they argue that what is usually put forward as human rights concepts in traditional Africa is nothing more than the notion of *human dignity* and worth which exist in all preindustrial societies.

---

Excerpted from Bonny Ibhawoh, "Restraining Universalism: Africanist Perspectives on Cultural Relativism in the Human Rights Discourse," in Paul Tiyanbe Zeleza and Philip J. McConnaughay, eds., *Human Rights, the Rule of Law, and Development in Africa* (Philadelphia: University of Pennsylvania Press), pp. 21–39. © 2004 University of Pennsylvania Press. Reprinted with permission of the University of Pennsylvania Press. Some of the author's notes have been omitted.

It is argued that all human societies including those in Africa have gone through a stage when, because of the low level of productive forces, collective ownership of the means of production and the communal organization of society were necessary for subsistence (Eze 1993, 92). This "communal" social structure naturally allowed for the development of humanistic ideals that did not necessarily equate with the modern conception of human rights. Any argument for a traditional precolonial concept of human rights is therefore only a question of confusing "human dignity" with "human rights." Even at that, it has been further suggested that, to the extent that modernization or Westernization has reached into, and transformed traditional communities in Africa, traditional approaches to guaranteeing human dignity for all their worth would seem objectively inappropriate for the modern African nation state. To continue to base human rights policy on the "communal" model of traditional Africa would be to ignore the changes that have occurred and are occurring in the way Africans live.

Another variant of this school of thought is the argument that traditional Africa, as indeed most premodern agrarian societies, did not evolve perceptions of human rights because these societies did not recognize the concept of a "human being" as a descriptive category to which some inalienable rights were attached. Instead, persons were defined by social status or group membership. Thus, traditional societies generally did not recognize rights held simply because one is a human being (Donnelly 1982). The kind of social relationship between the state and the individual on which the concept of human rights is based was therefore never created within the context of such traditional societies (Mutua 1995). Human rights, were thus alien to traditional African societies (as they were to feudal Europe), until Western modernizing incursions dislocated community and denied newly isolated individuals access to the customary ways of protecting their lives and human dignity. Indeed, human rights as defined by many liberal scholars, are understood as individual claims against the state as founded in the Universal Declaration of Human Rights and in this sense there is only one conception of human rights and that is Western (Shivji 1989, 16).

In contrast to these positions, several African and Third World writers have argued that the philosophy and conceptions of human rights are neither exclusive to Western liberal traditions nor relevant only with reference to post-1948 developments. They reject the notion that the concept of human rights, having been originated, developed and refined in the West was thereafter "transplanted" to Africa and the rest of the world. This view has been variously described as paternalistic, inherently ahistorical and philosophically bankrupt. . . .

The Africanist approach to the discourse on the cultural relativism of human rights can therefore be broadly divided into two schools. The first of these is the less radical approach, which is ideologically closer to the dominant universalist schools of the West. Proponents of this school, while arguing the validity of a uniquely African concept of human rights, also recognize the universality of a basic core of human rights. Kofi Quashigah (1991) for instance, concludes that human rights concepts, which are rooted in certain social facts that are peculiar to particular societies, cannot be expected to be universal. At the same time, he acknowledges that certain basic needs are indisputably universally ascribable to persons of every historical, geographical, and cultural background.

The second school is in more radical opposition to the universalist approach. It seeks to fundamentally challenge the Western-oriented state-individual perspective that otherwise dominates human rights discourse. The main argument here is rooted in a belief that the philosophical basis and worldviews of Western European and African societies are fundamentally different, that collectivist rather than individualistic conceptions of rights and duties predominate in Africa. Yougindra Khasualani (1983) and Makau Mutua (1995) are some of the writers in this category. The modern conception of human rights, they contend, contains three elements that are Western-oriented and makes it inappropriate to the African and other non-Western contexts. One, the fundamental unit of the society is the individual, not the family or community. Two, the primary basis of securing human existence in society is through rights, not duties. Three, the primary method of securing these rights is through a process of legalism where rights are claimed as inalienable entitlements and adjudicated upon, not reconciliation, repentance and education. . . .

Makau Mutua's (1995) position is a similar one. He argues that an examination of the norms governing the legal, political, and social structures in precolonial African societies, demonstrates that the concept of rights informed the notion of justice, which, though community centered, also supported a measure of individualism. He argues further that in traditional Africa, the concept of rights was founded not on the individual but on the community, to which the individual related on the basis of obligations and duties. Rights in this context included but were not limited to the right to political representation, which was often guaranteed by the family, age groups and the clan. Rather, the society developed certain central social features that tended to foster the promotion of both individual and collective rights. These included deference to age, commitment to the family and the community, and solidarity with other members of the community. The dominant social orientations toward rights emphasized the groupness, sameness, and commonality, as well as a sense of cooperation, interdependence, and collective responsibility.

These ideals served to strengthen community ties and social cohesiveness, engendering a shared fate and a common destiny. In these circumstances, the concept of human rights did not stand in isolation. It went with duties. For every right to which a member of society was entitled, there was a corresponding communal duty. Expressed differently, the right of a kinship member was the duty of the other and the duty of the other kinship member was the right of another (Cobbah 1987, 321). Although certain rights attached to the individual by virtue of birth and membership of the community, there were also corresponding communal duties and obligations. This matrix of entitlement and obligations which fostered communal solidarity and sustained the kinship system, was the basis of the African conception of human rights.

It has been pointed out that the philosophy behind this concept of rights and duties is based on the presumption that the full development of the individual is only possible where individuals care about how their action would affect others. Thus, in contrast with the Western conception of rights, which conceives rights in terms of abstract individualism without corresponding duties, the dominant African conception of human rights combines a system of rights and obligations, which gives the community cohesion and viability. This conception—that of the individual as a moral being endowed with rights but also bounded by duties actively uniting his needs with the needs of others—was the quintessence of the formulation of rights in precolonial African societies and can provide a fitting basis for the construction of national human rights regimes in contemporary African states.

These arguments for a peculiarly communal African concept of human rights, however, are confronted with their own theoretical and empirical limitations particularly in their relevance to the contemporary African societies. Rather than the persistence of traditional cultural values in the face of modern incursions, the reality in contemporary Africa—as it is in the rest of the developing world—is a situation of disruptive and incomplete westernization, "cultural confusion," or even the enthusiastic embrace of "modern" practices and values. In other words, the ideals of traditional culture and its community-centered values, advanced to justify arguments for the cultural relativism of human rights in the African context, far too often, no longer exists.

Although scholars have been at the forefront of exploring the cultural relativism of human rights in the African context, the assertion of "African values" gains prominence when it is articulated in the political rhetoric of African leaders and elites. It has been suggested that in asserting these values, leaders from the continent find that they have a convenient tool to silence internal criticism and to fan anti-Western nationalist sentiments. Some writers have even suggested that the picture of an idyllic traditional communitarian society, has been presented by African rulers and elite "from Kaunda to Nyerere" only to hide and rationalize their own unbridled violations of human rights. In the scathing words of Rhoda Howard (1990, 25; see also Howard 1984a,b):

> Some African intellectuals persist in presenting the communal model of social organization in Africa as if it were fact, and in maintaining that the group oriented, consensual, and re-distributive value system is the only value system and hence it ought to be the basis of a uniquely African model of human rights. These ideological denials of economic and political inequalities assist members of the African ruling class to stay in power.

In a similar vein, Donnelly has pointed out that arguments for the cultural relativism of human rights within the African context are far too often made by urban economic and political elites who have long left traditional culture behind. Their appeal to cultural practices is often a mere cloak for self-interest and arbitrary rule. In traditional cultures, communal customs and practices usually provided each person with a place in society and a certain amount of dignity and protection. Rulers on the continent have largely undermined this traditional protection such that the human rights violations of most African regimes are as antithetical to the cultural traditions that they idealize, as they are to the "Western" human rights conceptions that they despise. Donnelly (1984, 400) therefore cautions that:

> We must be alert to a cynical manipulation of a dying, lost or even mythical cultural past. We must not be misled by complaints of the inappropriateness of "western" human rights made by repressive regimes whose practices have at best only the most tenuous connection to the indigenous culture; communitarian rhetoric too often cloaks the depredations of corrupt and often westernized elite. In particular, we must be wary of self-interested denunciations of the excessive individualism of "western" human rights.

Howard and Donnelly are clearly, and perhaps quite justifiably suspicious of the political elite of African countries who use the constant references to communal society and the primacy of socioeconomic well-being over civil and political rights, to mask systematic violations of human rights in the interests of the ruling elite. . . .

## ■ The "African Cultural Fingerprint"

The second level of the Africanist discourse on the cultural relativism of human rights relates to the questions that have been raised over the validity and applicability to the African context, of modern human rights conceptions, as developed and interpreted in the West. In other words, even though the modern thrust and substance of human rights may have their philosophical roots in Western societies, are they definitely applicable to contemporary African states and societies?

Several Western liberal scholars contend that since all African countries have been or are modernizing on a western model which gives priority to the individual, the only conception of human rights which exists (i.e., the Western one) is of equal application to African societies whatever their historical antecedents or cultural circumstances may be. Some Africanists and proponents of cultural relativism have tended to agree with this. Edward Kannyo (1980), for instance, contends that to the extent that the Western model of the state has spread to other parts of the world, the factors which give rise to the need for constitutional guarantees and led to the evolution of the philosophy of human rights in the West have become equally relevant in other parts of the world.

Some Africanists, however, insist that in order to make it relevant to the circumstances in the continent, the content of universal human rights has to be tempered by specific African cultural experiences. Essentially, this means that the content of human rights has to bear what Mutua (1995) has described as the "African cultural fingerprint" which emphasizes the group, duties, social cohesion and communal solidarity as opposed to rigid individualism. This appears an eminently reasonable and practical approach to the issue for, indeed, one of the inadequacies of Western concepts and institutions uncritically adopted by most African states at the dawn of independence was that they borrowed little or nothing from the existing traditional norms and values. For this reason, some of these colonial-engineered concepts and institutions have continued to bear little or no relevance to the distinctive needs of the postcolonial African state. This situation calls for a regime of human rights founded on the basic universal human rights standards but enriched by the African cultural experience.

It needs to be emphasized, however, that there are substantive human rights limitations even in well-established cultural practices. Cultural practices which were acceptable in times past under different social and historical contexts cannot always be expected to conform with established modern human rights orientations. For example, while slavery and trials by ordeal have been customary in many societies in Africa as in other parts of the world, today these are cultural practices that cannot be justified on any grounds. The same applies to the practices of discrimination on the basis of sex, social status, caste or ethnic group, which were widely practiced, but are indefensible today. Yet, cultural relativism is a fact of human rights discourse and the peculiarities in cultural and ethical orientations invariably influence people's conception of rights and duties. For this reason, cultural differences may justify some deviations from universal human rights standards. However, cultural relativism must function as an expression and guarantee of local self-determination rather than as an excuse for arbitrary rule and despotism. Cultural derogation from universal human rights standards must be founded on an authentic cultural basis with adequate alternative constitutional and other legal provisions for guaranteeing basic human dignity where cultural orientations themselves fall short of these standards.

## ▓ Reconsidering the "Full Belly Thesis"

The third level of the argument in Africanist discourse on the cultural relativism of human rights stems from the tendency of some Africanists and African elites to stress the priority of social and economic rights over political and civil rights. The point of emphasis here is the Africanist angle to this debate that seeks to justify the curtailment of civil and political rights in the interest of the collective social and economic development within the context of the post-colonial state. Julius Nyerere, the former president of Tanzania puts this position across quite graphically when he asks:

> What freedom has our subsistence farmer? He scratches a bare existence from the soil provided the rains do not fail; his children work at his side without schooling, medical care or even good feeding. Certainly he has freedom to vote and to speak as he wishes. But these freedoms are much less real to him than his freedom to be exploited. Only as his poverty is reduced, will his existing political freedom become properly meaningful and his right to human dignity becomes a fact of human dignity. (quoted in Shivji 1989, 26)

Another African leader expressed a similar view when he opined that, "one man, one vote is meaningless unless accompanied by the principle of one man, one bread." The hub of these expressed sentiments is that given the peculiar constraints of poverty and underdevelopment in Africa, economic and social rights must take precedence over civil and political rights or the state-individual perspective that otherwise dominates Western notions of human rights. This argument is often advanced as part of the larger thesis on the relativity of human rights.

However, some Western liberal scholars in disagreement with this position have argued that political and civil rights are of as much significance as economic and social rights. They disagree with the argument that political and civil rights should wait until basic needs are secured, because civil and political rights are needed in order to implement reasonable development policies, to secure equitable distribution of wealth and promote economic growth. Civil and political rights are also needed to guarantee social and cultural rights and the maintenance of a stable social order necessary for society itself to exist. Howard (1984c, 467) has referred to the arguments for the primacy of economic rights by some Africanists as the "full belly thesis." This thesis is that a man's belly must be full before he can indulge in the "luxury" of worrying about his political freedoms.

The thesis is, however, in my opinion, a less than fair representation of the arguments of writers like Julius Nyerere. The reference point here is not so much a *full belly* as it is an *empty belly*. A man's belly need not be full for him to be concerned about his political and civil liberties, but it is important that it is not empty, either. Political and civil rights can best be guaranteed in a situation of relative economic and social stability where the people are guaranteed a basic level of well-being. This is particularly evident from the experiences in many post-colonial African states where the level of poverty is so severe and the standard of living so low that it often undermines the democratic electoral process. In some African countries, it has become common for poverty stricken rural voters to sell their votes for as little as a handful of salt or rice.

For this category of Africa's poorest, the need for immediate survival surpasses any other long-term political or civil rights considerations.

This, however, is not to suggest that political and civil rights are less significant than economic and social rights or that economic and social rights parameters should solely define the human rights aspirations of African states. The point being made is that the economic versus political rights debate in relation to Africa may not be quite as simplistic as Howard portrays it in her "full belly" thesis. The post-colonial African state manifests certain developmental limitations and other peculiar characteristics that must be taken into account in any study that seeks broad interpretations of the conditions and prospects for human rights in the continent. For one, it is useful to recognize that unlike in the West, the African state commands overwhelming power and influence which stands in rather marked distinction to the non-state sphere consisting of a largely undifferentiated and vulnerable peasantry. Under such circumstances, there are significant limitations to the level of political influence which civil society can or is in a position to wield without significant social and economic improvement.

At some point in the discourse, the arguments for and against the Africanist positions on the cultural relativism of human rights becomes something of a vicious circle, very much like the classical riddle of the chicken and the egg—which came first? Just as one may ask: Political rights and economic rights—which come first? Or: Individual rights and communal rights. Which should take precedence over the other? It is perhaps in the nature of the discourse that these questions will never be conclusively answered. Yet, as indicated earlier, one approach to addressing these questions would be to perceive human rights as a holistic and integrated concept in which civil, political, social, and economic rights constitute complementary aspects of the same broad concept. It is useful to realize that like individual and communal rights, both political rights and economic rights are interactive, interrelated and interdependent, not sequential.

An Afrocentric conception of human rights is a valid worldview. Its significance to the discourse on the cultural relativism of human rights, however, demands careful consideration. Rather than being the basis for abrogating or delegitimizing the emerging universal human rights regime, it should inform the cross-fertilization of ideas between Africa and the rest of the world. The present challenge for Africanist human rights scholars generally is to articulate for the international human rights community, an African sense of human rights or dignity, which flows from the African perspective, but one that the rest of the international community can also use. With the sanctity of Western individualist paradigms of human rights being increasingly questioned, the African sense of community obligation has much to offer the international discourse on human rights, particularly in the promotion of social and economic rights.

## ■ References

Cobbah, Josiah. 1987. "African Values and the Human Rights Debate: An African Perspective." *Human Rights Quarterly* 9, 3:309–331.

Donnelly, Jack. 1982. "Human Rights and Human Dignity: An Analytic Critique of Non-Western Human Rights Conceptions." *American Political Science Review* 76:303–316.

———. 1984. "Cultural Relativism and Universal Human Rights." *Human Rights Quarterly* 6, 4:400–419.

Eze, Osita C. 1993. "Is the Protection of Human Rights and Democracy Strange to African Traditions?" In *Human Rights and Democracy in Africa*, ed. Tunji Abayomi. Lagos: Human Rights Africa.

Howard, Rhoda. 1984a. "Is There an African Concept of Human Rights?" In *Foreign Policy and Human Rights: Issues and Responses,* ed. R.J. Vincent. Cambridge: Cambridge University Press.

———. 1984b. "Evaluating Human Rights in Africa: Some Problems of Implicit Comparisons." *Human Rights Quarterly* 6:160–179.

———. 1984c. "The Full Belly Thesis: Should Economic Rights Take Priority over Civil and Political Rights? Evidence from Sub-Saharan Africa." *Human Rights Quarterly* 5, 4:467–490.

———. 1990. *Human Rights in Commonwealth Africa*. Totowa, N.J.: Rowman and Littlefield.

Kannyo, Edward. 1980. *Human Rights in Africa: Problems and Prospects: A Report Prepared for the International League of Human Rights*. New York: The League.

Khasualani, Yougindra. 1983. "Human Rights in Asia and Africa." *Human Rights Law Journal* 14, 4:403–442.

Mutua, Makau. 1995. "The Banjul Charter and the African Cultural Fingerprint: An Evaluation of the Language of Rights and Duties." *Virginia Journal of International Law* 35, 2:339–380.

Quashigah, Kofi. 1991. "The Philosophical Basis of Human Rights and Its Relation to Africa." *Journal of Human Rights Law and Practice* (Lagos) 1–2.

Shivji, Issa. 1989. *The Concept of Human Rights in Africa*. Dakar: Codesria Book Series.

# 5 Witness to Torture

## 5.1

# Introduction
*The Editors*

Perhaps the most poignant human rights violation is that of torture or the violation of human security. Torture not only violates the individual in question, but institutes a system of constant fear within society. Its prevalence has been documented throughout history, and instances of systemic torture still exist today. In response, the international community addressed this particular violation within the UDHR and subsequent covenants. However, the tireless work of Amnesty International and other NGOs (nongovernmental organizations) led the way to the passage of an additional document, the *Convention Against Torture and Other Cruel, Inhuman or Degrading Treatment or Punishment* in 1984, highlighting the importance of addressing this particular issue in a separate campaign.

The ultimate form of torture is genocide. Modern examples of systematic torture can be found in Nazi Germany and during Pol Pot's reign in Cambodia. Both required that a certain amount of secrecy take place. For the Nazis, the removal of individuals to camps effectively removed the torture from the eyes and minds of the populace at large. Miklos Nyiszli, a Holocaust survivor, recounts the torture experienced at the hands of the Nazis at Auschwitz. As a doctor, Nyiszli was spared the gas chambers, only to bear witness to the horror of those led to their deaths upon arrival at Auschwitz. Nyiszli also recounts the atrocities committed at the hands of Dr. Josef Mengele, who used victims in the camps in lab experiments. In Cambodia, the expulsion of Westerners and journalists isolated the society from the rest of the world. In both instances, we see the state attempt to take complete control of political ideas. In an excerpt from *A Cambodian Odyssey*, Haing Ngor tells the story of his harrowing escape from the brutal Pol Pot regime. As with the previous testimonies, Ngor provides compelling evidence of the horrors of living with torture.

The prevalence of torture in authoritarian regimes such as Nazi Germany and Pol Pot's Cambodia, while never acceptable, is nevertheless often the norm. Bobby Sands provides a startling testimonial of imprisonment and torture in a democratic regime. Jailed in Northern Ireland during the 1980s, Sands recounts his treatment at the hands of the British. He describes the inhumanity of his imprisonment and his vulnerability at the hands of the guards. His account is an important reminder of what democratic regimes are capable of if human rights are not vigilantly guarded.

Images of Nazi-like camps were brought back into focus during the wars in the Balkans in the 1990s. In excerpts from *The Tenth Circle of Hell*, Rezak Hukanović relays his experience at Omarska, a notorious camp policed by the Serbian army. Here, the author employs a third-person narrative to describe the beatings and starvation that took place. Like Bobby Sands, the author provides not only a testimonial to torture, but also insight into the mind of the victim.

Finally, Jean Hatzfeld gives the reader a view of torture from the perpetrator's perspective. The Rwandan genocide in 1994 claimed over 800,000 lives and was carried out not by a trained and organized military, but by everyday citizens, primarily farmers, who took their machetes and became manhunters. Hatzfeld interviewed several participants who spoke frankly and openly about their experience, including their first kill; what it was like to kill a friend, woman, or even a child; as well as their remorse and regret.

Each of these pieces provides a harrowing account of the reality of state repression, which continues to be violated on a widespread basis today. In each case, the iniquitous actions of the state result in individuals being denied their fundamental personal integrity rights.

# 5.2

# Auschwitz:
# A Doctor's Eyewitness Account
*Miklos Nyiszli*

The strident whistle of a train was heard coming from the direction of the unloading platform. It was still very early. I approached my window, from which I had a direct view onto the tracks, and saw a very long train. A few seconds later the doors slid open and the box cars spilled out thousands upon thousands of the chosen people of Israel. Line up and selection took scarcely half an hour. . . .

Then they advanced for about 100 yards along a cinder path edged with green grass to an iron ramp, from which 10 or 12 concrete steps led underground to an enormous room dominated by a large sign in German, French, Greek and Hungarian: "Baths and Disinfecting Room." The sign was reassuring, and allayed the misgivings or fears of even the most suspicious among them. They went down the stairs almost gaily.

The room into which the convoy proceeded was about 200 yards long: its walls were whitewashed and it was brightly lit. In the middle of the room, rows of columns. Around the columns, as well as along the walls, benches. Above the benches, numbered coat hangers. Numerous signs in several languages drew everyone's attention to the necessity of tying his clothes and shoes together. Especially that he not forget the number of his coat hanger, in order to avoid all useless confusion upon his return from the bath.

"That's really a German order," commented those who had long been inclined to admire the Germans.

They were right. As a matter of fact, it *was* for the sake of order that these measures had been taken, so that the thousands of pairs of good shoes sorely needed by the Third Reich would not get mixed up. The same for the clothes, so that the population of bombed cities could easily make use of them.

There were 3,000 people in the room: men, women and children. Some of the soldiers arrived and announced that everyone must be completely undressed within ten minutes. The aged, grandfathers and grandmothers; the children; wives and husbands; all were struck dumb with surprise. Modest women and girls looked at each other questioningly. Perhaps they had not

Excerpted from *Auschwitz: A Doctor's Eyewitness Account.* © 1960 by N. Margareta Nyiszli; translation © 1993 by Richard Seaver. Reprinted from Miklos Nyiszli, *Auschwitz* (New York: Arcade Publishing).

exactly understood the German words. They did not have long to think about it, however, for the order resounded again, this time in a louder, more menacing tone. They were uneasy; their dignity rebelled; but, with the resignation peculiar to their race, having learned that anything went as far as they were concerned, they slowly began to undress. The aged, the paralyzed, the mad were helped by a Sonderkommando squad sent for that purpose. In ten minutes all were completely naked, their clothes hung on the pegs, their shoes attached together by the laces. As for the number of each clothes hanger, it had been carefully noted. . . .

At that very instant the sound of a car was heard: a deluxe model, furnished by the International Red Cross. An SS officer and an SDG (*Sanitätsdienstgefreiter:* Deputy Health Service Officer) stepped out of the car. The Deputy Health Officer held four green sheet-iron canisters. He advanced across the grass, where, every thirty yards, short concrete pipes jutted up from the ground. Having donned his gas mask, he lifted the lid of the pipe, which was also made of concrete. He opened one of the cans and poured the contents—a mauve granulated material—into the opening. The granulated substance fell in a lump to the bottom. The gas it produced escaped through the perforations, and within a few seconds filled the room in which the deportees were stacked. Within five minutes everybody was dead.

For every convoy it was the same story. Red Cross cars brought the gas from the outside. There was never a stock of it in the crematorium. The precaution was scandalous, but still more scandalous was the fact that the gas was brought in a car bearing the insignia of the International Red Cross.

In order to be certain of their business the two gas-butchers waited another five minutes. Then they lighted cigarettes and drove off in their car. They had just killed 3,000 innocents. . . .

The bodies were not lying here and there throughout the room, but piled in a mass to the ceiling. The reason for this was that the gas first inundated the lower layers of air and rose but slowly towards the ceiling. This forced the victims to trample one another in a frantic effort to escape the gas. Yet a few feet higher up the gas reached them. What a struggle for life there must have been! Nevertheless it was merely a matter of two or three minutes' respite. If they had been able to think about what they were doing, they would have realized they were trampling their own children, their wives, their relatives. But they couldn't think. Their gestures were no more than the reflexes of the instinct of self-preservation. I noticed that the bodies of the women, the children, and the aged were at the bottom of the pile; at the top, the strongest. Their bodies, which were covered with scratches and bruises from the struggle which had set them against each other, were often interlaced. Blood oozed from their noses and mouths; their faces, bloated and blue, were so deformed as to be almost unrecognizable. Nevertheless some of the Sonderkommando often did recognize their kin. The encounter was not easy, and I dreaded it for myself. I had no reason to be here, and yet I had come down among the dead. I felt it my duty to my people and to the entire world to be able to give an accurate account of what I had seen if ever, by some miraculous whim of fate, I should escape.

The Sonderkommando squad, outfitted with large rubber boots, lined up around the hill of bodies and flooded it with powerful jets of water. This was necessary because the final act of those who die by drowning or by gas is an involuntary defecation. Each body was befouled, and had to be washed. Once the "bathing" of the dead was finished—a job the Sonderkommando carried out by a voluntary act of impersonalization and in a state of profound distress—the separation of the welter of bodies began. It was a difficult job. They knotted thongs around the wrists, which were clenched in a vise-like grip, and with these thongs they dragged the slippery bodies to the elevators in the next room. Four good-sized elevators were functioning. They loaded twenty to twenty-five corpses to an elevator. The ring of a bell was the signal that the load was ready to ascend. The elevator stopped at the crematorium's incineration room, where large sliding doors opened automatically. The kommando who operated the trailers was ready and waiting. Again straps were fixed to the wrists of the dead, and they were dragged onto specially constructed chutes which unloaded them in front of the furnaces.

The bodies lay in close ranks: the old, the young, the children. Blood oozed from their noses and mouths, as well as from their skin—abraded by the rubbing—and mixed with the water running in the gutters set in the concrete floor. . . .

When the convoys arrived, soldiers scouted the ranks lined up before the box cars, hunting for twins and dwarfs. Mothers, hoping for special treatment for their twin children, readily gave them up to the scouts. Adult twins, knowing that they were of interest from a scientific point of view, voluntarily presented themselves, in the hope of better treatment. The same for dwarfs.

They were separated from the rest and herded to the right. They were allowed to keep their civilian clothes; guards accompanied them to specially designed barracks, where they were treated with a certain regard. Their food was good, their bunks were comfortable, and possibilities for hygiene were provided. . . .

The experiments, in medical language called *in vivo*, *i.e.*, experiments performed on live human beings, were far from exhausting the research possibilities in the study of twins. Full of lacunae, they offered no better than partial results. The *in vivo* experiments were succeeded by the most important phase of twin-study: the comparative examination from the viewpoints of anatomy and pathology. Here it was a question of comparing the twins' healthy organs with those functioning abnormally, or of comparing their illnesses. For that study, as for all studies of a pathological nature, corpses were needed. Since it was necessary to perform a dissection for the simultaneous evaluation of anomalies, the twins had to die at the same time. So it was that they met their death in the B section of one of Auschwitz's KZ barracks, at the hand of Dr. Mengele.

This phenomenon was unique in world medical science history. Twin brothers died together, and it was possible to perform autopsies on both. Where, under normal circumstances, can one find twin brothers who die at the same place and at the same time? For twins, like everyone else, are separated by life's varying circumstances. They live far from each other and almost never die simultaneously. One may die at the age of ten, the other at fifty. Under such conditions comparative dissection is impossible. In the Auschwitz camp, however, there were several hundred sets of twins, and therefore as many possibilities of dissection. That was why, on the arrival platform, Dr. Mengele separated twins and dwarfs from the other prisoners. That was why both special groups were directed to the right-hand column, and thence to the barracks of the spared. That was why they had good food and hygienic living conditions, so that they didn't contaminate each other and die one before the other. They had to die together, and in good health. . . .

I began the dissection of one set of twins and recorded each phase of my work. I removed the brain pan. Together with the cerebellum I extracted the brain and examined them. Then followed the opening of the thorax and the removal of the sternum. Next I separated the tongue by means of an incision made beneath the chin. With the tongue came the esophagus, with the respiratory tracts came both lungs. I washed the organs in order to examine them more thoroughly. The tiniest spot or the slightest difference in color could furnish valuable information. I made a transverse incision across the pericardium and removed the fluid. Next I took out the heart and washed it. I turned it over and over in my hand to examine it.

In the exterior coat of the left ventricle was a small pale red spot caused by a hypodermic injection, which scarcely differed from the color of the tissue around it. There could be no mistake. The injection had been given with a very small needle. Without a doubt a hypodermic needle. For what purpose had he received the injection? Injections into the heart can be administered in extremely serious cases, when the heart begins to fail. I would soon know. I opened the heart, starting with the ventricle. Normally the blood contained in the left ventricle is taken out and weighed. This method could not be employed in the present case, because the blood was coagulated into a compact mass. I extracted the coagulum with the forceps and brought it to my nose. I was struck by the characteristic order of chloroform. The victim had received an injection of chloroform in the heart, so that the blood of the ventricle, in coagulating, would deposit on the valves and cause instantaneous death by heart failure.

My discovery of the most monstrous secret of the Third Reich's medical science made my knees tremble. Not only did they kill with gas, but also with injections of chloroform into the heart. A cold sweat broke out on my forehead.

Luckily I was alone. If others had been present it would have been difficult for me to conceal my excitement. I finished the dissection, noted the differences found, and recorded them. But the chloroform, the blood coagulated in the left ventricle, the puncture visible in the external coat of the heart, did not figure among my findings. It was a useful precaution on my part. Dr. Mengele's records on the subject of twins were in my hands. They contained the exact examinations, X-rays, the artist's sketches already mentioned, but neither the circumstances nor causes of death. Nor did I fill out that column of the dissection report. It was not a good idea to exceed the authorized bounds of knowledge or to relate all one had witnessed. And here still less than anywhere else. I was not timorous by nature and my nerves were good. During my medical practice I had often brought to light the causes of death. I had seen the bodies of people assassinated for motives of revenge, jealousy, or material gain, as well as those of suicides and natural deaths. I was used to the study of well-hidden causes of death. On several occasions I had been shocked by my discoveries, but now a shudder of fear ran through me. If Dr. Mengele had any idea that I had discovered the secret of his injections he would send ten doctors, in the name of the political SS, to attest to my death.

In accordance with orders received I returned the corpses to the prisoners whose duty it was to burn them. They performed their job without delay. I had to keep any organs of possible scientific interest, so that Dr. Mengele could examine them. Those which might interest the Anthropological Institute at Berlin-Dahlem were preserved in alcohol. These parts were specially packed to be sent through the mails. Stamped "War Material—Urgent," they were given top priority in transit. In the course of my work at the crematorium I dispatched an impressive number of such packages. I received, in reply, either precise scientific observations or instructions. In order to classify this correspondence I had to set up special files. The directors of the Berlin-Dahlem Institute always warmly thanked Dr. Mengele for this rare and precious material.

# 5.3

# A Cambodian Odyssey

*Haing Ngor*

We had walked for only an hour when three Khmer Rouge stopped us. They were children, maybe ten years old. "Angka says no more traveling!" the soldiers said crossly. "Whatever village you are trying to reach, they are all destroyed. So you have to stop here and go to work."

They led us to a village on the edge of the jungle, and in the morning Huoy and I were ordered to work in a rock quarry. The supervisor issued us ordinary hammers, took us to piles of fist-size rocks and told us to break them into gravel. Chips shattered off the rocks when we hit them, flying into our hands and faces. There was no shade on the mountain, and it was very hot.

In the early afternoon they gave us our first meal of the day, a bowl of salted rice porridge. "Angka is poor, so you must sacrifice for your nation," the supervisor explained. "We just got free from the capitalist oppressors, and now we are starting to rebuild the nation."

I looked at my capitalist hands, blisters across my palms and fingers. Huoy's blisters were even worse. As a schoolteacher she had never had to hold more than a piece of chalk. That morning, as Huoy broke rocks, she wept quietly. She was not crying because of the hard work; our universe had been turned upside down. . . .

The Khmer Rouge made us go to *bonns*, an ancient religious word meaning ceremonies at a temple. These bonns were held at night, usually in some mosquito-infested clearing in the forest. They were brain-washing sessions at which we were lectured on the glorious rule of Angka.

At one bonn, a man stepped forward from a line of cadre dressed in the usual black, with red headbands and *kramas* (Cambodian all-purpose scarves) tied like sashes about their waists. "We don't need capitalist technology," he said. "Under our new system, we don't need schools. Our school is the farm. The land is our paper. The plow is our pen."

"We don't need any of the capitalist professions anymore," he went on. "We don't need engineers, and we don't need doctors. If someone has to have his intestines removed, I will do it." He made a cutting motion with an imag-

Excerpted from Haing Ngor, *A Cambodian Odyssey* (Macmillan, 1987). Reprinted with permission of the author's estate, Roger Warner, and the Joy Harris Literary Agency, 156 Fifth Ave., Suite 617, New York, NY 10010.

inary knife across his stomach. "All we need are people who want to work hard on the farm!

"And yet, comrades," he said, looking around at our faces, "there are some troublemakers who do not show the proper revolutionary mentality. Such people are our enemies, and some are right here in our midst!" There was uneasy shifting in the audience.

"These people cling to the old capitalist ways and the old capitalist fashions. We have some among us who still wear eyeglasses. They wear them to be handsome in the capitalist way; because they are vain. These people are leeches sucking energy from others!"

I took off my glasses and put them in my pocket. Around me, others with glasses did the same. My eyesight wasn't too bad; I was just a little nearsighted. I could still recognize people. . . .

I went to work in a rice field. Two teen-age soldiers took us men to paddies where there were eight wooden plows and three or four oxen by a hillock. "We don't have enough oxen," one soldier told us.

*Oh no*, I said to myself. *Are they going to use human beings?*

The soldier held a long whip of plaited leather in his hand, "You," he said, "go to the plow. You too, and you." He pointed at me.

I walked over to the plows and stood in back of the crosspiece. On my left stood an old female ox.

"Now go," said the soldier, cracking his whip overhead.

Struggling to keep up with the ox, I kept pushing, but the wooden crosspiece was too high. Reaching up to it strained my shoulders and back. Blisters had formed on my hands from previous work and I could feel them pop open and the fluid running out.

"Faster, faster," came the soldier's voice behind me.

SNAP! A searing pain across my back. "Hey," I yelled angrily. "Let me rest; then I can go back to working."

"Finish the field and then rest," the soldier replied. A woman in the next field was standing absolutely still, her hand clasped across her mouth as if she were trying to stop herself from screaming. It was Huoy.

That night she put a hot compress on the whip welts that curved over my shoulders and neck to the top of my chest. She was crying. "Today I prayed to my mother to take us with her," she said. "The Khmer Rouge should just kill us now and get it over with."

## ■ Be Strong in Your Mind

My normal weight dropped from 140 pounds to about 115 pounds. I began having to excuse myself while plowing. At first, I thought it was ordinary diarrhea, but when I noticed mucus and later dark, purplish blood, I knew I was very sick.

I wasn't the only one. In Phum Chhleav more people were sick than healthy. The hard work, unsanitary conditions and near absence of medicine caused illness on a scale I had never seen before in all my medical training.

The greatest factor in this public-health disaster was malnutrition. The Khmer Rouge fed us a bowl of salty broth with a few spoonfuls of rice at the bottom for lunch, and the same for dinner. That was all. They didn't allow us to gather wild foods for our private meals, though sometimes we did anyway. Without proper nutrition, we weakened.

By the time I got amoebic dysentery, I had used up all my medicines treating others who had been sick before me. Huoy went out to get medicine, but for more than an ounce of gold, which she kept hidden in a hip pocket, she found only a handful of tetracycline tablets. To supplement the tetracycline, Huoy made me a tea out of guava leaves and bark—an old folk remedy.

I was long past feeling any shame about my dysentery, even though it is an ugly and humiliating disease. Huoy bathed me day and night. She cooked the little bit of rice we had and fed it to me a spoonful at a time, with my head in her lap.

By the 30th day, my weight was down to 70 pounds, but some deep intuition told me I was going to outlast the infection. However, the next day something changed. I took my pulse; my heart was slowing down. In a few hours it would stop. I told Huoy, "I think I am going to die. Please, bring my father."

Papa looked down at me with his wrinkled face. He told me I wasn't going to die. But he went outside and set candles and incense on the ground under the mango tree and prayed. Mama knelt beside him, old and gray.

Huoy sat next to me, tears rolling down her cheeks. "Keep being strong in your mind," she said, "and you will never die." Suddenly there was a sound of footsteps and a big loud voice. "Come get your yams! One person from every family. Come get your rations!"

I lay back and begin thinking: yams are basically carbohydrate. Put in a fire, they turn into charcoal. Eating carbon from burned food sometimes cures diarrhea by trapping gases and reducing symptoms, while occasionally acting on the infectious agent itself.

When Huoy returned, she had one fist-size yam. She was looking at it with a glazed, intent expression. How long had it been since she had eaten a real meal? Two weeks? Three? She had been feeding almost everything to me.

I told her to put the yam in the fire, and to take it out when it was black all the way through. Then, despite her own hunger, she fed the yam to me in small pieces.

Soon, I felt stronger. The yam had helped turn the tide. After a week, Huoy helped me to walk. The 50 yards to the railroad track became my goal, and when I finally made it, I was tired but triumphant. Huoy was happy and smiling. We talked as we had in the old days, calling each other "Sweet." . . .

One day, about a month after we got to the front lines, Huoy and I were resting in our hammock. The next thing we knew, two boys were looking down at us.

"Angka wants to see you!" they shouted. "Hurry!"

I did not struggle when they tied me up. "I'll be back," I told Huoy.

The soldiers led me through the woods. My arms grew numb from the tight cords around my elbows, but I wasn't worried. Foraging for food was the worst they could accuse me of. We finally stopped at a collection of buildings in a clearing. The soldiers told me to wait.

In an hour a prison guard led me to a large grove of mango trees. At the base of each tree sat a prisoner, tied to the trunk. I could see that many of them had been brutalized and were suffering terribly. The guard loosened the rope around my elbows and tied a longer rope to my wrists and then around the tree trunk. I sat with my back to the mango tree and began to pray.

Something crawled onto my neck. Then it bit. Red ants! I twisted my head from side to side to try to crush them. More ants crawled onto my shoulder. They were coming down the tree. A lot of them were on me now, biting my scalp, my shoulders, my chest. I strained against the ropes, scratching and moving my feet in a frenzy, unable to move enough to crush them. The more I struggled, the more they swarmed over me.

When the afternoon sun had sunk below the tree branches, a sturdily built man walked into the mango grove. He wore new black clothes, black rubber-tire sandals and a wristwatch, and he carried a hatchet. He came over to me, demanding to know whether I was Vietnamese or Chinese. I said I was neither.

"What did you do before? Were you a soldier?"

"Taxi driver."

"*No!*" he roared. "You were not a taxi driver. I can tell you are *lying!*"

"I am telling you the truth, comrade," I insisted.

He called out for someone else, who arrived quickly. They tightened the rope, and pushed me over on my side. While the second one held my neck down in the dirt, the burly one put my hand on top of a mango tree root, then stepped on my wrist with his foot. He dropped down and swung the hatchet. There was an excruciating pain in my little finger, exploding into my brain.

"Why don't we cut off a toe?" asked the second man. "We shouldn't let him walk."

"Right," said the burly man. "Hold his leg." He swung the hatchet at my right ankle, laying bare the bone underneath. Then they left.

I could see my ankle, the white bone gleaming in the middle of the wound, the flesh red and bleeding around the edges. I tried to wiggle my little finger and, even with the general pain, knew that the fingertip wasn't there anymore. Drawn to the blood, red ants swarmed over my hand and bit like hot needles.

Of the late afternoon and sunset I remember little. My ankle hurt. My finger throbbed. It was a long, long night. The next afternoon two guards untied me from the tree and jerked me to my feet.

We left the prison by the same footpath I had entered. Every time I stepped on my right foot the pain flashed up to my hip. I knew they weren't simply going to let me go; this was part of the torture, to let me think I was going to get away.

"Stop here!"

I stopped. They kicked me from behind and I fell.

"Do you want to go home?"

"Yes," I said. "If you allow me to go, I will. But if you don't allow me, if you kill me, it's up to you."

They removed the rope. Apparently I had given the right answer. I had told them they had the power of life and death over me. "Don't look back," they said. "Just keep on walking. Go home."

## ▇ The King of Death

They gave me time off from work to recover from my injuries and, as before, Huoy proved a perfect nurse. I tried not to think about my experiences in prison.

But a few weeks later they came for me again. Just like before, they tied my elbows, kicked me, and marched me away in front of hundreds of people. Huoy was hysterical.

In Cambodian folk religion the King of Death is a judge from whom nothing is hidden. The souls he sends to hell become the victims of everlasting tortures. After spending the night in a prison building, chained and sleepless, I was brought before the King of Death. He wore a green Mao cap and Vietnamese rubber-tire sandals.

"Angka knows who you are," the King of Death began gently. "You were a military doctor. You held the rank of captain. So please, tell Angka the truth. Make it easier on yourself."

"Good comrade," I said, "I was not a captain, or a doctor. I was a taxi driver."

"You are a liar," the judge answered calmly. "Tell Angka the truth, and Angka will give you an excellent job. You are an educated person. You can help the country build its independence-sovereignty."

"Comrade if I were a doctor, I would tell you. I want to help Angka."

BAM! The kick came to my ribs. I fell over on my side and arched in agony. The guards took turns kicking me. Finally the judge rapped on the table and they dragged me away by the legs.

Later the guards led a group of us into a field, where we saw a double line of wooden structures with uprights and crosspieces, like soccer goal posts, except narrower and higher. On the ground in the middle of each was a pile of wood and rice hulls and a wooden cross with a length of rope.

Prisoners were tied to the crosses, the weight of their bodies sagging against the ropes. The upright crosses hung from the goal-post crossbars. Smoke and flames rose from the fires at the prisoners' feet.

I thought, *I hope Huoy never knows about this.* As the soldiers tied me to the cross, I fought them and shouted, "Just shoot! Get it over with!"

They hoisted me up until my feet swayed above the pile of wood and rice hulls, and then they lit the rice hulls with a cigarette lighter.

Rice hulls have a consistency like sawdust, and burn slowly, for days. Some who had been crucified longer had already died of starvation or thirst— generally women, heads dropped against their chests, bodies sagging heavily against the ropes. Beneath them the fires smoldered.

The weight of my body dragged down on the ropes around my arms and legs. My feet and my fingers were numb. Iridescent green flies settled on my back where the skin was bleeding from the beating. Gradually the fire spread below the surface of the rice hulls to the wood. There were no flames, but there was a new smell. My feet must have been burning, but I could not feel them.

The moon rose silent and calm above the trees. Then the wind picked up, stirring the treetops, and the coals glowed and the fire grew hotter. The crucified hung like strange butchered animals from the crosses under the nearly full moon.

*You gods,* I prayed, *any gods who can hear. Jesus. Allah, Buddha. Spirits of the forests. Spirits of my ancestors, hear me. Spirits of the wind, if the gods cannot hear, carry the news to them. Tell them what is happening. Please, gods, do not punish Huoy. She is innocent. Do not let her know I am one of the damned. I am in hell. And I do not know why.*

In the morning the guards took down those who had been crucified before us and who were still alive; these prisoners were then questioned. Next the guards tied plastic bags over their heads, and the prisoners began kicking spastically. I was too weak to care. What was left of me was a core—a heart that beat in my chest, and a brain that prayed.

After four days and four nights with no food or water they untied the ropes and let me down. The circulation returning to my arms and legs brought a pain that was worse than the numbness and hotter than the fire. I fell over on my back and didn't move.

"Are you a doctor?" a faraway voice asked. "A captain?"

I tried to form words, but my lips wouldn't work. Finally I whispered, "No. Just *shoot*," I told them. "I will be happy to die. Just shoot."

They tied a plastic bag over my head. I couldn't see anything, and when I tried to breathe, there was no air. I went wild, my feet kicking. Then they pulled the bag off and I took great gasping lungfuls of air.

Time passed. Five minutes, or five hours. I did not know the difference. A rubber-tire sandal shoved my shoulder. "This one isn't dead yet. Give him some water."

Two months later, I was released. When Huoy saw me, she wept with happiness. Then when I came closer, she sobbed and would not stop. The neighbors gathered around, silent. They boiled water, and helped Huoy to clean me. They brought gifts of medicine, a capsule of ampicillin, a couple of aspirin, some herbs. Most of them were crying, because they knew that what had happened to me could happen to them.

# 5.4

# One Day in My Life
*Bobby Sands*

I heard the rattle of the trolley and I knew breakfast was coming, and still no blankets or mattress. Don't forget to see which screws are on the wing today, when the door opens, I remind myself. We could do with a few quiet screws . . . I thought, as the cell door opened and two orderlies with sneers on their freshly washed faces planted the morning offering right into my hands—mug of tea in one hand and a bowl of porridge with two slices of bread lying on top of it in my other hand. A little rat-faced figure with a black hat poked his head round the open door he was leaning against and wearing a smirk said, 'Good morning! Would you care to put on the prison clothing and go to work, clean your cell, wash yourself or polish your boots? . . .

'You wouldn't! Ah well, we'll see after!'

The door slammed shut.

'Bastard,' I said, retreating to the corner to inspect the second catastrophe of the day—the breakfast. I salvaged whatever dry bit of bread I could, and having fished the two slices from the soggy porridge I threw the remainder, porridge and all, against the far wall. Disgusted, I literally forced the meagre bit of bread and lukewarm tea into me. It was bitter cold, so cold that in between sips of tea I had to keep pacing the floor. I thought of the three screws who had stood outside the door while I received my breakfast. Warders 'A—', 'B—', and 'C—'. That was all I needed. Three out-and-out torture-mongers and they'd be here all day. Bloody marvelous, I thought.

The screw who had just spoken to me was 'A—'. He was heartless, sly and intelligent when it came to torturing naked men. There was no physical stuff from him. All purely psychological attacks and cunning tricks. He was a right-out-of-Belsen type, and like the majority of the screws he took great pleasure in attacking the dignity of the naked Prisoners-of-War. He was on a constant ego trip, but then weren't they all once they donned their little black suits with the shining buttons, and were handed their baton and pistol?

The second screw that I had seen was 'B—', a sectarian bigot. He was of medium build, black hair, good looking and all go. He was also an alcoholic and handy with his baton, especially on the younger lads, and that was a regular practice of his.

The remaining screw, and perhaps the worst of the three, was 'C—'. He hated us more than 'B—' the bigot, and he constantly went out of his way to prove it. He never smiled, never spoke unless to make a derogatory remark or hurl abuse. He carried an extra large chip on his shoulder, which we had to bear.

Three perfect bastards, I thought, and I cursed the cold, my aching body and the pangs of hunger that never left me. . . .

How much must we suffer, I thought. An unwashed body, naked and wrecked with muscular pain, squatting in a corner, in a den of disease, amid piles of putrifying rubbish, forced to defecate upon the ground where the excreta would lie and the smell would mingle with the already sickening evil stench of urine and decaying waste food. Let them find a name for that sort of torture, I thought, rising and moving towards the window to seek fresh air, the beatings, the hosing-downs, starvation and deprivation, just let them bloody well put a name on this nightmare of nightmares. . . .

I was very tired, becoming easily exhausted, not having had exercise or fresh air for so long, and I was bored stiff. The thought of my afternoon visit left me barely able to think. But there is always someone worse off than yourself, I told myself, remembering only too well my dead comrades and their families.

'At least I can see you once a month,' my mother would say. 'Better where you are than Milltown Cemetery.'

But then there were times when Milltown would have been the preferable alternative when things became so unbearable that you just couldn't care less whether you lived or died just as long as you could escape the hellish nightmare. Aren't we dying anyway, I thought. Aren't our bodies degenerating to a standstill? I am a living corpse now. What will I be like in six months' time? Will I even be alive after another year? I used to worry about that, churning it around in my mind for hours on end. But no more! Because that is the only thing left that they can do to me: kill me. I have known this for some time and God knows that it isn't for the want of trying that they haven't achieved that on some one of us yet! But I am determined that I shall never give up. They can do what they will with me but I will never bow to them or allow them to criminalise me.

I find it startling to hear myself say that I am prepared to die first rather than succumb to their oppressive torture and I know that I am not on my own, that many of my comrades hold the same. And I thought of my dead comrades again. My friends who had stood beside me one day and were dead the next. Boys and girls just like myself, born and raised in the nationalist ghettos of Belfast to be murdered by foreign soldiers and lecky sectarian thugs. How many have been murdered at their hands throughout the occupied Six Counties. Too many! One boy or girl was one too many! How many more Irish people would die? How many more lives would be lost before the British had decided they had murdered enough and were forced to get out of Ireland forever? Inside and outside of gaol it was all the same—oppression bearing down upon you from every direction. Every street corner displaying an armed British soldier, every street having endured its share of suffering and grief at their hands.

I was proud to be resisting, to be fighting back. They couldn't defeat us outside; they are torturing us unmercifully inside their hell-holes and have failed to defeat us again. I was frightened but I knew I would never give up. I would face the imperial might of their entire torturous arsenal rather than succumb. . . .

The punishment block stood for torture, brutality and inhumanity. Even the screws knew it but would not say. I spent three days there a few months ago—three of the longest and most unbearable days of my entire life. The screws removed me from my cell naked and I was conveyed to the punishment block in a blacked-out van. As I stepped out of the van on arrival there they grabbed me from all sides and began punching and kicking me to the ground. Not one single word had been spoken, not even so much as a threat. I was a Republican blanket-man and that was all the go-ahead that was needed. I barely realised what had occurred or what was happening as they dragged me by the hair across a stretch of hard core rubble to the gate of the punishment block. One of them rang the bell to summon the screw inside to come out and open the gate to admit them. I lay at their feet, dazed, shocked and panting for breath. My heart was pounding and my body felt like it was on fire, torn to ribbons by the rough concrete that had cut and hacked at my naked skin. My face was warm and wet from the blood spurting from a gash on my head. I lay stock still, playing 'possum, hoping they'd be content thinking that I was unconscious. My cheek rested upon the cold hard black surface but my body was unaware of the biting cold. I mumbled a 'Hail Mary' to myself and a hurried 'Act of Contrition' as I heard the approaching jingle of keys. Several gloved hands gripped and tightened around my arms and feet raising my body off the ground and swinging me backwards in the one movement. The full weight of my body recoiled forward again, smashing my head against the corrugated iron covering around the gate. The sky seemed to fall upon me as they dropped me to the ground. The second impact sent a mass of tiny white stars exploding in front of my eyes like a fireworks display that suddenly became extinguished by a cloud of inky blackness. I regained consciousness lying on the floor of one of the cells in the punishment block.

I opened my eyes. My head was reeling. The bright light in the ceiling spiralled downwards and blinded me. The pain in my head was enormous and sickening. My whole body was seized by crippling pains and aches. I lay transfixed to the ground, afraid to move, the taste of blood on my swollen lips, fighting to work out where I was and what had happened. The concrete floor was intensely cold and I knew I would have to get off it or pay the consequences of perhaps pneumonia later. I rose slowly to my knees first. The walls came hurtling towards me. I fell. After an eternity I tried again though spasms of pain almost rendered my body useless. I made it to my knees. My skin was burning as the raw flesh from the mass of cuts and scrapes clung to the cold floor. I got up. I made it to my feet. I almost fell again but with the aid of the wall I staggered to the concrete block that served as a stool and slumped upon it. I felt as if I were dying. I was so distracted by pain and shock that I didn't know what to do. I simply couldn't think. The slightest movement of my body sent me shivering and gasping in agony. I was on the point of screaming out when the cell door opened revealing a white-coated figure of an orderly who stepped into the cell. The glorified screw with the white coat began to examine me, fiddling about my body, poking and probing, imitating the antics of a doctor, trying to impress the audience of screws who stood around the entrance of the cell.

Having made his observations, or whatever he had done, he arrogantly informed me that to see the doctor and receive treatment I would firstly have to bathe. I glared at him in disbelief. He repeated what he had said only in a sterner threatening voice. He knew what he was doing. He knew I was hurt and in need of immediate attention, but he was putting me under duress, holding me to ransom. No bath—no treatment. Besides, I was so sore I could barely move let alone bathe and I hadn't any intention of breaking my protest. Hurt or dying I was not going to concede to him or anyone else. I knew what was coming. His ultimatum changed to a command.

'Drop dead!' I said angrily. The hovering press-gang without so much as 'Where are you hurt?' and without any ceremony lifted me as a man would lift a bundle of rags and carried me to the already-full bath, dropping me into the water like a bar of soap. The shock of the ice-cold water engulfing my tattered body almost stopped my breath.

Every part of me stung unmercifully as the heavily disinfected water attacked my naked raw flesh. I made an immediate and brave attempt to rise out of the freezing, stinging water but the screws held me down while one of them began to scrub my already tattered back with a heavy scrubbing brush. I shrivelled with the pain and struggled for release but the more I fought the more they strengthened their iron grip. The tears came flooding to my eyes. I would have screamed had I been able to catch my breath. They continued to scrub every part of my tortured body, pouring buckets of ice cold water and soapy liquid over me. I vaguely remember being lifted out of the cold water—the sadistic screw had grabbed my testicles and scrubbed my private parts. That was the last thing I remembered. I collapsed.

I was taken to the prison hospital wrapped in a large fawn blanket where the doctor examined me. I remained there for two hours and patched up like a mummy, sporting a black eye and seven stitches in my head, I was returned to my punishment cell. I sat there wrapped in a solitary filthy blanket that reeked of urine and stale smoke. I had regained my composure although I was a little disorientated and still trying to piece together my awful ordeal. But that soon became overshadowed by the thoughts of what was to come. No one could do anything for me. I could not tell a soul as I was isolated, alone and vulnerable. I was simply at their mercy and I had already discovered and learned that they did not know the meaning of the word. Perhaps worst of all I was freezing cold, unable to walk and exercise to warm myself and I was feeling sorry for myself. The screws came back later in the day and once again dragged me out of the cell to appear naked before a Prison Governor to be tried in the normal farcical court. I stood naked before them, humiliated and embarrassed, my head bursting with the pain from my earlier beating. I was charged with 'disobeying an order'—that is refusing to co-operate with the screw who was endeavouring to probe and search my anal passage. In other words, I refused point-blank to allow this. But I was charged because it took three or four of them to hold me down to do it. The screw in question had been the white-coated one. It would have made little difference to me had he been a brain surgeon, as the motive was purely to degrade and humiliate me, which was all part of the general torture to break our resistance. I was found guilty—not that I expected anything else—and sentenced to three days to be spent in the punishment cells, to be fed on what was politely termed a 'number one diet', a starvation diet. I also lost one month's remission, the equivalent of a two month prison sentence! To wrap things up nicely, I was charged with assaulting the four screws who had almost murdered me that morning and, to rub it in, I was also charged with causing self-inflicted wounds to myself and informed in a roundabout way that if I dared to make a formal complaint I would also be charged with making false allegations against prison officers. How can you win, I thought, and felt like vomiting as they dragged me back to my cell again. . . .

The cell was freezing cold, bare and lonely. I'd been here once before, therefore I knew just how lonely and unbearable it would get. A board on the concrete floor served as my bed, a concrete slab as a table and a concrete block as a stool. A bible, po and water container were the only other visible items. I remained there for the three days, being beaten up twice more but not as severely as the initial hiding I received. . . .

When I returned to H-Block even the screws stared in shock at my death-like appearance. I was physically wrecked and mentally exhausted. The starvation, beatings, forcible bathing, the boredom and cold remained in my mind, scarring me deeply with hatred, bitterness and thoughts of revenge. Two weeks later I endured another fifteen days there. It was the same nightmare only multiplied by five. I lived like an insane animal, eating with my hands. Every other three days they starved me and once again I plodded through the dirt and filth, exercising to keep warm, taking the beatings, praying to myself, crying in my sleep, always fighting the urge to give in to them, to surrender.

But I survived. I beat them again. The torturous dungeons and the sadists who manned them had destroyed my body but had failed to break my spirit. It was three weeks later before I recovered from my torturous ordeal. My mind will never recover from it. God only knows how many of us have been subjected to that nightmare. . . .

I was about to sit down once more upon my mattress when the warning shout rang out.

'Bears in the air! Heavy gear!'

I knew just what that meant. I dived at the mattress and put it standing lengthways, in the farthest corner from the door, against the wall and put all the blankets behind it, wrapping the towel around my waist . . . I heard the first splash of lashing liquid at the cell facing me.

Heavy gear, all right! I could smell it already: ammonia-based detergent, a very strong and extremely dangerous disinfectant. The screws were lashing it in under and through the splits in the sides of the doors. I braved a quick glance through my little spy-hole as the lights in the corridor were turned on. It was a very foolish and dangerous thing to do because if the disinfectant hit me in the eyes it would burn my eyes out, blind me in a matter of seconds. 'B—' was lashing a full bucket of the sickening liquid in under the door facing me and shouting to the other screws to hurry up and fetch more. I heard the chokes and coughs of the man across from me. The boys on the other side of the wing were in trouble. Their windows were blocked up. The fumes from the disinfectant were similar to tear gas, they cut at the eyes and throat, bringing on fits of vomiting and temporary blindness. I heard the hose being unraveled at the top of the wing.

'Hose on the air,' I yelled and stepped back from the door. 'B—' was lashing the disinfectant in through the doors like a mad man, laughing all the while. He had been wearing a small face-mask which protected him from the fumes and no doubt he and his companions were clad in their blue nylon overalls. The hose burst into life and the thundering jets crashed against the bottom of the doors. I heard a swish and saw the greenish coloured liquid flooding in under the door. Immediately the terrible fumes struck me and I began coughing and spluttering, my eyes watering as I made my way to the window. My stomach was turning and I thought I was going to be sick as I fought for gasps of air at the window, my head pressed tightly against the concrete bars. Every single man must have been at his window coughing. That's all I could hear with the swish of the high-powered hose in the background. The tears were tripping me. I couldn't see a thing. Then the water came pouring in the sides of the door and came flooding across the blackened floor. I couldn't have cared less. I was shattered and coughing, my throat burning and dry. The water would dilute the disinfectant. I knew that. But it would be several minutes before the fumes cleared. The water from the hose was still streaming in under

the door then it ceased as the screw moved on to another cell. I was still coughing and spluttering but the fumes were clearing. . . .

It had been a hard day but wasn't every day the same and God only knew
what tomorrow would bring. Who would be the unlucky unfortunates tomorrow, supplying the battered bloody bodies for the punishment block? Who
would be hosed down, beaten up or torn apart during a wing shift? Tomorrow
would only bring more pain and torture and suffering, boredom and fear and
God knows how many humiliations, inhumanities and horrors. Darkness and
intense cold, an empty stomach and the four screaming walls of a filthy night-
mare-filled tomb to remind me of my plight, that's what lay ahead tomorrow
for hundreds of naked Republican Political Prisoners-of-War, but just as sure
as the morrow would be filled with torture so would we carry on and remain
unbroken. It was hard, it was very, very hard, I thought, lying down upon my
damp mattress and pulling the blankets around me. But some day victory
would be ours and never again would another Irish man or woman rot in an
English hell-hole. . . .

That's another day nearer to victory, I thought, feeling very hungry.

I was a skeleton compared to what I used to be but it didn't matter. Nothing really mattered except remaining unbroken. I rolled over once again, the
cold biting at me. They have nothing in their entire imperial arsenal to break
the spirit of one single Republican Political Prisoner-of-War who refuses to be
broken, I thought, and that was very true. They can not or never will break our
spirit. I rolled over again freezing and the snow came in the window on top of
my blankets.

'*Tiocfaidh ár lá*,'* I said to myself. '*Tiocfaidh ár lá.*'

---

*'Our day will come.'

# 5.5 ⸺

# The Tenth Circle of Hell

*Rezak Hukanović*

In earlier wars the locals had fought to defend Bosnia's border region from various enemies, but now . . . what exactly was happening now? Who were these mighty warriors who fled their farms, leaving behind half-empty beer bottles, to take up cannons and machine guns, to fire mortars and bullets, heedless of what they aimed at or how many rounds they shot? Once, not so long ago, people had made sacrifices; they had gone without food for the greater good. Now they were defying the legal authorities to arm what had once been everyone's army, the Yugoslav People's Army, taking refuge in the five-pointed star and the attribute "People's." And now that army was pounding Bosnians with the very same weapons they had acquired to defend themselves from any possible enemy—only the enemy, it turned out, had been living right next door, right down the street. Until just yesterday Bosnians had shared everything, drinking coffee together, going to parties and funerals together, visiting each other, marrying each other, but now. . . .

To the old song's words "Where the People's Army marches . . . ," Djemo would have added . . . "is a land where grass no longer grows." These were strange times. Bosnia trembled as if it had been hit by a powerful earthquake. But an earthquake comes and goes. This upheaval just kept on coming.

Was this bus trip the beginning of something still worse? The people beaten up—what were they guilty of? And what about the others, staring at the floor of the bus, their eyes filled with fear? The new Serbian authorities had nothing to blame them for, other than that their very existence was a reminder that Bosnia had long been home to Muslims and Croats as well as Serbs. Now Serbs were destroying mosques and churches and even digging up graveyards. Such crimes were well organized and harked back to times everyone thought had been forgotten. Irrational hatred flowed from the darkest parts of their souls and stared out from their bloodshot eyes. The reaction of most people was silence, fearful silence.

---

The bus stopped outside the administration building of the iron ore mine at Omarska, only a few miles from the village of the same name. On one side, looted cattle grazed in the mowed fields, while across from them the mining embankments—busy with workers until only days before—lay remote and isolated, seared by the unbearable heat. Two huge buildings stood in the center, separated by a wide asphalt lot with two smaller buildings. The prisoners were ordered to get off the bus with their arms raised over their heads, holding up three fingers on each hand. Two rows of fully armed soldiers opened a path through which they had to walk. Five men were pulled out of the line; the others were taken into one of the big buildings. Among the five selected, Djemo recognized Tewfik, a local actor whom everyone called "Cheapskate." Within minutes a burst of machine-gun fire rang out. Cheapskate would never "break a leg" on stage again.

With every arriving busload, the room got more and more crowded. Djemo's son arrived, along with his cousins Fadil, Mirsad, and Fudo, and Fudo's son Elijan. By Djemo's count, over twenty buses arrived before dark.

The pattern repeated itself the next day. Over the course of two days more than three thousand inhabitants of Prijedor and its outlying villages were arrested in their homes in these inconceivable raids and brought to the Serb prison at Omarska. Among the prisoners, whose only fault was being Muslim or Croat, were intellectuals, teachers, engineers, police officers, craftsmen. Djemo recognized the mayor of Prijedor, the Honorable Mr. Muhamed Čehajić. How absurd such a title seemed now.

The prisoners were given nothing to eat for the first four days. They slept on a tiled floor. Djemo found a cardboard box, broke it up, and put it on the floor for himself and his son to use as a bed. The stale air was hard to breathe and dried out their throats. On the fifth day they were ordered to line up for food. Their hunger was unbearable. Everyone swarmed to the door, and they were taken away in groups of thirty. Ari was in the third group; Djemo was way back in the tenth. When Djemo's group came up, they were told there was no more food. They went back to their places, writhing in pain. Later all prisoners would be given food once a day: a couple of cabbage leaves with a few beans, covered in tepid water, and a piece of bread that seemed to be made of soapsuds. They would be allowed only two minutes to eat.

Most of the time the prisoners were beaten on the way to and from the canteen where they ate. That route wound through a narrow corridor that branched off at the end and led to a staircase on the right. Upstairs, prisoners were interrogated. Back downstairs, on the left, was the canteen. The guards would pour water on a worn-out patch of glazed cement to make the corridor more slippery. If a prisoner fell, the guards would pounce on him like famished beasts at the sight of a carcass. Using whips made of thick electrical cable, they beat the fallen prisoner all the way up the stairs for the inevitable interrogation—or simply to finish the job they had already started. . . .

One time Djemo caught sight of the miserable prisoners in the garage through the wide door to his area. A group of about ten of them were chosen and taken out some forty yards in front of the garage. They were ordered to undress completely. The prisoners began taking off their worn, ragged clothes and putting them in a pile as four guards looked on. The guards were completely drunk, as anyone could tell by the way they moved. As the prisoners stripped, bashfully using their hands to try to cover their nakedness, the guards fixed their cynical glares upon them even more intently.

One big man, over six feet tall, refused to strip. His beard was long, a sign that he had been imprisoned for quite some time. He simply kept quiet and didn't move. He stood with his head bowed, mutely watching. One of the guards came up to him, put the barrel of his rifle to the man's neck, and said something to him. The man just stood there, without moving a single part of his body. "The poor guy's going to get it, they'll kill him," said someone behind Djemo. Djemo didn't turn around or respond but kept looking through the upper part of the glass door that separated the inmates from the guards. He was watching to see what would happen to this defiant figure and the other men from Kozarac.

The guard, seeing that the man was steadfast in his intention not to carry out the order, aimed his rifle upward and fired several shots into the air. Except for some quail in a nearby tree flying away out of sight, nothing happened. The man stood stubbornly in place without making the slightest movement. While bluish smoke still rose from the rifle barrel, the guard struck the clothed man in the middle of the head with the rifle butt, once and then again, until the man fell. Then the guard handed his rifle to another guard and moved his hand to his belt. A knife flashed in his hand, a long army knife.

He bent down, grabbing hold of the poor guy's hair with his free hand. Another guard joined in, continuously cursing. He, too, had a flashing knife in his hand. The two other guards backed off a little and trained their rifles on the nine naked prisoners, observing their every move. The guards with the knives started using them to tear away the man's clothes. After only a few seconds, they stood up, their own clothes covered with blood. The air resounded with a long, loud, and painful wail. It sent shivers through all who heard it.

Never in all his life was Djemo to see a more horrifying sight. The poor man stood up a little, or rather tried to stand up, still letting out excruciating screams. He was covered with blood. One guard took a water hose from a nearby hydrant and directed the strong jet at the poor prisoner. A mixture of blood and water flowed down his exhausted, gaunt, naked body as he bent down repeatedly, like a wounded Cyclops, raising his arms above his head, then lowering them toward the jet of water to fend it off; his cries were those of someone driven to insanity by pain. And then Djemo, and everyone else, saw clearly what had happened: the guards had cut off the man's sexual organ and half of his behind.

After that Djemo couldn't remember anything. The shocking sight of that horror momentarily numbed his mind. Only later was he told that the poor man, after succumbing to the torture, was taken to a garbage container, doused with gasoline, and burned. The other men were taken back to the garage.

When the interrogations began, the garage gradually started to empty. Eventually no more than fifty people were left, living witnesses to incarceration in the infamous garage. . . .

Wednesday, June 10, early evening. The interrogators had already left for the day, in the van that took them back and forth from Prijedor. One of the guards, drunker than usual, stuck his unkempt head through the door of the dorm and called for Djemo.

The same deathly silence that accompanied night calls descended on the dorm. Djemo felt a booming in his head, as if hundreds of hammers were pounding at his temples, at the top of his skull and the nape of his neck. His heart started pounding wildly; he could feel it beating in every part of his body. His blood pulsed through the labyrinth of capillaries across his face. He turned to his son and began to speak, his voice breaking: "Don't be scared, son, nothing will happen to me." Djemo hugged Ari tightly, feeling the delicate, rhythmic trembling of his fragile body.

"Ari, son, Daddy will be back, believe me." Timidly he took his son's arms off his shoulders, turned aside so that Ari wouldn't see the tears trickling down his cheeks, and started to walk away, not believing his own words. Somewhere at the back of his head he could almost feel the eyes of the poor souls whose silence spoke so eloquently. Gasps and deep sobs began from where he had been sitting, first softly, then louder and louder. Ari was weeping as the weak arms of those nearby reached out to keep him from going after his father. "Daddy, come back, please!" Djemo stopped for a second as his eyes tracked his son's voice. Something big and heavy, like a cannonball, lodged in his throat. He could hardly breathe. The tears that had trickled down his cheeks now flowed freely. Trying to flee such a merciless fate, he forced himself to utter: "I'll be back, son, I'll be back." Then he stepped forward past the guard, whose bearded face was flushed and whose eyes transmitted only darkness.

"In front of me," the guard ordered, pointing to the White House. On the way over he ranted and raved, cursing and occasionally pounding Djemo on the back with his truncheon. The hot, heavy air made everything even more unbearable. Djemo cast one more dull glance backward, into the distance, almost stopping. The guard pushed the barrel of his rifle hard into Djemo's back, until he felt a sharp pain and beads of sweat gathered on his face.

An overwhelming desire came over Djemo. He was on the verge of turning to spit in the bearded creature's face and punch him right in the middle of his ugly, drunken snout. But no—the voice of his son resounded in his ears like a seal ripped open within his torn heart. Defiantly, Djemo raised his head high above his shoulders and kept walking. The guard took him to the White House, to the second room on the left. (There were no prisoners in the White House then; they were only brought in later.) The next second, something heavy was let loose from above, from the sky, and knocked Djemo over the head. He fell.

Something flashed across his eyes, and everything became blurry. Blistering heat scorched his face and neck. He couldn't open his eyes. Half-conscious, sensing that he had to fight to survive, he wiped the blood from his eyes and forehead and raised his head. He saw four creatures, completely drunk, like a pack of starving wolves, with clubs in their hands and unadorned hatred in their eyes. Among them was the frenzied leader of the bloodthirsty pack, Zoran Žigić, the infamous Žiga whose soul, if he had one at all, was spattered with blood. He was said to have killed over two hundred people, including many children, in the "cleansing" operations around Prijedor. He took barely enough time between slaughters to put his bloody knife back into its sheath. Scrawny and long-legged, with a big black scar on his face, Žiga seemed like an ancient devil come to visit a time as cruel as his own. Anyone who came close to him also came close to death.

"Now, then, let me show you how Žiga does it," he said, ordering Djemo to kneel down in the corner by the radiator, "on all fours, just like a dog." The maniac grinned. Djemo knelt down and leaned forward on his hands, feeling humiliated and as helpless as a newborn. Just then they brought three more prisoners in from his dorm: Asaf, Kiki, and Bego. Being the last, Bego was immediately taken to the room across the way by Nikica, the youngest of the group of murderers. The sounds of beating and screaming soon reached the room Djemo was in. Asaf had to take the same position as Djemo, only at the other end of the radiator.

The tallest of the guards, another local murderer, name Duća, ordered Kiki to lie down on his back in the middle of the room. Then he jumped as high as he could and, with all his 250-odd pounds, came crashing down on Kiki's stomach and ribs. Another wild man wearing a headband came up to Asaf and started hitting him with a truncheon made out of thick electrical cable. Žiga kept hitting Djemo the whole time on the back and head with a club that unfurled itself every time he swung it to reveal a metal ball on the end. Djemo curled up, trying to protect his head by pulling it in toward his shoulders and covering it with his right hand. Žiga just kept cursing as he hit, his eyes inflamed by more and more hatred. The first drops of blood appeared on the tiles under Djemo's head, becoming denser and denser until they formed a thick, dark red puddle. Žiga kept at it; he stopped only every now and then, exhausted by his nonstop orgy of violence, to fan himself, waving his shirttail in front of his contorted face.

At some point a man in fatigues appeared at the door. It was Šaponja, a member of the famous Bosnamontaža soccer club from Prijedor; Djemo had once known him quite well. He came up to Djemo and said, "Well, well, my old pal Djemo. While I was fighting in Pakrac and Lipik, you were pouring down the cold ones in Prijedor." He kicked Djemo right in the face with his boot. Then he kicked him again in the chest, so badly that Djemo felt like his ribs had been shattered by the weight of the heavy combat boots. He barely managed to stay up on his arms and legs, to keep himself from falling. He knew that if he fell it would be all over. Žiga laughed like a maniac. Then he pushed Šaponja away and started hitting Djemo again with his weird club, even more fiercely than before.

The strange smell of blood, sweat, and wailing that enveloped the room only increased the cruelty of the enraged beasts. Djemo received another, even stronger kick to the face. He clutched himself in pain, bent a little to one side, and collapsed, his head sinking into the now-sizable pool of blood beneath him. Žiga grabbed him by the hair, lifted his head, and looked into Djemo's completely disfigured face: "Get up, you scum, and get out, everybody out," he shouted. Pulling Djemo up by the hair, Žiga raised him to his feet. Djemo could barely stand up, but he managed to take one step and then another, with Asaf and Kiki following.

"On all fours, I said—like dogs!" Žiga bellowed, like a dictator. He forced the three men to crawl up to a puddle by the entrance to the White House and then ordered them to wash in the filthy water. Their hands trembling, they washed the blood off their faces. "The boys have been eating strawberries and got themselves a little red," said Žiga, laughing like a madman before he chased them all back into the White House. Another prisoner, Slavko Ećimović, a Croat, and one of the first to rebel against local Serb rule, was in the same room where they had just been tortured. At least, it *seemed* like him. He was kneeling, all curled up, by the radiator. When he lifted his head, where his face should have been was nothing but the bloody, spongy tissue under the skin that had just been ripped off. Instead of eyes, two hollow sockets were filled with black, coagulated blood.

"You'll all end up like this, you and your families," Žiga said, taking on the airs of a military commander. "We killed his father and mother. And his wife. We'll get his kids. And yours, too, we'll kill you all." And with a wide swing of his leg, he kicked Djemo right in the face again with his boot. Djemo felt pieces of dried blood flying out of his mouth and nose and shards of broken teeth cutting his tongue. Then everything stopped—the blows, the curses, even the screams seemed to subside. As if through a fog, Djemo saw someone in an officer's uniform enter the room. In response to some tacit command, the beating had stopped. The prisoners were taken out to be washed at the same puddle and then returned to the dorms. Slavko Ećimović stayed in the White House and was never seen again.

Djemo went first. When he opened the door to the dorm, the murmur of voices inside stopped. A hush came over the room. He held his arms out, barely able to see the people backing up in front of him to clear the way. And then a shrill scream: "Daddy!" Djemo felt his son's arms clutch him before he sank into the deepest abyss. His body was overcome by absolute dark and silence. He didn't know how much time had gone by before he heard indistinct voices and felt something cold on his face and body. He tried to open his eyes. He felt a sharp pain in his head. As wet and cold compresses were applied to his face and back, Djemo managed to notice, though only with great effort, the many people around him and the tearful face of his son.

His recovery lasted twenty days. During that time he couldn't even move. Ari and some other prisoners had to carry him to the toilet. It didn't make Djemo feel very good, having everyone else do things for him. He couldn't even get to the canteen to eat, so his mates would save up pieces of bread or an occasional biscuit, depriving themselves in order to give him something to eat. Every day Ari brought his father half of his own meal.

When Djemo looked at himself in the mirror for the first time, he started crying. His face was covered with black contusions and bruises. Where his nose had been, there was only a huge swelling that almost shut his eyes. Several of his front teeth were broken. His whole back was black and blue. The tracks of the endless blows converged into a single, dark surface that spread over his entire back and neck. Dr. Sadiković told him later that his nose, a rib, and his right hand, at the wrist, were all broken, but that he would be all right: "You've pulled through. That's the most important thing. None of us thought you'd make it. At least now I can tell you, you're tough." The doctor made splints with wood ripped off the door and bandaged them around Djemo's broken hand with strips of cloth torn from his own shirt. . . .

After Djemo had been imprisoned for two months, the Serbs released everyone under eighteen and over sixty-five. . . . For Djemo, it was the happiest of days: his son Ari was among those released, as with Elijan, his cousin Fudo's son. They were called out early in the morning, taken to the runway, and kept there the whole day, the sun mercilessly beating down on them. It wasn't until late afternoon that two buses arrived to take them to Trnopolje, a camp the Serbs called a "reception center." From there the prisoners were sent home. Ari spent seventeen days in Trnopolje before he was released.

# 5.6 ⎯⎯⎯⎯

# Machete Season
*Jean Hatzfeld*

## ▇ How It Was Organized

**Élie:** We had to work fast, and we got no time off, especially not Sundays—we had to finish up. We canceled all ceremonies. Everyone was hired at the same level for a single job—to crush all the cockroaches. The intimidators gave us only one objective and only one way to achieve it. Anyone who detected something irregular, he brought it up quietly; anyone needing a dispensation, the same. I don't know how it was organized in other regions—in ours it was rudimentary.

**Jean-Baptiste:** When you get right down to it, it is a gross exaggeration to say we organized ourselves up on the hills. The plane came down April 6. A very small number of local Hutus went straight for retaliation. But most waited four days in their houses and in the nearest *cabarets*, listening to the radio, watching Tutsis flee, chatting and joking without planning a thing.

On April 10 the burgomaster in a pressed suit and all the authorities gathered us together. They lectured us, they threatened in advance anyone who bungled the job, and the killings began without much planning. The only regulation was to keep going till the end, maintain a satisfactory pace, spare no one, and loot what we found. It was impossible to screw up.

## ▇ The First Time

**Pancrace:** I don't remember my first kill, because I did not identify that one person in the crowd. I just happened to start by killing several without seeing their faces. I mean, I was striking, and there was screaming, but it was on all sides, so it was a mixture of blows and cries coming in a tangle from everyone.

Still, I do remember the first person who looked at me at the moment of the deadly blow. Now that was something. The eyes of someone you kill are immortal, if they face you at the fatal instant. They have a terrible black color.

---

They shake you more than the streams of blood and the death rattles, even in a great turmoil of dying. The eyes of the killed, for the killer, are his calamity if he looks into them. They are the blame of the person he kills.

**Léopord:** . . . This told us that the day would heat up. I took my machete, left the house, and went to the center of town. On this side and that, people were already giving chase.

At the marketplace I saw a man running toward me. He was coming down from Kayumba, all breathless and scared, looking only for escape, and he didn't see me. I was heading up, and in passing, I gave him a machete blow at neck level, on the vulnerable vein. It came to me naturally, without thinking. Aiming was simple, since the gentleman did not fight back. He made no defensive move—he fell without shouting, without moaning. I felt nothing, just let him lie. I looked around; killing was going on every which way. I kept chasing after runaways all day long.

It was sweaty-hard and stimulating, like an unforeseen diversion. I did not even keep count. Not during the action, not afterward, since I knew it would be starting up again. I cannot tell you, sincerely, how many I killed, because I forgot some along the way.

This gentleman I killed at the marketplace, I can tell you the exact memory of it because he was the first. For others, it's murky—I cannot keep track anymore in my memory. I considered them unimportant; at the time of those murders I didn't even notice the tiny thing that would change me into a killer.

## ■ Apprenticeship

**Élie:** The club is more crushing, but the machete is more natural. The Rwandan is accustomed to the machete from childhood. Grab a machete—that is what we do every morning. We cut sorghum, we prune banana trees, we hack out vines, we kill chickens. Even women and little girls borrow the machete for small tasks, like chopping firewood. Whatever the job, the same gesture always comes smoothly to our hands. The blade, when you use it to cut branch, animal, or man, it has nothing to say.

In the end, a man is like an animal: you give him a whack on the head or the neck, and down he goes. In the first days someone who had already slaughtered chickens—and especially goats—had an advantage, understandably. Later, everybody grew accustomed to the new activity, and the laggards caught up.

Only young guys, very sturdy and willing, used clubs. The club has no use in agriculture, but it was better suited to their way of trying to stand out, of strutting in the crowd. Same thing for spears and bows: those who still had them could find it entertaining to lend them or show them off.

**Léopord:** Me, I took up only the machete: first because I had one at the house, second because I knew how to use it. If you are skilled with a tool, it is handy to use it for everything—clearing brush or killing in the swamps. Time allowed everyone to improve in his fashion. The only strict rule was to show up with a good cutting machete. They were sharpened at least twice a week. This was not a problem, thanks to our own whetstones.

Whoever struck crooked, or only pretended to strike, we encouraged him, we advised him on improvements. He might also be obliged to take another turn at a Tutsi, in a marsh or in front of a house, and to kill the victim before his colleagues, to make sure he had listened well.

### ■ Taste and Distaste

**Fulgence:** We became more and more cruel, more and more calm, more and more bloody. But we did not see that we were becoming more and more killers. The more we cut, the more cutting became child's play to us. For a few, it turned into a treat, if I may say so. In the evening you might meet a colleague who would call out, "You, my friend, buy me a Primus or I'll cut open your skull, because I have a taste for that now!" But for many, it was simply that a long day had just come to an end.

We stopped thinking about obligations or advantages—we thought only about continuing what we had started. In any case, it held us so tight, we could not think about its effects on us.

**Léopord:** Since I was killing often, I began to feel it did not mean anything to me. It gave me no pleasure, I knew I would not be punished, I was killing without consequences, I adapted without a problem. I left every morning free and easy, in a hurry to get going. I saw that the work and the results were good for me, that's all.

During the killings I no longer considered anything in particular in the Tutsi except that the person had to be done away with. I want to make clear that from the first gentleman I killed to the last, I was not sorry about a single one.

### ■ Field Work

**Léopord:** Killing was less wearisome than farming. In the marshes, we could lag around for hours looking for someone to slaughter without getting penalized. We could shelter from the sun and chat without feeling idle. The workday didn't last as long as in the fields. We returned at three o'clock to have time for pillaging. We fell asleep every evening safe from care, no longer worried about drought. We forgot our torments as farmers. We gorged on vitamin-rich foods.

Some among us tasted pastries and sweets like candies for the first time in our lives. We got our supplies without paying, in the center of Nyamata, in shops where farmers had never gone before.

**Ignace:** Killing could certainly be thirsty work, draining and often disgusting. Still, it was more productive than raising crops, especially for someone with a meager plot of land or barren soil. During the killings anyone with strong arms brought home as much as a merchant of quality. We could no longer count the panels of sheet metal we were piling up. The taxmen ignored us. The women were satisfied with everything we brought in. They stopped complaining.

For the simplest farmers, it was refreshing to leave the hoe in the yard. We got up rich, we went to bed with full bellies, we lived a life of plenty. Pillaging is more worthwhile than harvesting, because it profits everyone equally.

## Women

**Jean-Baptiste:** During the killings, much jealousy spilled from the mouths of our women because of the constant talk about the Tutsi women's slender figures, their smooth skin thanks to drinking milk, and so on. When those envious women came upon a Tutsi searching for food in the forest, they called their neighbors to taunt her for crawling around that way all slovenly. Sometimes women shoved a neighbor to the bottom of the hill and threw her bodily into the waters of the Nyabarongo.

**Léopord:** The women vied with one another in ferocity toward the Tutsi women and children that they might flush out in an abandoned house. But their most remarkable enterprise was fighting over the fabrics and the trousers. After the expeditions they scavenged and stripped the dead. If a victim was still panting, they dealt a mortal blow with some hand tool or turned their backs and abandoned the dying to their last sighs—as they pleased.

## Acquaintances

**Alphonse:** We killed everything we tracked down in the papyrus. We had no reason to choose, to expect or fear anyone in particular. We were cutters of acquaintances, cutters of neighbors, just plain cutters.

Today some name acquaintances they supposedly spared, because they know these are no longer living to contradict them. They tell the tales to attract the favor of suffering families, they invent rescues to ease their return. We joke about those fake stratagems.

**Élie:** We were forbidden to choose men and women, babies and oldsters—everyone had to be slaughtered by the end. Time was hurrying us on, the job pulled us along, and the intimidators kept saying, "Anyone who lowers his machete because of somebody he knows, he is spoiling the willingness of his colleagues."

Anyway, someone who avoided the fatal gesture before a good acquaintance did it out of kindness to himself, not to his acquaintance, because he knew it brought no mercy to the other person, who'd be struck down anyhow. Quite the contrary, the victim might wind up cut more cruelly, for having slowed up the job for a moment.

## ■ Suffering

**Jean-Baptiste:** Extreme agonies were worked on important people, well-known businessmen. It was to punish them for past misdeeds or make them cough up their hidden savings. Also torments were done to people with whom there had been a stubborn grievance—a bargain that had not been settled or bad blood over some trampling by cows, for example. But not often. No orders were given about this. The bosses would say, "Kill, and fast, that's all. There's no point in taking your time."

**Pio:** There was voluntary suffering and involuntary suffering, so to speak. Because numerous Tutsis ended screaming from cuttings simply because of poor technique. They were the wounded left writhing, through haste, carelessness, or disgust with what had just been done more than through cruelty. Those were sufferings through sloppiness.

**Alphonse:** Saving the babies, that was not practical. They were whacked against walls and trees or they were cut right away. But they were killed more quickly, because of their small size and because their suffering was of no use. They say that at the church in Nyamata they burned children with gasoline. Maybe it's true, but that was just a few in the first-day turmoil. Afterward that did not last. In any case I noticed nothing more. The babies could not understand the why of the suffering, it was not worth lingering over them.

## ■ And God in All This?

**Léopord:** We no longer considered the Tutsis as humans or even as creatures of God. We had stopped seeing the world as it is, I mean as an expression of God's will.

That is why it was easy for us to wipe them out. And why those of us who prayed in secret did so for themselves, never for their victims. They prayed to ask for their crimes to be a bit forgotten, or to get just a little forgiveness—and they returned to the marshes in the morning.

Anyway, it was more than forbidden to speak kindly of the Tutsis to God or anyone else. Even after their deaths, even of a newborn. Even a priest was not to profit from his favor with God to pray for the soul of a Tutsi. He risked too much if someone overheard.

**Jean-Baptiste:** Only dogs and wild beasts ventured into the church and its slaughterhouse stench. When we walked alongside the parish wall to go to Kanzenze or down into the marshes, that stink turned us even farther away from reading the gospels.

Truly, the times no longer wanted us to worry about God, and we went along. Deep down we knew that Christ was not on our side in this situation, but since He was not saying anything through the priests' mouths, that suited us.

**Élie:** All the important people turned their backs on our killings. The blue helmets, the Belgians, the white directors, the black presidents, the humanitarian people and the international cameramen, the priests and the bishops, and finally even God. Did He watch what was happening in the marshes? Why did He not stab our murderous eyes with His wrath? Or show some small sign of disapproval to save more lucky ones? In those horrible moments, who could hear His silence? We were abandoned by all words of rebuke.

On Sunday mornings the radio programs no longer broadcast masses as before. But encouraging hearsay came from well-known monsignors who arrived from Kigali. Sometimes we heard hymns and services on the radio. Those were tapes without sermons, but the religious music soothed people who felt uneasy. It reminded them of ordinary Sundays—it did them some good.

## ■ Remorse and Regrets

**Ignace:** I think time will allow me to leave the difficult memories behind in Rilima, when I get to leave. I will fold the bad thoughts up inside the prison uniform. I think I will go home with my memory in fine shape, to pick up life again in good spirits.

But the memory of the mine shaft where the Tutsis were smoked alive, that one will never leave me. I can feel it well hidden behind my mind. It will eat at me on the hill. And that is a big thing. It is going to stalk me with no warning, since I live not far from the mines.

I had not foreseen that this memory would work at me so viciously. I believe it is because of the smell of the burns—I believe it is unnatural for men to kill men with fire.

**Élie:** In prison and on the hills, everyone is obviously sorry. But most of the killers are sorry they didn't finish the job. They accuse themselves of negligence rather than wickedness. Those who keep saying that they weren't there during the fatal moments, that they don't remember a thing, that they lost their machetes and tripe like that, they are bowing down with the hope of evading punishment—while waiting to start all over again. Repentance may wear many faces. But it is worthless if it is not the right kind.

**Léopord:** Some try to show remorse but tremble before the truth. They sneak around it, because of too many conflicting interests, and wind up flung backwards.

It was in a camp in Congo that I first felt my heart ache. I prayed, hoping to find relief, but in vain. After prayers or hymns, shame waited for me, without fail. So I began being sorry out loud, paying no attention to the mockery spewing from my comrades' mouths. In prison I told my whole truth. It came out freely. Ever since then, whenever someone asks me for it, it flows the same way.

Aside from this vile prison life, I have felt calm since I spoke up. I'm waiting peacefully to go home to my land. I do not fear any problem returning to work in the fields beside the neighbors on the hill. On the contrary, I am impatient for my next life.

## ▣ Words to Avoid Saying It

**Élie:** No one can admit the whole sad truth, not now, not ever. No one can speak all the precise words of his misdeeds without damning himself in other people's eyes. And that's too grim. But without fear of seeming more punishable, a small number are beginning to recount some ugly bits and pieces, to do penance for the blood they splattered. Those few are clearing a path of sincerity. It is a big thing.

On the hills or in prison, truth offers every participant a share. The survivors have the largest share because of what they endured, that's normal. The Tutsi wives who were saved, the international cameramen, the soldiers have shares. But if the offenders' share is missing, the revelations about those killings will go around in circles forever. The offenders know more than the basic facts they remember, more than the details about how things were managed. They have secrets in their souls.

**Adalbert:** Genocide is not an idea common to wars and battles. It is an idea the authorities have—to rid themselves of a danger once and for all. A convenient idea that need not be named or encouraged, except with the usual malicious outbursts. It's a quite ordinary idea when it flies from word to word, sometimes from joke to joke; it becomes extraordinary when it is caught on the tips of machetes.

This idea does not die with the killings, not after victory, not after defeat. It can be salvaged by future authorities for another destiny. But how can you kill an idea, used so extraordinarily, if you do not know how to kill its word, which can recall it to life? Killing enemies, killing offenders, killing neighbors—that you can understand. Killing ideas and words—that is beyond intelligence, a farmer's intelligence, anyway.

# 6 Gender-Based Repression

## 6.1 _____

# Introduction
### *The Editors*

Oftentimes, cultural and historical practices have created norms within society that make women particular targets of personal integrity rights. Norms regarding the women's role in society and the economy leave women with less protection than men. For example, in many societies men are still viewed as the breadwinners and women are structurally prevented from achieving economic independence. Moreover, many societies overly emphasize women's chastity while it is the sexual norm for males in that society to have multiple partners or mistresses. The result is that women in many societies continue to have less social and economic protection while being targeted for cultural expectations that are unequal.

The history of women's rights has been paltry to say the least. Only recently has the international community addressed the specific legal needs of women with the *United Nations Convention on the Elimination of All Forms of Discrimination Against Women* (1979). In this chapter, we examine issues that constitute gross human rights violations against women, including the slavery and sex trade of women and children, the rights of Muslim women, and the specific issue of female circumcision/genital mutilation (FGM).

The first article in this chapter by Kevin Bales addresses what he calls the "new slavery." He estimates that there are currently twenty-seven million slaves in the world today. Bales's main point is that slavery today is fundamentally different from slavery in the past. The primary motivation for this new wave of slavery, according to Bales, is economics: "Slaves keep your costs low and returns on your investments high." These slaves are primarily engaged in agricultural and non-technological sectors of the economy. According to Bales, since there are so many people living in poverty, slaves today are cheap and disposable. He contends that demands for cheap goods and our globalized economy continue to fuel slavery in the world.

Human trafficking has continued to thrive in this age of human rights. Today trafficking is manifest in both bonded labor and the global sex trade. Kazuko Watanabe provides a historical perspective of the trafficking of women in this study on military comfort women during World War II. The legacy of these comfort women can be seen in the modern sex tourism trade, catalog brides, and prostitution around military bases. In what is described as the institutionalization of sexual violence against women, Watanabe weaves the tale of mostly Korean women, an estimated 200,000, that were used by Japanese soldiers as sexual slaves. Watanabe explains that many of the women that were victims during World War II have remained silent due to cultural and religious norms regarding chastity. Only recently have they emerged to shed light on the issue of military comfort women. The testimony of these women provides a picture of sexual abuse that is not much different from the experience of sex workers today. Today, over 100,000 women arrive each year in Japan to work in the sex industry. Tricked by the promise of a job in a factory or department store, these young women are then sold into slavery. The US military bases in Asia also perpetuate the use of comfort women as they attract those involved in the sex trade.

In more general terms, Riffat Hassan addresses the issues of women's rights within the Islamic community. Hassan illuminates the quandary of Muslim women who feel alienated and discriminated against in the Western world, but simultaneously feel that "virtually all Muslim societies discriminate against women from cradle to grave." Defending the Islamic position, Hassan claims that the Quran is the "Magna Carte of human rights." She then delves into the Quran's protection of many rights, such as the right to life, respect, justice, freedom, privacy, sustenance, and work, as having foundations in the Islamic text. She is concerned, however, with the schism between the ideals outlined in the Quran and the practices of Muslims, particularly when it comes to women's rights. The excerpt included here examines that schism. Contrary to the teachings of Islam, Muslim women are the victim of honor-killings and a host of other forms of oppression and injustice. One of the problems with the discourse from the Muslim world is that women are not participants generally in the dialogue. Patriarchal Muslim societies have limited the access to education for most women. This is one of the obstacles that must be overcome in order to advance the dialogue of women's human rights in the Muslim world.

Patriarchal societies are also often blamed for the prevalence and continuing practice of FGM. In her article "Female Circumcision Comes to America," Linda Burstyn provides several firsthand accounts of this traditional practice. While common among certain societies, particularly in Africa, the practice is on the rise in America, as well as Europe, due to increases in immigration. Western societies now have to face the cultural relativist debate directly regarding a topic that in Burstyn's words is "taboo." Burstyn, citing documentation from the World Health Organization, summarizes the physical and psychological damage that opponents of FGM point to as reasons to abolish such practices. Burstyn interweaves personal testimony with adverse health consequences to illustrate the long-term damage that FGM can cause.

# 6.2 _____

# Disposable People: New Slavery in the Global Economy
## Kevin Bales

Slavery is a booming business and the number of slaves is increasing. People get rich by using slaves. And when they've finished with their slaves, they just throw these people away. This is the new slavery, which focuses on big profits and cheap lives. It is not about owning people in the traditional sense of the old slavery, but about controlling them completely. People become completely disposable tools for making money.

> On more than ten occasions I woke early in the morning to find the corpse of a young girl floating in the water by the barge. Nobody bothered to bury the girls. They just threw bodies in the river to be eaten by the fish.[1]

This was the fate of young girls enslaved as prostitutes in the gold mining towns of the Amazon, explained Antonia Pinto, who worked there as cook and a procurer. While the developed world bemoans the destruction of the rain forests, few people realize that slave labor is used to destroy them. Men are lured to the region by promises of riches in gold dust, and girls as young as eleven are offered jobs in the offices and restaurants that serve the mines. When they arrive in the remote mining areas, the men are locked up and forced to work in the mines; the girls are beaten, raped, and put to work as prostitutes. Their "recruitment agents" are paid a small amount for each body, perhaps $150. The "recruits" have become slaves—not through legal ownership, but through the final authority of violence. The local police act as enforcers to control the slaves. As one young woman explained, "Here the brothel owners send the police to beat us . . . if we flee they go after us, if they find us they kill us, or if they don't kill us they beat us all the way back to the brothel."[2]

The brothels are incredibly lucrative. The girl who "cost" $150 can be sold for sex up to ten times a night and bring in $10,000 per month. The only expenses are payments to the police and a pittance for food. If a girl is a trou-

Excerpted from Kevin Bales, *Disposable People: New Slavery in the Global Economy* (Los Angeles: University of California Press), pp. 1–33. © 1999 University of California Press. Reprinted with permission. Some of the author's notes have been omitted.

blemaker, runs away, or gets sick, she is easy to get rid of and replace. Antonia Pinto described what happened to an eleven-year-old girl when she refused to have sex with a miner: "After decapitating her with his machete, the miner drove around in his speedboat, showing off her head to the other miners, who clapped and shouted their approval."[3] . . .

We might think slavery is a matter of ownership, but that depends on what we mean by *ownership*. In the past, slavery entailed one person legally owning another person, but modern slavery is different. Today slavery is illegal everywhere, and there is no more *legal* ownership of human beings. When people buy slaves today they don't ask for a receipt or ownership papers, but they do gain *control*—and they use violence to maintain this control. Slaveholders have all of the benefits of ownership without the legalities. Indeed, for the slaveholders, not having legal ownership is an improvement because they get total control without any responsibility for what they own. For that reason I tend to use the term slave*holder* instead of slave*owner*.

In spite of this difference between the new and the old slavery, I think everyone would agree that what I am talking about is slavery: the total control of one person by another for the purpose of economic exploitation. . . .

## How Many Slaves?

*My best estimate of the number of slaves in the world today is 27 million.* This number is much smaller than the estimates put forward by some activists, who give a range as high as 200 million, but it is the number I feel I can trust; it is also the number that fits my strict definition of slavery. The biggest part of that 27 million, perhaps 15 to 20 million, is represented by *bonded labor* in India, Pakistan, Bangladesh, and Nepal. Bonded labor or debt bondage happens when people give themselves into slavery as security against a loan or when they inherit a debt from a relative (we'll look at this more closely later). Otherwise slavery tends to be concentrated in Southeast Asia, northern and western Africa, and parts of South America (but there are some slaves in almost every country in the world, including the United States, Japan, and many European countries). There are more slaves alive today than all the people stolen from Africa in the time of the transatlantic slave trade. Put another way, today's slave population is greater than the population of Canada, and six times greater than the population of Israel.

These slaves tend to be used in simple, nontechnological, and traditional work. The largest group work in agriculture. But slaves are used in many other kinds of labor: brickmaking, mining or quarrying, prostitution, gem working and jewelry making, cloth and carpet making, and domestic service; they clear forests, make charcoal, and work in shops. Much of this work is aimed at local sale and consumption, but slave-made goods reach into homes around the world. Carpets, fireworks, jewelry, and metal goods are made by slave labor, as well as grains, sugar, and other foods harvested by slaves are imported directly to North America and Europe. In addition, large international corporations, acting through subsidiaries in the developing world, take advantage of slave labor to improve their bottom line and increase the dividends to their shareholder.

But the value of slaves lies not so much in the particular products they make as in their sweat, in the volume of work squeezed out of them. Slaves are often forced to sleep next to their looms or brick kilns; some are even chained to their work tables. All their waking hours may be turned into working hours. In our global economy one of the standard explanations that multinational corporations give for closing factories in the "first world" and opening them in the "third world" is the lower labor cost. Slavery can constitute a significant part of these savings. No paid workers, no matter how efficient, can compete economically with unpaid workers—slaves. . . .

## ■ What Does Race Have to Do with It?

Today the morality of money overrides other concerns. Most slaveholders feel no need to explain or defend their chosen method of labor recruitment and management. Slavery is a very profitable business, and a good bottom line is justification enough. Freed of ideas that restrict the status of slave to *others*, modern slaveholders use other criteria to choose slaves. Indeed, they enjoy a great advantage: being able to enslave people from one's own country helps keep costs down. Slaves in the American South in the nineteenth century were expensive, in part because they originally had to be shipped thousands of miles from Africa. When slaves can be gotten from the next town or region, transportation costs fall. The question isn't "Are they the right color to be slaves?" but "Are they vulnerable enough to be enslaved?" The criteria of enslavement today do not concern color, tribe, or religion; they focus on weakness, gullibility, and deprivation. . . .

## ■ The Old Slavery Versus the New Slavery

Government corruption, plus the vast increase in the number of people and their ongoing impoverishment, has led to the new slavery. For the first time in human history there is an absolute glut of potential slaves. It is a dramatic illustration of the laws of supply and demand: with so many possible slaves, their value has plummeted. Slaves are now so cheap that they have become cost-effective in many new kinds of work, completely changing how they are seen and used. Think about computers. Forty years ago there were only a handful of computers, and they cost hundreds of thousands of dollars; only big companies and the government could afford them. Today there are millions of personal computers. Anyone can buy a used, but quite serviceable, model for

$100. Use that $100 computer for a year or two, and when it breaks down, don't bother to fix it—just throw it away.

The same thing happens in the new slavery. Buying a slave is no longer a major investment, like buying a car or a house (as it was in the old slavery); it is more like buying an inexpensive bicycle or a cheap computer. Slaveholders get all the work they can out of their slaves, and then throw them away. The nature of the relationship between slaves and slaveholders has fundamentally altered. The new disposability has dramatically increased the amount of profit to be made from a slave, decreased the length of time a person would normally be enslaved, and made the question of legal ownership less important. When slaves cost a great deal of money, that investment had to be safeguarded through clear and legally documented ownership. Slaves of the past were worth stealing and worth chasing down if they escaped. Today slaves cost so little that it is not worth the hassle of securing permanent, "legal" ownership. Slaves are disposable. . . .

First, no one tries to assert legal ownership of the bonded laborer. The slave is held under threat of violence, and often physically locked up, but no one asserts that he or she is in fact "property." Second, the bonded laborer is made responsible for his or her own upkeep, thus lowering the slaveholder's costs. The slaves may scrape together their subsistence in a number of ways: eking it out from the foodstuffs produced for the slaveholder, using their "spare time" to do whatever is necessary to bring in food, or receiving some foodstuffs or money from the slaveholder. The slaveholders save by providing no regular maintenance, and they can cut off food and all support when the bonded laborer is unable to work or is no longer needed.

Third, if a bonded laborer is not able to work, perhaps because of illness or injury, or is not needed for work, he or she can be abandoned or disposed of by the slaveholder, who bears no responsibility for the slave's upkeep. . . . Fourth, the ethnic differentiation is not nearly so rigid as that of the old slavery. As already noted, bonded laborers may well belong to a lower caste than the slaveholder—but this is not always the case. The key distinction lies in wealth and power, not caste.

Finally, a major difference between the old and new slavery is in the profits produced by an enslaved laborer. Agricultural bonded laborers in India generate not 5 percent, as did slaves in the American South, but over 50 percent profit per year for the slaveholder. . . .

## ■ The New Slavery and the Global Economy

Just how much does slave labor contribute to the global economy? Inevitably, determining the exact contribution of slaves to the world economy is very difficult because no reliable information is available for most types of slavery. Nevertheless, a few rough calculations are possible.

Agricultural bonded laborers, after an initial loan (think of this as the purchase price) of around $50, generate up to 100 percent net profit for the slaveholders. If there are an estimated 18 million such workers, the annual profit generated would be on the order of $860 million, though this might be distributed to as many as 5 million slaveholders. If 200,000 women and children are enslaved as prostitutes, a not unreasonable guess, and if the financial breakdown found in Thai prostitution is used as a guide, then these slaves would generate a total annual profit of $10.5 billion.

If these sums are averaged to reflect a world population of 27 million slaves, the total yearly profit generated by slaves would be on the order of $13 billion. This is a very rough estimate. But we might put this sum into global perspective by noting that $13 billion is approximately equal to the amount the Dutch spent last year on tourism, or substantially less than the personal worth of Microsoft founder Bill Gates.

Although the direct value of slave labor in the world economy may seem relatively small, the indirect value is much greater. For example, slave-produced charcoal is crucial to making steel in Brazil. Much of this steel is then made into the cars, car parts, and other metal goods that make up a quarter of all Brazil's exports. Britain alone imports $1.6 billion in goods from Brazil each year, the United States significantly more.[4] Slavery lowers a factory's production costs; these savings can be passed up the economic stream, ultimately reaching shops of Europe and North America as lower prices or higher profits for retailers. Goods directly produced by slaves are also exported, and follow the same pattern. It is most likely that slave-produced goods and goods assembled from slave-made components have the effect of increasing profits rather than just lowering consumer prices, as they are mixed into the flow of other products. I'd like to believe that most Western consumers, if they could identify slave-produced goods, would avoid them despite their lower price. But consumers do look for bargains, and they don't usually stop to ask why a product is so cheap. We have to face facts: by always looking for the best deal, we may be choosing slave-made goods without knowing what we are buying. And the impact of slavery reverberates through the world economy in ways even harder to escape. Workers making computer parts or televisions in India can be paid low wages in part because food produced by slave labor is so cheap. This lowers the cost of the goods they make, and factories unable to compete with their prices close in North America and Europe. Slave labor anywhere threatens real jobs everywhere. . . .

## ▓ From Knowledge to Freedom

Looking at the nature of new slavery we see obvious themes: slaves are cheap and disposable; control continues without legal ownership; slavery is hidden behind contracts; and slavery flourishes in communities under stress. Those social conditions have to exist side by side with an economy that fosters slavery. Order sometimes breaks down in European or American communities, but slavery doesn't take hold. This is because very, very few people live in the kind of destitution that makes them good candidates for slavery. In most Western countries the extreme differential in power needed to enslave doesn't exist, and the idea of slavery is abhorrent. When most of the population has a reasonable standard of living and some financial security (whether their own or assured by government safety nets), slavery can't thrive.

Slavery grows best in extreme poverty, so we can identify its *economic* as well as social preconditions. Most obviously, there have to be people, perhaps nonnative to an area, who can be enslaved as well as a demand for slave labor. Slaveholders must have the resources to fund the purchase, capture, or enticement of slaves and the power to control them after enslavement. The cost of keeping a slave has to be less than or equal to the cost of hiring free labor. And there must be a demand for slave products at a price that makes slaveholding profitable. Moreover, the potential slave must lack perceived alternatives to enslavement. Being poor, homeless, a refugee, or abandoned can all lead to the desperation that opens the doors to slavery, making it easy for the slaver to lay an attractive trap. And when slaves are kidnapped, they must lack sufficient power to defend themselves against that violent enslavement.

It may seem that I am too insistent on setting out these conditions and themes in the new slavery. But the new slavery is like a new disease for which no vaccine exists. Until we really understand it, until we really know what makes it work, we have little chance of stopping it. And this disease is spreading. As the new slavery increases, the number of people enslaved grows every day. We're facing an epidemic of slavery that is tied through the global economy to our own lives.

## ▓ Notes

1. Alison Sutton, *Slavery in Brazil: A Link in the Chain of Modernisation* (London: Anti-Slavery International, 1994), 102.

2. Ibid., 97.

3. Sue Branford, "Brazilian Congress Tells of Half-Million Child Prostitutes," *Guardian* January 29, 1993, p. 12.

4. See Great Britain Department of Trade and Industry 1997. *Overseas Trade Statistics of the United Kingdom.* London: H.M. Stationery Office; Economist Intelligence Unit. 1997. in *Country Forecast Brazil, Third Quarter* 1997. Graham Stock (ed.). London: EIU.

# 6.3 _____

# Trafficking in Women's Bodies, Then and Now: The Issue of Military "Comfort Women"
*Kazuko Watanabe*

In December 1991, Korean women identified themselves as military comfort women for the first time. They unveiled the sexual war crimes committed by members of the Japanese Imperial Army and filed a lawsuit against the Japanese government at the Tokyo District Court. They asked for an official apology to each individual victim, compensation, prosecution of perpetrators, proper education of the public on the nature of this war crime, the rewriting of the history of war crimes to include this one, and the building of memorial tablets for deceased victims. The voices of comfort women are only now being heard after 50 years of silence.

Kim Haku Soon, the only plaintiff who revealed her name in the 1991 court case, related her experiences. Her story included the following: "When I was 17 years old, the Japanese soldiers came along in a truck, beat us and then dragged us into the back. . . . I was told that if I were drafted, I could earn lots of money at the textile company. . . . The first day I was raped and the rapes never stopped."[1]

Each woman was made to service an average of 30 to 40 soldiers per day. The men would stand in line outside a small room, waiting for their turn. In her interview, Soon explained her feelings of anger and agony: "I was born as a woman but never lived as a woman. . . . I feel sick when I come close to a man. Not just Japanese men but all men—even my own husband, who saved me from the brothel—made me feel this way. I shiver when I see the Japanese flag. . . . Why should I feel ashamed? I don't have to feel ashamed."[2]

Since Soon gave her testimony, dozens of Korean women have followed her example including a Korean Japanese woman, Song Siin Do, who now lives in Japan. Most of these women have reached the age of 70. Their pains

Excerpted from Kazuko Watanabe, "Trafficking in Women's Bodies, Then and Now: The Issue of Military 'Comfort Women,'" *Peace and Change* 20 (4): 501–514. © 1995 Blackwell Publishers. Reprinted with permission. Some of the author's notes have been omitted.

and scars must be overcome for them to "rebuild their mined lives before it becomes too late."[3]

The term "military comfort women," a literal translation of *Jugun Ianfu*, is a euphemism for forced military sexual slavery during World War II. It actually meant the collective and systematic rape of women and the regulation of rape by the Japanese Imperial Army. Clearly, the term "military comfort women" was coined by Japanese military officials as well as agents of the sex industry to disguise its dreadful reality.[4] It was originally called *Teishintai*, which means "voluntary labor corps." Even today, Korean women would rather use this latter term.

Thus were women brought from Japan's Asian neighbors—Korea, China, Taiwan, Indonesia, Malaysia, and the Philippines—to the battlefields where Japanese armies were stationed. Their total number is estimated to have been more than 200,000. Fewer than 30 percent survived the end of the war.[5] I focus on the Korean comfort women of World War II because they were the most numerous, comprising 80 percent of the total, and because I have been more involved in their movement.

One of the witnesses, a Japanese military doctor during World War II, Tetsuo Aso, declared that these women were treated as "female ammunition" and that their dehumanized bodies were used as "public toilets."[6] They were also important laborers who carried weapons even on the front lines. In addition, Kim Yonja testified that even her blood was taken for Japanese soldiers.[7]

The Japanese Imperial Army divided comfort women into a hierarchical order according to class, race, and nationality—and according to the rank of the soldiers they were made to serve. Korean and most other Asian women were assigned to lower class soldiers. Japanese and European women went to high-ranking officers. Most of the European women were Dutch who were imprisoned in a prisoner of war camp in the Netherlands East Indies. This latter group has also sued the Japanese government. . . .

World War II was not the first use of comfort women by the Japanese army. Indeed, the practice had been institutionalized as early as the turn of the century. In the invasion of Siberia in 1918, the Imperial Army took along Japanese prostitutes. Most of these women, called *Karayukisan* ("foreign-bound prostitutes"), were daughters of poor farmers.

Beginning with the Japanese invasion of China in 1932, the "recruiting" of women as prostitutes from Korea (which had been annexed by Japan in 1910) became systematized. The purpose was to arouse the soldiers' fighting spirits by providing them with an outlet for the frustration fostered by hierarchical military life. The system was also designed to prevent Japanese soldiers from collectively raping Chinese women, especially after the highly publicized Nanking massacre in 1937. The use of comfort women was also begun to protect Japanese soldiers from venereal disease because the Korean recruits were young women who were not sexually experienced and were, therefore, free from such disease. Today, this practice is reminiscent of the trafficking in young girls as prostitutes as protection against AIDS.

The practice of military sexual abuse and trafficking in women did not end with the comfort women operation in World War II. The trafficking of women has been expanded on an unprecedented scale in times of "peace." Associated with Karayukisan is Japayukisan, the term identifying Asian women bound for Japan, mostly to serve as "sex workers," usually as either entertainers or prostitutes. It is also a contemporary form of trafficking in women. (The term Japayukisan is a racist and sexist expression because it has strongly been associated with prostitution and evil action. However, I use it deliberately to call attention to the plight of these women in Japan.) The total number of sex workers who arrive in Japan every year is estimated to be more than 100,000 women. Wealthy Japan is now the most notorious country in the world for recruiting and exploiting such women. . . .

Comfort women and contemporary sex workers have been recruited often by similar deceits: if they followed the brokers, they could easily find well-paid, responsible jobs. Sex tourism to other Asian countries by Japanese men is a contemporary version of the Japanese Imperial Army's sexual exploitation of Asian women. Symbolically, the difference lies only in the way the men dress: instead of military uniforms, they now wear business suits. Both cases show us men commodifying and dehumanizing women's bodies.

Actually, men's bodies and sexuality are also victims of militarist and consumerist capitalist societies. Men are, supposedly, unable to control their sexual impulses and are in need of prostitutes. Male soldiers were dehumanized to make them good fighters and then stimulated by sexual desire that was fulfilled by comfort women. These soldiers acted just like Japanese businessmen called "economic animals" during the postcolonial era.

Both the soldiers who were forced to die for the emperor on the battlefields and today's businessmen who die for their companies from *karoshi* (overwork) have often been rewarded with prostitutes. Thus gendered bodies were used to expand the state's power during World War II, and this process continues today in the postwar economic expansion by Japanese corporations into other Asian countries. Also, so-called South (or Third World) countries cannot provide enough resources to their people and therefore encourage them to earn foreign currency by commodifying their bodies. Thus both North and South countries share responsibility for this practice.

Legally and psychologically, comfort women and Japayukisan who were trafficked have been left in uninformed isolation. They were brought into an environment where they lost their identities as well as their cultures and languages. Japayukisan are forced to use falsified passports and then the passports, their legal source of identification, are taken away as soon as they enter Japan. They are trapped and imprisoned in small apartments and bars.[8] Similarly, most of the comfort women of World War II were called by Japanese names and forbidden to speak their own languages. As a result, such women were and are quite powerless and completely vulnerable.

Culturally, Confucian ideology, which promotes and characterizes the patriarchal system in Asian countries, has created a double standard. Its taboos have made people put a priority on women's chastity, which has resulted in women separating themselves from their own bodies. It has also inhibited them from speaking about their own sexuality while trapping them as men's property. It is one of the reasons why survivors of sexual military slavery have been silenced for half a century.

Because of this chastity myth, comfort women caught by Japanese militarism faced only two alternatives: either they submitted or they killed themselves to protect their chastity, which Confucianism taught them to consider more important than their lives.[9] After the war, some survivors of sexual slavery committed suicide or stayed away from their own families and led solitary lives because they were so ashamed of the loss of their virginity.

Even during the present era, Japayukisan have been stigmatized as prostitutes in their own societies. Even if they succeed in fleeing pimps and return to their homelands, many of them find themselves so traumatized that they return to Japan. To the extent that their bodies are denied in their society, women are dehumanized. Comfort women have especially suffered from victimization, totally deprived of not only their sexual desire but also the ability to procreate. Many of them have been sterilized and feel even more degraded because they were denied motherhood.

Even more pathetic and discouraging is that today many Japanese women regard trafficked Asian women as cultural and historical "others" and try not to see them and not to hear their cries. Research has shown that more than half of Japanese women try not to believe in comfort women although they have heard their stories.[10] Japanese wives often help their husbands pack for sex tours in other Asian countries. They do not seem to mind as long as their husbands buy women of another ethnicity or nationality. Thus women are overtly categorized as either prostitutes or bearers of children. The double standard exists not just in gender and sexuality but also in race and ethnicity. Thus was constructed the durable sexism and racism that has allowed wartime and present Japan to traffic in women's bodies. . . .

Trafficking in women and violence against women also occur at military bases. This was pointed out at the Asian Tribunal in March 1994 by Takasato Suzuyo, an Okinawan municipal councilor and activist.[11] She has been protesting practices at the U.S. military bases on the island. This problem should not be left out of an examination of sexual exploitation and violence for several reasons. First, it shows that the institution of military sexual slavery transcends a historical time and place, wartime and peacetime. Second, it clarifies the close relationship between militarization and commodification of women's bodies and the inherent gender perspectives of militarism. It shows that military bases systematize violence in general and justify violence against women in particular. Third, it reveals that women in Japan (including Okinawa) are still victims of war. The Okinawa women's protest against sexual exploitation around the U.S. military bases may enable Japanese women to transcend the historical designation of Okinawan women as victims and mainland women as victimizers because all women share the responsibility to attack prostitution and sexual slavery.

## ■ Notes

1. Jugun Ianfu Mondai Uriyosong Network [Comfort Women Issue Uriyosong Network], *Kono Han o Tokutameni [To Liberate This Bitterness]* (Tokyo: Gakuyo shobo, 1993), 5–6; Kaiho Shuppansha, ed., *Kim Hak-Soon San no Shogen [The Testimony of Kim Haku-Soon]* (Tokyo: Kaiho Shuppansha, 1993).

2. *Kono Han o Tokutameni*, 8.

3. *Comfort Women Issue Uriyosong Network Newsletter,* no. 5 (April 1993): 1; *Sojo [Written Complaints]* (Tokyo: Zainichi no Ianfu Salban o Sasueru Kai [Support Group for the Lawsuit of Korean Former Comfort Women Resident in Japan], 1993).

4. Kazuko Watanabe, "Militarism, Colonialism and Trafficking of Women: Military 'Comfort Women' Forced into Sexual Labor by Japanese Soldiers," *Bulletin of Concerned Asian Scholars* 26, no. 4 (1994), 3–16.

5. Suzuki Yuko, *Chosenjin Jugun Ianfu [Korean Military Comfort Women]* (Tokyo: Iwanami Shoton, 1991).

6. Nishino Rumiko, *Jugun Ianfu: Moro Heishitati no Shogen [Military Comfort Women: Testimony of Former Soldiers]* (Tokyo: Akashi Shoten, 1991), 42–43; Jugtin Ianfu Mondai Kodo Network [Military Comfort Women Issue Action Network], ed., *Jugun Ianfu Mondai Ajia Rental Kaigi Hokokushu [Report on Asian Association Conference on Comfort Women Issue]* (Tokyo: Association of Anti-Prostitution Activity, 1993), 17.

7. Kim Yonja's speech was given at the Human Rights World Conference in Vienna in 1992; see also Women's Human Rights Committee of Japan, ed., *Joseino Jinken Ajia Hotei [Women's Human Rights Asian Tribunal]* (Tokyo: Akashi Shoten, 1994), 123.

8. Abe Yuko, "Struggle with Trafficking in Women: From Activities of 'Mizura'," in *Josei/Bouryoku/Jinken [Women/Violence/Human Rights],* ed. Kazuko Watanabe (Tokyo: Gakuyo shobo, 1994), 156–66.

9. Yun Chong-ok, "Chosenjin Jugun Ianfu" ["Korean Military Comfort Women"], in *Chosenjin Jugun Ianfu Mondai Shiryoshu [Collection of Papers on Korean Military Comfort Women],* vol. 3:194–202 (Tokyo: Sanichi Shobo, 1992); "Teishintai Shuzaiki" ["Survey of Teishintai"], in *Cho senjin Josei ga mita "Ianfu Mondai" [Korean Women's View of "Comfort Women" Issue]* (Tokyo: Sanichi shobo, 1992), 11–94.

10. *Shukan Post [The Weekly Post]* survey, February 28, 1992. A well-known essayist, Kamisaka Fuyuko, wrote that the institution of comfort women was a necessary evil to protect respectable women from sexual abuse by Japanese soldiers.

11. Takasato Suzuyo, "Military Bases: Violence Against Women," in *Josei/ Bouryoku/Jinken,* 178–93; Takasato Suzuyo, "Okinawa in the Military Base," in *Joseino Jinken Ajia Hotei,* 95–103.

# 6.4 ───

# Rights of Women Within Islamic Communities
*Riffat Hassan*

## ■ Western Perception of Islam (and of Muslim Women)

Since the 1970s, there has been a growing interest in the West in Islam and Muslims. Much of this interest has been focused, however, on a few subjects such as Islamic Revival, Islamic Fundamentalism, The Salman Rushdie Affair, and Woman in Islam, rather than on understanding the complexity and diversity of the World of Islam. Not only the choice of subjects, but also the manner in which these subjects have generally been portrayed by Western media or popular literature calls into question the motivation which underlies the selective Western interest in Islam and Muslims. It is difficult to see this interest as being positively motivated given the widespread negative stereotyping of Islam and Muslims in the West. . . .

Given the reservoir of negative images associated with Islam and Muslims in "the Collective Unconscious" of the West, it is hardly surprising that, since the demise of the Soviet Empire, "the World of Islam" is being seen as the new "Enemy" which is perhaps even more incomprehensible and intractable than the last one. The routine portrayal of Islam as a religion spread by the sword and characterized by "Holy War," and of Muslims as barbarous and backward, frenzied and fanatic, volatile and violent, has led, in recent times, to an alarming increase in "Muslim-bashing"—verbal, physical, and psychological—in a number of Western countries.

In the midst of so much hatred and aversion toward Islam and Muslims in general, the outpouring of so much sympathy, in and by the West, toward Muslim women appears, at a surface level, to be an amazing contradiction. Are Muslim women also not adherents of Islam? Are Muslim women also not victims of "Muslim-bashing"? Few of us can forget the brutal burning of Turkish Muslim girls by German gangsters or the ruthless rape of Bosnian Muslim

Excerpted from Riffat Hassan, "Rights of Women Within Islamic Communities," in John Witte, Jr., and Johan D. Van Der Vyver, eds. *Religious Human Rights in Global Perspectives* (Leiden: Brill Publishers), pp. 1–33. © 1996 Brill Publishers. Reprinted with permission. Some of the author's notes have been omitted.

women by Serbian soldiers. In what way, then, am I—a Muslim woman—to interpret the "sympathy" shown to Muslim women by the popular rhetoric of the West?

As a Muslim woman who has lived for the greater part of her life in the West, I find it difficult to believe on the basis of my experience, that there is much genuine concern for Muslim women in many Western countries or peoples. The concern which exists in a country with a large Muslim population—such as England—is that the cultural norms and values of the British society not be jeopardized or compromised by "foreigners" like the Muslims. A large number of Muslims living in England happen to be blue-collar workers who are devout religiously and highly conservative insofar as attitudes toward women are concerned. This was the case when I was a student at the University of Durham in England during the 1960s. At that time neither the religious devotion of the Muslims nor their attitude toward women caused much concern to British society. But things changed radically and dramatically after the publication of *The Satanic Verses* by Salman Rushdie, in the fall of 1989. The intense reaction of the Muslims to this book which degraded, with a calculated deliberateness, that which was most sacred to them in their religious tradition, caused grave alarm to the British who began to see the Muslims in Britain as a threat to their "secular democracy." One very effective way to get back at the Muslims was to hit them where it would hurt the most—by politicizing the issues of Muslim women. Images of "poor, oppressed" Muslim women began to attract more and more publicity, not in England but in other Western countries with sizeable Muslim minorities, as Muslims generally were denounced as anti-Western, anti-rational, anti-modern, even anti-human.

## ▓ Rights of Women: Qur'anic Ideal Versus Muslim Practice

Muslim men never tire of repeating that Islam has given more rights to women than has any other religion. Certainly, if by "Islam" is meant "Qur'anic Islam," the rights that it has given to women are, indeed, impressive. Not only do women partake of all the general rights mentioned in the foregoing section, they are also the subject of much particular concern in the Qur'an. Underlying much of the Qur'an's legislation on women-related issues is the recognition that women have been disadvantaged persons in history to whom justice needs to be done by the Muslim "*ummah*." Unfortunately, however, the cumulative (Jewish, Christian, Hellenistic, Bedouin, and other) biases which existed in the Arab-Islamic culture of the early centuries of Islam infiltrated the Islamic tradition, largely through the Hadith literature, and undermined the intent of the Qur'an to liberate women from the status of chattels or inferior creatures and make them free and equal to men.

A brief review of Muslim history and culture brings to light many areas in which—Qur'anic teaching notwithstanding—women continued to be subjected to diverse forms of oppression and injustice, often in the name of Islam, and, what is far worse, in the name of a just, merciful, and compassionate God. While the Qur'an, because of its protective attitude toward all downtrodden and oppressed classes of people, appears to be weighted in many ways in favor of women, many of its women-related teachings have been used in patriarchal Muslim societies against, rather than for, women. Muslim societies, in general appear to be far more concerned with trying to control women's bodies and sexuality than with their human rights. Many Muslims when they speak of human rights either do not speak of women's rights at all,[1] or are mainly concerned with how a woman's chastity may be protected.[2] (They are apparently not very worried about protecting men's chastity.)

Women are the targets of the most serious violations of human rights which occur in many Muslim societies. Muslims say with great pride that Islam abolished female infanticide; true, but it must also be mentioned that one of the most common crimes in a number of Muslim countries (for example Pakistan) is the murder of women by their husbands. These so-called "honor-killings" are, in fact, extremely dishonorable and are frequently used to camouflage other kinds of crimes.

Female children are discriminated against from the moment of birth, for it is customary in Muslim societies to regard a son as a gift, and a daughter as a trial, from God. Therefore, the birth of a son is an occasion for celebration while the birth of a daughter calls for commiseration if not lamentation. Many girls are married when they are still minors, even though marriage in Islam is a contract and presupposes that the contracting parties are both consenting adults. Even though so much Qur'anic legislation is aimed at protecting the rights of women in the context of marriage[3] women cannot claim equality with their husbands. The husband, in fact, is regarded as his wife's gateway to heaven or hell and the arbiter of her final destiny. That such an idea can exist within the framework of Islam—which, in theory, rejects the idea of there being any intermediary between a believer and God—represents both a profound irony and a great tragedy.

Although the Qur'an presents the idea of what we today call a "no-fault" divorce and does not make any adverse judgments about divorce, Muslim societies have made divorce[4] extremely difficult for women, both legally and through social penalties. Although the Qur'an states clearly that the divorced parents of a minor child must decide by mutual consultation how the child is to be raised and that they must not use the child to hurt or exploit each other,[5] in most Muslim societies, women are deprived of both their sons (generally at age 7) and their daughters (generally at age 12). It is difficult to imagine an act of greater cruelty than depriving a mother of her children simply because she is divorced. Although polygamy was intended by the Qur'an to be for the protection of orphans and widows,[6] in practice Muslims have make it the Sword of Damocles which keeps women under constant threat. Although the Qur'an gave women the right to receive an inheritance not only on the death of a close relative, but also to receive other bequests or gifts during the lifetime of a benevolent caretaker, Muslim societies have disapproved greatly of the idea of giving wealth to a woman in preference to a man, even when her need or circumstances warrant it. Although the purpose of the Qur'anic legislation dealing with women's dress and conduct[7] was to make it safe for women to go about their daily business (since they have the right to engage in gainful activity as witnessed by Surah 4: *An-Nisa'*: 32) without fear of sexual harassment or molestation, Muslim societies have put many of them behind veils and shrouds and locked doors on the pretext of protecting their chastity, forgetting that according to the Qur'an[8] confinement to their homes was not a normal way of life for chaste women but a punishment for "unchastity."

Despite the fact that women such as Khadijah and 'A'ishah (wives of the Prophet Muhammad) and Rabi'a al-Basri (the outstanding woman Sufi) figure significantly in early Islam, the Islamic tradition has, by and large, remained rigidly patriarchal until now, prohibiting the growth of scholarship among women particularly in the realm of religious thought. This means that the sources on which the Islamic tradition is mainly based have been interpreted only by men who have arrogated to themselves the task of defining the ontological, theological, sociological, and eschatological status of Muslim women. It is hardly surprising that until now the majority of Muslim women have accepted this situation passively, almost unaware of the extent to which their human (also Islamic, in an ideal sense) rights have been violated by their male-dominated and male-centered societies. Kept for centuries in physical, mental, and emotional bondage, and deprived of the opportunity to actualize their human potential, even the exercise of analyzing their personal experiences as Muslim women is, perhaps, overwhelming for these women. (Here it needs to be mentioned that while the rate of literacy is low in many Muslim countries, the rate of literacy of Muslim women, especially those who live in rural areas where most of the population lives, is amongst the lowest in the world.)

Much of what has happened to Muslim women becomes comprehensible if one keeps one fact in mind: Muslims, in general, consider it a self-evident fact that women are not equal to men, who are "above" women or have a "degree of advantage" over them. There is hardly anything in a Muslim woman's life that is not affected by this belief; hence it is vitally important, not only for theological reasons but also for pragmatic ones, to subject it to rigorous scholarly scrutiny and attempt to identify its roots. . . .

Woman and man, created equal by God and standing equal in the sight of God, have become very unequal in Muslim societies. The Qur'anic description of man and woman in marriage reads thus: "They are your garments/And you are their garments" (Surah 2: *Al-Baqarah*: 187) implies closeness, mutuality, and equality. However, Muslim culture had reduced many, if not most, women to the position of puppets on a string, to slave-like creatures whose only purpose in life is to cater to the needs and pleasures of men. Not only this, it has also had the audacity and the arrogance to deny women direct access to God. It is one of Islam's cardinal beliefs that each person—man or woman—is responsible and accountable for his or her individual actions. How can the husband become the wife's gateway to heaven or hell? How can he become the arbiter not only of what happens to her in this world but also of her ultimate destiny? Surely such questions must arise in the minds of Muslim women, but so far they have not been asked aloud. My own feeling is that not only Muslim men, but also Muslim women—with a few exceptions—are afraid to ask questions the answers to which are bound to threaten the existing balance of power in the domain of family relationships in most Muslim societies.

Despite everything that has gone wrong with the lives of countless Muslim women through the ages due to patriarchal Muslim culture, I believe strongly that there is hope for the future. There are indications from across the world of Islam that an increasing number of Muslims are beginning to reflect seriously upon the teachings of the Qur'an as they become disenchanted with capitalism, communism, and Western democracy. As this reflection deepens, it is likely to lead to the realization that the supreme task entrusted to human beings by God, of being God's deputies on earth, can only be accomplished by establishing justice which the Qur'an regards as a prerequisite for authentic peace. Without the elimination of inequities, inequalities, and injustices that pervade the personal and collective lives of human beings, it is not possible to talk about peace in Qur'anic terms. It is important to note that there is more Qur'anic legislation pertaining to the establishment of justice in the context of family relationships than on any other subject. This points to the assumption implicit in much Qur'anic legislation, namely, that if human beings can learn to order their homes justly so that the human rights of all within its jurisdiction—children, women, and men—are safeguarded, then they can also order their society and the world at large, justly. In other words, the Qur'an regards the home as a microcosm of the "*ummah*" and the world community, and emphasizes the importance of making it "the abode of peace" through just living.

## ▓ Notes

1. For example, R. A. Jullundhri, "Human Rights in Islam," in A. D. Falconer, ed., *Understanding Human Rights* (Dublin, 1980).

2. For example, A. A. Maududi, *Human Rights in Islam* (Lahore, 1977).

3. See, e.g., Surah 4: *An-Nisa'*: 4, 19; Surah 24: *An-Nur*: 33; Surah 2: *Al-Baqarah*: 187; Surah 9: *At-Tawbah*: 71; Surah 7: *Al-A raf*: 189; Surah 30: *Ar-Rum*: 21.

4. See, e.g., Surah 2: *Al-Baqarah:* 231, 241.
5. The reference here is to Surah 2: *Al-Baqarah*: 233.
6. The reference here is to Surah 4: *An-Nisa'*: 2–3.
7. See, e.g., Surah 24: *An-Nur*: 30–31; Surah 33: *Al-Ahzah*: 59.
8. The reference here is to the Qur'an, Surah 4: *An-Nisa'*: 15.

# 6.5 ⸻

# Female Circumcision Comes to America

*Linda Burstyn*

It is a late-summer night, nearly midnight in Washington, D.C., when the taxi-cab comes for Mimi Ramsey. She steps into it with a worried look in her eyes and her mouth firmly set. She is on her way to yet another stranger's house, where she will again—for the umpteenth time in the past year—talk about the most personal and most secret of African customs, offering herself as a sort of human roadblock in the traffic of tradition.

At the house Ramsey is kissed on both of her cheeks by her hostess, an Ethiopian immigrant like herself, and ushered into a dimly lit living room dec-orated with rugs and cloths from their homeland. There she spends the next several hours huddled together with the young mother, Genat, talking in con-spiratorial whispers.

"Mother says she will do it anyway, herself—when I'm out of the house—if I don't agree to get it done soon," Genat confides to the woman she hopes will help her. "She says she will take a razor blade and do it." Ramsey nods. She has heard this story many times before, and responds by reciting a long list of reasons why the older woman must be stopped, trying to give Genat the courage to buck tradition and disobey her mother. "You cannot let her do this to your child. Please. It is wrong. You know how painful it is. How damaging. Your daughter may hate you for life for what you allow to happen to her."

Genat shakes her head. She doesn't want her baby girl, just born in this country, to be circumcised, as is customary in her native land, but her mother is adamant.

"She believes in it so strongly," Genat says. "She said if I don't do these things, the girl will grow up horny. She'll be like American girls. And how will I be able to go back to work if my mother is not here to care for my child?"

It is not until many hours later, after a long, sleepless night and a fruitless morning discussion with the older woman, that Ramsey, discouraged, finally ends this peculiar house call. "Please send your mother home," she advises

Excerpted from Linda Burstyn, "Female Circumcision Comes to America," *The Atlantic Monthly* (October 1995): 28–35. Reprinted with permission from the author. Some of the author's notes have been omitted.

Genat. "Go on welfare if you have to, but don't let your mother stay in the house and do this to your baby." . . .

Americans who are aware of the practice, which has been performed on some 100 million to 130 million women and girls worldwide, assume that it is a fact of life only for girls who live in faraway places—a form of barbarism that doesn't touch American homes, schools, or doctor's offices. This is simply not true. As more and more African immigrants move to this country, bringing with them their food, practices, and traditions, perhaps hundreds more daughters of African parents are circumcised in the United States every year.

Many of the immigrant mothers who are making these decisions about their daughters know little or nothing about their own anatomy. They are told that if the clitoris is left alone, it will grow and drag on the ground; that if their daughters are left uncircumcised, they will be wild, and will crave men; that no man from their home country will marry them uncircumcised (although many African men say that they prefer uncircumcised women for sex and marriage); that circumcision aids in menstruation and childbirth (although the opposite is true in both cases); and that it is a religious—usually Islamic—requirement (although none of the major Islamic texts calls directly for FGM). And so these women and their husbands come to the United States filled with misinformation, and remain blindly dedicated to continuing this torturous tradition. . . .

Frequently families will chip in to bring someone from the homeland to the United States to perform circumcisions, because it's cheaper to import a circumciser than it is to send several girls abroad. A taxi driver in Washington, D.C., who hotly defends the practice says that he recently had his daughters circumcised that way. "I stood over her to make sure she cut enough," he says. "I wasn't going to let my daughters have those things!" . . .

Mimi Ramsey has made it her avocation to visit African businesses and communities in this country and proselytize against FGM.

Ramsey typifies many who, after hearing about FGM in the media, have finally been able to talk about an experience long suppressed. For years she had gone to doctors for help with the aftereffects of her radical circumcision. For years doctors, either because they were stunned by what they saw or because they were trying to be culturally sensitive, said nothing to Ramsey about what had been done to her and simply prescribed various topical creams and jellies to ease her pain. But in February of last year all that changed.

"I went to a doctor for the problem I have down there," Ramsey says. "He asked me, 'Why did they do this to you? Why did they remove all your genitalia?' He was in shock." After returning to her apartment, depressed and confused, Ramsey, a devout Christian, prayed for some answers. Later that night she saw a television program about FGM and the Nigerian woman's asylum case in Oregon. It answered many of her questions. "I was angry and still am. The morning after the show I got up and called all the African women from my address book who live in the United States. I asked them, 'Are you a victim too?' And they said yes. I said, 'Let's talk about it. I'm not going to shut up anymore.'"

Most of the talk about circumcision in this country has focused on male circumcision, as people have made the case that it causes physical and psychological pain to infant boys. When it comes to women, "circumcision" is at best a misnomer.

"Cutting off the clitoris is equivalent to cutting off much of the penis," Asha Mohamud says.

This is why opponents and medical leaders use the more descriptive and more accurate term "female genital mutilation." Although in a tiny percentage of cases FGM consists of a small cut to the hood of the clitoris, typically it is much more severe. It usually involves the complete removal of the clitoris, and often the removal of some of the inner and outer labia. In its most extreme form—infibulation—almost all the external genitalia are cut away, the remaining flesh from the outer labia is sewn together, or infibulated, and the girl's legs are bound from ankle to waist for several weeks while scar tissue closes up the vagina almost completely. A small hole, typically about the diameter of a pencil, is left for urination and menstruation. The cutting is usually done with a razor, a kitchen knife, or a pair of scissors. It is rare for any anesthesia to be used. The age at which FGM is performed varies among countries and communities. In some countries it is done on infants in the days or weeks after birth; in others, such as Senegal, it is part of an elaborate rite of passage that comes with puberty. In parts of Nigeria and Burkina Faso, FGM is practiced during the seventh month of a woman's first pregnancy, in the belief that if the baby at birth comes in contact with its mother's clitoris, it will die. . . .

"I think some people leave some traditions behind, but some traditions are stronger than others," Mohamud says. "This is one that's very strong. The community here sees explicit sex on television, they hear a lot of alien things, and so it becomes more urgent for mothers to do this to their daughters so the girls don't fall into loose groups. They think if they don't follow the tradition, they don't know what will happen." . . .

A desire to educate both the officials in her adopted country and immigrants from her native one drives Mimi Ramsey. The New York–based international women's-rights group Equality Now is raising money to fund Ramsey's efforts so that she will be able to spend more time doing what she does best: taking her message to the streets.

In a dark restaurant in Los Angeles paper place mats are decorated with maps of Ethiopia. Shiny red-vinyl booths are filled with brightly dressed residents of the local immigrant community. Original Ethiopian artwork and African posters cover the walls. The smell of cooked meat and the sound of quiet laughter surround the booth where Ramsey sits, with her just-served lunch. Her own conservative dress is more likely to be found in Orange County than in Addis Ababa. She bows her head and prays aloud: "Please, God, save girls from being tortured. Please, God. Please. Thank you."

Just minutes after she begins her meal of traditional Ethiopian bread dipped in a stew of vegetables and meat, she gets up and approaches a table of four Ethiopian men. She exchanges pleasantries in their native language, Amharic, but quickly the conversation turns tense. A few English words are mixed with the foreign ones. A man says, "Tradition." Ramsey replies, "Let's talk about it," and squeezes in next to the men.

"In this country you see a lot of young women unmarried, pregnant," Yashanu, an Ethiopian taxi driver in his mid-forties, says, leaning back in his chair. "Maybe if American girls were circumcised, this wouldn't happen. When I was growing up, a girl had to stay within the family. She could be home no later than five or six in the afternoon. But in this country there are no rules." He shakes his head. "When you circumcise a woman, they're less active sexually and more interested in their schoolwork."

Mimi describes the physical pain, the burning and irritation, she still feels from what was done to her when she was six years old. She takes a small tube of cream from her purse and shows it to them. The cream is supposed to soothe her damaged nerve endings. "I can't enjoy sex," she tells them. "I feel nothing. I will never forgive my mother for doing this to me. Will you join me in stopping people from doing this to little girls? We have to help them," she says, smiling, touching one of the young men on his arm.

By the time Mimi stands up, thirty minutes later, the three younger men, all of whom knew vaguely about FGM because they had had sex with women who were circumcised, are horrified. They each promise earnestly to call their families back in Ethiopia to talk with them about the practice. But the older man remains unconvinced. . . .

Soraya Mire, the Somali film maker, is one of a handful of women trying to find the finances and forums to educate an immigrant population that views FGM as a comforting tie to the morality and traditions of its homeland. She uses screenings of her documentary as opportunities to discuss the issue. Like others, Mire is motivated by her own experience as a mutilated woman.

"They use vegetable thorns to sew because they are very strong," Mire says, describing the process of infibulation that she experienced. "The stitches stay in until marriage. Then three days before the wedding they ask the groom, Do you want to open her or do you want us to open her? A good man will say, You go ahead and do it. Others want to tear the woman open themselves." . . .

Last year Mire went into hiding after receiving death threats from Somalis who were angry about what they saw as her traitorous behavior. She is now cautious when she's out in public and is reluctant to divulge the whereabouts of her secluded Los Angeles–area home. . . .

Back home in San Jose, some time later, Ramsey hears again from Genat, in Washington. Genat has sent her mother back to Ethiopia. She happily reports that her daughter is safe. Crying, Ramsey thanks her, returns the phone to its cradle, and bows her head in prayer.

# 7 Children as Targets

## 7.1

# Introduction
*The Editors*

This chapter examines children as targets of human rights violations. Children today face a myriad of human rights abuses ranging from economic deprivation to repression. Children around the world face the lion's share of human rights abuses and are often the last voices to be heard. Today children increasingly find themselves trafficked into slavery, sold into bonded labor, or conscripted as child soldiers. Amidst growing international attention, little real change has occurred, perhaps because children often depend on others to voice and protect their rights. Even though almost every country in the world has ratified *The United Nations International Convention on the Rights of the Child* (1989) and its optional protocols, this document has done little to protect children from gross human rights violations worldwide.

Zehra Kabasakal Arat provides an excellent overview of the issues surrounding child labor. She begins with an exploration of the relationship between poverty and child labor, a discussion of the costs of child labor, as well as how integral and pervasive the practice is in many developing countries. Arat also addresses the policies of international institutions, such as the World Bank and International Monetary Fund (IMF), which contribute to the persistent nature of child labor. She further summarizes attempts to end child labor, beginning with the first attempt to establish a minimum working age in 1919 up to the 1999 *Worst Forms of Child Labor Convention*. Ultimately, Arat argues that in order to eradicate child labor, the problems of exploitation and poverty must be addressed.

Andew Bushell also addresses how poverty promotes the exploitation of children, in this case examining the prevailing practice of child marriages in Afghanistan and Pakistan. The long-standing cultural practice of betrothing young girls and boys in marriage has evolved to young girls marrying much older men due to the changes in society over the past several decades. The nature of child marriage is increasingly motivated by economic concerns, where poor families are paid by older males who want to marry their young children. The author points out the detrimental consequences of child marriage, including increased likelihood of domestic violence and illiteracy, as young girls drop out of school to take on the traditional roles expected of wives. Ultimately, the end result is often death as young girls give birth before their bodies mature. International organizations are paying greater attention to the legal question of child marriage. Yet the issue of child marriage as a human rights violation remains highly controversial.

Lee Tucker examines the bonded labor problem in India, where poverty compels parents to sell their children into bondage. Although there are a plethora of laws enacted to protect against child labor, there is little enforcement. Besides poverty, the traditional caste system, lack of education, and various myths regarding the advantages of child labor contribute to and enable the proliferation of child labor. Tucker provides several examples of the industries that favor child labor, including *beedi* (cigarette rolling), silver, silk, and hand-woven woolen carpets. For each industry, he carefully documents the number of children involved, the working conditions and abuse by the employers, the health consequences, testimonies of child laborers, and the basic ineffectiveness of the existing laws governing each industry as well as the use of child labor. Tucker suggests a holistic approach, focusing on enforcement of existing laws and prevention of selling children into labor bondage in the future. In the excerpt included here, the practice of using child labor for *beedi* production is explored.

The trafficking of children goes beyond bonded labor. The article by R. Barri Flowers focuses on children in the sex trade. Children are exposed to any number of human rights violations, including child prostitution, child pornography, rape, murder, psychological abuses, and exposure to disease, particularly AIDS. Flowers points out the difficulty in measuring the number of children involved in the sex industry, but he does provide some statistics, including the fact that there are 1 million child prostitutes in Asia, 500,000 in Brazil, and anywhere from several hundred thousand to 2 million in the United States. Flowers also focuses on the organizational aspect of child sexploitation: child sex tourism. Child sex tourism is most prevalent in Southeast Asia—Thailand and the Philippines in particular. The majority of the "tourists" come from the wealthiest countries, with one quarter traveling from the United States. Child pornography is discussed as well. In both cases, one of the most likely consequences for children is the risk of AIDS and the contraction of other sexually transmitted diseases. As with the case of bonded labor in India, Flowers points out that current legislation does little to help or protect children lost in the web of the child sex trade. More success is found in the actions of NGOs and IGOs that focus on the needs of children.

The human rights of children today are further endangered by war. Steven Hick examines the nature of war and how it contributes to the plight of children today. He argues that the current wars, those within nations rather than between nations, are driven by changes in the politics of globalization. He points to the institutions of the free trade regime, specifically free trade and the IMF, as contributors to modern-day wars. The former motivates armies to protect corporate and landowner interests to the detriment of the majority of citizens within these states. The latter institutes structural adjustment programs that weaken economies, creating the conditions for war. Hick contends that the forces of globalization contribute to and exacerbate a wealth gap that falls heavily on the shoulders of children. In the excerpt included here, Hick examines the interrelationship among poverty, conflict, and abuse. The number of children growing up in poverty, in conditions ripe for conflict, makes them a target for abuse and torture during conflict. Children are susceptible to the most egregious human rights violations, such as systematic rape, ethnic cleansing, and genocide. Children are also likely to suffer from malnutrition, disease, and injuries from land mines. Many children are also drawn into the conflict directly as child soldiers. Ultimately, children join the ranks of refugees and internally displaced persons. Hick also examines the long-lasting effect of war on children, the trauma of conflict that they take into adulthood.

# 7.2 ‹‹‹‹‹‹‹

# Child Labor as a Human Rights Issue: Efforts, Mistakes, and Solutions
*Zehra F. Kabasakal Arat*

## ■ The Problem and Its Scope

"Child labor" typically refers to the work rendered by minors under age 15 (or 18). Since it tends to be illegal and takes place in the informal sector of the economy, it has been difficult to obtain accurate data on the number of child laborers. Global estimates range from 200 to 500 million. According to the International Labour Organization (ILO), in the 1990s, 250 million children—140 million boys and 110 million girls—between the ages of five and fourteen were working; 120 million of them worked full-time (ILO 1998). A new ILO study noted an 11 percent decline in the number of child laborers between 2000 and 2004; it set the total number at 218 million and indicated a major decline in the Latin America and Caribbean regions (ILO 2006). However, the problem prevails in both industrial and developing countries, and under severer circumstances in the latter group. An estimated 15 to 20 percent of children in developing countries work for no pay, usually as domestic help or farm workers, and rural children constitute about two-thirds of all child laborers and start working at a younger age (Boukhari 1999).

Bonded child labor is an acute problem in India and Pakistan, where millions of bonded child laborers work long hours as virtual slaves in activities ranging from agriculture to carpet weaving. Because of the fraudulent accounting schemes of the creditor-employers, some children end up spending their entire childhood or lives working to pay off their family's debts. Some conservative estimates put the number of bonded child laborers at 15 million in India (Human Rights Watch 1996), 5 million in Indonesia, and 500,000 in Sri Lanka (ILO 1998). In Thailand, children are routinely bought and sold to work in private houses, restaurants, factories, and brothels. Domestic work particularly affects girls, and due to its "hidden" nature, is very difficult to estimate.

This is an abridged and updated version of Zehra F. Kabasakal Arat, "Analyzing Child Labor as a Human Rights Issue: Its Causes, Aggravating Principles, and Alternative Proposals." *Human Rights Quarterly* 24 (1) (February 2002): 177–204. I am grateful to my assistant, Kathryn Eaker, for her help in preparing this version.

People oppose child labor for several reasons, ranging from moral to economic. They claim that it

- steals the childhood of millions of children;
- subjects children to economic exploitation, because they are paid at the lowest rates;
- replaces adult labor, because employers view children as cheap and docile;
- pushes wages down for all laborers;
- causes physical deformations and long-term healthcare problems in children due to unhealthy, unsafe, dangerous, and poisonous work environments;
- perpetuates poverty, because child laborers, deprived of education or healthy physical development, are likely to become adults with low earning prospects; and
- lowers the labor cost, thus allowing countries to attract investors and benefit from "unfair trade" due to their low production cost.

## ▓ Who Uses or Sustains Child Labor?

Child labor is sustained by three key players: employers, parents, and the state. However, international financial agencies also have a significant role.

Employers use child labor because it is cheap and profitable. Child labor is prevalent in industries such as carpet weaving, silk production, synthetic gemstone manufacturing, and jasmine picking due to a belief that nimble fingers, small hands, and thin arms can do the delicate jobs better. Children are preferred also for being more docile.

Child labor is provided by lower classes and poor households, which are disproportionately high among immigrant and ethnic minority groups. The lack of "living wages," disability benefits, a healthy and safe work environment, healthcare, and childcare allowances for adult workers increases families' dependency on child labor. Thus, parents allow or force their children to work and rely on them as unpaid laborers in family farms and businesses or as wage-earners.

Governments often turn a blind eye. Individuals and national or transnational corporations bribe officials to ignore violations, and pressure governments to relax employment restrictions and restrict labor rights and union activities. Most countries mandate primary education and have laws that ban child labor. Yet, governments not only fail to enforce these laws, but deny the existence of the problem. Some even hire child laborers in state-owned enterprises. Despite many laws forbidding forced and child labor, the Indian government, for example, recruits children as young as six years for "training" programs in carpet making, and thus effectively runs a business entirely based on child labor (Tucker 1997). In Egypt, which has an estimated 1.5 million workers under the age of fourteen working in agriculture or related areas, the Ministry of Agriculture, which owns about 10 percent of Egypt's cotton fields, relies upon children as young as five years old to pick cotton (Mekay 1997). Military and armed conflicts are often sustained by recruiting the young. The majority of the estimated 250,000 child soldiers around the world are recruited by private militia or opposition groups (Smolin 2000), but the United States and other states routinely recruit children in their late teens.

Transnational corporations and international financial agencies, such as the IMF and the World Bank, influence state policies and create socioeconomic conditions that do not protect children's rights but encourage child labor. As a condition for lending, the IMF and the World Bank ask the borrowing government to seek economic stability and apply "fiscal discipline," by implementing structural adjustment policies (SAPs), which include freezing wages, reducing government spending, and privatizing government enterprises. While reducing government spending typically means reducing social expenditures (e.g., health and education) and eliminating government subsidies on basic goods and services, privatization almost always results in major layoffs, forcing low-income households to tighten their belts more and more. The IMF's insistence on reducing aggregate demand in order to curb inflation comes at the expense of poor households, which then turn to child labor for additional income. At least in India and Zimbabwe, the link between the SAPs and the explosion of child labor has been well documented (Tucker and Ganesan 1997; Bellamy 1997, 28).

The SAPs adversely affect children's education by reducing government spending and forcing parents to rearrange their priorities. Poor parents send children to work instead of school, or keep them at home to watch their younger siblings so their mothers can earn wages. Given the patriarchal nature of societies, girls' education is likely to be sacrificed first. A study of seventeen countries that had implemented the SAPs in the 1980s identified "a clear tendency for a deterioration in the ratio of girls to boys in secondary education after the onset of recession" (Vickers 1991, 29).

The World Bank's development mission and programs appear more complex in terms of its approach to the issues of poverty and development than those of the IMF. Since the 1960s, its studies have pointed to the persistent nature of poverty, human resource development needs, and the enormous social gains promised by improving education and income opportunities for women (e.g., improved nutrition and health of children, higher labor and land productivity, and lower fertility rates). However, the Bank has been slow in incorporating these findings into project design and funding policies. Until recently, it allocated only about a combined 8 percent of its development assistance funds to projects in primary healthcare, education, clean water, and sanitation

(UNDP 2000, 79). In 1997, critics of the Bank claimed that by failing to monitor labor conditions in the silk industry in India, the Bank had "in effect, underwritten an industry which relied on bonded child labor at all stages of operation" (Tucker and Ganesan 1997, 19). In response to criticism by Human Rights Watch and others, the Bank hired an official in 1998 to oversee the process to avoid lending to businesses that use child labor (Prashad 1999).

Recently, the World Bank has changed its approach and started to move away from large-scale projects to support education and healthcare by increasing funding. Although promising, these shifts are not likely to be effective if the Bank and other international agencies, which are heavily influenced by the US Treasury Department, continue to subscribe to the principles known as the "Washington Consensus," a set of neoliberal economic policies (e.g., SAPs) that clearly weaken the control that governments of developing countries have over the economy and favor the freedom of capital. Moreover, facing global price competition and trying to attract foreign capital, governments, with reduced budgets and declining regulatory power, do not or cannot enforce laws on mandatory education, minimum working age, and healthy and safe work conditions.

In order to increase their competitiveness in global markets, governments have been redefining their welfare policies, social security systems, retirement policies, and labor laws. These "labor law reforms" reduce the negotiating power of unions, limit workers' benefits, and undermine job security. Although historically unionization rates increased as a country became more industrialized, according to the ILO reports, trade union membership has been falling both in industrial and developing countries in recent years. The new "labor law reforms" are likely to push down unionization levels further. The welfare of workers and the elimination of child labor, however, would demand resisting and reversing this declining trend.

## ▓ The Root Causes of Child Labor: Poverty and Related Issues

The ILO and other concerned groups agree that child labor is primarily driven by poverty. In addition to poverty, child labor is supported by a host of interrelated problems, such as an unskilled adult labor force, exploitative work conditions, weak labor laws and unions, inadequate social services, and improper economic policies—circumstances that are more abrasive in developing countries.

Many adults in developing countries are unemployed or underemployed and cannot make a decent living. For example, in Sal Hagar, an Egyptian village with 50,000 people, over 30 percent of adult males are unemployed, while others work for low wages in the grain fields, and child laborers work in the cotton fields earning up to $1.50 for an eight-hour day. Although very low, children's earnings still constitute an important source of income for these poor families (Mekay 1997). The UNDP's Human Poverty Index indicates that human poverty affects at least a third of the population in more than one-third of the developing world, and 2.5 billion people live on less than $2 a day (UNDP 2005, 4). Contributing around 20 to 25 percent of family income (ILO 1998), children's labor becomes crucial.

The demographics and population trends of developing countries also work against their children. According to UNICEF, 87 percent of the world's population under age eighteen live in developing countries (UNICEF 1997, 24). The proportion of youth and elderly populations to the working-age population provides the "dependency ratio" in the domestic economy; a high percentage of youth means that more people depend on the work of fewer people. To avoid starvation, countries with high dependency ratios should either increase the productivity level of the working-age population or allow some of the underage population to participate in the workforce.

Population control policies would also help. The global interest in population control in developing countries, however, has yielded mostly coercive and ineffective programs. Although an increase in women's education is directly related to decline in fertility rates, education in general, and girls' education in particular, have been neglected by governments and many internationally sponsored development programs.

National laws mandating primary education are not enforced, especially outside urban centers. Rural schools are few and most are severely underfunded. Many schools are overcrowded, inadequately staffed and supplied, and offer poor-quality education. "Free" education may mean the absence of tuition and fees, but the costs of uniforms, books, and supplies are expected to be paid by parents. The opportunity cost (i.e., time a child could use earning money instead of in school) plus school expenses impose huge financial burdens on parents. Consequently, it is not surprising that 110 million children of primary school age in developing countries are not enrolled (UNDP 2005, 43).

## ■ Efforts to End Child Labor

The international community has attempted to address child labor in several ways. The ILO first established a minimum age for children to be employed in 1919 (Convention 5), and in 1973 issued the Minimum Age Convention (138), in which it prohibited economic activity performed by a person under the age of fifteen for being hazardous to the physical, mental, and moral well-being of the child (Convention 138).

An especially popular human rights convention, the 1989 UN Convention on the Rights of the Child (CRC), included several articles against economic exploitation and abuse of children. The Convention broke UN records by entering into force on 25 September 1990, less than a year after being adopted, and it got close to achieving universal ratification with 193 state parties—the only exceptions being the United States and Somalia. Despite this high level of state support for the CRC, only a minority of the world's children fully enjoy the rights that it provides, such as Article 32, which obligates states to protect children "from economic exploitation and from performing any work that is likely to be hazardous or to interfere with the child's education, or to be harmful to the child's health or physical, mental, spiritual, moral, or social development."

After failing to achieve consensus for its Minimum Age Convention—it is ratified by only 103 states because it is considered too complex and difficult to implement (though now the number of ratifications has reached 147)—the ILO adopted a new convention in 1999, Worst Forms of Child Labor Convention, which entered into force on 19 November 2000. The Convention prioritizes the struggle against the *worst forms of child labor* and calls for their elimination for all persons under the age of eighteen.

Human rights advocates emphasize the interrelatedness and interdependency of human rights, and these principles have been promoted in various international declarations and conventions. The Vienna Declaration and Programme for Action of 1993 asserts: "All human rights are universal, indivisible, and interdependent and interrelated. The international community must treat human rights globally in a fair and equal manner, on the same footing, and with the same emphasis." The interdependency of rights is revealed by the child labor problem in a unique form: Denying the right to employment or a livable wage for adults inevitably results in the violation of children's rights by setting the conditions for allowing child labor to exist. However, policies that focus on child labor tend to undermine the interdependency of rights and try to deal with symptoms rather than causes.

Conscientious people in industrial countries have proposed and pursued banning child labor through trade sanctions, import restrictions, and consumer boycotts. These solutions merely palliate the guilt of citizens in wealthy countries and perpetuate the suffering of poor children and their families. Selectively addressing the child labor issue in export-oriented industries is problematic for four primary reasons. First, according to the ILO, export industries employ only 5 percent of child workers, ignoring the majority of the full-time working children located in the commercial agricultural sector. Second, many export items produced solely by adult labor depend on raw materials and intermediary goods created by child laborers. Third, trade bans on goods produced by child labor decrease demand for such goods, consequently decreasing the demand for all labor in general, triggering a decline in wages and furthering the decline of the export sector in developing countries. Finally, banning child labor in export industries could push children to seek employment in less protected informal sectors (e.g., illegal operations and prostitution). The US Child Labor Deterrence Act of 1993, for example, attempted to eliminate child labor by banning imports of goods produced by children aged fourteen years and younger. Concerned about the ban, Bangladeshi garment producers fired 50,000 child laborers (Bellamy 1997; Bachman 2000). UNICEF researchers later discovered that these "freed" children were "trapped in a harsh environment with no skills, little or no education and precious few alternatives"; many of them took work as stone-crushers, street hustlers, and prostitutes—industries more hazardous and exploitative than garment production (Bellamy 1997, 60).

Simple bans or restrictions imposed upon export industries that employ child labor also fail to reach children who are employed in other areas, such as domestic work. Domestic child workers, most of whom are girls, suffer greater abuse; in addition to working for long hours and living in unsuitable conditions, they are exposed to physical, emotional, and sexual abuse by their employers or other household members and are deprived of their parents' affection and support. They earn very little, sometimes paid with leftover food and used clothing. They constitute the most vulnerable and exploited children of all, and also the most difficult to protect (Bellamy 1997).

Some "fair trade" advocates, mostly in developed countries, who support sanctions linking trade to restrictions on child labor or other social clauses, are not necessarily interested in promoting the rights of the child or labor rights. They want to limit imports from those countries with cheaper labor costs. The US Executive Order 13126, Prohibition of Acquisition of Products Produced by Forced or Indentured Child Labor, signed by President Bill Clinton in 1999, was merely a public relations tool. The order appeared to prevent the US government from purchasing goods made by the "worst forms" of child labor but exempted those produced in Mexico (a party to the North American Free Trade Agreement) and countries that are World Trade Organization (WTO) members.

## ■ How to Approach the Child Labor Issue

Recently, child workers from urban areas have begun to organize by asserting their opposition to trade sanctions and claiming their right to work. This now international movement started with Niños y Adolescents Trabajadores (Child and Teenage Workers) in Peru in the 1970s, then spread to other Latin American countries. Child laborers in Africa and Asia demand that the UN and other organizations distinguish between exploitative and beneficial forms of work. More than 1,000 child workers who participated in a 1994 conference organized by the Campaign Against Child Labor in Chennai, India, demanded local schools, free books and uniforms, an "interesting" education, jobs for their parents, day-care for their siblings, and their own workplace rights and ability to unionize (Prashad 1999).

A comprehensive approach to ending child labor would include eliminating poor families' reliance on their wages, enforcing the principle of mandatory education, and providing improved and free education. Government investment in education should be encouraged, supported, and reinforced by unilateral and multilateral aid and by the international lending agencies. Educational programs and schools like the ones established by the ILO under its 1992 International Program on the Elimination of Child Labor (IPEC) should be expanded as a preventative measure as well as to help rehabilitate child laborers (ILO 2006).

UNICEF argues that improved access to education is the most effective way to eradicate child labor. Pointing out that the failure in providing primary education stems from a lack of political will rather than scarce resources, UNICEF reported in 1997 that an estimated addition of $6 billion a year—less than 1 percent of what the world spends every year on weapons—would have put every child in school by the year 2000 (Bellamy 1997, 55). In addition to accessibility, measures such as providing meals or stipends to cover lost wages would make schooling more attractive to parents.

The lasting solution to the problem of child labor would be to eliminate poverty, and that can be achieved only if the adult labor force is paid meaningful wages and has access to credit, training programs, healthcare, social security, and safety nets. The inference from an economic modeling of child and adult labor substitutability concludes that "the first-best policy is to attack the problem at its source. This entails improving the condition and scope for adult labor" (Basu and Hoang Van 1998, 425).

Of course, no proposal that attempts to improve working conditions and no labor law, domestic or international, that protects labor rights can be effectively enforced without proper monitoring by groups other than the employers and government. Both of them can be too willing to undermine the well-being of the workers for profit and other short-term interests. Moreover, the shortage of trained and committed government inspectors, repeatedly reported as an enforcement problem, would necessitate enrolling other competent and committed observers. They can be logically found in labor unions.

The right to form and join unions is a human right, but labor unions are also crucial to promoting workers' rights, improving working conditions, increasing wages, and enforcing minimum-age rules. Thus, unionization should be promoted, for all ages, first to improve the conditions of child laborers, but eventually to eliminate the need for child workers. By emphasizing antidiscrimination in wages (including age discrimination) and seeking healthy and safe work conditions and environments for all workers, unions would push for contracts and laws that would make child labor less attractive to the employers. Unions in industrial countries, instead of lobbying for trade sanctions, should direct their energy and resources to resisting the trend of deunionization and restrictive labor legislation both at home and abroad.

As aptly put by Vijay Prashad, "refusing to split apart the 'special' question of child labor from exploitation in general may be the key which unlocks the child labor issue—placing the onus not on the aberration of exploiting children, but on a world system which makes this and other forms of hyper-exploitation all too typical" (Prashad 1999, 23). In fact, this is the point that *some* of the protestors at the IMF, World Bank, and WTO summit meetings have been trying to convey to the "masterminds" of the world economy and globalization.

In 2000, the United Nations adopted eight Millennium Development Goals (MDGs), which include eradicating extreme poverty and hunger, achieving universal primary education, promoting gender equality and empowerment of women, and increasing foreign aid. They are all directly related to child labor issues and can help provide substantial relief. The 2005 assessments of the MDGs, however, indicate that the global commitments have been far from satisfactory, and the benchmarks set for 2015 are not likely to be met.

## ■ References

Bachman, S. L. 2000. "A New Economics of Child Labor: Searching for Answers Behind the Headlines." *Journal of International Affairs* 53 (3) (Spring): 545–572.

Basu, Kaushik, and Pham Hoang Van. 1998. "The Economics of Child Labor." *American Economic Review* 88 (3) (June): 412–427.

Bellamy, Carol. 1997. *The State of the World's Children 1997*. New York: UNICEF.

Boukhari, Sophie. 1999. "Child Labor: A Lesser Evil?" *UNESCO Courier* (May), pp. 37–39.

Human Rights Watch. 1996. *The Small Hands of Slavery: Bonded Child Labor in India*. New York: Human Rights Watch, pp. 1, 122.

ILO. 2006. *The End of Child Labor: Within Reach*. Report I(B) of the International Labor Conference, 95th Session, Geneva.

———. 1998. *Child Labor: Targeting the Intolerable*. Report IV of the International Labor Conference, 86th Session, Geneva.

Mekay, Emad. 1997. "An Economic Essential? (Child Labor in Egypt)." *The Middle East* 272 (November): 38–40.

Prashad, Vijay. 1999. "Calloused Conscience: The Limited Challenge to Child Labor." *Dollars & Sense* 225 (September): 21–23.

Smolin, David M. 2000. "Strategic Choices in the International Campaign Against Child Labor." *Human Rights Quarterly* 22 (4) (November): 942–987.

Tucker, Lee. 1997. "Child Slaves in Modern India: The Bonded Labor Problem," *Human Rights Quarterly* 19 (3): 572–629.

Tucker, Lee, and Arvind Ganesan. 1997. "The Small Hands of Slavery: India's Bonded Child Laborers and the World Bank." *Multinational Monitor* 18 (January–February): 17–20.

UNDP. 2005. *Human Development Report 2005*. New York: Oxford University Press.

———. 2000. *Human Development Report 2000*. New York: Oxford University Press.

UNICEF. 1997. *The State of the World's Children 1997*. New York: Oxford University Press.

Vickers, Jeanne. 1991. *Women and the World Economic Crisis*. London: Zed Books.

# 7.3 ⸻

# Child Marriage in Afghanistan and Pakistan
*Andrew Bushell*

Entering the Kacha Ghari Afghan refugee camp, filled as it is with mud buildings reinforced by straw and dung baked to a brown-pink terra-cotta by the harsh Central Asian sunlight, is like walking into the 14th century. Turbaned shopkeepers hawk wares from pushcarts and lean-tos, meat crawling with flies hangs in the entrance to the butcher's shop, and raw human waste streams down narrow streets between the waddle and daub houses. Want hangs heavy in dry, dusty air.

It is therefore not surprising that Kacha Ghari children love school. The girls' primary school of about 150 students, run by the United Nations High Commissioner for Refugees, forms a sort of oasis. Classrooms, though spare, are made of cement and brick. Floors are stone rather than dirt. If only for a few hours a day, laundry, cooking and husbands seem far away for this second grade class.

Husbands?

According to Mrs. Habiba, the second grade teacher, and Mrs. Q'rmrun, the principal, over two-thirds of the nine-year-old girls sitting on the stone floor in a classroom an hour from Tora Bora were either already married or soon to become wives. Almost all of the older children were married, and only about one-third of the children who attended school in second grade continued to sixth grade. Social convention, rather than lack of opportunity, is the real bar to education for female Afghan refugee children.

Child marriage in Afghanistan and Pakistan is a traditional way of arranging marriages that is centuries old. Two children are married and then sent back to live with their parents until puberty. Girls would often live with their mothers-in-law until they started to menstruate, and the men they married would not only be well known to the family; they would often be the same age as the girls. But a combination of war, privation and disassociation over the past 25 years has eroded social norms of Afghan refugees.

Excerpted from Andrew Bushell, "Child Marriage in Afghanistan and Pakistan," *America* 186 (8) (March 11, 2002): 12–14. © 2002 America Magazine.

Salima, a 10-year-old girl in second grade, will be marrying a 60-year-old man in five months. She says she will be happy to marry Iqbal. When asked why, Salima said: "Iqbal's children already have wives to help them and Iqbal says the only thing I will have to do is cook and wash for him and keep him warm at night. It will be better than taking care of my four older brothers and my younger brother and sister." She will not return to school.

Since Iqbal is decades older than Salima and clearly not the ideal suitor, he paid Salima's father 1,500 rupees, or about $25, for the privilege of marrying her. The main reason for Salima's father's decision was that he could not afford to pay for a wedding feast, which according to Afghan tradition is to be paid by the father of the bride. Obtaining hard currency is a perennial problem for the refugees, because Pakistani guards at the camp entrances regularly demand bribes to let the refugees go to work and often beat them upon return. The money Iqbal gave Salima's family will provide clothes and shoes that will make it possible for an older brother to go to work.

According to Unicef—the United Nations Children's Fund—over 54 percent of girls over the age of 15 are married. There are no statistics for rates of marriage of girls between 8 and 15 in Central Asia, but such figures would assuredly be high in Afghanistan, Pakistan and Bangladesh. Surveys of five Afghan refugee camps on the Pakistan border of girls aged 8 to 13 indicate rates of marriage that exceed 50 percent, with the largest concentration of marriages occurring between 10 and 11 years.

For both boys and girls, child marriage has profound physical, intellectual, psychological and emotional consequences as well as destroying opportunities for education. Physically, premature pregnancy means higher rates of maternal mortality. In fact, it is the leading cause of death in girls aged 15 to 19 worldwide, and while much of that is due to poor health care, physical immaturity is the key risk for girls under 15. According to Claire O'Kane, a social worker in the office of Save the Children Sweden in Peshawar, Pakistan, child wives are three times as likely to have serious psychological problems as those refugees who marry after age 16.

Abuse of child wives is also common. Though there are no figures for Afghanistan, in Egypt 29 percent of married adolescents have been beaten by their husbands; of those, 41 percent were beaten during pregnancy. A study in Jordan indicated that 26 percent of reported cases of domestic violence were committed against wives under 18.

What happens to children who run away from amorous elders? Afghans have a specific word for this act that translates loosely as "honor killing"— usually invoked to prosecute adultery of a mature spouse by her own family. Though the words regicide, patricide and fratricide all exist in English for the killing of a sovereign, father or brother respectively, no specific words exist for the killing of a wife or daughter by her parents. The closest terms are uxoricide, murder of a wife by her husband, and parricide, the murder of a close relative. If no word exists, neither does redress. Just last year, the male head of a prominent Pakistani family murdered his daughter in a lawyer's office, only to be acquitted. According to Carol Bellamy, executive director of Unicef, "there has been no attempt to examine child marriage as a human rights violation until recently."

And only in recent months has Unicef taken the position that early marriage constitutes a violation of a girl's human rights—primarily because it can deprive her of the right to give full and free consent to marry, which is guaranteed under the 1948 Universal Declaration of Human Rights. "While clearly a violation of human rights," according to Anthony Arend, a legal expert and professor of international law at Georgetown University's School of Foreign Service, "it is not only unclear whether children are protected against marriage at any age, but whether they were intended to be protected."

Though poverty is the driving factor in the abandonment of these norms, selling a daughter into early marriage merely reinforces the refugee's penury by decreasing the aggregate education in the village. To date, though the United Nations has provided many guidelines, it has created few practical barriers to child wedlock.

But help may come from an unlikely source. Consent of a mother is often necessary for her child to be wed. Many older women earnestly regret early marriages that robbed them of literacy. If they can stand up to their husbands, innocence may yet bloom in the dust of Kacha Ghari.

# 7.4 _____

## Child Slaves in Modern India: The Bonded Labor Problem
_Lee Tucker_

### ■ The Context of Bonded Child Labor: Poverty, Tradition and Caste

Bonded labor is a variation on slavery. In India, it is a traditional worker-employer relationship that dates back more than 1,500 years, and continues today with more than sixty-five million people in its grip.[1] It is closely linked to caste; an estimated 80 percent of India's bonded laborers are Dalits (previously, the "untouchables") or are indigenous tribal people, the adivasi. In some industries, including carpet weaving, 98 percent of the bonded child laborers are members of these castes and tribes.[2] So close is the relationship between caste and occupation, that some academics believe the caste system itself evolved as a formalization of already-existing patterns of domination and control, including rigid stratification of occupations. Caste considerations are also a factor behind weak enforcement of the anti-bondage statutes.

Poverty and a lack of access to credit also contribute to the prevalence of bonded labor. The majority of Indians are extremely poor and earn bare subsistence wages. When additional financial needs arise (to compensate for seasonal declines in earnings or crops, to pay for medical expenses, or to pay for wedding or funeral ceremonies), there are no savings to fall back on, and the money must be borrowed.

There are few borrowing options for the poor. Even if a bank or cooperative society is accessible—and for most they are not—the poor laborer cannot qualify for a loan, having no security or collateral to offer. With no institutionalized credit sources to turn to, the laborer is forced to take loans from a local moneylender or bondmaster. Moneylenders charge twenty percent monthly interest or more. Bondmasters charge a much higher rate than this, but it is less visible because it is taken out in labor value. Many laborers fall into debt bondage as a direct result of borrowing from moneylenders: they borrow the

Excerpted from Lee Tucker, "Child Slaves in Modern India: The Bonded Labor Problem," _Human Rights Quarterly_ 19 (3) (1997): 572–629. Reprinted with permission of The Johns Hopkins University Press. Some of the author's notes have been omitted.

money, are unable to pay it back because of the accelerated interest rate, then find themselves forced to turn to debt bondage—of themselves or of a child— to obtain enough money to repay the original loan. . . .

## ■ "Nimble Fingers" and Other Myths of Child Labor

Employers prefer child labor because it is cheaper than adult labor, easier to exploit, and readily replenishable. Children labor as long and as hard as adults but earn a third or less of an adult's wages. Children are unaware of their rights, and in fact do not enjoy all of the rights to which adults are entitled: under current Indian law children may not form labor unions, and legislatively established minimum wages for adults do not apply to them. Some employers specify their preference not just for children, but for girl children in particular, on the grounds that they are the most "docile" of workers.

A gentler set of reasons is used to justify child labor as a phenomenon that benefits everyone. These myths of child labor are fiercely and widely believed. From parents of working children to the highest government officials, the same myths are heard: children must be trained at the "right" age or they will never learn a skill; children must be trained in a profession "appropriate" to their background and class; children are particularly well-suited for certain kinds of work because of their "nimble fingers"; and child labor is an inevitable product of poverty.

The "nimble fingers" theory is applied to some of the harshest industries employing children. This includes the carpet, silk, beedi, and silver industries. This theory asserts that children make the best product in these occupations, thanks to their small and agile fingers, which are, theoretically, better able to tie the tiny knots of wool, unravel the thread from the boiling silk cocoons, or solder tiny silver flowers to thin chains. Under this view, child labor is a production necessity.

The myth about being trained at the "right" age (at six or seven years) contends that children who go to school, postponing their craft training until adolescence, will either be unable to adequately learn a skill or will be at an irreparable disadvantage in comparison with those who did begin working as young children.

Finally, there is the myth that poverty alone causes child labor. Against the background of lack of opportunity and societal and governmental neglect, however, many children's rights activists scoff at the assertion that child labor stems from poverty alone. One long-time worker in the carpet-belt offered this assessment: "Poverty does not cause bonded child labour. If there are no social welfare facilities in the area, if there is no employment for the adults, if there is no education for children . . . what else will the children do, but work? They have no other option."[3] . . .

## ■ Beedi

> The agent would beat me with a stick if I was not there on time, he beat me
> if I could not roll 1500 beedies a day, and he beat me if I was tired. I had to
> roll eight beedies a minute. If I failed he would beat me. If I looked around,
> he beat me. He made me put a matchbox under my chin; if it fell, he would
> beat me.
>
> *—Panjaran, ten years old, pledged at the*
> *age of six for a 500 rupee advance.*

A beedi is a hand-rolled cigarette. With more than 500 billion beedi cigarettes produced and smoked each year, beedi is one of India's most significant
domestic products.[4] More than 325,000 children labor in the beedi industry,
most in the southern state of Tamil Nadu.[5]

Beedi rolling is stationary work; the children sit cross-legged on the ground
or floor all day, with a large and smoothly woven shallow basket in their laps.
The basket holds a pile of tobacco and a stack of rectangular rolling papers cut
from the large leaves of the tendu plant. The child takes a paper, sprinkles tobacco into it, rolls it up tightly, and ties it with string. The tips are closed either
by the roller herself or by a younger child, typically four to seven years old;
young children often begin their beedi careers by working as tip closers.

The pace is rapid, and most of the older children—those over ten—roll
1,500 to 2,000 beedies each day. In order to encourage speed, employers keep
close vigil over the child workers, scolding them or hitting them if they slow
down. Some children are forced to work with a matchbox tucked between their
chin and their neck; in order to hold the box in place, they must keep their head
down and focused on the work. If the matchbox falls, the employer knows the
child has looked away and will punish her or him.

Children working under bondage in the beedi industry work between ten
and fourteen hours a day, with short breaks for lunch and dinner. They work
six and a half days a week year-round, but are only paid for six—the half day
on Sunday is a designated "catching up" day. When children fail to report to
work, either because of sickness or out of rebellion at the harsh conditions,
their employer often will go to their house and forcibly return them to work.

Often, entire families are dedicated to the production of beedi. Usually it
is the children who work as bonded laborers, with adults managing to buy their
own freedom by the time they reach maturity or marry. For these poor families, bondage is a cyclical phase, with successive generations repeating the
steps: as children they are bonded, as young adults they buy or win their release, and as mature adults they eventually succumb to financial pressures and
turn their own children over to the beedi bondmasters.

The structure of debt repayment in the beedi industry is different than in
other bonded industries, where at least some of the child's labor value serves

to whittle away at the principal amount owed. In beedi, the "advances" given to secure the child workers are not paid off by the child's labor, no matter how long he works for the bondmaster. In fact, they are not really advances at all, but loans, against which the child's labor functions as both surety and interest.

Regardless of the amount borrowed, these loans must be paid back in a single lump-sum payment. The child will not be released otherwise, no matter how many thousands of rupees his labor brings to the agent over the years. This lump-sum debt cancellation is an onerous requirement. Often, the only way a parent can come up with sufficient funds is by securing a larger loan from another agent or by bonding another child.

Bonded beedi rollers are paid between 20 and 30 percent of the wages they would be entitled to on the open market. The remaining 70 to 80 percent of the value of their wages is kept by the agents, presumably as interest. This system results in effective annual interest rates ranging from 300 to 500 percent. The meager daily wages of the children are further reduced by "penalties," which are often bogus, but are stated to be for sloppy work or other minor infractions.

A look at the production and earnings of some bonded beedi rollers demonstrates just how lucrative this arrangement is for the bondmaster.

Twelve-year-old Raju was pledged at the age of eight in exchange for a 1,500 rupee loan. He rolled 1,000 beedies a day, for which he earned six rupees. The government-established minimum wage for rolling beedi in Tamil Nadu is 30.90 rupees per thousand beedies.[6] After paying Raju his six rupees, then, the agent cleared a minimum of twenty-five rupees of labor-cost savings every day, enough to compensate him for the original loan in a mere two months. Instead, Raju worked for the agent for four years, netting his employer about 40,000 rupees in the process. . . .

Punishment is common for a variety of infractions: arriving late, working slowly, making a mistake in the work, or talking to other workers. Even missing work because of illness can lead to punishment. Most children reported frequent scoldings and beatings, usually blows with the employer's open hand on the arms or head, or beatings on the arms with sticks. Other researchers have found more extreme examples of abuse at the hands of employers. Until the early 1990s, the matchbox-under-the-chin form of compulsion and control was quite common, and even measures such as chaining children in place were not unusual.[7] As recently as 1993, a social worker found a fourteen-year-old beedi roller who was kept shackled in leg irons. The boy, who had been bonded for 2,000 rupees, had once attempted to escape, and his employer had kept him in shackles ever since.[8] These abuses have decreased markedly in villages where social activists have been working to increase public awareness, but there is no evidence to suggest that the practices have changed significantly in more remote villages, where intervention has not taken place.

Sumathi, a twelve-year-old girl, is the oldest sibling of five. Three of the five children are girls, and the three sisters all rolled beedi. The youngest, eight years old, worked at home as a tip closer. The second, nine years old, was bonded to an agent three years ago for an advance of 1,000 rupees; she worked full time as a tip closer, earning only three rupees a week. Sumathi herself was bonded when she was seven in exchange for a 1,000 rupee advance. She rolled 1,500 beedies a day, for which she earned five rupees.

> My father and mother force me to go to work with the agent. The agent often beats me. If I tell my father, he allows me to stay home the following day, but then they are pushing me to go again. My father and mother say I have to go. I don't want to go. I am afraid of my agent. But my parents force me to go, if I don't go they scold me and beat me.
> Every week the agent gives my wages to my parents. If it is less money than usual, they beat me.
> In my family there are seven members, so it is difficult to even get enough food to eat. That's why my father goes to the agent—to ask for more money. But the agent won't give it, because he says I don't work hard enough. But every day I am being sent back to the agent. . . .

Beedi is one of the twenty-five industries classified by the Child Labour Act as hazardous. Beedi rollers suffer chronic back pain from sitting hunched over their work all day. The long hours of maintaining this unnatural position sometimes interfere with normal growth patterns, causing stunted growth or physical deformities among those who spend their childhoods rolling beedi. As adults, these children will be restricted in the types of work they are physically able to do; they will not be able to perform hard manual labor and may in fact be restricted to beedi rolling for their entire productive lives.[9] Large muscle groups are neglected and atrophy during years of sitting six and a half days a week, for twelve or more hours a day. In the words of one local beedi activist, the children grow up "small, puny, and malnourished."[10]

In addition to back ailments, many of the children interviewed complained of pain in their hands and wrists, which suffer from the constant repetitive motion of rolling and tying the cigarettes. "My hands would hurt so bad sometimes I thought I couldn't work," said Chintamani, a twelve-year-old boy who had been rolling beedies for three years. But, as Chintamani's mother pointed out, he had to work despite the pain. "If the child misses work because he is in pain or sick with fever or disease, the agent will beat him and take him back," she said.

The damage to the body is cumulative and progressive.

> As the worker gets older her/his fingers become numb and, unlike a young worker, an older worker has to make three or four attempts to roll a beedi. The nature of beedi work is such that a worker cannot take his/her eyes off it

even for a moment if he/she is to make the required number of beedies for a day. This takes its toll on people's eyesight as they grow older.[11]

The most serious health hazard of the beedi industry is lung disease. Beedi rollers spend their lives constantly inhaling tobacco dust, and study after study has shown them to suffer a high rate of tuberculosis, asthma, and other lung disorders.[12] Of the twenty-six child beedi rollers we interviewed, six (23 percent) had parents who were either dead or dying as a result of tuberculosis.[13] If the cycle continues unchanged, in twenty-five years these children will themselves be dying, while their own sons and daughters breathe tobacco dust and grow feeble. . . .

In sum, the fight against bonded child labor must be holistic, with a focus on two fronts: enforcement and prevention. Those employers who continue to bind children to themselves with debt, paying just pennies for a hazardous and grueling work day, must be prosecuted. Children must be removed from bondage and rehabilitated to avoid a subsequent relapse. Finally, the educational and survival needs of all children at risk must be addressed in order to stop the cycle of bondage.

## ▓ Notes

1. See "Citizen's Body on Bonded Labour," *Times of India*, 18 Nov. 1994.

2. See "Citizen's Body on Bonded Labour," *Times of India*, 18 Nov. 1994.

3. Interview with Shamshad Khan, Founder and Secretary, Centre for Rural Education & Development Action (CREDA), in Mirzapur, Mirzapur district, Uttar Pradesh, India (19 Dec. 1995).

4. "50,000 Cr Beedies Consumed Annually," *Indian Express*, 1 Feb. 1995. One crore, abbreviated as "cr," equals ten million rupees. Annual sales equal forty billion rupees.

5. See Neera Burra, *Born to Work: Child Labour in India* xxiv (New Delhi: Oxford Univ. Press 1955) (citing estimate of 327,000 child workers in the beedi industry); R. Vidyasagar, A Status Report on Child Labour in Tamil Nadu 8 (written for UNICEF (Madras), 1995) (reporting that there are 248,000 child beedi workers in Tamil Nadu).

6. See Pradeep S. Mehta, "Cashing in on Child Labor," *Multinational Monitor,* Apr. 1994, at 24, 25.

7. Interview with longtime social welfare activist (name withheld), in Madras, India (21 Nov. 1995).

8. See Jacob Varghese, "Freedom at Mid-Day," *Worldvision: A Worldvision of India Magazine,* 1993, at 6, 6–7.

9. Interview with social activist, *supra* note 7.

10. *Id.*

11. Vidyasagar, *supra* note 5, at 9.

12. See *id.* (citing a study of one beedi manufacturing village wherein 25 percent of all beedi rollers had tuberculosis).

13. Interviews with child bonded laborers (names withheld), in North Arcot district, Tamil Nadu, India (25 Nov. 1995).

# 7.5 _____

# The Sex Trade Industry's Worldwide Exploitation of Children

### R. Barri Flowers

## ■ International Scope of Child Sexual Exploitation

How big is the problem of child sexploitation globally? Many sources—including government and nongovernment organizations, researchers, and experts in the commercial sexual exploitation of children—have produced figures estimating its incidence and prevalence from country to country and internationally (Campagna and Poffenberger 1988; ECPAT 1996; Ennew et al. 1996; Flowers 1998; Smolenski 1995; U.S. Department of Justice 1999).

The clear indications are that the worldwide exploitation of children by the sex trade industry has reached numbers that merit serious attention and action, if not epidemic proportions. According to UNICEF, there are over 1 million child prostitutes in Asia alone (Flowers 1998). End Child Prostitution, Child Pornography and Trafficking of Children for Sexual Purposes (ECPAT) estimated that there are 800,000 child prostitutes in Thailand, 400,000 in India, and 60,000 in the Philippines (ECPAT 1996; Smolenski 1995). . . .

Other figures on child prostitution are just as notable. Up to 500,000 children are being exploited in the sex trade industry in Brazil, while as many as 200,000 teenage prostitutes are plying their trade in Canada (Flowers 1998; Kotash 1994). In the United States, estimates of juvenile prostitutes range from the hundreds of thousands to 2 million selling their bodies on the streets (Flowers 1986, forthcoming; Smolenski 1995). Child sexual exploitation is also believed to be flourishing in Western Europe, Eastern Europe, and Africa (Flowers 1998; U.S. Department of Justice 1999). . . .

Most studies of child sexploitation focus mainly on child prostitution without adequately accounting for the global danger of child pornography and the correlation between the two through child sex rings and the trafficking of children (Flowers 1994; Smolenski 1995; U.S. Department of Justice 1999). There is also the issue of illegal versus legal use of children for purposes of

Excerpted from R. Barri Flowers, "The Sex Trade Industry's Worldwide Exploitation of Children," *Annals of the American Academy of Political and Social Science* 575 (2001): 147–157. Some of the author's notes have been omitted.

sexual exploitation. For example, in some countries, child prostitution is technically legal, making it difficult to separate what is outlawed from what is tolerated (Flowers 1998; Goodall 1995; Leuchtag 1995; Miller 1995). Perhaps the greatest limitation in assessing the true measure of international child sexual exploitation is the lack of cooperation between countries and researchers in gathering and quantifying data.

## Child Sex Tourism

A major component of the international sexual exploitation of children is the child sex tourism industry, defined by the United Nations as "tourism organized with the primary purpose of facilitating the effecting of a commercial-sexual relationship with a child" (U.S. Department of Justice 1999, 32). Child sex tourism is particularly prominent in Thailand, the Philippines, and other countries in Southeast Asia. Between 6.2 percent and 8.7 percent of Thai females, for example, are estimated to be sex workers (Robinson 1993). Many of these prostitutes can earn up to 25 times the salaries of other occupations in Thailand. However, some are recruited from poor rural areas and become indentured sex slaves, supporting their entire families (Flowers 1998). In the Philippines, sex tourism and the trafficking of Filipino girls and women continue to be used to spur economic development, in spite of efforts to curb the practice (Smolenski 1995).

According to a report on child sex tourism in Southeast Asia, Americans account for the largest group of foreign tourists (*ECPAT Newsletter*, 1996). In data gathered from 1991 to 1996, of 240 tourists who sexually abused and exploited children in Asia in the prior seven years and faced arrest, imprisonment, deportation, or fled the country, around one-fourth were American child sex tourists. Other tourists came from Germany, Britain, Australia, France, and Japan. Most foreign tourists who sexually exploit children tend to travel from wealthy, economically developed Western nations to impoverished countries such as those in Southeast Asia with well-established and commercialized sex tourism industries (Smolenski 1995; U.S. Department of Justice 1999). . . .

## Global Child Pornography

Untold numbers of children around the world are being sexually exploited through child pornography (Burgess 1984; Flowers 1998; Johnson 1992; O'Brien 1983; Smolenski 1995). Often referred to as "kiddie porn" and "child porn," child pornography includes photographs, magazines, books, videotapes, audiotapes, motion pictures, and images on Web sites on the Internet that depict children in sexually explicit acts with other children, adults, animals, and/or foreign objects (Flowers 1994; Tannahill 1980). Victims of child pornographers are subjected to many forms of sexual abuse, perversions, and exploitation such as rape, sadism, pedophilia, triolism, torture, and even murder (Flowers 1998). In many instances, child prostitutes are initiated into the sex trade by being coerced into performing pornographic sexual acts as a way to normalize prostitution and lower the child's resistance (Rickel and Hendren 1993). Other prostituted youths are enticed into entering the kiddie porn business as a way to make extra money or support drug habits (Flowers 1998; Johnson 1992). Some children are forced into child pornography by pimps and operators of child sex rings or child sex tourism, where they are turned into sex slaves (Burgess 1984; Burgess and Grant 1988; Flowers 2001).

Child pornography is, by most accounts, a multi-billion-dollar global enterprise. In Germany alone, estimated sales of child porn exceed $250 million, with the number of consumers ranging from 30,000 to 40,000 (Serrill 1993). The biggest market for child pornography is the United States, where an estimated $6 billion is generated annually (Flowers 1998). Eighty-five percent of the worldwide sales of child pornography comes from America. Each year, an estimated 30,000 children are sexually exploited by child pornographers in Los Angeles alone (Flowers 1990). . . .

Syndicated child sex rings are in many cases international in scope and highly organized in recruiting children, producing child pornography, delivering other sexual services, and maintaining a large customer base (Flowers 2001; Lanning 1992).

The use of the Internet by pornographers and other sexual exploiters of children has increased the globalization of child pornography and the child sex tourism industry, while making it more difficult for law enforcement authorities to track down perpetrators (Flowers 1998). . . .

## ■ Other Consequences of Sexual Exploitation

Children who are victims of commercial sexual exploitation face a number of health and psychological hazards in addition to AIDS. The rate of sexually transmitted diseases such as herpes, chlamydia, crabs, gonorrhea, and syphilis is high among prostituted children worldwide (Flowers 1998; World Health Organization 1996). This is attributed in great measure to the limited or nonuse of condoms among underage prostitutes. Many girls involved in prostitution are at increased risk for other infectious diseases such as pelvic inflammatory disease (U.S. Department of Justice 1999). Pregnancy is also common among young female prostitutes, as is developing complications in giving birth (Widom and Kuhns 1996; World Health Organization 1996). In poorer countries, sexually exploited girls—including those abducted from other countries—are especially vulnerable to pregnancy and disease, due to lack of birth control or safe sex practices, language barriers, and poverty.

Sexually exploited children worldwide are prone to being raped, assaulted, robbed, and even killed (Flowers 1998; Volkonsky 1995). Many are runaways or have been thrown out of sexually, physically, or mentally abusive homes; they become dependent on alcohol or drugs as prostitutes, sex slaves, or other victims of the child sex trade (Flowers 1994, 1998; Harlan, Rodgers, and Slattery 1981; James 1980).

Child prostitutes and other sexually exploited children are also susceptible to a number of psychological effects such as severe depression, low self-esteem, post-traumatic stress disorder, and attempted suicide (Flowers 2001; World Health Organization 1996). . . .

## ▇ Fighting for Sexually Exploited Children's Rights

One of the more prominent international responses in recent years to protecting children from sexual exploitation and misuse has been the 1989 U.N. Convention on the Rights of the Child (CRC). Currently ratified by 191 countries . . . the CRC strongly condemns the sexual exploitation of children through prostitution or other illegal sexual practices (Flowers 1998; U.S. Department of Justice 1999).

Another important initiative in developing global strategies to fight child sex tourism and other child sexploitation came in 1996 when the First World Congress Against Commercial Sexual Exploitation of Children took place in Stockholm, Sweden. The congress called on governments worldwide to coordinate efforts to stop the commercial sexual exploitation of children in all capacities. Delegates from more than 120 countries vowed to cooperate in stiffening criminal sanctions against child sexual exploiters—including pimps, child sex tourist operators, pedophiles, and customers—while assisting sexually exploited child victims (Flowers 1998).

Other notable efforts at attacking the sexual exploitation of children include the Task Force to End Sexual Exploitation in Thailand, which represents 24 government and private agencies, and the Programme for Action for the Prevention of the Sale of Children, Child Prostitution, and Child Pornography, which was adopted in 1992 by the U.N. Commission on Human Rights (U.S. Department of Justice 1999).

These actions notwithstanding, global commercial child sexual exploitation by the sex trade industry continues to proliferate almost unabated. Flesh peddlers, pornographers, and promoters of child sex—along with an insatiable market of child tourists and international clients—are taking away the freedom and violating the rights of those children victimized. . . .

While we cannot know for certain precisely how many children are currently being exploited by the international sex trade industry, even conservative estimates from many countries suggest that the problem is one that is likely affecting hundreds of thousands and, quite possibly, millions of children around the world.

# ■ References

Burgess, Ann W. 1984. *Child Pornography and Sex Rings*. Lexington, MA: Lexington Books.

Burgess, Ann W. and Christine A. Grant. 1988. *Children Traumatized in Sex Rings*. Arlington, VA: National Center for Missing & Exploited Children.

Campagna, Daniel and Donald Poffenberger. 1988. *The Sexual Trafficking in Children*. Westport, CT: Auburn House.

*ECPAT Newsletter*. 1996. The Paedo File. Presented at ECPAT International, Aug., Bangkok, Thailand.

Ennew, Judith, Kusum Gopal, Janet Heeran, and Heather Montgomery. 1996. *Children and Prostitution: How Can We Measure and Monitor the Commercial Sexual Exploitation of Children?* 2d ed. New York: UNICEF.

Flowers, R. Barri. 1986. *Children and Criminality: The Child as Victim and Perpetrator*. Westport, CT: Greenwood Press.

———. 1990. *The Adolescent Criminal: An Examination of Today's Juvenile Offender*. Jefferson, NC: McFarland.

———. 1994. *The Victimization and Exploitation of Women and Children: A Study of Physical, Mental and Sexual Maltreatment in the United States*. Jefferson, NC: McFarland.

———. 1998. *The Prostitution of Women and Girls*. Jefferson, NC: McFarland.

———. 2001. *Sex Crimes, Predators, Perpetrators, Prostitution, and Victims: An Examination of Sexual Criminality in America*. Springfield, IL: Charles C. Thomas.

Goodall, Richard. 1995. *The Comfort of Sin: Prostitutes and Prostitution in the 1990s*. Kent: Renaissance Books.

Harlan, Sparky, Luanne L. Rodgers, and Brian Slattery. 1981. *Male and Female Adolescent Prostitution: Huckleberry House Sexual Minority Youth Services Project*. Washington, DC: U.S. Department of Health and Human Services.

James, Jennifer. 1980. *Entrance into Juvenile Prostitution*. Washington, DC: National Institute of Mental Health.

Johnson, Joan J. 1992. *Teen Prostitution*. Danbury, CT: Franklin Watts.

Kotash, Myrna. 1994. Surviving the Streets. *Chatelaine* 67:103–7.

Lanning, Kenneth V. 1992. *Child Sex Rings: A Behavioral Analysis*. Alexandria, VA: National Center for Missing & Exploited Children.

Leuchtag, Alice. 1995. Merchants of Flesh: International Prostitution and the War on Women's Rights. *The Humanist* 55(2):11–16.

Miller, Laura. 1995. Prostitution. *Harper's Bazaar* 3400(March):208–10.

O'Brien, Shirley. 1983. *Child Pornography*. Dubuque, IA: Kendall/Hunt.

Rickel, Annette U. and Marie C. Hendren. 1993. Aberrant Sexual Experiences. In *Adolescent Sexuality*, ed. Thomas P. Gullotta, Gerald R. Adams, and Raymond Montemayor. Newbury Park, CA: Sage.

Robinson, Lillian S. 1993. Touring Thailand's Sex Industry. *The Nation* 257:494–96.

Serrill, Michael S. 1993. Defiling the Children. *Time* 141:52–54.

Smolenski, Carol. 1995. Sex Tourism and the Sexual Exploitation of Children. *Christian Century* 112:1079–80.

Tannahill, Reay. 1980. *Sex in History*. New York: Stein and Day.

U.S. Department of Justice. 1999. *Prostitution of Children and Child Sex Tourism: An Analysis of Domestic and International Responses*. Alexandria, VA: National Center for Missing & Exploited Children.

Volkonsky, Anastasia. 1995. Legalizing the "Profession" Would Sanction the Abuse. *Insight on the News* 11:20–22.

Widom, Cathy S. and Joseph B. Kuhns. 1996. Childhood Victimization and Subsequent Risk for Promiscuity, Prostitution and Teenage Pregnancy: A Prospective Study. *American Journal of Public Health* 86:1607–10.

World Health Organization. 1996. Commercial Sexual Exploitation of Children: The Health and Psychological Dimensions. Paper presented at the World Congress Against Commercial Sexual Exploitation of Children, Aug., Stockholm.

# 7.6 ─────

# The Political Economy of
# War-Affected Children
*Steven Hick*

The impact of war on children has been devastating. Children are drawn into war as soldiers. They suffer from malnutrition, disease, sexual violence, and the depredations of forced flight. Sometimes they are deliberately killed. The new wars are particularly deadly for children because little distinction is made between combatants and civilians. In recent decades, the proportion of war victims who are civilians has increased from 5 percent to over 90 percent. During the 1990s, more than 2 million children died as a result of armed conflicts, and more than three times as many were permanently disabled or seriously injured (Machel 1996, 13).

Today's wars regularly involve horrifying levels of violence and brutality, from systematic rape, to the destruction of crops and the poisoning of wells, to ethnic cleansing and outright genocide. Increasingly, children are themselves drawn in as fighters, becoming not just the targets of warfare but also the perpetrators of atrocities. . . .

## ▓ Refugee and Internally Displaced Children

Approximately 1 in every 300 children on earth is displaced by armed conflict (1 in 150 of the general population is so displaced) (Machel 2000, 9). Armed conflict causes large numbers of people to flee their homes to escape danger. These people become either refugees or internally displaced persons (IDPs). People staying within their own countries are considered "internally displaced," while those who flee to other countries become "refugees." The majority of these fleeing armed conflicts become IDPs rather than refugees. Most refugee and displaced children travel with their families, but many lose their parents. Unaccompanied minors typically account for up to 5 percent of a refugee population and often more—as children are lost, separated, or orphaned in the panic of flight (Ressler, Tortorici, and Marcelino 1993, 142).

Excerpted from Steven Hick, "The Political Economy of War-Affected Children," *Annals of the American Academy of Political and Social Science* 575 (2001): 106–121. Some of the author's notes have been omitted.

Today there are about 40 million refugees and displaced persons who are predominantly women and children (Machel 2000, 9). Children make up more than half of the refugee and IDP populations. Many die within the first days and weeks of displacement due to malnutrition and disease, especially measles, diarrheal diseases, respiratory infections, and malaria. Displaced children are also the most likely to be raped, tortured, murdered, or recruited as child soldiers. Girls and women are in constant danger of sexual attack and abuse, leading to pregnancy and HIV infection. The youngest children are also affected when they witness an attack on a mother or sister.

Refugees and IDPs are predominantly in Africa and Asia, although they can be found throughout the world. The greatest numbers of IDPs stemming from armed conflict are in Sudan (an estimated 4 million), Angola (1.5 million to 2 million), Colombia (1.8 million), Iraq (900,000), Afghanistan (540,000 to 750,000), Burma (500,000 to 1 million), Bosnia and Herzegovina (830,000), Azerbaijan (568,000), Sri Lanka (more than 500,000) and Burundi (800,000).

Camps for refugees and IDPs should be safe, but the violence, sexual assault, and alcohol and substance abuse there often reach high levels. Women in camps in Burundi told how they were forced to exchange sex for food or protection. Camps are also often highly militarized, and children are particularly vulnerable to recruitment by armed forces or other armed groups. Many refugee and internally displaced children lose their chances of receiving an education, proper nutrition, and health care. In Colombia, for example, some 85 percent of refugee children do not receive primary education. Camps often lack adequate reproductive health care for women and girls.

Many children have lived their entire lives in a state of displacement, never knowing a normal, stable family environment. On top of that, many families have been displaced not only once but twice or three times, making them more vulnerable each time. . . .

Although refugees are often in a desperate situation, IDPs are generally worse off. They may remain within or close to areas of conflict and have to move repeatedly. They are often more difficult to reach due to fighting or government policies. Unlike refugees, they have no specific agency or body of law to protect and assist them. . . .

## Child Soldiers

One of the most alarming trends in armed conflict is the participation of children as soldiers or in supporting roles for armies. A child soldier is a boy or girl under the age of 18 who is compulsorily or voluntarily recruited or otherwise used in hostilities by armed forces, paramilitaries, civil defense units, or other armed groups (Machel 2000, 6).

In the new wars, armies, rebels, paramilitary groups, and militia groups have abducted or recruited over 300,000 child soldiers. While the majority are adolescents, many are 10 years of age or younger. Increasingly, however, adults are deliberately conscripting or taking children as combatants or soldiers. Some commanders have even noted the desirability of child soldiers because they are "more obedient, do not question orders and are easier to manipulate than adult soldiers" (Brett, McCallin, and O'Shea 1996, 88). Beyond their use as soldiers, armies are using children for sexual services, as forced "wives," and also as spies, messengers, porters, and cooks. The number of children used to support and service armies (as opposed to being used as soldiers) is unknown.

The number of children used as soldiers is unknown. It has remained constant over time, while the cumulative impact has increased steadily. The estimated figure of 300,000 child soldiers reflects the number of children being used in combat at any one time. As new conflicts begin and children are killed or wounded, grow older, and are replaced by other children, the cumulative total is much higher and the destruction carries over from one generation to the next. Poorer children are particularly vulnerable. Adolescent boys working in the informal sector, selling cigarettes, gum, or lottery tickets on the streets, are a particular target. For example, in Myanmar, groups of 15- to 17-year-old children have been surrounded in their school yards and conscripted as soldiers against their will (Brett, McCallin, and O'Shea 1996, 23).

One reason for the growing problem of child soldiers is the proliferation of inexpensive and light weapons. Previous weapons were too heavy and cumbersome for children to use. The lighter and cheaper assault rifles, such as the Soviet made AK-47 or the American M-16, are light and simple to use. The rifles have also become much cheaper and more widely available. Their availability has steadily increased in war zones. Since their introduction in 1947, around 55 million AK-47s have been sold; in one African country, for example, they cost no more than U.S.$6 each (United Nations Research Institute for Social Development 1995, 113).

While most child soldiers are recruited by conscription, abduction, or coercion, some also volunteer. For them, joining an army may be the only way to escape starvation and death, and a military unit may serve as a refuge, providing a kind of surrogate family. In Uganda in 1986, the National Resistance Army had an estimated 3000 children, many under age 16, including 500 girls. Most of these children had been orphaned and looked on the army as a replacement for their parents (Dodge 1991, 55). Hunger, poverty, and lack of opportunities not only drive children to volunteer but may also compel parents to offer their children for service. Children volunteer when they believe that this is the only way to guarantee regular meals, clothing, or medical attention (Brett, McCallin, and O'Shea 1996, 33).

Many children joined armed groups in Cambodia in the 1980s as the best way to secure food and protection. Similarly, in Liberia in 1990, children as young as 7 were seen in combat because, according to the director of the Liberian Red Cross, "those with guns could survive." In Myanmar, parents volunteer their children for the rebel Karen army because the guerrillas provide clothes and two square meals a day; in 1990, an estimated 900 of the 5000-strong Karen army were under the age of 15 (Dodge 1991, 11).

Girls abducted into armed groups are mainly forced into sexual slavery, subjected to physical and emotional violence, and forced to provide other personal services. The majority become infected with sexually transmitted diseases and, increasingly, with HIV/AIDS. . . .

## ▒ Sexual Violence Against Children During Armed Conflict

Sexual attacks and exploitation are used methodically during armed conflict to humiliate and terrorize. Women and girls are continually threatened by rape, assault, sexual exploitation, trafficking, sexual humiliation, and mutilation. The main perpetrators of sexual attacks and exploitation are male combatants or soldiers, whether from government military groups, rebel groups, paramilitary groups, or private armies. Sexual violence against girls has traumatic long-term damaging effects on their psychological and physical development. The spread of HIV/AIDS from sexually active soldiers to girls is another growing problem.

Those who authorize or perpetrate sexual brutality during armed conflict are committing crimes against humanity and are violating international law. For example, a statute of the International Criminal Court explicitly recognizes sexual violence as a war crime. The International Criminal Tribunals for the former Yugoslavia and for Rwanda have highlighted the use of rape during those conflicts and brought gender-based charges against the instigators of war crimes. In the former Yugoslavia, the International Tribunal attempted to prosecute people on specific charges of rape and sexual assault. Despite estimates of up to 20,000 victims, the tribunals were able to indict only eight people. Even with this dismal result, the judgments represent a historic precedent in prosecuting sexual violence within armed conflicts. For the first time, perpetrators of sexual violence were charged and brought to justice.

Armed conflict often leaves women and children vulnerable to commercial sexual trafficking and sexual exploitation. . . .

The rape of women and girls is a widespread instrument of war. Machel (1996) argues that "the failure to denounce and prosecute wartime rape is partly a result of its mischaracterization as an assault against honour or a personal attack rather than a crime against the physical integrity of the victim" (sec. 103). . . .

## ▒ Children Traumatized by War

During every conflict, children witness and experience terrible atrocities. They witness the torture, murder, or rape of a loved one; they see dead bodies; they see people being beaten or being in situations where they thought they would die. All these events leave children with some degree of trauma. In many cases, they are left in a state of shock. For example, in a survey of 1505 children in Sarajevo, where almost 1 child in 4 has been wounded in the conflict, UNICEF found that 97 percent of the children had experienced shelling nearby, 29 percent felt "unbearable sorrow," and 20 percent had terrifying dreams. Some 55 percent had been shot at by snipers, and 66 percent had been in a situation where they thought they would die (UNICEF 1993, 3-4). In a 1993 study in Angola, UNICEF found that 66 percent of the children had seen people being murdered, 91 percent had seen dead bodies, and 67 percent had seen people being tortured, beaten, or hurt. In all, more than two-thirds of children had lived through events in which they had defied death (UNICEF 1993, 3–4).

The physical, sexual, and emotional violence to which children are exposed undermines the very foundations of their lives. It causes painful psychosocial damage and erodes their trust in adults. The word "psychosocial" highlights the dialectic relationship between psychological and social elements. Psychological elements are those that affect emotion, behavior, thoughts, memory, learning ability, perceptions, and understanding. Social elements include altered relationships due to death, separation, estrangement, and other losses; family and community breakdown; damage to social values and customary practices; and the destruction of social facilities and services. Social effects also extend to economic aspects as people become impoverished.

Armed conflict causes a variety of reactions in each child. The response depends on the child's age, gender, personality, personal and family history, cultural background and experience, as well as the character and length of the incident. A traumatized child has a range of symptoms, including increased separation anxiety, developmental delays, sleep disturbances, nightmares, decreased appetite, withdrawn behavior, and a lack of interest in play (Machel 2000, 19). Younger children can have learning difficulties; older children and adolescents can show anxious or aggressive behavior and depression. . . .

## ■ Conclusion

The rights of children are being trampled in the new warfare. Millions of youngsters are killed, violated, displaced, maimed, and traumatized. International organizations (such as the United Nations and UNICEF), national governments, and a range of nongovernmental organizations are involved in efforts to raise public awareness and mobilize international action on the plight of children affected by armed conflict. While rapid and important progress is being made to protect children and to ameliorate the effects of war on them, little attention is given to addressing the root causes of today's wars. Until the economic and political effects of globalization are seriously addressed, this new kind of warfare and its effusive effects on children will continue.

## ■ References

Brett, Rachel, Margaret McCallin, and Rhonda O'Shea. 1996. *Children: The Invisible Soldiers*. Geneva: Quaker U.N. Office and the International Catholic Child Bureau.

Dodge, Cole P. 1991. Child Soldiers of Uganda and Mozambique. In *Reaching Children in War: Sudan, Uganda and Mozambique*, ed. C. P. Dodge and M. Raundalen. Uppsala: Sigma Forlag.

Machel, Graça. 1996. *Impact of Armed Conflict on Children*. United Nations Report No. A/51/306. Available at http://www.unicef.org/graca.

———. 2000. *The Impact of Armed Conflict on Children: A Critical Review of Progress Made and Obstacles Encountered in Increasing Protection for War-Affected Children*. Winnipeg: Government of Canada. Available at http://www.war affectedchildren.gc.ca/machel-e.asp.

Ressler, Everett M., J. M.Tortorici, and A. Marcelino. 1993. *Children in War: A Guide to the Provision of Services*. New York: UNICEF.

UNICEF. 1993. Psychosocial Programme. Emergency Operations in Former Yugoslavia Kit. New York: UNICEF.

UNICEF. United Nations Research Institute for Social Development. 1995. *States of Disarray: The Social Effects of Globalization*. Geneva: UNRISD.

# 8 Globalization and Human Rights

## 8.1 ———

## Introduction
### The Editors

As we look toward future studies of human rights, two trends fundamentally alter the way human rights norms will be respected and changed: globalization and terrorism. Chapter 8 focuses on globalization, while Chapter 9 examines the connection between human rights and terrorism. Globalization, or the increasing interconnectedness among states, has changed not only the speed with which individuals become informed of human rights abuse worldwide, but also the framework within which states respond to such abuse. States in a globalized world face increased pressures to perform economically, which may exacerbate a state's incentive to repress its citizens. At the same time, globalization results in often instantaneous information transmission, making it more difficult for repressive regimes to hide their repression. States with extensive economic ties may have the ability to positively influence each other's human rights policies. Advocates of globalization argue that investment or trade with a state will lead to more jobs, basic services, and infrastructure. This exchange of goods is coupled with an exchange of ideas and values and can help facilitate the developing norm of respect for human rights worldwide. Opponents of globalization point to increasing disparity among rich and poor states and argue that these economic relationships are a means for rich states to maintain their favorable economic position relative to poorer states. In general, globalization may leave states increasingly less willing to place a primacy on human rights concerns as economic payoffs from trade and investment take precedence over moral concerns.

Julie Harrelson-Stephens examines the neoliberal theory that globalization will leave everyone better off. She explicitly examines the extent to which two aspects of globalization, trade and multinational investment, affect a state's willingness to repress its citizens. She outlines the theoretical arguments derived from the liberal perspective as well as summarizes the critiques of liberalism. She then develops a measure for globalization, the external economic penetration index, based on a state's level of both trade and investment. Using an ordered-probit model, she tests the extent to which globalization affects personal integrity rights. She finds that states with higher levels of external economic penetration realize lower levels of repression.

Not all assessments of globalization come to such optimistic conclusions. Robert McCorquodale and Richard Fairbrother also discuss the effects of globalization on human rights. These authors point out that decisions made by investors are based primarily on financial concerns and often at the cost of the local population. They argue that economic investment, as well as structural adjustment programs implemented by the IMF, can leave the most vulnerable segments of the population even worse off and may result in human rights concerns being further marginalized.

Erika Rosenthal further explores the negative aspects of globalization in her examination of a pesticide poisoning in the Andean mountains of Peru. Focusing on the issue of accountability, Rosenthal illustrates how multinational corporations (MNCs) can effectively remove themselves from culpability when such disasters occur. She suggests that in order to overcome this, NGOs and the global community at large must begin to address issues like pesticide poisoning in terms of human rights. Specifically, she contends that MNCs should be as accountable as states and that the legal framework needs to include MNCs as well.

Neve Gordon takes a contemporary global economic issue, outsourcing, and places it in the context of human rights violations. The realities of the modern transnational corporation (TNC) mean that much of the domestic work is outsourced, effectively removing the TNC from responsibility and accountability for a host of economic and social human rights violations. Gordon points out that not only do TNCs export human rights violations, but so do governments by outsourcing certain services, such as prisons, healthcare, and the military. For example, since the United States outlaws the use of torture, suspects are outsourced to countries such as Saudi Arabia and Egypt. Gordon suggests that in order to address this new wave of human rights violations, human rights organizations need to provide an alternative to the neoliberal message that tends to ignore social and economic rights in favor of the needs of business.

The last article focuses on poverty. Peter Singer, in a thought-provoking essay, suggests that average Americans not only have the ability but the obligation to do something about world poverty. He raises philosophical and moral questions regarding distributive justice and concludes that money spent on luxuries should be given away to charity.

# 8.2 ⎯⎯⎯⎯

# Achieving Human Rights:
# The Globalization Debate
*Julie Harrelson-Stephens*

At the end of World War II, the United States emerged as a world leader, putting into place international institutions based on its own liberal economic philosophy. The opening up of borders to trade and investment began an accelerated process of economic globalization. In the last few decades, this globalization or interconnectedness between states has increased at an enormous rate. This increase has been so drastic as to lead some researchers to question the future importance of state boundaries (Ruggie 1986, 1998). Recent headlines underscore the importance of this increased interconnectedness. Antiglobalization protests in Washington and Italy, for example, illustrate the tendency of many around the world to associate globalization with global suffering. The implications of this change are not yet fully understood. First economic relationships and now political ones are continually blurring the distinction between domestic and international as well as state and societal forces.

Concurrent with the rise of globalization, there has been increasing importance placed on the human rights behavior of states. Human rights were once viewed as the prerogative of sovereign states. However, since World War II, an international human rights norm has emerged. I argue that the two phenomena, globalization and human rights, are not unrelated. Increased globalization has, to a large part, facilitated improvements in the human rights records of a state. Moreover, states are becoming more and more willing to link economic relationships to human rights practices of other states. This paper draws on the neoliberal perspective, which suggests that liberalized economic relationships improve economic and social well-being in a country, such that everyone is better off. These economic relationships allow for not only the exchange of marketplace goods, but also the exchange of ideas. Moreover, the current world leader or hegemon in the international system will create and enforce norms of behavior and regimes. In the case of the United States, two of the most visible norms that are encouraged include the promotion of democratic institutions and the protection of human rights (Bueno de Mesquita 2000).

The purpose here is to examine the liberal idea that the interplay between globalization and human rights is increasingly important, as economies become more interdependent. Such interdependence creates incentives for cooperation and communication as it links people together. As such, investment and trade, for instance, may provide an opportunity to affect the human rights practices in a given country. Thus, understanding the nature and extent of the impact of globalization on human rights is critical in explaining differences in the human rights practices around the globe.

## ◼ The Liberal Paradigm

There are generally two theoretical arguments suggested by the liberal paradigm that are discussed here. The first argument suggests that economic exchanges also allow for an exchange of ideas, which is important to both economic development as well as human rights. As economic relationships are pursued, a diffusion of norms across borders exposes different cultures to prevailing norms. Robert Keohane and Joseph Nye's (1977) theory of complex interdependence suggests that the increased *interdependence* among states results in policies that are more *sensitive* to each state. The interdependence itself leaves states more aware and influenced by international norms than they would be if they were to maintain an isolated existence. The sensitivity among states can help facilitate a diffusion of values, including human rights. For example, increased interdependence increases the ability of the world to be aware of gross human rights violations and condemn them as quickly as they happen. This tendency is aided by relatively instantaneous media. As such, globalization has increased the ability of the international community to pressure a repressive state to alter its behavior.

This diffusion of norms regarding human rights, in turn, also extends into the economic realm. A state's leaders may be more apt to attract foreign investment, for example, if they appear more willing to play by the international rules of the game. This signal can help decrease uncertainty to potential investors and trading partners and is an indication that the state is willing to play by the current rules of the game—specifically capitalism. In other words, multinational corporations prefer to invest in states that appear to be similar to their own. Acceptance by a state of international norms suggests to investors that a particular country is less likely to nationalize its industry or, of more importance here, regularly violate the rights of the citizenry.

While the diffusion of human rights norms is one consequence of international economic exchanges, a second effect on human rights policies stems from the economic nature of interdependence itself. In particular, the liberal paradigm suggests that economic development will eventually lead to an increase in societal demands for human rights. In fact, Robert Gilpin (1987, 27) explains that this perspective "may, in fact, be defined as a doctrine and set of principles for organizing and managing a market economy in order to achieve maximum efficiency, economic growth, and individual welfare." This logic begins with the idea that states engage in interdependent behavior generally for the purpose of an economic payoff. Economic liberalism posits that such economic payoffs are the primary goal of states. Likewise, in such states political considerations are secondary to economic ones. This drive for economic payoffs, according to this perspective, overrides a state's need to repress. In a state with a healthy economy, the needs of the population are more likely to be met, decreasing the need for repression by the state (Henderson 1991). Countries that open their economies to economic penetration by other countries are likely to experience higher levels of economic development. This development will facilitate the growth of a middle class, which will increasingly demand respect for personal integrity within a state. Clair Apodaca (2001, 590), for example, suggests that "economic liberalization will lead to an expanded middle class that will, if democratic theory is correct, demand greater civil and political liberty, undermining authoritarian control." Thus, a central tenet of the liberal theory is the idea that economic incentives and social welfare go hand in hand.

These general arguments can be specifically applied to two aspects of globalization: trade and investment. The arguments in favor of trade liberalization are consistent with the liberal paradigm. According to the liberal perspective, free trade not only brings a basket of goods to the citizens of a country, facilitating economic development, it also brings the potential for norms and ideas to penetrate borders. In addition, countries that pursue a liberalized trade strategy help facilitate the development of a middle class, which is likely to demand increased civil and political rights. It is hypothesized, based on the liberal perspective, that increased trade openness will facilitate improved personal integrity rights within a country.

A second facet of globalization is multinational investment. Arguments in favor of multinational investment focus on the increased availability of information created by globalization. Debora Spar, for example, argues that MNCs bring with them a spotlight phenomenon, where MNC investment is followed by increased media attention and pressure to change abusive practices. For example, "when reports surfaced that Reebok was purchasing soccer balls stitched by 12-year-old Pakistani workers, the firm sprang into action. It created a new central production facility in Pakistan and established a system of independent monitors" (Spar 1998, 9). This is consistent with the liberal perspective that suggests investment is a win-win situation for states. From this perspective, investment not only facilitates improved economic conditions within the host state, but also provides for a diffusion of norms and ideas.

In both cases, critics of globalization suggest that increases in trade and investment cause profit, and not the human condition, to become the main goal of a state. When profit becomes the goal, the result is poor working conditions, detrimental terms of trade, and widespread use of child labor all in the name of profit. Moreover, many developing states would argue that the lion's share of that profit is expropriated to developed states, leaving the developing countries worse off on every level. For instance, powerful multinational firms often strip a country of its resources while extracting the profit back to the multinational's home state. Thus, the theoretical arguments in favor of globalization are by no means a given.

## ■ Previous Research

The literature on the relationship between trade and human rights focuses primarily on measures of state repression or negative sanctions and is motivated by dependency and world systems theory (Ziegenhagen 1986; Carleton 1989; Pion-Berlin 1989; Davenport 1995). Eduard Ziegenhagen (1986) and David Pion-Berlin (1989) find a positive, but limited, relationship between trade dependency and state repression. The former uses the Taylor and Jodice (1983) measure for negative sanctions and measures trade dependency by the degree of trade concentration in various export categories. Pion-Berlin includes two sources of information for the dependent variable: first, the *New York Times* Index, which is used to count individual incidences of state repression, and second, Amnesty International reports of abuse. As the independent variable, Pion-Berlin uses international trade agreements as a proxy for dependency, which is suspect and unconvincing as it is difficult to establish dependency based upon trade agreements alone. The actual amount of exports and imports, as well as the unevenness of the trade relationship, is necessary to determine the extent of trade dependency.

David Carleton (1989), examining only Latin American countries, finds similar results to Ziegenhagen (1986) and Pion-Berlin (1989), substituting Freedom House measures for the dependent variable and percentage of exports made of manufactured goods for trade dependency. Carleton is concerned with a new twist to the traditional international division of labor. He argues that a new division of labor is emerging, namely the labor in the Third World engaged in the manufacturing portion of MNC production processes. Carleton theorizes that states will engage in repressive behavior to maintain a political and economic environment that is attractive to MNCs. He finds that increases in manufacturing investment and the pursuit of export-oriented industrialization are associated with higher levels of state repression.

Ziegenhagen finds that trade concentration in particular exports in a country does lead to increased repression by that state. Similarly, Christian Davenport's (1995) results are inconsistent regarding the relationship between export specialization and repression. Pion-Berlin (1989) finds limited evidence that trade leads to repression. He measures dependency using international trade agreements. In the first two cases, the measure used does not capture overall trade, but instead concentrates on specific export trade sectors. Similarly, Pion-Berlin analyzes international trade agreements, which may in fact have little relation to a state's trade liberalization or to a state's degree of trade dependency. The liberal perspective suggests that greater overall trade will result in improved human rights, without respect to particular export sectors or trade agreements. Thus, in order to test the liberal perspective, overall trade, not just a particular area of trade, must be examined.

Apodaca (2001) provides an explicit examination of the liberal perspective and human rights. She examines a global sample of 152 countries from 1990 to 1996. Utilizing the Political Terror Scale (PTS) as the dependent variable, she concludes that trade helps guarantee human rights. However, her ability to draw conclusions regarding the liberal paradigm is limited by her trade measure. To capture trade, she relies on developing countries' exports to industrialized countries. This measure misses the crux of liberal theory, which suggests the win-win proposition that all trade is positive. Her analysis also omits the important control variable of economic development (see Mitchell and McCormick 1988; Henderson 1991; Poe and Tate 1994; Poe, Tate, and Keith 1999; Donnelly 1999; Davenport 1995), again raising the possibility of misleading statistical results. Thus, while there has been some attention to testing dependency theories regarding trade and human rights, tests of the liberal paradigm remain scant and inconclusive.

A second indicator of globalization is the level of international investment in a state. The empirical relationship between investment and human rights remains tenuous. Robert McCorquodale and Richard Fairbrother (1999) argue that globalization, conceptualized as both multinational investment and World Bank loans, creates opportunities for improved human rights conditions but in some cases can in fact exacerbate repression. Scant research exists that explicitly examines the relationship between human rights and investment. There are a few notable exceptions. The first is by William Meyer (1996), who tests two competing perspectives. The engines-of-development thesis suggests that MNCs promote human rights in the third world, whereas the Hymer thesis suggests that MNCs will facilitate uneven development, as profits are returned to the MNC's home state. Ultimately, Meyer's research supports the engines-of-development thesis. However, Meyer's study relies on a limited sample and time period, utilizes US investment rather than worldwide investment, and omits important control variables, all of which undermine our ability to have confidence in his results.

In response to Meyer, Jackie Smith, Melissa Bolyard, and Anna Ippolito (1999) replicate Meyer's research using a different dependent variable and worldwide investment. They find that investment is correlated with poor human rights records in states. However, the authors simply replicate Meyer's small sample, arbitrary lag, and time frame. In addition, they fail to include key control variables, such as previous human rights violations, internal and external violence, and democracy, suggested by the field. Thus, like Meyer's, it is difficult to generalize from these results.

## ■ Methods and Data

For the purpose of this study, I concentrate on security rights, or the right not to be tortured, murdered, or disappeared by your state. Utilizing a model of most countries in the world, from 1976 to 1996, allows me to draw the most generalizable conclusions. The PTS is employed as the dependent variable. This measure is a five-point ordinal scale created to indicate increasing degrees of personal integrity violations. The variable ranges from 1, representing the lowest level of human rights abuse, to 5, representing the most abusive regimes. Turning to the key variables of interest, I examine the extent to which countries with the highest level of economic penetration would realize the lowest levels of personal security rights violations in order to test the liberal perspective. The two most consistent measures of liberalization are trade and investment. An index is created based on a country's level of trade openness and level of investment to reflect liberalized trade.[1] The resulting variable ranges from two to eight, with eight representing the greatest amount of external economic penetration.

Last, I include the independent variables most consistently found in the literature on repression, and these are summarized in Table 8.2.1. In brief, it is

**Table 8.2.1   Data Sources**

| Variable Name | Data | Source |
|---|---|---|
| Personal Integrity Abuse | Ordinal Scale (1–5) based on content analysis | Political Terror Scale (PTS) |
| Investment | Foreign Direct Investment ÷ Gross Domestic Product (GDP) | World Development Indicators 1998 CD-ROM |
| Trade | (Imports + Exports) ÷ GDP | Summers and Heston Penn World Tables |
| Democracy | Ordinal Scale (0–10) | Polity III data Jaggers and Gurr 1996 |
| Economic Standing | Gross National Product per capita (in thousands of US dollars) | Data provided by Poe, Tate, and Keith (1999) |
| Civil War | 1 in years with civil war, else 0 | Data provided by Poe, Tate, and Keith (1999) |
| International War | 1 in years with international war, else 0 | Data provided by Poe, Tate, and Keith (1999) |

hypothesized that previous repression, civil wars, and international wars will increase the probability a state will choose to repress. On the other hand, democracy and economic standing both mitigate a state's willingness to repress. Thus, I estimate the following model:

$$\text{Personal Integrity Abuse} = \beta_1 \text{ Personal Integrity Abuse}_{t-1} + \beta_2$$
$$\text{External Economic Penetration}_{t-1} + \beta_3 \text{ Democracy} + \beta_4$$
$$\text{Economic Standing} + \beta_5 \text{ Civil War} + \beta_6 \text{ International War} + \beta_2 + \varepsilon$$

Due to the ordinal nature of the dependent variable, I utilize an ordered-probit model introduced in the social sciences by McKelvey and Zavoina (1975).[2] The ordered-probit analyses with the external economic penetration index are shown in Table 8.2.2. The chi-squares indicate that each of these

**Table 8.2.2   Ordered Probit Analyses of Personal Integrity Abuse with External Economic Penetration Index**

|  | Model A<br>All Countries | Model B<br>Non-OECD |
|---|---|---|
| Personal Integrity Rights$_{t-1}$ | 1.198*<br>(0.041)[a] | 1.140*<br>(0.041) |
| Democracy | –0.052*<br>(0.007) | –0.042*<br>(0.007) |
| Civil War | 0.731*<br>(0.097) | 0.774*<br>(0.095) |
| International War | 0.280*<br>(0.078) | 0.262*<br>(0.082) |
| Economic Standing | –0.041*<br>(0.005) | –0.017*<br>(0.007) |
| External Economic Penetration | –0.040*<br>(0.011) | –0.054*<br>(0.011) |
| Cut Point 1 | 0.835 | 0.682 |
| Cut Point 2 | 2.557 | 2.365 |
| Cut Point 3 | 4.244 | 4.034 |
| Cut Point 4 | 5.723 | 5.488 |
| N | 2610 | 2195 |
| McKelvey and Zavoina R$^2$ | 0.71 | 0.68 |
| Wald chi-square | 1608.61 | 1125.92 |
| prob > .05 | 0.000 | 0.000 |

*Notes:* a. Robust Standard Errors are shown in parentheses.
*p < .05
**p < .10

**Table 8.2.3  Marginal Effects, External Economic Penetration, and Personal Integrity Rights**

| | 1<br>Rule<br>of Law | 2<br>Limited<br>Imprisonment | 3<br>Extensive<br>Imprisonment | 4<br>Murder or<br>Disappearance,<br>Political Activist | 5<br>Murder or<br>Disappearance,<br>Entire Society |
|---|---|---|---|---|---|
| Entire Sample<br>External Economic Penetration[a] | 0.04 | 0.12 | –0.12 | –0.03 | –0.00 |
| Non-OECD Countries<br>External Economic Penetration | 0.02 | 0.15 | –0.08 | –0.09 | –0.01 |

*Note:* a. For ordinal variables the marginal effect is calculated as a change from the minimum value.

models taken as a whole is statistically significant. The McKelvey and Za-voina $R^2$ further indicates that the models are performing relatively well.[3] In both models, the coefficients of the control variables are statistically significant and in the expected direction. Consistent with past research, previous human rights abuses are indicative of future human rights abuse. Countries involved in a civil war or international war are more likely to experience state repression, whereas countries with higher levels of democracy or economic standing realize less repression.

Of importance here, the external economic penetration index is statistically significant and negatively associated with repression. This means that countries with greater degrees of external economic penetration tend to experience lower levels of personal integrity abuse, all things being equal. This relationship holds when all countries are examined as well as when only developing countries are included. This lends support to the liberal paradigm, which suggests greater economic interdependence should result in a basket of goods, including improved human rights practices. To examine the substantive effects of external economic penetration, marginal effects are reported in Table 8.2.3.

The marginal effects indicate that economic liberalization in a country can have a significant impact on a country's willingness to repress its citizens. A country that moves from the lowest score of 2 on the external economic penetration index to the highest score of 8 increases its likelihood of living under the rule of law by 4 percent in all countries and 2 percent in developing countries. That same move considerably increases the likelihood that a state will experience only limited imprisonment (from 12 percent in all countries to 15 percent in developing countries) and decreases the likelihood that a state will have extensive imprisonment or target political activists for murder or disappearance. These results, taken as a whole, indicate strong support for arguments derived from the liberal paradigm. Economic liberalization in a state appears to substantially decrease that state's willingness to repress its citizens.

## ■ Conclusion

This analysis examines the liberal hypothesis that countries with overall liberalized economies should experience improved personal integrity rights, all things being equal. The marginal effects indicate that the combined impact of trade and investment has the potential to make a significant difference in the level of personal integrity abuse in a country. Again support is found for the liberal perspective as greater economic penetration leads to less human rights abuse.

# ▉ Notes

1. Trade openness is based on the Heston and Summers (1994) measure, which is calculated by the sum of imports and exports divided by the gross domestic product in a given year. Investment is measured as a country's total foreign direct investment as a percentage of gross domestic product. Then, I divide the variables for investment and trade openness into quartiles. Two new variables are created, coded one for the lowest quartile, and up to four for the highest quartile. The external economic penetration index adds the two rankings together.

2. A pooled cross-sectional time series analysis (PCT) design is utilized to analyze these models. This design allows researchers to examine a phenomenon across two dimensions: space and time. PCT has been called an "extraordinarily robust research design, allowing the study of causal dynamics across multiple cases" (Stimson 1985, 916). However, this design presents unique challenges to researchers. Specifically, two threats to inference arise. First, because of the time series nature of the data, there may be autocorrelation. In addition, heteroscedasticity can result from the cross-national nature of the data. Both of these problems may bias results of the significance tests. To control for this, Nathaniel Beck and Jonathan Katz (1995) propose a lagged endogenous variable to deal with the autocorrelation. In addition, robust standard errors correct for heteroscedasticity.

3. Several authors suggest that the McKelvey and Zavoina $R^2$ is the most appropriate measure of fit when an ordered regression model is used. See McKelvey and Zavoina (1975), Veall and Zimmermann (1996), and Windmeijer (1995) for a complete discussion.

# ▉ References

Apodaca, Clair. 2001. "Global Economic Patterns and Personal Integrity Rights After the Cold War." *International Studies Quarterly* 45:587–602.

Beck, Nathaniel, and Jonathan Katz. 1995. "What to Do (and Not to Do) with Time-Series Cross-Section Data." *American Political Science Review* 89:634–647.

Bueno de Mesquita, Bruce. 2000. *Principles of International Politics: People's Power, Preferences, and Perceptions.* Washington, DC: Congressional Quarterly Press.

Carleton, David. 1989. "The New International Division of Labor, Export-Oriented Growth, and State Repression in Latin America," in George Lopez and Michael Stohl, eds. *Dependence, Development, and State Repression.* New York: Greenwood Press.

Davenport, Christian. 1995. "Multi-Dimensional Threat Perception and State Repression: An Inquiry into Why States Apply Negative Sanctions." *American Journal of Political Science* 39:683–713.

Donnelly, Jack. 1999. "Human Rights, Democracy, and Development." *Human Rights Quarterly* 21:608–632.

Gilpin, Robert. 1987. *The Political Economy of International Relations.* Princeton: Princeton University Press.

Henderson, Conway. 1991. "Conditions Affecting the Use of Political Repression." *Journal of Conflict Resolution* 35:120–142.

Heston, Alan, and Robert Summers. 1994. The Penn World Table (Mark 5.6).

Jaggers, Keith, and Ted Robert Gurr. 1995. POLITY III: Regime Change and Political Authority, 1800–1994. [computer file] (Study #6695). 2nd ICPSR version. Boulder, CO: Keith Jaggers/College Park, MD: Ted Robert Gurr [producers], 1995. Ann Arbor, MI: Inter-University Consortium for Political and Social Research [distributor], 1996.

Keohane, Robert O., and Joseph S. Nye. 1977, 1989, 2001. *Power and Interdependence*. New York: Longman Press.

McCorquodale, Robert, and Richard Fairbrother. 1999. "Globalization and Human Rights." *Human Rights Quarterly* 21:735–766.

McKelvey, R. D., and W. Zavoina. 1975. "A Statistical Model for the Analysis of the Ordinal Level Dependent Variables." *Journal of Mathematical Sociology* 4:103–120.

Meyer, William H. 1996. "Human Rights and MNCs: Theory Versus Quantitative Analysis." *Human Rights Quarterly* 18:368–397.

Mitchell, Neil J., and James M. McCormick. 1988. "Economic and Political Explanations of Human Rights Violations." *World Politics* 40:476–496.

Pion-Berlin, David. 1989. *The Ideology of State Terror: Economic Doctrine and Political Repression in Argentina and Peru*. Boulder, CO: Lynne Rienner Publishers.

Poe, Steven C., and C. Neal Tate. 1994. "Repression of Human Rights to Personal Integrity in the 1980s: A Global Analysis." *American Political Science Review* 88:853–872.

Poe, Steven C., C. Neal Tate, and Linda Keith. 1999. "Repression of the Human Right to Personal Integrity Revisited: A Global Cross-National Study Covering the Years 1976–1993." *International Studies Quarterly* 43:291–315.

Ruggie, John G. 1998. *Constructing the World Polity: Essays on International Institutionalization*. New York: Routledge.

———. 1986. "Continuity and Transformation in the World Polity: Toward a Neorealist Synthesis," in Robert O. Keohane, ed. *Neorealism and Its Critics*. New York: Routledge, pp. 131–157.

Smith, Jackie, Melissa Bolyard, and Anna Ippolito. 1999. "Human Rights and the Global Economy: A Response to Meyer." *Human Rights Quarterly* 21:207–219.

Spar, Debora. 1998. "The Spotlight and the Bottom Line: How Multinationals Export Human Rights." *Foreign Affairs* 77:7–12.

Stimson, James A. 1985. "Regression in Time and Space: A Statistical Essay." *American Journal of Political Science* 29:914–947.

Taylor, Charles Lewis, and David Jodice. 1983. *World Handbook of Political and Social Indicators III*. New Haven, CT: Yale University Press.

Veall, Michael R., and Klaus F. Zimmermann. 1996. "Pseudo-R2 Measures for Some Common Limited Dependent Variable Models." *Journal of Economic Survey* 10:241–259.

Windmeijer, Frank A. 1995. "Goodness-of-fit Measures in Binary Choice Models." *Econometric Reviews* 14:101–116.

Ziegenhagen, Eduard. 1986. *The Regulation of Political Conflict*. New York: Praeger.

# 8.3

## Globalization and Human Rights
*Robert McCorquodale and Richard Fairbrother*

### ■ Economic Rights and Economic Growth

Economic rights include the individual right to an adequate standard of living and the individual and group right to development.[1] The right to an adequate standard of living concerns access to the basic essentials for sustaining life, including food, shelter, clothing, and health care. The right to development, while still contentious as a human right, means that "every human person and all peoples are entitled to participate in, contribute to, and enjoy economic, social, cultural and political development, in which all human rights and fundamental freedoms can be fully realized."[2] Accordingly, it can be argued that economic growth will increase protection of economic rights because economic growth brings increased access to health care, food, and shelter, either directly through employment and increased income or indirectly through the improvement and extension of these facilities to more people. For most developing states, particularly those in Africa, economic growth is often fostered through large-scale external investment. This investment comes from globalized economic institutions, such as inter-governmental institutions, including the World Bank and the IMF, or transnational corporations.[3] This argument, therefore, concludes that economic growth through globalization leads to the protection of economic rights such as the right to an adequate standard of living and the right to development.

However, the reality is somewhat different in most instances. There are at least three reasons for this: the type of investment, the basis for investment decisions, and the type of economic growth. First, a great deal of the investment arising from globalized economic sources for the purposes of "development" is allocated only to certain types of projects, such as the building of dams, roads, and runways, and the creation of large-scale commercial farms. There is little or no investment in primary health care, safe drinking water, and basic education. Furthermore, these globalized investment-based projects "create

Excerpted from Robert McCorquodale and Richard Fairbrother, "Globalization and Human Rights," *Human Rights Quarterly* 21 (3) (1999): 735–766. Reprinted with permission of The Johns Hopkins University Press. Some of the authors' notes have been omitted.

some risks of (legally cognizable) harm to some categories of project-affected people, and some projects generate many risks of very serious harms to many people."[4] The World Bank itself has recognized the risks involved. With regard to large-scale irrigation projects, the World Bank has recognized that:

> [s]ocial disruption is inevitable in large-scale irrigation projects. . . . Local people often find that they have less access to water, land and vegetation resources as a result of the project. Conflicting demands on water resources and inequalities in distribution can easily occur both in the project area and downstream . . . altering the distribution of wealth.[5]

An example of this occurred when representatives of the Penan people of Malaysia told then Senator and now US Vice-President Gore: "We are not being killed by weapons, but when our lands are taken, it is the same as killing us."[6] Their statements "exemplif[ied] the grave human rights offenses that sometimes occur in the effort [by governments and transnational corporations] to develop national resources."[7] Thus, the type of investment generated by globalized economic institutions tends to infringe upon economic rights rather than protect them.

Second, decisions about investment by these globalized organizations are based almost exclusively on financial concerns, including generating profits for banks in the developed states and for other transnational corporations. As such, these concerns are external to the state in which the investment is made, and subsequently fail to focus on social welfare within the state. A classic example of this decision-making process is seen in an infamous internal World Bank memo:

> [S]houldn't the World Bank be encouraging more migration of the dirty industries to the [less developed countries]? . . . The measurement of the costs of health impairing pollution depends on the foregone earnings from increased morbidity and mortality. From this point of view, a given amount of health-impairing pollution should be done in the country with the lowest wages. I think the economic logic behind dumping a load of toxic waste in the lowest-wage country is impeccable and we should face up to that. . . . I've always thought that under-populated countries in Africa are vastly under-polluted; their air quality is probably vastly inefficiently [high] compared to Los Angeles or Mexico City.[8]

This memo, written by then World Bank Chief Economist and now US Deputy Treasury Secretary (and US Treasury Secretary–designate) Lawrence Summers, makes excellent neo-classical economic logic. But this logic can have disastrous consequences for environmental and human rights protection. For example, research has shown that United States–based chemical companies have been exporting pesticides banned in the US to developing states by altering production techniques and changing production sites to avoid strict US labeling laws.[9] Unlabeled containers of hazardous pesticides then become available for purchase over the counter in, for example, parts of Africa.[10] Often, due to lack of proper information by consumers, the pesticides are improperly used and the containers are reused to carry drinking water.[11]

In a globalized economy, the patience of investors to obtain returns on their investment is considerably reduced. In Africa, where long-term investment in infrastructure is needed, investors from developed states can be harsh in their economic decisions. For example, a French diplomat apparently said that "[e]conomically speaking, if the entire black Africa, with the exception of South Africa, were to disappear in a flood, the global cataclysm will be approximately nonexistent."[12] It should also be realized that many of the economic decisions made by the globalized economic institutions are made on the basis of very dubious information and analysis. The quantity and speed of information today does not always improve decision-making.

In broader human rights terms, globalized economic institutions often implement plans that hurt those whose economic rights are most vulnerable. For example, Howard notes that "[i]n Africa today, schools are closing down as governments retrench in the face of structural adjustment programmes imposed by the International Monetary Fund."[13] Because the government is the largest employer in most African states, "[n]ot only do thousands of people lose their jobs . . . , but often all services are drastically cut, especially those of the already underfunded health sector."[14] Those who are the worst affected when governments are forced to change their priorities are usually the poor, women, and agricultural workers. For example, Zimbabwe used to provide free education for all until adherence to an IMF structural adjustment program caused this to end. As a result, many Zimbabwean girls are no longer being educated because parents make gender-based financial choices. This occurs despite the clear evidence that the education of girls is an investment that "yield[s] the highest rate of return in a developing country."[15]

Indeed, structural adjustment programs have significant gender impact, and often fail to withstand criticism in the same economic terms that they purport to uphold. The United Nations Special Rapporteur on the Realization of Economic, Social and Cultural Rights reported that:

> [s]tructural adjustment programs continue to have a significant impact upon the overall realization of economic, social and cultural rights, both in terms of the ability of people to exercise them, and of the capability of governments to fulfil and implement them. . . . Human rights concerns continue to be conspicuously underestimated in the adjustment process.[16]

Thus, human rights (in the case of Zimbabwe, the rights to education and freedom from discrimination) are violated as a consequence of the policies of the globalized economic institutions.

Additionally, the fact that the economic decision-making process is being taken away from governments and put in the hands of financial "experts" in globalized economic institutions also means that the people and the governments of developing states are not effectively involved in decisions affecting their lives.[17] This has an impact on both state sovereignty and human rights. People are not able to exercise their right to development because they are not afforded the opportunity to participate in decisions concerning their development. In addition, governments, as well as minorities within a state, are marginalized as power is transferred to bureaucrats and special interest groups. This impact is compounded with the increasing privatization of public functions and public goods. As a result, the ability of governments to protect human rights, even if guaranteed by a constitution and enforced by an independent judiciary, becomes more restricted.[18] Of course, many governments, even when they are in control of economic decision-making, do not take the interests or economic rights of their people into account. However, globalization can restrict the choices open to governments and people, particularly in the human rights area, and thus make it more difficult to attribute responsibility for violations of human rights.

Ironically, it appears that the World Bank has now become concerned about the decreasing role of the state. It now argues that:

> [a]n effective state is vital for the provision of goods and services—and the rules and institutions—that allow markets to flourish and people to lead healthier, happier lives. Without it, sustainable development, both economic and social, is impossible. . . . [T]he state is central to economic and social development, not as a direct provider of growth but as a partner, catalyst, and facilitator.[19]

According to the World Bank, "globalization is [only] a threat to weak or capriciously governed states"[20] which fail to "set the rules that underpin markets and permit them to function."[21] However, the World Bank's support of a role for the state in the decision-making process of economic globalization is problematic because the state's role is seen purely in terms of allowing markets to "flourish." The state's role in allocating resources, dealing with social goods, and protecting human rights is all sublimated to the "market."[22] Indeed, the World Bank's concern for the role of the state is purely self-interested; the World Bank itself has noted that "if the history of development assistance teaches anything . . . it is that external support can achieve little where the domestic will to reform is lacking."[23] In this context, such reform must be in accord with the World Bank's own economic philosophies, rather than in terms of the social welfare or the protection of human rights of the people in the State.

The third and final reason that globalization does not necessarily promote economic rights is because there are different types of economic growth. The United Nations Human Development Report 1995 dealt with the impact of damaging forms of economic growth. It found that damaging economic growth includes:

> that which does not translate into jobs, that which is not matched by the spread of democracy, that which snuffs out separate cultural identities, that which despoils the environment, and growth where most of the benefits are seized by the rich.[24]

An example of damaging economic growth, where growth, as it were, is not growth, is where crops are planted for export to gain foreign exchange revenue while the people are deprived of their staple diet. This has happened in both Zimbabwe and Brazil. This kind of damaging economic growth is contrary to the right of self-determination which provides that "[i]n no case may a people be deprived of its own means of subsistence."[25] Another kind of damaging economic growth in which the benefits of economic growth are seized by the rich was exemplified in South Africa during the apartheid regime. There, economic growth was for many years achieved through the exploitation of a large unskilled, insecure, dispossessed, and dependent work force consisting of oppressed blacks.[26] Thus globalization can have the effect of increasing economic inequality when the economic interests which are protected are those of the rich and economically powerful, who are usually the elite urban males.

Economic growth through globalization processes can even encourage human rights abuses beyond state borders by providing economic incentives for trade in goods injurious to humans, such as land mines and military weapons. For example, in 1997, the South African arms manufacturer, Denel, sought to sell to Syria up to $640 million worth of updated weaponry for that country's fleet of T72 tanks. The deal eventually collapsed, partly because of strong criticism from the United States.[27] The South African government responded to the criticism by saying that South Africa was a sovereign state which would not determine its foreign policy with reference to the wishes of other states.[28] This reaction is ironic considering that the globalization of human rights concerns and the impact of the international legal order were integral to the improvement of human rights and the historic change of government in South Africa.

In sum, economic globalization can lead to improved conditions for those in developing states, but it can also encourage economic exploitation and oppression. Globalization may lead to apparent improvements in economic growth, but at a cost to the economic rights of many within a state. Indeed, "[t]he overwhelming thrust of the evidence would appear to support the claim that World Bank and IMF policies are violating human rights."[29] The influence of the economic philosophies of the globalized economic institutions is such that even the concepts of human rights can be affected. For example, the right to development is now partly defined on the notion that "development" means industrialization, westernization, and economic growth. Only a very few of the globalized economic institutions take human rights issues directly into account in their investment decisions, though this may be changing. If human rights issues are not taken into account in these investment decisions, it is likely that human rights will become more endangered as a consequence of those decisions.

## ▓ Notes

1. *See* Matthew Craven, The International Covenant on Economic, Social, and Cultural Rights: A Perspective on Its Development (1995); Economic, Social and Cultural Rights: A Textbook (Asbørjn Eide et al. eds., 1995). *See also* Jerry Dohnal, *Structural Adjustment Programs: A Violation of Rights*, 1 Austl. J. Hum. Rts. 57 (1994).

2. Declaration on the Right to Development, G.A. Res. 41/128 (Annex), *adopted* 4 Dec. 1986, U.N. GAOR, 41st Sess., Supp. No. 53, art 1.1, U.N. Doc. A/41/53 (1987), *reprinted in* 3 Weston III.R.2. The right has been subsequently affirmed by the international community. *See, e.g.*, Vienna Declaration, *supra* note 21, Part I, ¶ 10.

3. *See* Timothy M. Shaw & Clement E. Adibe, *Africa and Global Issues in the Twenty-First Century*, 51 Int'l J. 1, 12 (1996). They point out that most "African economies must rely on the [World Bank and IMF] for external financing since they cannot obtain capital from the world's financial markets."

4. James C.N. Paul, *The Human Right to Development: Its Meaning & Importance,* 25 J. Marshall L. Rev. 235, 238 (1992).

5. The World Bank, Technical Paper No. 140, 2 Environmental Assessment Sourcebook 96 (1991).

6. Brian B.A. McAllister, *The United Nations Conference on Environment and Development: An Opportunity to Forge a New Unity in the Work of the World Bank Among Human Rights, the Environment, and Sustainable Development,* 16 Hastings Int'l & Comp. L. Rev. 689, 691 (1993).

7. *Id.* at 691.

8. *See Let Them Eat Pollution*, Economist (London), 8 Feb. 1992, at 66 (quoting a World Bank memo written by Lawrence Summers). *See also, Pollution and the Poor*, Economist (London), 15 Feb. 1992, at 18.

9. *See* James H. Colopy, *Poisoning the Developing World: The Exportation of Unregistered and Severely Restricted Pesticides from the United States,* 13 UCLA J. Envtl. L. & Pol'y 167, 171, 181 (1995).

10. *See id.* at 177.

11. *See id.* at 177. Also, while developing states use only around twenty percent of all pesticides used in the world, over seventy percent of the world's pesticide-related deaths and fifty percent of acute pesticide poisoning occur in developing states.

12. Victor Chesnault, "Que faire de l'Afrique noire?," *Le Monde*, 28 Feb. 1990, at 2, *quoted in* Michael Chege, *Remembering Africa*, 71 Foreign Aff. [America and the World 1991/92], at 148 (1992).

13. Rhoda E. Howard, *Civil Conflict in Sub-Saharan Africa: Internally Generated Causes*, 51 Int'l J. 26, 32 (1996).

14. Mahmood Monshipouri, Democratization, Liberalization & Human Rights in the Third World 54 (1995) (quoting Fran Hoskin). *See also* Anne Orford, *Locating the International: Military and Monetary Interventions after the Cold War*, 38 Harv. Int'l L.J. 443, 464–75 (1997).

15. Josette L. Murphy, Gender Issues in World Bank Lending 22 (1995) (footnote omitted).

16. Danilo Türk, *The Realization of Economic, Social and Cultural Rights: Final Report*, U.N. Doc E/CN.4/Sub.2/1992/16 (1992).

17. *See* Lawrence Tshuma, *The Impact of IMF/World Bank Dictated Economic Structural Adjustment Programmes on Human Rights: Erosion of Empowerment Rights, in* The Institutionalisation of Human Rights in Southern Africa 219, 229 (Pearson Nherere & Marina d'Engelbronner-Kolff eds., 1993).

18. *See* Philip Alston, *The Myopia of Handmaidens: International Lawyers and Globalization*, 8 Eur. J. Int'l L. 435, 443 (1997).

19. The World Bank, World Development Report 1997, at 1 (1997).

20. *Id.* at 11.

21. *Id.* at 34.

22. This position could also be seen in the negotiation for a Multilateral Agreement on Investment which would enable transnational corporations to enforce limitations on governments' actions, even if these limitations are contrary to the wishes of the people. *See* David Rowan, *Meet the New World Government*, Guardian Weekly (Manchester), 22 Feb. 1998, at 14. However, the International Labour Organization has recently adopted a declaration which states that "all Members . . . have an obligation . . . to respect, to promote and to realize, in good faith . . . the principles concerning the fundamental [labor] rights": *ILO Declaration on Fundamental Principles and Rights at Work* (June 1998) *available on* <http://www.ilo.org>.

23. The World Bank, *supra* note 19, at 15.

24. Larry Elliott, *Bridging the North-South Divide*, Guardian Weekly (Manchester), 11 Aug. 1996, at 14.

25. International Covenant on Economic, Social and Cultural Rights, *adopted* 16 Dec. 1966, G.A. Res. 2200 (XXI), U.N. GAOR, 21st Sess., Supp. No. 16, art. 1(2), U.N. Doc. A/6316 (1966), 993 U.N.T.S. 3 (*entered into force* 3 Jan. 1976) [hereinafter ICESCR].

26. *See* Heribert Adam, *Cohesion and Coercion, in* The Elusive Search for Peace: South Africa, Israel and Northern Ireland 227 (Hermann Giliomee & Jannie Gagiano eds., 1990).

27. *See* Arms Transfer Project of the Stockholm International Peace Research Institute (SIPRI), Frosunda, Sweden, available at <http://www.sipri.se> (as verified by the authors' correspondence with Siemon Wezeman of the Arms Transfer Project of SIPRI, Mar. 1999; copy on file with authors).

28. *See id.*

29. Dohnal, *supra* note 1, at 82.

# 8.4 ⸻

## The Tragedy of Tauccamarca:
## A Human Rights Perspective on the
## Pesticide Poisoning Deaths of 24
## Children in the Peruvian Andes
*Erika Rosenthal*

Tauccamarca is a remote village in the windswept Andean highlands of Peru, three hours by foot from the nearest road. On October 22, 1999, 24 of the village's 48 children were poisoned and killed when they drank a powdered milk substitute, part of their school lunch, that had been contaminated by an organophosphate pesticide.[1] When the children began to foam at the mouth and writhe in pain, their parents ran carrying them down the mountain to the nearest village with a health post. Most of the children died en route in their parents' arms. Eighteen other children were poisoned but survived. Preliminary evaluations indicate that they may suffer significant long-term developmental consequences of organophosphate poisoning.[2]

Interviews conducted by the press, the police, and the local Peruvian rights ombudsman's office give a fairly clear picture of what happened. A village woman mixed a white powdered pesticide into a bag of powdered milk substitute that is served as part of the children's school breakfast, and left it by her doorway to kill or sicken a dog that had been chasing her chickens. A child walked by, noticed the bag of powdered milk, and brought it to school, where it was mixed with several other bags of powdered milk the next day and fed to the children, with devastating results. The woman, like almost everyone else in her village, speaks only Quechua, not Spanish (the language on the label) and is illiterate. She had no idea of the extreme toxicity of the pesticide.

The pesticide in question appears to be methyl parathion, which is imported, formulated, and sold in Peru by Bayer S.A., a wholly owned subsidiary of the German chemical company. Although Bayer denies that methyl parathion was responsible for the poisonings, a Peruvian Congressional Investigative

Excerpted from Erika Rosenthal, "The Tragedy of Tauccamarca: A Human Rights Perspective on the Pesticide Poisoning Deaths of 24 Children in the Peruvian Andes," *International Journal of Occupational and Environmental Health* 9 (2003): 53–58. Some of the author's notes have been omitted.

Subcommittee report concluded that there is significant evidence of responsibility on the part of the agrochemical company Bayer and on the part of the Ministry of Agriculture.[3] The report recommends that the government and Bayer indemnify the families of the dead children, and recommends significant reforms to remedy Peru's lax and ineffective pesticide control policy.

Methyl parathion is a category Ia, or "extremely hazardous," pesticide according to the World Health Organization. Nonetheless, in Peru methyl parathion—a white powdered pesticide with no strong chemical odor—was sold in one-kilogram plastic bags, with pictures of vegetables above the label, and no pictogram indicating the acute danger of the product to human health.

On paper, Peruvian pesticide regulations direct that WHO Category Ia pesticides such as methyl parathion must be registered as "restricted use" products, which can legally be sold to only a buyer who has received a "technical prescription" from a licensed agronomist, accredited by the Ministry of Agriculture.

In practice, though, the Peruvian ministry charged with enforcing pesticide regulations—like those of most developing southern countries—simply doesn't have the human or financial resources to carry out its mandate. Postregistration enforcement of pesticide regulations is practically nonexistent. According to the villagers, no licensed agronomist has ever visited Tauccamarca, and methyl parathion is freely available for sale without a technical prescription in the nearby markets.[4]

When questioned by the Congressional Investigative Committee, SENASA, the department of the Peruvian Ministry of Agriculture responsible for pesticide regulation, openly stated that it is impossible for them to guarantee regulatory control over the way these pesticide products are sold and used.[5] The Congress report concluded that SENASA didn't carry out its mandate to enforce the country's pesticide laws, allowing the free circulation of dangerous products and putting the health of farmers and the population in general at risk.[6]

Bayer has responded, both in the press and in court documents, that the company complies with all legal and technical requirements of Peruvian law, and that they operate under a policy of "Responsible Care" in Peru. Moreover, Bayer asserts that the deaths of the children were caused not by uncontrolled availability of a restricted-use pesticide in the countryside per se, but by the misuse of the product by the village women, which cut off any legal responsibility that might adhere to the company. In other words, because a pesticide, which could reasonably be predicted to be misused, was in fact misused, the deaths of the children become just an unfortunate accident.

## ■ Unfortunate Accidents or a Systematic Pattern of Human Rights Abuses Ignored?

Although only a small percentage of global pesticide use is in the developing south, the great majority of pesticide poisonings occur there.

This fact has been a staple of international public health investigation and regulatory hand wringing for decades. In 1990 the World Health Organization estimated 3 million pesticide poisonings per year, causing 220,000 deaths,[7] and in 1994 estimated between 3 and 5 million occupational poisonings annually.[8] And a recent study conducted with support of the Pan-American Health Organization in the seven Central American countries estimates that when underreporting of pesticide poisonings is factored into the equation there are 400,000 poisonings per year in Central America alone.[9] This suggests that the global dimensions of the pesticide problem may be much greater than previously projected.

The pesticide industry, and Bayer itself, have acknowledged the danger posed by highly toxic pesticides, especially those such as methyl parathion that are classified as the most acutely toxic, or category Ia and Ib, by the World Health Organization. Bayer was pressured to stop selling methyl parathion in Germany as of 1989 due to the product's extreme toxicity, but continues to market the product internationally. Bayer had even published a statement proclaiming its goal of phasing out sale of its products in the WHO Toxicity Class 1 in the developing south.[10] And the high number of methyl parathion poisoning incidents in Central America, as shown in a Danish video in 1997, caused the major Danish manufacturer, Cheminova, to withdraw its methyl parathion product from Nicaragua.[11]

In the United States, responding to numerous incidents of severe health harm caused by methyl parathion, the Environmental Protection Agency in 1997 instituted some of the strictest restrictions ever applied to a pesticide. These included a requirement to add an odorant, or "stenching" agent, to the pesticide to discourage home use, and the use of tamper resistant containers that require special equipment for removal of the product. Most uses of methyl parathion were subsequently banned in 1999.

Given these facts, it's safe to assume that Bayer was well aware of the public health risk posed by methyl parathion, especially under the socioeconomic conditions prevalent in the developing south, where pesticide users are often poorly educated or illiterate; don't speak or read the language of the pesticide label; and have no access to protective equipment. Compounding the danger, most southern governments lack the regulatory and enforcement infrastructure necessary to control sale and use of these pesticides. Even where a pesticide is registered as a restricted-use product, as methyl parathion was in Peru, the reality in the countryside, as noted by the Peruvian Ministry of Agriculture, is that there is no control.

Under these conditions, pesticide users will predictably misuse the pesticide, often with devastating results. As the poisoning data and tragedies such as Tauccamarca indicate, "safe use" of toxic pesticides is simply not possible under the prevailing unsafe conditions in these countries.

Yet Bayer widely promoted its methyl parathion formulation throughout Peru, targeting marketing on use in Andean crops cultivated primarily by small farmers, most of whom are illiterate. Bayer packaged a white powdered pesticide that resembles powdered milk and has no strong chemical odor in one-kilogram bags, labeled in Spanish and displaying a picture of vegetables. The labels provided no usable safety information, such as pictograms, for the majority of users in these remote villages, and little indication of the danger of the product.

It's hard to argue that Bayer could not foresee the misuse of the product in a country with a large population of illiterate, Quechua-speaking users.[12] Moreover, for a very small investment, Bayer and other pesticide companies could have adequately packaged their product in special containers, with labels that included pictograms to help to convey the danger of the product to illiterate users, and added a stenching agent to discourage off-label home use as was required in the United States. They did nothing. Their failure to take protective action, or alternatively to take precautionary measures and withdraw the product from the market, should not be accepted as business as usual, but rather should be understood as systematic disrespect for fundamental human rights. . . .

Why aren't business practices such as the marketing of a pesticide where the probability of foreseeable misuse and injury is so high as to be a virtual certainty considered human rights violations? Why don't agrochemical companies take steps to prevent the foreseeable misuse of extremely toxic products, given the severe health risks presented and the well known socioeconomic conditions throughout the developing south?

The agrochemical industry wields significant political and economic influence throughout the world, and mounts well-funded campaigns to persuade governments that its products are economic necessities, that "safe use" of extremely toxic pesticides is possible, and that pesticide poisonings are just unfortunate accidents, the sad outcome of user error.

In practice, the international community has allowed the agrochemical industry's assertion of a right to enter a toxic product into the stream of commerce to trump fundamental human rights. The agrochemical industry's approach around the world is designed to maximize profits and minimize costs, while nominally fulfilling regulatory requirements that are known to be ineffective and insufficient.

Driven by short-term profit motives, industry will seek to continue production, discharges, or overseas sales of chemicals long after they are known to damage human health or the environment. When it comes to pesticides in the developing south, there are no unsafe uses per se; poisonings are not random accidents—but rather foreseeable events caused by introducing highly toxic products into unsafe conditions throughout the developing south. Just because these are daily acts of commerce doesn't mean they can't also be understood as continuing and systematic human rights violations.

## ■ Conclusion

The world community should begin to frame corporate accountability issues in human rights terms, and not allow corporations to hide behind paper compliance with weak, unenforced national laws. A human rights analysis can help achieve better national and international control of dangerous pesticides and better corporate accountability. If business practices such as the marketing of a pesticide where foreseeable misuse is expected were understood as human rights violations, it would require an immediate and serious reevaluation of international pesticide and toxic substance control regimes. The rights to life, health and security of person should be understood to include the right not to be poisoned by the agrochemical industry.

## ■ Notes

1. Boyd S. Pesticide poisoning raises questions: the deaths of 24 children in a remote Andean village highlight the hazards of poor agrochemical controls. Latinamerica Press. 1999; 31, no. 42/Nov. 15.

2. Wesseling C, Boluarte A, Sanchez D. Efectos neuroconductuales y neuropsicologicos en niños intoxicados con el plaguicida organofosforado paration. Tauccamarca, Cuzco, Peru: Informe Preliminar. 20 de octubre de 2001.

3. Peruvian Congress, Agrarian Commission, Final Report. Investigative Subcommittee on the Sad Events in Tauccamarca-Cusco, Relating to the Deaths of 24 Children and 18 Poisoned Children Due to the Ingestion of Food Contaminated with Pesticides. May 2002, Lima, Peru.

4. A civil lawsuit was filed on behalf of the parents of the deceased children on October 22, 2001. Less than 48 hours later (a landspeed record for the judicial system in Peru) the judge issued an order proclaiming the case inadmissible on various procedural grounds—lack of certain documents, such as marriage certificates, that the parents had lost—and also decided the underlying legal issue—of causation between Bayer's marketing of the pesticide in the region and the eventual poisoning of the children. The judge was not competent under the Peruvian Code of Civil Procedure to consider substantive issues at this stage of the proceedings. The families appealed the illegal decision and won, reinstating the case. As of November 2002, the court had yet to set the first hearing date.

5. Peruvian Congress report, p. 61.

6. Peruvian Congress report, p. 51.

7. Jeyaratnam F. Acute pesticide poisoning: a major global health problem. World Health Statist Q. 1990; 43:139–44.

8. International Labour Organization. ILO warns on farm safety; agriculture mortality rates remain high; Pesticides pose major health risks to global workforce. Released simultaneously in Geneva, Switzerland, and Itasca, IL. 8usA. (ILO/97/23). October 22, 1997. <http://www.ilo.org/public/english/burcau/inf/pr/1997/23.htm>.

9. Based on preliminary results from a multicentric study, based on 32,245 questionnaires in six countries, that indicated 98% underreporting of pesticide poisonings and 7,000 reported poisonings in 2000. Murray D, Wesseling C. Pesticide Illness Surveillance in the Developing World: Putting the Data to Work, 2002. To be published. The same epidemiologic surveillance program has identified methyl parathion as one of the 12 pesticides that cause the most acute pesticide poisonings in Central America.

10. Bayer. Responsible Care in the Crop Protection Business Group 2000. In: Dewa. Product Stewardship.

11. Kirshner A. Methyl parathion in Central America: Cheminova responds. Global Pesticide Campaigner. 1997; 7(3, September).

12. In fact, Bayer's own guidelines for corporate responsibility and responsible care state that: "The purchaser of the product must be advised of any risks associated with its use, and every product must bear the necessary warning labels." Guidelines for Legal Compliance and Corporate Responsibility at Bayer. <http://www.bayer.com/en/unternehmen/unternehmenspolitik/grundsaetze/verantwort.html#produkt>. Their guidelines for product stewardship state that: "Distributors and customers must be given the necessary information and advice to enable them to transport, store, handle, use and dispose of our products safely." Guidelines for Responsible Care in Environmental Protection and Safety. <http://www.bayer.com/en/unternehmen/unternehmenspolitik/grundsaetze/umwelt.html#produktverantwortung>.

# 8.5

# Strategic Violations: The Outsourcing of Human Rights Abuses

*Neve Gordon*

In her book *Mercenaries, Pirates, and Sovereigns,* Janice Thomson describes how "sea dogs" such as Francis Drake extorted large ransoms from Spanish colonial cities by threatening to destroy them if they failed to pay up. The sea dogs were virtually indistinguishable from other pirates, except that they were acting under the auspices of the British crown. Queen Elizabeth orchestrated their so-called private campaigns. And due in large part to these state-sanctioned ravages, by the late 16th-century England had gained naval superiority over Spain. In a sense, Drake was a subcontractor; the Queen outsourced work, employing him and other sea dogs to execute certain tasks which, in today's parlance, constituted blatant violations of human rights.

The economic neologism outsourcing denotes, according to the Oxford English Dictionary, "the obtaining of goods or contracting of work from sources outside a company or area." Replacing the word work with violations and adding the word government before company, imparts a definition which helps explain a pervasive strategy used these days to violate basic human rights: outsourcing, the contracting of violations from sources outside a government, company, or area. . . .

Outsourcing has often been put to use to abdicate social and moral responsibility. Its benefits are legal, political, and economic. From a legal perspective, employing subcontractors is an effective device since it obfuscates the connection between the perpetrator and the contravening act, making it extremely difficult to hold the violator legally accountable for the abuses it sanctions. From a political perspective, outsourcing is beneficial because, even if abuses are exposed they are frequently presented to the public as having been carried out by someone else—i.e., the subcontractor. In this manner, subcontracting the violations helps a country deflect the shaming technique, considered by many the most effective tool employed by human rights organizations. From a slightly different perspective, insofar as a major role of rights groups is to create norms that shape policies and interests as well as ensure that these

---

Excerpted from Neve Gordon, "Strategic Violations: The Outsourcing of Human Rights Abuses," *The Humanist* 63 (2003): 10–14. Some of the author's notes have been omitted.

norms are respected, outsourcing is used in order to conceal the perpetrator's breach of these norms. Finally, the use of subcontractors is economically advantageous not only because it cuts production costs but also because it enables the corporation to avoid both legal prosecution and embarrassment, both of which can have an unfavorable effect on capital. . . .

Along the same lines, political and civil violations are also subcontracted around the globe. Torture, still illegal in the United States, has been contracted out to countries like Saudi Arabia, Morocco, and Egypt. Nation reporter Eyal Press stated that the Central Intelligence Agency had already transferred one hundred suspects to ally countries whose brutal torture methods have been amply documented in the State Department's own annual human rights reports. "We don't kick the [expletive] out of them," one government official told the *Washington Post*. "We send them to other countries so they can kick the [expletive] out of them."

This is what Press found out: Many captives have been sent to Egypt, where, according to the State Department, suspects are routinely "stripped and blindfolded; suspended from a ceiling or doorframe with feet just touching the floor; beaten with fists, whips, metal rods, or other objects; subjected to electric shocks." In at least one case, a suspect was sent to Syria where, the State Department says, torture methods include "pulling out fingernails; forcing objects into the rectum . . . using a chair that bends backwards to asphyxiate the victim or fracture the spine." A story in *Newsday* published just after this arrest quoted a former CIA official who, describing a detainee transferred from Guantánamo Bay to Egypt, said, "They promptly tore his fingernails out and he started telling things."

The second Bush administration, with its ongoing attack on civil liberties, didn't invent the wheel. Not only have past administrations employed this tactic but other countries have as well. Consider Israel, which founded the mercenary South Lebanese Army (SLA) in 1978, employing it to control the "security zone" or "enclave" comprising about 10 percent of Lebanese territory. The Al-Khiam prison was the SLA's permanent interrogation and detention facility, in which prisoners were held outside any legal framework. Torture was systematically practiced in Al-Khiam; the methods employed included electric shock, suspension from an electricity pole, dousing with water, painful postures, beating with an electric cable, and sleep deprivation. Amnesty International reports that torture practiced by Israel's subcontractor resulted in physical injury and, on a number of occasions, the death of detainees.

Military training and support of governmental security forces and mercenaries, used extensively by the United States and the former Soviet Union after World War II, are also mechanisms of outsourcing violations. Smaller and less powerful nations used these tools as well. The brutal Buhtulaizi government was armed and supported by the South African apartheid regime, and the paramilitaries in East Timor operated under the directives of the Indonesian military.

More recently, private military contractors (PMCs), frequently run by retired military generals, have been utilized to do the dirty work previously carried out by foreign mercenaries. PMCs are the new big business on the block. Their job is to provide stand-ins for active soldiers, engaging in everything from actual fighting and battlefield training to logistical support and military advice at home and abroad. Writing for *Mother Jones,* Barry Yeoman suggests that they enjoy an estimated $100 billion in business each year, with much of this money going to Fortune 500 firms like Lockheed Martin, Raytheon, Halliburton, and DynCorp. In the U.S. war on Iraq, the United States employed an estimated twenty thousand corporate workers in the region; that is one civilian for every ten soldiers—a tenfold increase over the 1991 Iraq War.

The advantage of subcontracting to PMCs is clear: it allows the executive branch to avoid public debate or legislative controls. While Congress capped the number of U.S. soldiers who could be sent to Colombia at five hundred, the Pentagon together with the Colombian government have been employing additional corporate soldiers from DynCorp to carry out anti-drug operations. According to Peter Singer from the Brookings Institute, the firm utilizes armed reconnaissance planes and helicopter gunships designed for counterguerrilla warfare and has been involved in several firefights with local rebels. DynCorp has lost several planes and employees to rebel fire, but there has been no public outcry about the losses simply because "corporate soldiers" were killed rather than "real soldiers."

In Bosnia, the addition of two thousand corporate soldiers helped evade the congressional limit of twenty thousand troops. The issue isn't only that the Pentagon uses PMCs to undercut restrictions made via democratic procedures, but also that corporate soldiers are accountable solely to the corporations that retain them, rather than to governments. Employees of DynCorp in Bosnia were caught operating a sex-slave ring of underage women and even videotaping a rape. Leslie Wayne of the *New York Times* reported that while the DynCorp employees trafficked in women—including buying one for $1,000—the company turned a blind eye. Since the DynCorp employees involved weren't soldiers, their actions weren't subject to military discipline. Nor did they face local justice; they were simply fired and sent home. . . .

An additional example wherein outsourcing is used to systematically violate human rights is the private prison complex, which currently holds over one hundred thousand inmates. In this case, both political and civil rights as well as economic and social rights are violated. *The Nation*'s Eric Bates argues that the real danger of prison privatization isn't merely the inhumanity on the part of guards but rather the added financial incentives that reward inhumanity. He states,

> The same economic logic that motivates companies to run prisons more efficiently also encourages them to cut corners at the expense of workers, pris-

oners and the public. Private prisons essentially mirror the cost-cutting practices of health maintenance organizations: Companies receive a guaranteed fee for each prisoner, regardless of the actual cost. Every dime they don't spend on food or medical care or training for guards is a dime they can pocket. . . .

Outsourcing is, however, not employed merely as a strategy to help the perpetrator abdicate responsibility for the violations it authorizes; it also assists the aggressor in maintaining a respectable aura in the public eye. It isn't the United States that tortures al-Qaeda suspects, Egypt does; it isn't the transnational corporation that neglects the health of its employees but rather its subsidiary in Thailand. Governments and transnational corporations use subcontractors in order to conceal pernicious practices because the success of power, as Michel Foucault convincingly argued, "is in proportion to its ability to hide its own mechanisms." Thus, outsourcing should be considered a technique employed by power in order to conceal its own mechanisms. It is motivated by the unwavering efforts of governments and corporations to remain in control. . . .

The practice of outsourcing violations engenders new challenges for the human rights community. If the party carrying out the act isn't the only culpable entity, then the process of identifying those responsible becomes much more complicated. Moreover, identifying the agent employing the subcontractor is only the first step in a long and arduous struggle against violations, since it often remains extremely difficult to prosecute or effectively employ the shaming technique. Consequently, human rights organizations need to develop new strategies and promote the introduction of clear directives within international law that take into account this phenomenon and can aid in holding governments, corporations, and other international financial institutions accountable.

# 8.6

# The Singer Solution to World Poverty

*Peter Singer*

In the Brazilian film "Central Station," Dora is a retired schoolteacher who makes ends meet by sitting at the station writing letters for illiterate people. Suddenly she has an opportunity to pocket $1,000. All she has to do is persuade a homeless 9-year-old boy to follow her to an address she has been given. (She is told he will be adopted by wealthy foreigners.) She delivers the boy, gets the money, spends some of it on a television set and settles down to enjoy her new acquisition. Her neighbor spoils the fun, however, by telling her that the boy was too old to be adopted—he will be killed and his organs sold for transplantation. Perhaps Dora knew this all along, but after her neighbor's plain speaking, she spends a troubled night. In the morning Dora resolves to take the boy back.

Suppose Dora had told her neighbor that it is a tough world, other people have nice new TV's too, and if selling the kid is the only way she can get one, well, he was only a street kid. She would then have become, in the eyes of the audience, a monster. She redeems herself only by being prepared to bear considerable risks to save the boy.

At the end of the movie, in cinemas in the affluent nations of the world, people who would have been quick to condemn Dora if she had not rescued the boy go home to places far more comfortable than her apartment. In fact, the average family in the United States spends almost one-third of its income on things that are no more necessary to them than Dora's new TV was to her. Going out to nice restaurants, buying new clothes because the old ones are no longer stylish, vacationing at beach resorts—so much of our income is spent on things not essential to the preservation of our lives and health. Donated to one of a number of charitable agencies, that money could mean the difference between life and death for children in need.

All of which raises a question: In the end, what is the ethical distinction between a Brazilian who sells a homeless child to organ peddlers and an American who already has a TV and upgrades to a better one—knowing that

Excerpted from Peter Singer, "The Singer Solution to World Poverty," *The New York Times,* September 5, 1999.

the money could be donated to an organization that would use it to save the lives of kids in need?

Of course, there are several differences between the two situations that could support different moral judgments about them. For one thing, to be able to consign a child to death when he is standing right in front of you takes a chilling kind of heartlessness; it is much easier to ignore an appeal for money to help children you will never meet. Yet for a utilitarian philosopher like myself—that is, one who judges whether acts are right or wrong by their consequences—if the upshot of the American's failure to donate the money is that one more kid dies on the streets of a Brazilian city, then it is, in some sense, just as bad as selling the kid to the organ peddlers. But one doesn't need to embrace my utilitarian ethic to see that, at the very least, there is a troubling incongruity in being so quick to condemn Dora for taking the child to the organ peddlers while, at the same time, not regarding the American consumer's behavior as raising a serious moral issue.

In his 1996 book, Living High and Letting Die, the New York University philosopher Peter Unger presented an ingenious series of imaginary examples designed to probe our intuitions about whether it is wrong to live well without giving substantial amounts of money to help people who are hungry, malnourished or dying from easily treatable illnesses like diarrhea. Here's my paraphrase of one of these examples:

Bob is close to retirement. He has invested most of his savings in a very rare and valuable old car, a Bugatti, which he has not been able to insure. The Bugatti is his pride and joy. In addition to the pleasure he gets from driving and caring for his car, Bob knows that its rising market value means that he will always be able to sell it and live comfortably after retirement. One day when Bob is out for a drive, he parks the Bugatti near the end of a railway siding and goes for a walk up the track. As he does so, he sees that a runaway train, with no one aboard, is running down the railway track. Looking farther down the track, he sees the small figure of a child very likely to be killed by the runaway train. He can't stop the train and the child is too far away to warn of the danger, but he can throw a switch that will divert the train down the siding where his Bugatti is parked. Then nobody will be killed—but the train will destroy his Bugatti. Thinking of his joy in owning the car and the financial security it represents, Bob decides not to throw the switch. The child is killed. For many years to come, Bob enjoys owning his Bugatti and the financial security it represents.

Bob's conduct, most of us will immediately respond, was gravely wrong. Unger agrees. But then he reminds us that we, too, have opportunities to save the lives of children. We can give to organizations like UNICEF or Oxfam America. How much would we have to give one of these organizations to have a high probability of saving the life of a child threatened by easily preventable diseases? (I do not believe that children are more worth saving than adults, but since no one can argue that children have brought their poverty on themselves, focusing on them simplifies the issues.) Unger called up some experts and used the information they provided to offer some plausible estimates that include the cost of raising money, administrative expenses and the cost of delivering aid where it is most needed. By his calculation, $200 in donations would help a sickly 2-year-old transform into a healthy 6-year-old—offering safe passage through childhood's most dangerous years. To show how practical philosophical argument can be, Unger even tells his readers that they can easily donate funds by using their credit card and calling one of these toll-free numbers: (800) 367-5437 for Unicef; (800) 693-2687 for Oxfam America.

Now you, too, have the information you need to save a child's life. How should you judge yourself if you don't do it? Think again about Bob and his Bugatti. Unlike Dora, Bob did not have to look into the eyes of the child he was sacrificing for his own material comfort. The child was a complete stranger to him and too far away to relate to in an intimate, personal way. Unlike Dora, too, he did not mislead the child or initiate the chain of events imperiling him. In all these respects, Bob's situation resembles that of people able but unwilling to donate to overseas aid and differs from Dora's situation.

If you still think that it was very wrong of Bob not to throw the switch that would have diverted the train and saved the child's life, then it is hard to see how you could deny that it is also very wrong not to send money to one of the organizations listed above. Unless, that is, there is some morally important difference between the two situations that I have overlooked.

Is it the practical uncertainties about whether aid will really reach the people who need it? Nobody who knows the world of overseas aid can doubt that such uncertainties exist. But Unger's figure of $200 to save a child's life was reached after he had made conservative assumptions about the proportion of the money donated that will actually reach its target.

One genuine difference between Bob and those who can afford to donate to overseas aid organizations but don't is that only Bob can save the child on the tracks, whereas there are hundreds of millions of people who can give $200 to overseas aid organizations. The problem is that most of them aren't doing it. Does this mean that it is all right for you not to do it?

Suppose that there were more owners of priceless vintage cars—Carol, Dave, Emma, Fred and so on, down to Ziggy—all in exactly the same situation as Bob, with their own siding and their own switch, all sacrificing the child in order to preserve their own cherished car. Would that make it all right for Bob to do the same? To answer this question affirmatively is to endorse follow-the-crowd ethics—the kind of ethics that led many Germans to look away when the Nazi atrocities were being committed. We do not excuse them because others were behaving no better.

We seem to lack a sound basis for drawing a clear moral line between Bob's situation and that of any reader of this article with $200 to spare who does not donate it to an overseas aid agency. These readers seem to be acting at least as badly as Bob was acting when he chose to let the runaway train hurtle toward the unsuspecting child. In the light of this conclusion, I trust that many readers will reach for the phone and donate that $200. Perhaps you should do it before reading further.

Now that you have distinguished yourself morally from people who put their vintage cars ahead of a child's life, how about treating yourself and your partner to dinner at your favorite restaurant? But wait. The money you will spend at the restaurant could also help save the lives of children overseas! True, you weren't planning to blow $200 tonight, but if you were to give up dining out just for one month, you would easily save that amount. And what is one month's dining out, compared to a child's life? There's the rub. Since there are a lot of desperately needy children in the world, there will always be another child whose life you could save for another $200. Are you therefore obliged to keep giving until you have nothing left? At what point can you stop?

Hypothetical examples can easily become farcical. Consider Bob. How far past losing the Bugatti should he go? Imagine that Bob had got his foot stuck in the track of the siding, and if he diverted the train, then before it rammed the car it would also amputate his big toe. Should he still throw the switch? What if it would amputate his foot? His entire leg?

As absurd as the Bugatti scenario gets when pushed to extremes, the point it raises is a serious one: only when the sacrifices become very significant indeed would most people be prepared to say that Bob does nothing wrong when he decides not to throw the switch. Of course, most people could be wrong; we can't decide moral issues by taking opinion polls. But consider for yourself the level of sacrifice that you would demand of Bob, and then think about how much money you would have to give away in order to make a sacrifice that is roughly equal to that. It's almost certainly much, much more than $200. For most middle-class Americans, it could easily be more like $200,000.

Isn't it counterproductive to ask people to do so much? Don't we run the risk that many will shrug their shoulders and say that morality, so conceived, is fine for saints but not for them? I accept that we are unlikely to see, in the near or even medium-term future, a world in which it is normal for wealthy Americans to give the bulk of their wealth to strangers. When it comes to praising or blaming people for what they do, we tend to use a standard that is relative to some conception of normal behavior. Comfortably off Americans who give, say, 10 percent of their income to overseas aid organizations are so far ahead of most of their equally comfortable fellow citizens that I wouldn't go out of my way to chastise them for not doing more. Nevertheless, they should be doing much more, and they are in no position to criticize Bob for failing to make the much greater sacrifice of his Bugatti.

At this point various objections may crop up. Someone may say: "If every citizen living in the affluent nations contributed his or her share I wouldn't have to make such a drastic sacrifice, because long before such levels were reached, the resources would have been there to save the lives of all those children dying from lack of food or medical care. So why should I give more than my fair share?" Another, related, objection is that the Government ought to increase its overseas aid allocations, since that would spread the burden more equitably across all taxpayers.

Yet the question of how much we ought to give is a matter to be decided in the real world—and that, sadly, is a world in which we know that most people do not, and in the immediate future will not, give substantial amounts to overseas aid agencies. We know, too, that at least in the next year, the United States Government is not going to meet even the very modest United Nations–recommended target of 0.7 percent of gross national product; at the moment it lags far below that, at 0.09 percent, not even half of Japan's 0.22 percent or a tenth of Denmark's 0.97 percent. Thus, we know that the money we can give beyond that theoretical "fair share" is still going to save lives that would otherwise be lost. While the idea that no one need do more than his or her fair share is a powerful one, should it prevail if we know that others are not doing their fair share and that children will die preventable deaths unless we do more than our fair share? That would be taking fairness too far.

Thus, this ground for limiting how much we ought to give also fails. In the world as it is now, I can see no escape from the conclusion that each one of us with wealth surplus to his or her essential needs should be giving most of it to help people suffering from poverty so dire as to be life-threatening. That's right: I'm saying that you shouldn't buy that new car, take that cruise, redecorate the house or get that pricey new suit. After all, a $1,000 suit could save five children's lives.

So how does my philosophy break down in dollars and cents? An American household with an income of $50,000 spends around $30,000 annually on necessities, according to the Conference Board, a nonprofit economic research organization. Therefore, for a household bringing in $50,000 a year, donations to help the world's poor should be as close as possible to $20,000. The $30,000 required for necessities holds for higher incomes as well. So a household making $100,000 could cut a yearly check for $70,000. Again, the formula is simple: whatever money you're spending on luxuries, not necessities, should be given away.

Now, evolutionary psychologists tell us that human nature just isn't sufficiently altruistic to make it plausible that many people will sacrifice so much for strangers. On the facts of human nature, they might be right, but they would be wrong to draw a moral conclusion from those facts. If it is the case that we ought to do things that, predictably, most of us won't do, then let's face that fact head-on. Then, if we value the life of a child more than going to fancy restaurants, the next time we dine out we will know that we could have done something better with our money. If that makes living a morally decent life extremely arduous, well, then that is the way things are. If we don't do it, then we should at least know that we are failing to live a morally decent life—not because it is good to wallow in guilt but because knowing where we should be going is the first step toward heading in that direction.

When Bob first grasped the dilemma that faced him as he stood by that railway switch, he must have thought how extraordinarily unlucky he was to be placed in a situation in which he must choose between the life of an innocent child and the sacrifice of most of his savings. But he was not unlucky at all. We are all in that situation.

# 9 Human Rights in the War on Terror

## 9.1

## Introduction
### The Editors

A final aspect of states becoming increasingly connected is the problem of terrorism. In this age of globalization, terrorists are both increasingly disenfranchised and increasingly able to communicate and coordinate with terrorists in other parts of the world. The first piece in this section examines how growing concerns regarding international terrorism may be related to human rights issues around the world. Rhonda L. Callaway and Julie Harrelson-Stephens attempt to identify under which conditions terrorism thrives. We argue that the genesis of terrorist organizations is found in both subsistence and security rights, as well as political rights. Countries with low levels of political rights and medium levels of subsistence and security rights are the prime breeding ground for terrorist activity. We also examine the interplay between domestic causes of terrorism and international-level attributes that further enable or constrain terrorist behavior. As the war on terror indicates, terrorism is one aspect of globalization that we can no longer ignore. As goods and values move with increasing ease across borders, so too do terrorists. This piece deals with the importance of human rights as a topic of study and how ignoring those rights can increase the likelihood of continued and future terrorism.

The aftermath of September 11 brings the topic of torture back to America. The conditions at Guantanamo Bay, Cuba, and the revelation of torture as a tool of interrogation at Abu Ghraib prison in Iraq have not only brought torture and international human rights law to the forefront of the human rights agenda, but made them leading topics of foreign policy and national security as well. Elisa Massimino focuses on the climate within the Bush administration that has allowed such types of torture and cruelty to exist. She points to the "degradation of the Geneva Convention" as one element, along with a loose interpretation of the definition of torture. Ultimately, Massimino suggests that this behavior will undermine any credibility that the United States has when it comes to outlawing torture around the globe.

The selection by Julie Mertus and Tazreena Sajjad outlines the effects of the US war on terror on the achievement of human rights. These authors contend that since 9/11, the international movement toward human rights has been stunted by policies designed to fight the war on terror. The retrenchment of acceptance of human rights norms is evidenced in a variety of ways. Mertus and Sajjad begin with a discussion of the use of torture, rendition, and generally questionable detention practices associated with the US war on terror. Next they examine the tendency since 9/11 for the US government to invade the privacy of its citizens, including expanded search-and-seizure capability as well as monitoring of e-mails, financial records, and bookstore activity. Finally, Mertus and Sajjad conclude with a discussion of US treatment of noncitizens since 9/11. These authors contend that the rights of noncitizens have dramatically decreased in the past few years, resulting in a climate of fear. Overall, these authors paint a bleak picture for the prospects of human rights as the war on terror resulted in the national security interests of the United States trumping progress that had been previously made in that arena.

Since World War II, the international community has increasingly recognized limits on state sovereignty, and the language of international human rights has become increasingly accepted worldwide. Yet, the international community's willingness to limit state sovereignty continues to move slowly and oftentimes sporadically. Globalization means the world is becoming a smaller place, and information continues to be transmitted in new and instantaneous ways. The pressures that globalization put on the state and the state's response to those pressures will be critical for the future realization of human rights. At the same time, global terrorism is increasing and increasingly dangerous in a time when terrorists can network around the world. The connection between terrorism and human rights will increasingly dominate the world stage. How states and the international community respond to these threats will be the essential factor that shapes the future of human rights.

# Human Rights Violations as a Catalyst for Terrorist Activity

*Rhonda L. Callaway and Julie Harrelson-Stephens*

Since September 11, there has been increasing attention paid to terrorism and terrorist activity around the world. It has become the primary focus of US foreign policy, while the war in Iraq seems to be fueling terrorist activity in all parts of the world. Although researchers have long argued over the nature, definition, and causes of terrorism, we have seen a recent explosion in the number of studies on terrorism. Nonetheless, the study of terrorism remains underdeveloped, focusing primarily on typologies of terrorists and terrorism (Rubenstein 1974; Schultz 1978, 1990; Sederberg 1994; Laqueur 1999, 2001).

A history of colonial subjugation, slow economic development, and years of dictatorial rule has left many states in domestic turmoil, both politically and economically. The rapid rate of globalization over the past several decades has exacerbated, if not highlighted, many of these domestic inadequacies and inequalities. States have responded in a variety of ways ranging from more economic and political openness to, in the most extreme cases, complete state failure. This spectrum of state response suggests that states at the losing end of the spectrum might be characterized by limited civil and political rights, poor quality of life, and in some cases, gross human rights violations. It is within these societies that we expect to see greater potential of terrorist activity due to the human rights conditions within the state. The domestic environment provides a breeding ground that serves as necessary, but not sufficient, conditions for terrorism. In most cases, we can expect that the domestic conditions within the state might lead to domestic political unrest, with disenfranchised citizens calling for reform by the government or the provision of additional social services. Richard Schultz (1978) refers to this type of violence as either *subrevolutionary terrorism* or *revolutionary terrorism*. The objective of the former is to affect the political system, while the objective of the latter is to facilitate complete domestic political change.

This paper was originally presented at the annual International Studies Association meeting in Montreal, 2004. A later version with a test of the theory developed in it was published as Rhonda L. Callaway and Julie Harrelson-Stephens, "Toward a Theory of Terrorism: Human Security as a Determinant of Terrorism," *Studies in Conflict and Terrorism* 29 (2006): 773–796.

We develop a theoretical framework for the causes of terrorism. Specifically, we argue that human rights violations create an environment that makes terrorist activity more likely. Much like the definition of terrorism, a universal definition of human rights remains elusive. By human rights, we mean the rights that one has simply because one is human (Donnelly 1989, 1998). However, in order to formulate any testable hypotheses, we turn to types of rights that ultimately can be measured and quantified. Here, we examine three subsets of human rights: political rights, security rights, and subsistence rights, in turn. We might collectively refer to these as *basic rights* (Shue 1980). In the end, we argue that violations of these rights are directly related to the genesis and growth of terrorism.

One of the main stumbling blocks to the study of terrorism is the controversy over how we define terrorism (Rubenstein 1974; Laqueur 2001; Cooper 2001; Crenshaw 1995; Combs 2003). This dilemma has resulted in a field of study that is "descriptive, prescriptive and obliquely emotive in form" (Schultz 1990, 49) and one that has precluded empirical analysis (O'Brien 1998). The oft-quoted line "one man's terrorist is another man's freedom fighter" seems to leave the field of terrorism in a quandary. This problem is exacerbated by states using the term politically to caste one's enemies in a negative light, but refusing to use the term to describe one's allies. If we conclude that terrorism is indefinable, then terrorism is rendered immeasurable, and there is no point in trying to advance any sort of empirical study of terrorism. On the other hand, we contend that terrorism can be defined in an empirically neutral way if it is based on the target rather than on one's emotional or cultural attachments to a particular group.[1]

In this study, we utilize the definition of terrorism provided by Bruce Bueno de Mesquita (2000, 339). According to this definition, terrorism is "any act of violence undertaken for the purpose of altering a government's political policies or actions that target those who do not actually have the personal authority to alter governmental policy." This definition has the benefit of distinguishing terrorists from other types of combatants by their targets. The purpose of terrorism, for Bueno de Mesquita, is to incite the population to pressure its own government for policy changes.

In order to proceed, we first assess the extent to which political rights affect the probability of terrorist activity. We then explore the link between security rights and terrorism, followed by a discussion of subsistence rights and their relationship to terrorism. We conclude with a discussion of how each of these rights, taken collectively, can create an environment that encourages terrorism.

## ■ Political Rights and Terrorism

Our first argument focuses on the relationship between political rights and terrorism. Political rights ensure that citizens are able to participate in government, usually in the form of voting, protesting, and otherwise legitimately opposing the government in power. Inherently, democracies are more open and transparent, and as such, more accepting of political protests (Gurr 1979; Hamilton 1978; Turk 1982; Ross 1993; Eubank and Weinberg 1994). Citizens who are able to protest within their regime are less likely to resort to terrorism. The more open the political system, the less likely individuals are to go outside the system to participate in the political process (Essman 1994). Thus, democracies are less likely to engender terrorist groups.[2]

Conversely, a citizen in a state with limited political rights is less likely to have an opportunity to work within the system to effect change. More closed political systems, therefore, motivate citizens to seek redress outside the norms of the system. A prolonged denial of political rights and civil liberties provides a foundation of domestic political dissent. The more closed the system, the more likely this political dissent will take on a violent nature. In some cases, minorities, especially ethnic minorities, are often disenfranchised, which possibly leads to a violent response. A group that is systematically excluded from the political process may feel it has no choice but to pursue unconventional means of participation, including, in the extreme, terrorism. After the overthrow of Juan Perón in Argentina, for example, the Aramburu government targeted Peronists and excluded them from participating in the political system. It was within this context that a small group of Peronists formed a resistance group called the Montoneros. Eventually this group would embrace terrorism in an attempt to effect change in the political system of Argentina (Whittaker 2001).

In Sri Lanka, the Sinhalese majority has systemically repressed and abused the Tamil minority by instituting an "illiberal language policy (Sinhalese only), the refusal to give all Tamils in Sri Lanka citizenship, and the attempt to repatriate some of them to India, even though they had been born in Sri Lanka" (Whittaker 2003, 94). The great traditions, specifically the cultural and social, separating the Sinhalese from the Tamils have led to a violent reaction by the latter. While the violence and revolutionary tendencies of the Tamils were originally based on Marxism, they have been replaced by a violent form of self-determination (Whittaker 2003). In the Sri Lankan case, we see a minority restricted politically by a majority, leading to domestic political violence or what Schultz (1978) refers to as "revolutionary" terrorism.

In sum, we expect that in democratic states, terrorist activity is less likely due to their relative levels of openness and transparency. As states become less democratic, we would expect an increase in the likelihood of terrorism as a response to political repression. Thus, we hypothesize the relationship between political rights and terrorism to be a linear one.

## ■ Conditions in the State: Security Rights of the Individual

The second category of human rights we examine is security rights, or what are often referred to as *personal integrity rights*. Security rights violations include torture, state murder, and disappearances (Gastil 1980; Gibney and Dalton 1996). Both leftist (Stalin's Russia) and right-wing autocratic regimes (Pinochet's Chile, Argentina under Perón, Franco's Spain) have been guilty of such atrocities throughout history. The human rights literature shows a clear connection between political rights and security rights, specifically that the more democratic a state is, the more likely it will respect human rights (Henderson 1991, 1993; Mitchell and McCormick 1988; Poe and Tate 1994; McCormick and Mitchell 1997; Poe, Tate, and Keith 1999). However, this relationship among political rights, security rights, and terrorist activity is a complex one. Here, we argue that even once the effect of political rights is controlled for, state repression has an independent effect, exacerbating terrorist activity.

When security rights are violated, an incentive is created for people to seek extra-systemic means of political expression. When a state uses violence against its citizens, opposition groups often feel justified in responding in kind. The Red Brigade in Italy, for example, argued that their use of violence was justified because the state had resorted to violence (Whittaker 2001). The effect of state repression goes beyond the persecuted individual directly; it also impacts the entire populace due to the fear or terror that state repression creates throughout society (Lopez and Stohl 1992; Poe and Tate 1994).

In addition, terrorism is likely to be greatest in states that have some degree of repression short of the most abusive regimes. For example, the Irish Republican Army operates in a relatively open society, which facilitates its continued existence. On the other hand, terrorism research suggests that under extreme repressive conditions, domestic terrorism is rare (Weinberg 1991). Extremely repressive regimes do a good job of combating domestic political unrest. It is difficult to imagine that groups of citizens in Saddam Hussein's Iraq would pursue terrorist actions on a widespread basis. In Iraq, where repression was so complete and arbitrary, citizens were too fearful for their lives to engage in terrorist activities. Similarly, under the Khmer Rouge, Cambodians were unlikely to attempt to attack the state. In states where repression is the most extreme, terrorist activity against the state is unlikely. Thus, we contend that the relationship between security rights violations and terrorism is nonlinear in that at low levels of repression there is a greater likelihood of terrorism, which increases as repression increases until a certain threshold is reached.

## ■ Conditions in the State: Subsistence Rights of the Individual

The last type of rights we discuss is subsistence rights or basic human needs. Although subsistence rights are a subset of human rights, violations against them are fundamentally different from other types of violations. On the one hand, security rights violations are proactive actions against certain citizens by the government. Oftentimes, the targets of such abuse are the potential political opposition and may only encompass a small percentage of the population. On the other hand, violations against basic human needs most often refer to the inability of government to provide for the citizenry and suggest not proactive abuse, but rather neglect. This neglect can be intentional in many cases (Zimbabwe, for example) or simply a result of the state's inability to provide for basic human needs (as in Haiti). Regardless, citizens suffer. This suffering is prime breeding ground for discontent. Those suffering may choose to blame the current regime, but may also blame other states for their condition. Again, we don't suggest that this relationship is a linear one, but rather an inverted U. Similar to the theorized relationships presented in the full-belly thesis (Howard 1983) and the more-murder-in-the-middle thesis (Fein 1995), citizens at both extremes of subsistence are less likely to engage in terrorist activity.

Those at the lower end of the spectrum are simply struggling for personal survival and have little time or energy to expend on the political process in general. Alexis de Toqueville argued just this in his analysis of the French Revolution, where those clamoring for more rights were the emerging middle class, not the poorest in society. Those at the upper end of the spectrum are generally more satisfied in terms of basic human needs and therefore are less likely to engage in terrorist activity. It is those states in the middle where terrorist activity is more likely. The middle area represents people who have been exposed to wealth and whose expectations often rise faster than their economic well-being. For example, members of the Red Brigade tended to be the working-class or middle-class students in the university system (Whittaker 2001; Combs 2003). Likewise the Baader-Meinhof group of the 1970s in West Germany was "composed of middle and upper-class intellectuals" (Combs 2003, 59). Thus, we argue that, in terms of basic human needs, terrorism is more likely in the middle.

Combining the violation of political rights and security rights and suboptimal levels of basic human needs, the conditions are ripe for terrorism. We hypothesize that terrorism is likely to occur in states with medium levels of repression, as these citizens feel justified in responding to state terror with terrorist acts. Further, in states with medium levels of subsistence, citizens are more likely to feel deprived relative to others and that sense of injustice fosters terrorism. Finally, terrorism is likely to ferment in these areas particularly when individuals feel that other options of dissent are limited due to the relatively closed political system within the state. It is at the nexus between these three rights that we see prime breeding ground for terrorist activity.

## ▓ Notes

1. That is not to say it will be easy, or even that there will not be difficult cases, but merely to acknowledge that social sciences are replete with difficult-to-define con-

cepts, such as *power, war,* and even *human rights.* To conclude that a concept that is difficult to define is a concept that is impossible to define is to doom the study of terrorism to its infancy indefinitely.

2. On the other hand, open political systems may create an environment in which terrorists have an easier time operating. This has led some theorists to argue that democracies are more likely to experience acts of terrorism on their soil. Violations of such rights generally occur in repressive regimes, both of the ideologically right and left. In open political systems, individuals have legitimate means to work within the system to express their preferences.

# ■ References

Bueno de Mesquita, Bruce. 2000. *Principles of International Politics: People's Power, Preferences, and Perceptions.* Washington, DC: CQ Press.

Combs, Cindy C. 2003. *Terrorism in the Twenty-First Century.* Upper Saddle River, NJ: Prentice-Hall.

Cooper, H.H.A. 2001. "Terrorism: The Problem of Definition Revisited." *American Behavioral Scientist* 44:891–893.

Crenshaw, Martha. 1995. *Terrorism in Context.* University Park: Pennsylvania State University Press.

Donnelly, Jack. 1998. *International Human Rights,* 2nd Edition. Boulder, CO: Westview Press.

———. 1989. *Universal Human Rights in Theory and Practice.* Ithaca and London: Cornell University Press.

Essman, Milton J. 1994. *Ethnic Politics.* Ithaca: Cornell University Press.

Eubank, William L., and Leonard B. Weinberg. 1994. "Does Democracy Encourage Terrorism?" *Terrorism and Political Violence* 6 (4): 47–35.

Fein, Helen. 1995. "More Murder in the Middle: Life Integrity Violations and Democracy in the World, 1987." *Human Rights Quarterly* 17:170–191.

Gastil, Raymond. 1980. *Freedom in the World: Political Rights and Civil Liberties, 1980.* Cambridge, MA: Harvard University Press.

Gibney, Mark, and Matthew Dalton. 1996. "The Political Terror Scale," in David Cingranelli, ed. *Human Rights and Developing Countries.* Greenwich, CT: JAI Press.

Gurr, Ted Robert. 1979. "Some Characteristics of Political Terrorism in the 1960s," in Michael Stohl, ed. *The Politics of Terrorism.* New York: Marcel Dekker, pp. 119–143.

Hamilton, Lawrence C. 1978. "Ecology of Terrorism: A Historical and Statistical Study." Ph.D. dissertation. University of Colorado.

Henderson, Conway. 1993. "Population Pressures and Political Repression." *Social Science Quarterly* 74:322–333.

———. 1991. "Conditions Affecting the Use of Political Repression." *Journal of Conflict Resolution* 35:120–142.

Howard, Rhoda. 1983. "The Full-Belly Thesis: Should Economic Rights Take Priority over Civil and Political Rights? Evidence from Sub-Saharan Africa." *Human Rights Quarterly* 5:467–490.

Laqueur, Walter. 2001. *A History of Terrorism.* New Brunswick: Transaction Publishers.

———. 1999. *The New Terrorism: Fanaticism and the Arms of Mass Destruction.* New York: Oxford University Press.

Lopez, George A., and Michael Stohl. 1992. "Problems of Concept and Measurement in the Study of Human Rights," in Thomas B. Jabine and Richard P. Claude, eds. *Human Rights and Statistics: Getting the Record Straight.* Philadelphia: University of Pennsylvania Press.

McCormick, James M., and Neil Mitchell. 1997. "Human Rights Violations, Umbrella Concepts, and Empirical Analysis." *World Politics* 49:510–525.

Mitchell, Neil J., and James M. McCormick. 1988. "Economic and Political Explanations of Human Rights Violations." *World Politics* 40:476–498.

O'Brien, Sean P. 1998. "Foreign Policy Crises and the Resort to Terrorism." *Journal of Conflict Resolution* 40:320–335.

Poe, Steven C., and C. Neal Tate. 1994. "Repression of Human Rights to Personal Integrity in the 1980s: A Global Analysis." *American Political Science Review* 88: 853–872.

Poe, Steven C., C. Neal Tate, and Linda Keith. 1999. "Repression of the Human Right to Personal Integrity Revisited: A Global Cross-National Study Covering the Years 1976–1993." *International Studies Quarterly* 43:291–314.

Ross, Jeffrey Ian. 1993. "Structural Causes of Oppositional Political Terrorism: Towards a Causal Model." *Journal of Peace Research* 30:3317–3329.

Rubenstein, Richard E. 1974. *Alchemists of Revolution: Terrorism in the Modern World.* New York: Basic Books.

Schultz, Richard. 1990. "Conceptualizing Political Terrorism," in Charles Kegley, ed. *International Terrorism.* New York: St. Martin's.

———. 1978. "Conceptualizing Political Terrorism." *Journal of International Affairs* 32 (1): 7–15.

Sederberg, Peter C. 1994. *Fires Within: Political Violence and Revolutionary Change.* New York: HarperCollins College Publishers.

Shue, Henry. 1980. *Basic Rights: Subsistence, Affluence, and U.S. Foreign Policy.* Princeton: Princeton University Press.

Turk, Austin T. 1982. "Social Dynamics of Terrorism." *Annals AAPSS* 463:119–128.

Weinberg, Leonard. 1991. "Turning to Terror: The Conditions Under Which Political Parties Turn to Terrorist Activities." *Comparative Politics* 23:423–438.

Whittaker, David J. 2001, 2003. *The Terrorism Reader.* New York: Routledge.

# 9.3 _____

## Leading by Example?
## U.S. Interrogation of Prisoners
## in the War on Terror

*Elisa Massimino*

When "trophy photos" taken by soldiers involved in the abuse of Iraqi prisoners at Abu Ghraib prison—one of the most notorious under Saddam Hussein's regime—were made public in late April 2004, the Pentagon had already completed two investigations into allegations of abuse at the prison. The graphic and disturbing photographs, some aired on prime-time American television, show naked Iraqi prisoners in humiliating poses, many with smiling uniformed soldiers looking on and pointing or giving a "thumbs up" sign. In one of the photographs, two naked prisoners are posed to make it look as though one is performing oral sex on another. Another shows a hooded prisoner standing on a box with wires attached to his wrists; the army says the prisoner was told that if he fell off the box, he would be electrocuted. Two pictures show dead prisoners—one with a battered and bruised face, the other whose bloodied body was wrapped in cellophane and packed in ice. One shows an empty room, splattered with blood. Reportedly, there is video as well.

These gruesome photographs were splashed across the front pages of newspapers in the Middle East and around the world, the headlines screaming "TORTURE." But the abuse was not news to the Pentagon. According to news accounts, a scathing 53-page report by Major General Antonio M. Taguba, completed in February, concluded that there was ongoing systematic and criminal abuse of detainees at the Abu Ghraib prison. As Seymour Hersh reported in the *New Yorker* magazine in May, General Taguba's report confirmed that abuses were taking place at the prison, including: threatening male detainees with rape, sodomizing a male detainee with a broomstick or chemical light, threatening detainees with dogs, and pouring chemicals from broken light bulbs onto detainees.[1] As a result of this investigation, six soldiers are facing

Excerpted from Elisa Massimino, "Leading by Example? U.S. Interrogation of Prisoners in the War on Terror," *Criminal Justice Ethics* 23 (Winter/Spring 2004): 32, 74–76. Reprinted with permission of The Institute of Criminal Justice Ethics, 555 West 57th Street, Suite 607, New York, NY 10019-1029.

courts-martial on charges that include cruelty toward prisoners, dereliction of duty, and indecent acts.

Are the soldiers who engaged in these acts just "sick bastards," as their commanding officer recently said,[2] or is there something more profoundly disturbing going on here? Why did the soldiers feel free to document their crimes on camera? Some answers to these questions will likely emerge in the prosecution of the soldiers involved. But it appears from the information already available that this was abuse with a particular purpose—to "create conditions favorable for successful interrogation"—that is, to break down a prisoner's will.

## ■ The Descent to Lawlessness

As shocking as these abuses are, to anyone who has followed closely the Bush Administration's descent into lawlessness in its prosecution of the "war on terrorism," they are not surprising. Three factors contribute to an environment in which such torture and cruelty can proliferate.

First is the Administration's persistent degradation of the Geneva Conventions and other international standards governing its conduct toward prisoners. Beginning with the initial transfer of prisoners from Afghanistan to Guantanamo, White House officials argued that the Geneva Conventions were not relevant to the war on terrorism. Later, under pressure from Secretary of State Colin Powell and other current and former military officers who revere the Geneva Conventions as a source of protection in case of capture, the Administration announced that it "believes in the principles" of the Geneva Conventions, but neither Taliban fighters nor al Qaeda suspects were eligible for their protections. Thus, as we continue to learn from Guantanamo, Bagram, and now Abu Ghraib, believing in the principles of the Geneva Conventions and actually complying with them are two different things—and there is no in-between. Complying with the Geneva Conventions requires that all of the detainees on Guantanamo and elsewhere have a recognized legal status. This, the Administration has steadfastly refused to do. But if the United States wants to be able to rely on the protections in the Geneva Conventions, then it must comply with them—not just in word, but in deed. Failing to do so not only places U.S. soldiers at greater risk, but contributes to a situation in which the details and importance of the Geneva Conventions are completely unrecognized by soldiers, like those at Abu Ghraib, charged with guarding and interrogating prisoners.

Second is the way in which the United States has played fast and loose with the prohibition on torture and cruel, inhuman, or degrading treatment. For example, one government official described the interrogation of an alleged high-ranking al Qaeda operative as "not quite torture, but about as close as you can get." Various administration officials—as well as some detainees who have been released—report that prisoners in U.S. custody have been beaten; thrown into walls; subjected to loud noises and extreme heat and cold; deprived of sleep, light, food, and water; bound or forced to stand in painful positions for long periods of time; kept naked; hooded; and shackled to the ceiling. Euphemistically called "stress and duress" techniques, U.S. officials who admit to these practices seem to think they are permissible so long as they don't cross the line into "outright torture." They are mistaken. When President Bush's father pushed the Convention Against Torture through the Senate, he committed to interpret the phrase "cruel, inhuman or degrading treatment or punishment" in ways consistent with the Eighth Amendment's prohibition on cruel and unusual punishment. To put these "stress and duress" techniques into constitutional context, the U.S. Supreme Court ruled in 2002 that handcuffing a prisoner to a hitching post in a painful position for eight hours clearly violated the protection against cruel and unusual punishment.[3] While there are certainly some interrogation methods that are unpleasant but not illegal, "stress and duress" interrogation techniques are clearly illegal. Pentagon General Counsel William J. Haynes III asserts that U.S. policy is "to treat all detainees and conduct all interrogations wherever they may occur, in a manner consistent with" the prohibition on cruel treatment.[4] But because many detainees are interrogated without the presence of lawyers or even the confidentiality-bound International Committee of the Red Cross (ICRC), it is difficult to know if that policy is known to interrogators, let alone whether they comply with it.

The third factor contributing to the kinds of interrogation abuses that are now coming to light is the Administration's focus on using interrogation almost exclusively for the purpose of obtaining information, rather than to obtain a confession or other evidence admissible in court. When the goal of interrogation is prosecution, the rules are familiar: Miranda, lawyers, a day in court. But what are the rules when there is no day in court in a detainee's future? Almost immediately after September 11, 2001, Attorney General Ashcroft and other senior officials at the Justice Department began talking about a fundamental shift in approach when dealing with terrorist suspects, from prosecution to prevention. Facilitated by an "enemy combatant" policy that so far has allowed the government to keep even U.S. citizens in incommunicado detention for prolonged periods, the Administration argues that detainees have no rights—to counsel, to appear before a judge, to speak to anyone at all—that might interfere with the sense of dependency and lack of control designed to make a detainee "lose hope."

## ■ Justifying Torture

Most discussions of interrogation and torture begin with the so-called "ticking time bomb" scenario, which posits a situation in which a detainee has information that, if revealed, could spare those about to be slaughtered. Is torture permissible if it would save those lives? People who focus on this hypothetical often do so in order to expose as "soft" those wide-eyed moralists unwilling to "do what is necessary" for the greater good. Since September 11, some lawyers and even judges have argued that if the taboo against torture has not already been broken, it should be now. Harvard law professor Alan Dershowitz proposed "torture warrants" for the ticking time bomb scenario, so that the abuses could be undertaken with judicial and societal sanction.[5] Federal Judge Richard Posner has said that anyone who doubts torture is permissible when the stakes are high enough should not be in a position of responsibility.[6] The end—saving innocent lives—justifies the means.

This is tough talk. But those who advocate for torture in these circumstances are the ones who are out of touch with reality. Many experienced interrogators have pointed out that the "ticking time bomb" scenario, with its factual (if not moral) clarity, is a fantasy, a situation that simply never presents itself in the real world. Abu Ghraib prison, on the other hand, is reality, and it is a reality where the means—torture and humiliation—quite likely will help to undermine the ends that the U.S. government is pursuing—Iraqi acceptance of a U.S. military presence in a free and democratic Iraq.

## ◼ Outlawing Torture

Just before the beating deaths of two Afghan prisoners who died under interrogation at Bagram Air Force Base were made public, I told a friend of mine— a senior military officer at the Pentagon—how disturbed I was by the fact that so many Americans with whom I talked casually believed, without distress or the slightest bit of cognitive dissonance, that the United States was torturing suspects for information. I asked my friend whether he believed that prisoners being held by the United States were being tortured. "I can't believe that," he said. "I could never be involved in a mission that relied on torture and abuse. It's a betrayal of everything we stand for."

Not only that, it's also illegal. When the U.S. Senate gave its advice and consent to ratification of the United Nations Convention Against Torture and Other Cruel, Inhuman or Degrading Treatment or Punishment, it recognized that ratification would have to await the passage and implementation of legislation, required by the treaty, making torture a crime. Congress did so in 1994. Title 18, Section 2340 of the United States Code defines torture as "an act committed by a person acting under the color of law specifically intended to inflict severe physical or mental pain or suffering (other than pain or suffering incidental to lawful sanctions) upon another person within his custody or physical control." Section 2340A makes torture, attempted torture, and conspiracy to commit torture a federal crime, punishable by up to 20 years in prison; if the victim dies as a result of torture, the punishment could be death. The law applies only to torture committed outside the United States, but includes acts by U.S. citizens. While the conduct of U.S. soldiers is governed by the Uniform Code of Military Justice (hence the charges of "cruelty" and "indecent acts" in the Abu Ghraib prison abuse case), it appears that other U.S. personnel—private contractors and intelligence officials—may also have been involved in the abuse. In the 10 years that the anti-torture law has been on the books, not a single person has been charged under its provisions. That may now change.

## ■ No Exceptions

Regardless of the words used to prohibit it, the ban on the use of torture is absolute. Unlike other provisions of international human rights law—such as the right to be free from arbitrary arrest or detention—that can be suspended during a declared emergency that "threatens the life of the nation," no exigency can justify torture.

This prohibition applies to the outsourcing option as well. International law prohibits the United States, as a signatory of the Convention Against Torture, from sending a person to a country where there is a substantial likelihood that he will be tortured. Congress reiterated this obligation in legislation in 1998, requiring regulations from all relevant executive agencies detailing how this obligation would be implemented.[7] The Departments of Justice and State both issued regulations; the Pentagon and the CIA never complied. Over the last 18 months, a number of Administration officials have confirmed that the United States is handing some al Qaeda suspects in military or CIA custody over to other governments for interrogation. These transfers are known as "extraordinary rendition"—a highly legalistic term for a completely extra-legal arrangement. Some of the countries where the detainees are sent—Egypt, Syria, Morocco—are places where, according to the State Department's annual country reports on human rights practices, torture and other prisoner abuse is routine. Some detainees have been transferred with a list of questions that their American interrogators want answered; in other cases, U.S. officials maintain more of a distance, simply receiving the fruits of the interrogation. It is unclear whether U.S. officials are ever present at these sessions. But even if they are not, it is a fiction that "extraordinary rendition" allows the United States to preserve clean hands, despite one U.S. official's claim that "We don't kick the [expletive] out of them. We send them to other countries so they can kick the [expletive] out of them."[8] Interestingly, when those countries comply, they may get a free pass from the State Department. In 2002, new instructions were issued to U.S. embassy personnel who draft the human rights reports: "Actions by governments taken at the request of the United States or with the expressed support of the United States should not be included in the report."[9]

When pressed to explain how its policy of "extraordinary rendition" to countries known to practice torture comports with its obligations under both the Convention Against Torture and domestic law, the Administration's response is either disingenuous or rather naive. In a letter to Senator Patrick Leahy responding to just this question, Pentagon General Counsel Haynes said that when it transfers a detainee to a third country, U.S. policy is "to obtain specific assurances from the receiving country that it will not torture the individual being transferred to that country."[10] In other words, we just take Syria's word for it. As Senator Leahy responded, "mere assurances from countries that are known to practice torture systematically are not sufficient."[11] Though Haynes has said that the United States will follow up on any evidence that these "diplomatic assurances" were not being honored, it seems that it would be awfully rare that such evidence would ever emerge, since the detention is likely to be incommunicado.

However, though rare, such evidence is not impossible. In September of 2002, U.S. officials arrested Maher Arar, a dual citizen of Canada and Syria, as he was changing planes at JFK airport in New York, en route home to Canada. Although he was traveling on his Canadian passport, U.S. officials—apparently CIA and Justice Department working together—secretly transferred Arar first to Jordan then to Syria, a move that evoked strong protest in Canada. Arar arrived in Syria after being interrogated for 11 days at a CIA interrogation center in Jordan. He then spent 10 months in a Syrian jail, during which time he alleges he was repeatedly tortured. Under increasing public pressure from Canadians and human rights groups, Syria finally released Arar, claiming they never had any interest in him anyway, but had only jailed and interrogated him to curry favor with the United States. This case provides an opportunity to test whether the United States is serious about the safeguards it says it employs when it transfers detainees to the custody of other governments. Did the United States government seek "diplomatic assurances" from Syria before handing Arar over? It hasn't said. If it did, has it complained to Syria that its treatment of Arar violates those assurances? It appears not. Perhaps that is because, as Arar alleges, the transfer to Syria was for the purpose of interrogation under torture. While in Syrian custody, Arar confessed to being a terrorist and having trained in an al Qaeda camp, all of which he now denies. With the Syrian government's later dismissal of Arar's importance, it appears even the Syrians did not believe his confessions.

## ▓ Credibility

If another country is willing to torture a prisoner in whom it has no independent interest just to appease the United States, imagine what effect we are having on repressive governments anxious to legitimize their own abusive conduct towards political dissidents and others they wish to silence. As the world stares in horror at pictures of grinning American soldiers engaging in war crimes, it is becoming increasingly deaf to the President's proclamation that "America will always stand firm for the non-negotiable demands of human dignity."[12] Last summer, the President issued a clear and forceful statement reaffirming the "inalienable human right" to be free from torture. "The United States is committed to the world-wide elimination of torture and we are leading this fight by example," President Bush said in a statement commemorating the U.N. International Day in Support of Victims of Torture.[13] Now, nearly a year later, the world has good reason to doubt the integrity of the President's pledge.

# ■ Notes

1. Seymour M. Hersh, "Torture at Abu Ghraib," *New Yorker* (May 10, 2004) <http://www.newyorker.com/fact/content/?040510fa_fact>.

2. Brigadier General Janis Karpinski, as reported in Philip Shenon, "Officer Suggests Iraq Jail Abuse Was Encouraged," *New York Times* (May 2, 2004) <http://www.nytimes.com/2004/05/02/international/middleeast/02ABUS.html?pagewanted=print&position=>.

3. Hope v. Pelzer, 122 S. Ct. 2508 (2002).

4. Letter of June 25, 2003, to Senator Patrick J. Leahy, Ranking Member, U.S. Senate Committee on the Judiciary. Archived at <http://www.fas.org/irp/congress/2004_cr/s021004.html>.

5. Alan M. Dershowitz, "Commentary," *L.A. Times* (November 8, 2001) <http://www.latimes.com/news/opinion/la000089139nov08.story?coll=la%2Dheadlines%2Doped%2Dmanual>.

6. Richard Posner, "The Best Offense," *New Republic* (September 2, 2002): 30 [Review of: *Why Terrorism Works: Understanding the Threat, Responding to the Challenge*, by Alan M. Dershowitz].

7. Foreign Affairs Reform and Restructuring Act (October 19, 1998), Section 2242(a).

8. Quoted in Editorial, "Torture Is Not an Option," *Washington Post* (December 27, 2002): A24 <http://www.washingtonpost.com/ac2/wp-dyn/A42024-2002Dec26?language=printer>.

9. Instruction in the guideline to drafters for the Department of State's 2002 Country Reports on Human Rights Practices.

10. Letter of June 25, 2003.

11. Patrick J. Leahy, Congressional Record (February 10, 2004) (Senate), S784 <http://www.fas.org/irp/congress/2004_cr/ s021004.html>.

12. State of the Union Address, January 29, 2002 <http://www.whitehouse.gov/news/releases/2002/01/20020129-11.html>.

13. Statement by the President, June 26, 2003 <http://www.whitehouse.gov/news/releases/2003/06/20030626-3.html>.

# 9.4 ⎯⎯⎯⎯

# Human Rights Post–September 11

*Julie Mertus and Tazreena Sajjad*

In an effort to promote "American freedom and security," US foreign policy post–September 11 has had draconian implications for the struggle for human rights, both at home and abroad. Not only do many of the counterterrorism steps enacted by the United States directly abridge human rights, but the United State's myopic focus on countering terrorism at all costs has had tremendous indirect costs for human rights advocates as well. Secure in their belief that the United States will look the other way when a "friend in the war on terror" commits human rights violations, states claiming a place on the "US side" in the terror have become increasingly assured that they can violate human rights with impunity. In particular, many countries since 9/11 have taken advantage of this opportune moment to intensify their own crackdowns on political opponents, separatists, and religious groups. In addition, in several countries, leaders have exploited the situation to advance punitive policies against refugees, asylum-seekers, and other foreigners. The infringement of the mechanics of the war on terror, in the guise of emergency measures, is fast ensuring that the human rights protections for political and social minorities that do exist are being quickly rolled back.

Although the number of functioning international and domestic human rights mechanisms has reached an all-time high, and the promotion of human rights throughout the world has never been more critical, the realization of human rights has never been in greater danger. The fight for human rights and the protection of human dignity is now faced by an indomitable challenge in a distorted world defined narrowly in terms of "national" security. As a self-proclaimed leader of human rights and democracy, the United States plays a central position in this rollback on rights. This essay identifies three areas where the United States is a particularly bad role model for the rest of the world: (1) human rights in incarceration and detention; (2) government secrecy vs. citizens' privacy; and (3) nondiscrimination and, in particular, the rights of noncitizens. These specific examples demonstrate that the price being paid for security is excruciatingly high, and the human rights movement is indisputably a victim of this new emphasis on "national security" over human rights.

## ▧ Human Rights in Incarceration

The treatment of prisoners captured by the US government in the "war on terror" raises several critical human rights concerns. The use of torture against accused terrorists held in US custody in Iraq, Afghanistan, and Guantanamo Bay has been widely reported.[1] Significant evidence exists that the abuses have been widespread and that the United States has taken only limited steps to investigate and punish implicated personnel.[2] For example, a study by the Detainee Abuse and Accountability Project (DAA), a nongovernmental watchdog group initiated in March 2005 for the purpose of analyzing credible allegations of abuse of detainees, concluded:

- Detainee abuse has been widespread. The DAA Project has documented more than 330 cases in which US military and civilian personnel are credibly alleged to have abused, tortured, or killed detainees. These cases implicate more than 600 US personnel and involve more than 460 detainees.
- Only a fraction of the more than 600 US personnel implicated in these cases—40 people—have been sentenced to prison time.
- Of the hundreds of allegations of abuse collected by the DAA Project, only about half appear to have been adequately investigated.
- In cases where courts-martial—the military's equivalent of criminal trials—have convened, the majority of prison sentences have been for less than a year, even in cases involving serious abuse. Only 10 US personnel have been sentenced to a year or more in prison.
- No US military officer has been held accountable for criminal acts committed by subordinates under the doctrine of command responsibility. Only three officers have been convicted by court-martial for detainee abuse.
- Although approximately 20 civilians, including CIA agents, have been referred to the Department of Justice for criminal prosecution for detainee abuse, the Department of Justice has shown minimal initiative in moving forward in abuse cases. The Department of Justice has not indicted a single CIA agent for abusing detainees; it has indicted only one civilian contractor.[3]

Of additional concern is the fact that many prisoners often have been held in secret prisons and without notification to the accused's family or to any officials in the country of origin. The CIA's involvement in these detention centers is notable. Investigative journalists have uncovered persuasive evidence of CIA involvement in secret detention facilities at sites in eight countries, including Thailand, Afghanistan, and several democracies in Eastern Europe, as well as in Guantanamo. The existence and locations of the facilities—referred to as "black sites" in classified White House, CIA, Justice Department, and congressional documents—are known to only a handful of officials in the United States and, usually, only to the president and a few top intelligence officers in each host country. Virtually nothing is known about who is kept in the facilities, what interrogation methods are employed with them, or how decisions are made about whether they should be detained or for how long.[4]

While the International Committee of the Red Cross/Crescent (ICRC) has visited some of the more open facilities, their visits have been undermined in ways contrary to the letter and spirit of binding law.[5] In other cases, the existence of the detention facility is acknowledged by the United States—as in the case of more than a dozen detention facilities in Iraq—but very little else is known, particularly of the nature of the detainees' legal rights and status. There are cases in which the existence of the detention facility itself is not officially acknowledged but has been reported by multiple sources—for example, Kohat and Alizai in Pakistan; Jalalabad, Asadabad, and Kabul in Afghanistan;[6] the US Naval Base on Diego Garcia; and US military ships, particularly the USS *Batan* and the USS *Peleiliu*.[7] Furthermore, the United States has "been covertly transferring terrorism suspects to other countries for interrogation—notably Jordan, Egypt, and Syria—which are known for employing coercive methods."[8] US involvement in these transfers—known as extraordinary renditions—serves as a poor example to other states and comprises an additional violation of international law and human rights protections.

The classification of these prisoners has created roadblocks to human rights enforcement.[9] By classifying US prisoners in the war on terror as "detainees," a term unrecognized by international law, the Bush administration maintained that they were not entitled to protections of the Geneva Conventions, including the rights of due process and limited judicial oversight. Every international human rights body has rejected the Bush administration's attempt to classify these detainees as "unlawful combatants."[10] In May 2006, the Committee Against Torture (CAT), the international body of experts that monitors state compliance with the Convention Against Torture and Other Cruel, Inhuman or Degrading Treatment or Punishment, flatly rejected the Bush administration's claim that the Torture Convention is not applicable in times of armed conflict, stating unequivocally that "the Convention applies at all times, whether in peace, war or armed conflict, in any territory under its jurisdiction. . . ."[11] CAT called on the United States to close all secret prisons; hold accountable senior military and civilian officials who authorized, acquiesced, or consented to acts of torture committed by their subordinates; and end its practice of transferring detainees to countries with known torture records. It also specifically criticized the indefinite detention of prisoners in Guantanamo Bay and called for its closure.

## ◼ Government Secrecy vs. Citizens' Privacy

Since 9/11 the Bush administration has moved more quickly than any administration since World War II to make government activities, documents, and other information secret.[12] At the heart of this trend toward expanding the secrecy of government conduct has been a series of executive branch initiatives impinging on public access to information. These efforts combine to restrict access to information through a simultaneous increase in the classification of documents and a decrease in the declassification of documents.[13] As a result, information upon which human rights organizations rely for their watchdog roles is more difficult to obtain and, once obtained, is incomplete or distorted.

Newly enacted legislation has steadily limited the public's access to government information in all fifty states. Hundreds of thousands of public documents have been removed from government websites. Other public information has been edited, and access to some materials has been made more difficult. Some government materials yanked from the Internet, such as Environmental Protection Agency reports on the consequences of industrial accidents at chemical plants, may be viewed only in government reading rooms. Visitors must have an appointment and have to be accompanied by a government escort. Attorney General John Ashcroft's Justice Department set the tone for the focus on secrecy in October, telling US agencies to be more cautious about releasing records and other materials. In addition, legislatures have passed more than 1,000 laws changing access to information, approving more than twice as many measures that restrict information as laws that open government books.[14]

The ability of US citizens to enjoy lives free from unwarranted government interference has declined rapidly, even as the ability of their governments to act secretly has been enhanced. The US "Patriot Act," one of the first pieces of domestic legislation enacted in the "war on terror," greatly expanded the ability of federal officials to carry out searches and seizures on private homes without prior notice.[15] Among other measures, this legislation, which set the standard for similar copycat laws in other countries, permitted state authorities to "scrutinize people's reading habits by monitoring public library and bookstore records, . . . [while also] allow[ing] for 'sneak and peak' tactics such as physical search of property and computers, . . . monitoring of email, and access to financial and educational records," all without the notification of the suspect.[16] Specifically, under Section 213 of the Patriot Act, the government can delay notice of a search if it can show "reasonable cause to believe that providing immediate notification of the execution of the warrant may have an adverse result."[17]

As long as the low standard of "reasonable cause" or "reasonable necessity" is met, police officers can secretly enter a person's home or office while he or she is away and search through and seize private belongings.[18] These new powers are not limited to antiterrorism investigations, but rather apply to all federal investigations, including routine criminal cases. Furthermore, Congress did not create a sunset provision for this section.[19] This means that, unlike some other powers granted in the Act, the Section 213 powers are permanent. Also under new regulations issued by the Attorney General, the FBI can now carry out surveillance on any religious, civic, or political organization in the United States, without even the slightest suspicion of wrongdoing.[20] A key component of the new surveillance has been a crackdown on the work of domestic and international human rights organizations.

## ▓ Nondiscrimination and the Rights of Noncitizens

The restrictive measures taken by the Bush administration against US citizens pale in comparison with the new policies against noncitizens. As Athena Roberts has noted, "By applying different standards to citizens and non-citizens, the United States appears to be endorsing the idea that certain fundamental rights are tied to one's status as a citizen rather than one's status as a human being."[21] This serves to undermine the notions of equality and universality that lie at the heart of human rights.

Many of the abuses already discussed in this essay were restricted largely to noncitizens. One of the most prominent examples of this is the transport of "detainees" from Afghanistan and other countries to the US Naval Base in Guantanamo Bay, restricted to noncitizens.[22] But the daily discriminatory treatment of noncitizens is in fact more staggering and creates at times insurmountable challenges for those trying to enter the country. For all noncitizens who travel into the United States, fingerprints and photographs are now standard procedures upon entry into the country. "[T]hrough a series of nationality-specific information and detention sweeps—from special registration requirements to "voluntary" interviews to the detention of all those seeking asylum from a list of predominantly Muslim countries—the administration has acted on an assumption that all such individuals are of concern."[23] Further, foreigners already inside US borders are now subject to deportation without an administratively accountable process. Judicial reviews are no longer necessary for such cases, and suspected illegal immigrants may be held in detention, without notification of their families, for unspecified amounts of time, while their cases are pending.

In the dragnet of institutionalizing extensive security measures and making America "safe and free," no other communities have been as badly affected as the Arabs and Muslims, both citizens and noncitizens, since 9/11. The fact that the hijackers were all Arab and Muslim has greatly fortified the US position identifying these two groups from a particular range of countries to be treated with increased suspicion and hostility. The groups that have been subject to the worst discrimination are those that fit within overlapping bases of discrimination, such as noncitizens from Arab and Muslim countries. These mistreatments have included mass arrests, secret and indefinite detentions, prolonged detention of "material witnesses," closed hearings and use of secret evidence, government eavesdropping on attorney-client conversations, FBI home and work visits, wiretapping, seizures of property, removals of aliens with technical visa violations, and mandatory special registration. At least 100,000 Arabs and Muslims living in the United States have personally experienced one of these measures.[24]

In addition to these special measures, which clearly identified Arabs and/or Muslims to be the enemies of the United States, the current administration instituted a National Security Entry-Exit Regulation System, which only applied to nonimmigrant aliens from certain (predominantly Arab and Muslim) countries and other nonimmigrant aliens who represented an elevated national security risk.[25] This program requires males over age 16 who were from these countries and in the United States on temporary visas to report to Immigration and Naturalization Service offices in order to be fingerprinted, photographed, and questioned under oath. Failure to register is a deportable offense. The climate for noncitizens in the United States today is no longer framed by hope and possibilities, but tainted by fear and uncertainty.

## ■ Conclusion

The state of human rights, especially the civil and political rights of Americans and citizens of the rest of the countries of the world, is undisputedly facing a crisis. Despite the developments made in the field of international agencies, networks, institutions, covenants, and the establishment of international norms of conduct, in the newly emerging global order, the progress made in the protection of human rights and human dignity has not only been halted, but is actually being rolled back. The post-9/11 world has created the opportunity for national governments to implement draconian measures to curtail the rights of opposition groups, minorities, and others whom they believe work against their own interests.[26] Many countries have used the pretext of fighting terrorism in order to extend new security assistance and cooperation to abusive governments and to engage in human rights violations directly themselves.[27] For example:

- In Canada, the *Public Safety Act* compels air carriers to provide information on passengers, without warrants or restrictions, in cases involving terrorism.[28]
- The European Parliament has now adopted new rules to store phone and Internet data for up to two years, for the purpose of counterterrorism surveillance.[29]
- The Australian government has used the rhetoric of counterterrorism to justify its hardline policies on refugee and asylum issues and has sought extended powers of detention for its security agency.[30]

- Pakistan passed a new Anti-Terrorist Ordinance in 2002, which allows the police to arrest terrorist suspects and detain them for up to a year without charge.[31]
- China has stepped up its campaign against Uighur separatists in Xinjiang province by invoking the war on terror, blurring the distinction between peaceful activists and those with genuine connections to international terrorist organizations.[32]
- The Indian government enacted the new Prevention of Terrorism Act (POTA), which closely resembles a discredited, earlier security law that led to tens of thousands of politically motivated detentions, torture, and other human rights violations against perceived political opponents in the late 1980s and early 1990s.[33]

These and other counter–human rights measures being institutionalized politically and legally promise to ensure that the movement forward for human rights will be seriously derailed in the near future.

## ■ Notes

1. "U.S.: More Than 600 Implicated in Detainee Abuse; Investigations Lag Two Years After Abu Ghraib Photos," Human Rights Watch, April 26, 2006. Available at http://hrw.org/english/docs/2006/04/26/usint13268.htm. Viewed on June 1, 2006.

2. Ibid.

3. "By the Numbers: Findings of the Detainee Abuse and Accountability Project," April 26, 2006. Available at www.humanrightsfirst.info/pdf/06425-etn-by-the-numbers.pdf. Viewed on June 2, 2006.

4. The *Washington Post* has not published the names of the Eastern European countries involved in the covert program, at the request of senior US officials. They argued that the disclosure might disrupt counterterrorism efforts in those countries and elsewhere and could make them targets of possible terrorist retaliation. Dana Priest, "CIA Holds Terror Suspects in Secret Prisons; Debate Is Growing Within Agency About Legality and Morality of Overseas System Set Up After 9/11," November 2, 2005, p. A01. Available at www.washingtonpost.com/wp-dyn/content/article/2005/11/01/AR2005110101644.html.

5. "Ending Secret Detentions," Human Rights First, June 2004. Available at www.humanrightsfirst.org/us_law/PDF/EndingSecretDetentions_web.pdf.

6. James Risen and Thom Shanker, "Hussein Enters Post 9/11 Web of U.S. Prisons," *New York Times,* December 17, 2003. Available at http://query.nytimes.com/gst/abstract.html?res=F40E13F93D5B0C7B8DDDAB0994DB404482&fta=y.

7. See Expeditionary Strike Force One, U.S. Naval Special Operations Command Office of Public Affairs, "ESG 1 Strikes from the Sea," January 5, 2004 (reporting coalition force "takedowns" of vessels carrying drugs, including one with fifteen individuals "with possible links to Al Qaeda," and reporting: "Ten of the individuals from . . . two takedowns have been transferred to a secure, undisclosed location for further questioning by U.S. officials"), available at http://64.233.167.104/search?q=cache:TvjFs WzKUU4J:https://www.navsoc.navy.mil/esg1/pdf/dhowtakedown.pdf+questioning+

Peleliu&hl=en; "Searching a Suspected Compound: Marines Investigate Abandoned Taliban Compound amid Speculation over Omar Search," ABC News.com, January 1, 2002, available at http://more.abcnews.go.com/sections/world/dailynews/strike_main 020101.html; Grant Holloway, "Australia to Question al Qaeda Fighter," CNN.com, December 19, 2001, available at www.cnn.com/2001/WORLD/asiapcf/auspac/12/19/aust .talbandit20.12/; "Australian Taliban Fighter Handed over to U.S. Military Forces in Afghanistan," Associated Press, December 17, 2001, available at http://multimedia. belointeractive.com/attack/military/1217australia.ht.

8. Lawyers Committee for Human Rights, *Assessing the New Normal: Liberty and Security for the Post–September 11 United States,* Part 2 (New York: 2003).

9. Human Rights Watch, "Background Paper on Geneva Conventions and Persons Held by U.S. Forces." Available at http://hrw.org/backgrounder/usa/pow-bck.htm.

10. James Ross, "Bush, Torture and the Lincoln Legacy," Human Rights Watch, August 1, 2005. Available at http://hrw.org/english/docs/2005/08/05/usdom11610.htm. Viewed on May 22, 2005.

11. Conclusions and Recommendations of the Committee Against Torture, 36th Session, May 18, 2006, CAT/C/USA/CO2. Available at www.ohchr.org/english/bodies/ cat/docs/AdvanceVersions/CAT.C.USA.CO.2.pdf (hereafter "May 2006 CAT Conclusions and Recommendations").

12. Laura Parker, Kevin Johnson, and Toni Locy, "Post-9/11, Government Stingy with Information," *USA Today.* Available at www.usatoday.com/news/nation/2002/ 05/16/secrecy-usatcov.htm. Viewed on May 26, 2006.

13. Lawyers Committee for Human Rights, *Assessing the New Normal.*

14. Robert Tanner, "Less Information Access Since 9/11, AP Study Says," *Seattle Times*, March 12, 2006. Available at http://seattletimes.nwsource.com/html/nationworld/ 2002860012_sunshine12.html. Viewed on May 26, 2006.

15. Electronic Privacy Information Center, "The USA PATRIOT Act." Available at www.epic.org/privacy/terrorism/usapatriot/#overview.

16. "Denial of Rights: Amend the US Patriot Act Now!" *"War on Terror" Human Rights Issues,* Amnesty International. Available at www.amnestyusa.org/waronterror/ patriotact.

17. Electronic Privacy Information Center, "The USA PATRIOT Act." Available at www.epic.org/privacy/terrorism/usapatriot/#overview.

18. Ibid.

19. Ibid.

20. Ibid.

21. Athena Roberts, "Righting Wrongs or Wronging Rights? The United States and Human Rights Post–September 11th," *European Journal of International Law* 15 (September 2004): 721.

22. Sean Murphy, "Contemporary Practice of the United States Relating to International Law: U.S. Department of Defense Rules on Military Commisions," *American Journal of International Law* 96 (2002): 706, at 733.

23. Ibid.

24. Ibid.

25. See 67 Fed. Reg. 52584 (12 August 2002); 67 Fed. Reg. 67766 (6 November 2002), 70526 (22 November 2002), 77642 (18 December 2002). These countries included Afghanistan, Algeria, Bahrain, Bangladesh, Eritrea, Iran, Iraq, Lebanon, Libya, Morocco, North Korea, Oman, Pakistan, Qatar, Saudi Arabia, Somalia, Sudan, Syria, Tunisia, United Arab Emirates, and Yemen.

26. See generally Human Rights Watch, "Country Studies: The Human Rights Impact of Counter-Terrorism Measures in Ten Countries," in *In the Name of Counter-*

*Terrorism: Human Rights Abuses Worldwide.* March 25, 2003, at 10–25; Lawyers Committee for Human Rights, *Assessing the New Normal,* at 75–76.

27. "Asia Security Talks Risk Giving Green Light to Repression: Human Rights Abused in the Name of Fighting Terrorism," Human Rights Watch, June 16, 2003. Available at http://hrw.org/english/docs/2003/06/16/austra6151.htm. Viewed on May 25, 2006.

28. M. Kerr, "The State of Privacy Since 9/11," McCarthy Tetrault Publications, January 31, 2006. Available at www.mccarthy.ca/pubs/publication.asp?pub_code= 2381. Viewed on May 26, 2006.

29. Ibid.

30. "Asia Security Talks Risk Giving Green Light to Repression."

31. Ibid.

32. Ibid.

33. Ibid.

# Index

Abu Ghraib, 271, 280–281, 283–284
Afghanistan, 30; and child marriages, 201, 213–215; and the Taliban, 129, 130
African Charter on Human and Peoples' Rights, 76
African cultural fingerprint, 111, 136–137
African values, 8, 109–111, 124, 132–140; and communalism, 133–135
AIDS, 30; and child sexploitation, 188, 202, 231
Amnesty International: Annual Reports, 28, 31–32, 41, 48, 50, 52–58; as an organization, 122, 141
Apartheid, 23, 252, 262; and international law, 75–76, 92
Argentina, 56; and terrorism, 275
Asian values, 8, 109, 111, 124, 132; as challenge to West, 113–115; critique of, 188–119; elements of, 112, 115–117
Auschwitz. *See* Holocaust
Authoritarianism, 117, 120*n*4

Balkans. *See* Yugoslavia
Bangladesh, 93–94, 214; and bonded labor, 181, 210
Basic human needs. *See* Subsistence rights
Basic rights, 2, 274; and corresponding duties, 12–15; definition, 16, 59; as

security rights, 17; as subsistence rights, 18–20
*Beedi*, 220–221
Bentham, Jeremy, 23, 25
Bin Laden, Osama, 129
Bonded labor, 178, 183, 204; causes of, 216–217; and children, 201–202, 204; definition of, 181; estimate of, 181; and health consequences, 218–221; and profit, 184
Boomerang maneuver, 100
Bosnia, 122, 125; and IDPs, 229; and outsourcing torture, 263; and war crimes, 162–168, 191–192
Brazil, 252; and sexploitation, 202, 222; slavery in, 184

Cairo Declaration on Human Rights in Islam, 131
Cambodia: and child soldiers, 230; and the Khmer Rouge, 4–5, 31, 34, 141, 148–154, 276; and refugees, 93–94; and tribunals, 70
Canada, 285; and sexploitation, 222; and the War on Terror, 292
Child labor, 201–202; causes of, 205–206, 217; and education, 206, 207, 211; estimates of, 204; and international law, 208–210; and poverty, 207, 211; solutions to, 210–212
Children, 5, 13–14, 255–259; child marriages, 201–202, 213–215;

# About the Book

Bringing together key selections that represent the full range of philosophical debates, policy analyses, and firsthand accounts, the editors offer a comprehensive and accessible set of readings on the major themes and issues in the field of international human rights. The reader has been carefully designed to enhance students' understanding not only of human rights, but also of differing perspectives on the topic.

**Rhonda L. Callaway** is assistant professor of political science at Sam Houston State University. **Julie Harrelson-Stephens** is assistant professor of political science at Stephen F. Austin University.